Innovation, Alliances, and Networks in High-Tech Environments

Recent decades have been characterized by an increasing number of strategic alliances, mergers and acquisitions and more general collaborative networks. This phenomenon has primarily involved knowledge-intensive and high-tech industries where innovation is a key competitive weapon. This book focuses on the role of these partnerships and provides new insights into how they contribute to increasing innovation performance.

Despite their growing popularity, there are few contributions that examine these collaborative strategies. Existing studies tend to investigate the impact of alliances on financial performance, providing insight into the development and deployment of alliances, or exploring the governance of strategic alliances and mergers and acquisitions. This book fills this gap in existing literature by examining specific contributions of the absorptive capacity of firms, knowledge networks and spillovers.

This book will be of interest to graduate students and researchers interested in Industrial Economics, Strategic Management and Management of Technology and Innovation.

Fiorenza Belussi is full professor of strategy and innovation management at the department of economics and management, University of Padua, Italy.

Luigi Orsi is a post doctoral fellow at the department of economics and management, University of Padua, Italy.

Routledge Studies in Global Competition

Edited by John Cantwell,
Rutgers, The State University of New Jersey, USA
and
David Mowery
University of California, Berkeley, USA

For a complete list of titles in this series, please visit www.routledge.com

Innovation, Alliances, and Networks in High-Tech Environments

Edited by
Fiorenza Belussi and Luigi Orsi

Routledge
Taylor & Francis Group

LONDON AND NEW YORK

First published 2016 by Routledge

2 Park Square, Milton Park, Abingdon, Oxfordshire OX14 4RN
52 Vanderbilt Avenue, New York, NY 10017

Routledge is an imprint of the Taylor & Francis Group, an informa business

First issued in paperback 2019

British Library Cataloguing in Publication Data
A catalogue record for this book is available from the British Library

Library of Congress Cataloguing in Publication Data
Innovation, alliances, and networks in high-tech environments / edited by Fiorenza Belussi and Luigi Orsi.
pages cm
Includes bibliographical references and index.
1. High technology industries—Management. 2. Technological innovations.
3. Strategic alliances (Business) 4. Business networks. I. Belussi, Fiorenza, editor. II. Orsi, Luigi, editor.
HD62.37.I535 2015
658—dc23
2015015079

ISBN: 978-1-138-84660-9 (hbk)
ISBN: 978-0-367-87196-3 (pbk)

Typeset in Times New Roman
by Swales & Willis Ltd, Exeter, Devon, UK

Contents

Figures

Tables

Contributors

Ahreum Lee, Temple University, USA.

Alessandra Perri, University of Venice, Italy.

Andrea Ganzaroli, University of Milan, Italy.

Anna Minà, Sapienza University of Rome, Italy.

Daniela Baglieri, University of Messina, Italy.

Fiorenza Belussi, University of Padua, Italy.

Francesca Gambarotto, University of Padua, Italy.

Giovanni Battista Dagnino, University of Catania, Italy.

Hongryol Cha, Temple University, USA.

Ivan De Noni, University of Milan, Italy.

Izzet Darendeli, Temple University, USA.

Kristin Brandl, Copenhagen Business School, Denmark.

Kristina Rakic, University of Padua, Italy.

Luigi Orsi, University of Padua, Italy.

Marcelo Cano Kollmann, Temple University, USA.

Maria Francesca Savarese, University of Padua, Italy.

Naohiro Shichijo, Waseda University, Japan.

Ram Mudambi, Temple University, USA.

Robert D. Hamilton III, Temple University, USA.

Seojin Kim, Temple University, USA.

Silvia Rita Sedita, University of Padua, Italy.

Soumaya Ben Letaifa, University of Quebec at Montreal, Canada.

Stefania Michelazzo, University of Padua, Italy.

Stefano Solari, University of Padua, Italy.

T. J. Hannigan, Temple University, USA.

Vittoria Giada Scalera, Politecnico di Milano, Italy.

Yasunori Baba, University of Tokyo, Japan.

Introduction

This book focuses on three important interrelated characteristics of the strategic management of high-tech firms: on the one hand, their propensity towards high levels of innovativeness, and on the other, the pursuit of an open organizational design based on technological strategic alliances and open research networks. There is now a rich body of literature on the motivations of firms' alliances (Kanter, 1994; Dyer, 1997; Doz and Hamel, 1998; Gulati, 1998; Das and Teng, 2001). Firms enter alliances to access resources and foreign markets and to increase both economies of scale and their speed in placing new products into markets, but also to reduce risks and costs. We utilize here a knowledge perspective (Eisenhardt and Schoonhoven, 1996; Mowery et al., 1996; Powell et al., 1996) to address the benefits and risks of firms' alliances, studying, in particular, the technological dynamics enabled by alliances to firms belonging to high-tech sectors (and, above all, to the biopharma industry, Baum et al., 2000) and the asymmetries stemming from the heterogeneity of partner selection (Inkpen and Beamish, 1997). We combine three theoretical research paths: (1) the topic of alliances; (2) the network analysis approach (Sydow and Windeler, 1998; Cross et al., 2002; Capaldo, 2007; Tiwana, 2008) looking at the configuration of networks between firms and at the connectivity between actors, resources and activities; and (3) the open innovation study tradition (Hagedoorn and Duysters, 2002a; Chesbrough, 2003) and acknowledge the complexity inherent in the innovation process itself, where a multiplicity of resources is working to recombine different pieces of knowledge stemming from various disciplines (Carnabuci and Operti, 2013).

The formation of R&D alliances is considered to be a contractual agreement alternative to a more concentrated and verticalized mode of governance, where R&D activities are internalized in large laboratories owned by the largest firms. For many firms, alliances are a necessary step in order to boost innovative performance (Shan et al., 1994), new product development (Deeds and Hill, 1996; Rothaermel and Deeds, 2004) and, more generally, performance (Baum et al., 2000). Contributions based on the resource-based view of the firms (Barney, 1991; Wernerfelt, 1995) and on the knowledge-based view of the firms (Levitt and March, 1988; Nelson, 1991; Nonaka, 1991; Conner and Prahalad, 1996; Grant, 1996; Cloodt et al., 2006) provide some useful insights to understand this phenomenon. In order to generate and sustain a competitive advantage with respect to other companies, firms rely heavily on unique and innovative capabilities, i.e. specific expertise and competences related to the development and introduction of new processes and products (Rumelt, 1974; Hagedoorn and Duysters, 2002a). Such capabilities might be either endogenous or exogenous. Moreover, knowledge is often tacit, especially in technological- and knowledge-intensive contexts and thus difficult to be transferred from one firm to another (Larsson *et al.*, 1998). Markets are also imperfect mechanisms: thus, alliances or acquisitions may be better options. Despite the evidence that alliance portfolios are beneficial for firms, the question of *who allies with whom* within entrepreneurial technology ventures remains largely unexplored (Gans and Stern, 2003). These partnerships that often involve co-development contracts, challenge the traditional business models centred around the idea of developing a product in-house and create business model options that can significantly reduce R&D expenses, increase innovation output and open up new markets: the so-called markets for technology (Arora *et al.*, 2001).

In part I, we look at the phenomenon of firms' alliances, reflecting on the long-term impact exerted by alliances between advanced firms, R&D alliances and technological alliances, at the meso-level.

First, we consider the transformation of a specific high-tech industry – the old pharma – and we describe the emergence of a new biotech niche. In Chapter 1 Belussi and Orsi, using a long-term perspective, describe the complex evolution of both sectors. The new technological paradigm based on molecular biology has been considered as a competence-destroying mechanism for pharmaceutical firms (Powell *et al.*, 1996; Stuart *et al.*, 1999). To sustain their competitive advantage, they had no alternative but to ally with new entrant biotech firms that possessed the R&D competences and capabilities they lacked. Thanks to these strategic alliances, pharmaceutical firms have been able to enrich their product pipeline. Emerging technologies, such as biotechnology, had offered significant opportunities for cooperation between small and large incumbent firms. However, Chapter 1 shows not only the emergence of a new red biotech niche but also its evanescent dissolution into the integrated parallel 'knowledge system' of a new biopharmaceutical filière.

Second, we deal with the geography of international connectedness within innovation networks, as they emerge in the longitudinal analysis of co-patenting in innovative metropolitan US areas. In Chapter 2 Brandl *et al.*, using a comprehensive dataset comprising the population of the United States Patent and Trademark Office (USPTO) co-patents, are able to generate a knowledge map of the inventor networks for each American area. They find that in the 1975–1990 period, inventor numbers concentrated above all in large population centres (New York, Chicago, Los Angeles and Philadelphia), while in the decades between 1990 and 2010, inventor numbers rose more rapidly in the West and South so that, by the end of the period, the dominant innovative centres of the country were San Jose, Austin, Seattle, Portland, San Diego and the Silicon Valley area of San Francisco.

Third, we study the nature of competition and cooperation in a specific entrepreneurial ecosystem, considering the Canadian ICT industry, as illustrated in Chapter 3 by Dagnino, Minà and Ben Letaifa. These authors show the path of development of the local entrepreneurial ecosystem, which has offered a highly favoured and interacting environment to firms. Government leaders and other institutions (e.g. universities, research centres and professional support services, such as lawyers, accountants and banks) played an important role in shaping a supporting environment from which entrepreneurship could emerge. They have attracted external stakeholders (such as new entrepreneurs and investors), providing rules of interaction that have generated new opportunities for collaboration between firms.

Part II is dedicated to the deepening of our knowledge with regard to the phenomenon of alliance and acquisition in the biopharma industry. Traditionally, research on factors that affect partner selection in alliances emphasizes the role that partners play in bringing together critical resources and capabilities (i.e. *capability-seeking* aspects). However, many aspects in the literature still remain understudied: are biotech firms forming alliances with technologically similar partners or do they choose partner diversity as a means to build complementary capabilities? And how much does this influence the probability that a biotech firm will subsequently be acquired? In Chapter 4 Baglieri, Belussi and Orsi, using a large dataset, refer to about 4,000 international biotech alliances, affirming that biotech firms, in terms of innovative performance, are better off with an alliance portfolio characterized by a certain degree of partners' similarity (bio-to-bio alliances), where complementary knowledge can be developed. However, the main empirical result emerging from the subsequent analysis conducted in Chapter 5 by Belussi and Orsi to test the innovative performance of a large sample of Italian biotech firms, highlights that the alliance innovative output, measured in terms of the number of new products (in both the pipeline and the market), is exposed to the effect of diminishing returns, showing an inverted U-shape.

In Chapter 6 Baglieri, Belussi and Orsi consider which alliance partners become attractive targets for acquisitions in biotech. Interestingly, the existence of a prior alliance does not appear to be a key feature, while acquirers seems to evaluate more targets with large and technological heterogeneous ego-networks of alliances and with networks of alliances characterized by a high degree of centrality.

There are still very few contributions that look at M&As as strategies to drive firms' innovative performances. Existing studies tend to investigate the impact of M&As on financial performance (e.g. Lindgren, 1982; Shrivastava, 1986; Haspeslagh and Jemison, 1991; Greenwood *et al.*, 1994; Hakanson, 1995) or explore strategic alliances, instead of considering particularly the activity of M&A (e.g. Hagedoorn and Schakenraad, 1994; Rosenkopf and Almeida, 2003; Rothaermel and Deeds, 2004, 2006; Hagedoorn and Wang, 2012).

Academic literature has widely examined motivations for acquisition decisions both at a firm- and management-level (Hayward and Hambrick, 1997). From the firm-level perspective, the most common and evident drivers include growth and scale advantages, i.e. economies of scale and scope (Walter and Barney, 1990), financial synergies (Slusky and Caves, 1991), improved bargaining power, the elimination of overlaps and the utilization of complementary assets (Trautwein, 1990). It is in fact clear, for instance, that M&As might allow acquirers to expand their product pipeline and market share or to increase their bargaining power, thanks to size growth, as well as to rapidly access those complementary resources and knowledge that are useful to sustain their competitive advantage. Nevertheless, such firm-level motives have not been proved by numerous empirical studies concerning acquisition behaviour (Slusky and Caves, 1991; Hayward and Hambrick, 1997). Consequently, scholars have become interested in other explanations (Schildt and Laamanen, 2006). For instance, some have suggested that acquisitions might result from managements' incentive compensation schemes (Sanders, 2001) and the building of a 'managerial empire' or job-security concerns (Amihud and Lev, 1981); others have found a potential reason for M&A activity in the will of escalating commitment (Roll, 1986; Haspeslagh and Jemison, 1991; Haunschild, 1994). M&As that allow companies to internalize external knowledge, avoiding high transaction costs, generally characterize the transmission of tacit know-how (Bresman *et al.*, 1999; Hagedoorn and Duysters, 2002b).

Besides overcoming the lack of knowledge, M&As allow R&D costs and risk reduction and the enlargement of the number of potential products in the pipeline (Ahuja and Katila, 2001; Ranft and Lord, 2002). Furthermore, M&As might reduce uncertainty and help companies to increase their control over their environment or to reduce their dependency on it (Hagedoorn and Duysters, 2002b). Finally, successful M&As result in an improvement of companies' exploratory learning, and thus of their long-term technological performance (Hagedoorn and Duysters, 2002b).

However, post-acquisition knowledge transfer does not always occur (Al-Laham *et al.*, 2010). A fundamental aspect of the management of knowledge is to evaluate the benefits of the acquiring firms from the process of knowledge transfer/creation. In Chapter 7 Savarese, Belussi, Rakic and Orsi analyze the post-acquisition performance of acquirers in a representative sample of international biotech firms. Their study utilizes both quantitative (number of family patents) and qualitative measures (number of forward patent citations). They argue that the development of the firm's knowledge base through in-house investments might be a suboptimal choice, compared with a model of open innovation in which firms, sourcing new knowledge from outside from instances of M&A, can discover new avenues of research, escaping from the risk of inertial behaviour. The use of external sources, and particularly the knowledge of the acquired firms, may broaden the firm's knowledge base, enhancing the viability of its new ventures. Their analysis shows that M&As positively affect the innovative performance of the acquirers, both considering quantitative and qualitative indicators.

In Chapter 8 Orsi, Ganzaroli and De Noni investigate another aspect of post-acquisition performances of acquirers, and specifically the post-M&A 'absorption-related invention capacity'. The influence of several factors is tested, and the main result emerging from the empirical research is that technological similarities (measured in terms of technological patent classes' relatedness – similarity within the four-digit subclass) strongly influence the absorption capabilities of the acquirers, whereas complementarity (measured in terms of patent classes' relatedness within the one-digit section, excluding all cases of similarity) seems to have no relevance.

But are alliances becoming a complete mechanism for knowledge exploration and exploitation? From the extensive literature we have surveyed we can argue that exploration is better developed within alliances, but acquisition processes drive a more exhaustive exploitation. Through acquisition, firms can reduce the risk of the wrong selection and subsequent difficulties in knowledge integration (Hennart, 1988). Information asymmetry and opportunism inhibit market-mediated resource transactions (Williamson, 1973) and the cost of using the market increases as resources become more firm-specific and complex. Thus, acquisitions allow firms to obtain the required capabilities (Teece, 1987). Through M&As, firms gain access to external sources of innovation (Arora and Gambardella, 1994; Hitt *et al.* 1996; Graebner and Eisenhardt, 2004), develop and extend their resources and capabilities (Vermeulen and Barkema, 2001; Uhlenbruck *et al.*, 2006) and overcome local searching boundaries (Rosenkopf and Nerkar, 2001; Rosenkopf and Almeida, 2003).

On the same line of analysis, in Chapter 9, Belussi, De Noni, Ganzaroli and Orsi consider if M&As are driving more exploitation or exploration. The relationship between knowledge similarity and exploitative innovation appears to be an inverted U-shape. Thus, too many similarities do not enhance exploitative processes after a certain threshold (and neither do explorative processes). On the contrary, the relationship between knowledge complementarity and explorative innovation is negative and, after a certain threshold, is positive and therefore U-shaped.

Part III is dedicated to the study and analysis of alliances as important instruments for surviving in high-tech and turbulent industries. We examine the role of different forms of collaborations between firms and, also, between firms and universities, which support the formation of R&D partnerships in the high-tech environment. These strategic networks of collaboration, involving the growth of dynamic capabilities, play an important role. Collaborations can be a wellspring of innovation and provide companies with access to a portfolio of new ideas and inventions, as in the case of TOTO (a Japanese company) described in Chapter 10 and presented by Sedita, Yasunori, and Naohiro. Alliances can help companies to acquire external knowledge in an easy manner, strengthening their ability to survive in high-tech environments. The specific characteristics of these collaborations in the software industry are discussed in Chapter 11 by Gambarotto, Solari and Orsi. The aim of this work is to compare the weak software industry of two Southern European countries (Italy and Spain), with the stronger German industry. Using an interview panel for each country, five fundamental aspects characterizing the production model are analyzed: finance, labour and relationships with clients, suppliers and competitors. In Chapter 12 Savarese, Michelazzo, Belussi and Rakic show how interfirm alliances are shaping the different systems of innovation of the biotech industry in three European countries: Italy, France and (jointly) Denmark-Sweden.

Part IV illustrates two interesting cases studies in which alliances and acquisitions have been utilized by firms to extend their knowledge and to build external capabilities. Here, again, networks, alliances and innovation become deeply interwoven. Chapter 13 by Belussi, Sedita, Ganzaroli and Orsi, considers the case of L'Oréal. The reuse of knowledge in L'Oréal has opened up a new speciation of family products, to arrive at a radical shift in the creation of bio-cosmetics, where the nutritional aspects of some drugs and materials (coming from the research of a large multinational such as Nestlé) have been recombined with the experience of large producers of traditional cosmetics. In the case of Fidia Advanced Biopolymers, Anika Therapeutics, described in Chapter 14 by Belussi, we see how through the initial phase of development based on international R&D alliances in tissue engineering, the firm has built a paradigmatic model of open innovation. However, this was not sufficient to guarantee a viable path of growth. The firm was still suffering from being only a contract research organization. A radical change occurred when it was acquired by a large American biotech. Anika Therapeutics has, thus, guided the innovation strategy of its target towards a more profitable strategy that turns research into new therapies at reasonable costs.

References

Ahuja G., Katila R., 2001. Technological acquisitions and the innovation performance of acquiring firms: A longitudinal study. *Strategic Management Journal*, 22(3): 197–220.

Al-Laham A., Schweizer L., Amburgey T. L., 2010. Dating before marriage? Analyzing the influence of pre-acquisition experience and target familiarity on acquisition success in the "M&A as R&D" type of acquisition. *Scandinavian Journal of Management*, 26(1): 25–37.

Amihud Y., Lev B., 1981. Risk reduction as a managerial motive for conglomerate mergers. *The Bell Journal of Economics*, 12(2): 605–617.

Arora A., Gambardella A., 1994. Evaluating technological information and utilizing it: Scientific knowledge, technological capability, and external linkages in biotechnology. *Journal of Economic Behavior & Organization*, 24(1): 91–114.

Arora A., Fosfuri A., Gambardella A., 2001. *Markets for Technology: Economics of Innovation and Corporate Strategy*, The MIT Press, Cambridge, MA.

Barney J., 1991. Firm resources and sustained competitive advantage. *Journal of Management*, 17(1): 99–120.

Baum J., Calabrese T., Silverman B., 2000. Don't go it alone: Alliance network composition and startups' performance in Canadian biotechnology. *Strategic Management Journal*, 21(3): 267–294.

Bresman H., Birkinshaw J., Nobel R., 1999. Knowledge transfer in international acquisitions. *Journal of International Business Studies*, 30(4): 439–462.

Capaldo A., 2007. Network structure and innovation: The leveraging of a dual network as a distinctive relational capability. *Strategic Management Journal*, 28(6): 585–608.

Carnabuci G., Operti E., 2013. Where do firms' recombinant capabilities come from? Intraorganizational networks, knowledge, and firms' ability to innovate through technological recombination. *Strategic Management Journal*, 34(13): 1591–1613.

Chesbrough H., 2003. The era of open innovation. *The MIT Sloan Management Review*, 127(3): 34–41.

Cloodt M., Hagedoorn J., Van Kranenburg H., 2006. Mergers and acquisitions: Their effect on the innovative performance of companies in high-tech industries. *Research Policy*, 35(5): 642–654.

Conner K. R., Prahalad C. K., 1996. A resource-based theory of the firm: Knowledge versus opportunism. *Organization Science*, 7(5): 477–501.

Cross R., Borgatti S. P., Parker A., 2002. Making invisible work visible: Using social network analysis to support strategic collaboration. *California Management Review*, 44(2): 25–46.

Das T., Teng B., 2001. Trust, control, and risk in strategic alliances: An integrated framework. *Organization Studies*, 22(2): 251–283.

Deeds D. L., Hill C. W., 1996. Strategic alliances and the rate of new product development: An empirical study of entrepreneurial biotechnology firms. *Journal of Business Venturing*, 11(1): 41–55.

Doz Y. and Hamel G., 1998. *Alliance Advantage. The Art of Creating Value through Partnering*, Harvard Business School Press, Cambridge, MA.

Dyer J. H., 1997. Effective interfirm collaboration: How firms minimize transaction costs and maximise transaction value. *Strategic Management Journal*, 18(7): 535–556.

Eisenhardt K. M., Schoonhoven C. B., 1996. Resource-based view of strategic alliance formation: Strategic and social effects in entrepreneurial firms. *Organization Science*, 7(2): 136–150.

Gans J., Stern S., 2003. The product market and the market for ideas: Commercialization strategies for technology entrepreneurs. *Research Policy*, 32(2): 333–350.

Graebner M. E., Eisenhardt K. M., 2004. The seller's side of the story: Acquisition as courtship and governance as syndicate in entrepreneurial firms. *Administrative Science Quarterly*, 49(3): 366–403.

Grant R. M., 1996. Prospering in dynamically-competitive environments: Organizational capability as knowledge integration. *Organization Science*, 7(4): 375–387.

Greenwood R., Hinings C. R., Brown J., 1994. Merging professional service firms. *Organization Science*, 5(2): 239–257.

Gulati R., 1998. Alliances and networks. *Strategic Management Journal*, 19(4): 293–317.

Hagedoorn J., Schakenraad J., 1994. The effect of strategic technology alliances on company performance. *Strategic Management Journal*, 15(4): 291–309.

Hagedoorn J., Duysters G., 2002a. External sources of innovative capabilities: The preference for strategic alliances or mergers and acquisitions. *Journal of Management Studies*, 39(2): 167–188.

Hagedoorn J., Duysters G., 2002b. The effect of mergers and acquisitions on the technological performance of companies in a high-tech environment. *Technology Analysis & Strategic Management*, 14(1): 67–85.

Hagedoorn J., Wang N., 2012. Is there complementarity or substitutability between internal and external R&D strategies? *Research Policy*, 41(6): 1072–1083.

Hakanson L., 1995. Learning through acquisitions: Management and integration of foreign R&D laboratories. *International Studies of Management and Organization*, 25(1–2): 121–157.

Haspeslagh P. C., Jemison D. B., 1991. *Managing acquisitions: Creating Value through Corporate Renewal* (Vol. 416), Free Press, New York, NY.

Haunschild P. R., 1994. How much is that company worth?: Interorganizational relationships, uncertainty, and acquisition premiums. *Administrative Science Quarterly*, 39(3): 391–411.

Hayward M. L., Hambrick D. C., 1997. Explaining the premiums paid for large acquisitions: Evidence of CEO hubris. *Administrative Science Quarterly*, 42(1): 103–127.

Hennart J. F., 1988. A transaction costs theory of equity joint ventures. *Strategic Management Journal*, 9(4): 361–374.

Hitt M. A., Hoskisson R. E., Johnson R. A., Moesel D. D., 1996. The market for corporate control and firm innovation. *Academy of Management Journal*, 39(5): 1084–1119.

Inkpen A., Beamish, P. W., 1997. Knowledge, bargaining power, and the instability of international joint ventures. *Academy of Management Review*, 22(1): 177–202.

Kanter R. M., 1994. Collaborative advantages: The art of alliances. *Harvard Business Review*, July: 96–108.

Larsson R., Bengtsson L., Henriksson K., Sparks J., 1998. The interorganizational learning dilemma: Collective knowledge development in strategic alliances. *Organization Science*, 9(3): 285–305.

Levitt B., March J. G., 1988. Organizational learning. *Annual Review of Sociology*, 14: 319–340.

Lindgren U., 1982. *Foreign Acquisitions: Management of the Integration Process*, Institute of International Business, Stockholm, Sweden.

Mowery D. C., Oxley J. E., Silverman B. S., 1996. Strategic alliances and interfirm knowledge transfer. *Strategic Management Journal*, 17(S2): 77–91.

Nelson R. R., 1991. Why do firms differ, and how does it matter? *Strategic Management Journal*, 12(2): 61–74.

Nonaka I., 1991. The knowledge-creating company. *Harvard Business Review*, 69(6): 96–104.

Powell W., Koput K., Smith-Doerr L., 1996. Interorganizational collaboration and the locus of innovation: Networks of learning in biotechnology. *Administrative Science Quarterly*, 41(1): 116–145.

Ranft A. L., Lord M. D., 2002. Acquiring new technologies and capabilities: A grounded model of acquisition implementation. *Organization Science*, 13(4): 420–441.

Roll R., 1986. The hubris hypothesis of corporate takeovers. *Journal of Business*, 59(2): 197–216.

Rosenkopf L., Nerkar A., 2001. Beyond local search: Boundary-spanning, exploration, and impact in the optical disk industry. *Strategic Management Journal*, 22(4): 287–306.

Rosenkopf L., Almeida P., 2003. Overcoming local search through alliances and mobility. *Management Science*, 49(6): 751–766.

Rothaermel F. T., Deeds D. L., 2004. Exploration and exploitation alliances in biotechnology: A system of new product development. *Strategic Management Journal*, 25(3): 201–221.

Rothaermel F. T., Deeds D. L., 2006. Alliance type, alliance experience and alliance management capability in high-technology ventures. *Journal of Business Venturing*, 21(4): 429–460.

Rumelt R. P., 1974. *Strategy, Structure, and Economic Performance*, Division of Research, Graduate School of Business Administration, Harvard University, Boston, MA.

Sanders W. G., 2001. Behavioral responses of CEOs to stock ownership and stock option pay. *Academy of Management Journal*, 44(3): 477–492.

Schildt H. A., Laamanen T., 2006. Who buys whom: Information environments and organizational boundary spanning through acquisitions. *Strategic Organization*, 4(2): 111–133.

Shan W., Walker G., Kogut B., 1994. Interfirm cooperation and startup innovation in the biotechnology industry. *Strategic Management Journal*, 15(5): 387–394.

Shrivastava P., 1986. Postmerger integration. *Journal of Business Strategy*, 7(1): 65–76.

Slusky A. R., Caves R. E., 1991. Synergy, agency, and the determinants of premia paid in mergers. *The Journal of Industrial Economics*, 39(3): 277–296.

Stuart T. E., Hoang H., Hybels R. C., 1999. Interorganizational endorsements and the performance of entrepreneurial ventures. *Administrative Science Quarterly*, 44(2): 315–349.

Sydow J., Windeler A., 1998. Organizing and evaluating interfirm networks: A structurationist perspective on network processes and effectiveness. *Organization Science*, 9(3): 265–284.

Teece D., 1987. *The Competitive Challenge*, Ballinger Publishing Company, Cambridge, MA.

Tiwana A., 2008. Do bridging ties complement strong ties? An empirical examination of alliance ambidexterity. *Strategic Management Journal*, 29(3): 251–272.

Trautwein F., 1990. Merger motives and merger prescriptions. *Strategic Management Journal*, 11(4): 283–295.

Uhlenbruck K., Hitt M. A., Semadeni M., 2006. Market value effects of acquisitions involving internet firms: A resource-based analysis. *Strategic Management Journal*, 27(10): 899–913.

Vermeulen F., Barkema H., 2001. Learning through acquisitions. *Academy of Management Journal*, 44(3): 457–476.

Walter G. A., Barney J. B., 1990. Research notes and communications management objectives in mergers and acquisitions. *Strategic Management Journal*, 11(1): 79–86.

Wernerfelt B., 1995. The resource-based view of the firm: Ten years after. *Strategic Management Journal*, 16(3): 171–174.

Williamson O. E., 1973. Markets and hierarchies: Some elementary considerations. *The American Economic Review*, 63(2): 316–325.

Part I
Alliances and networks

1 The emergence of the red biotech niche and its evanescent dissolution into the integrated parallel 'knowledge system' of a new biopharmaceutical filière

An evolutionary perspective

Fiorenza Belussi and Luigi Orsi

Introduction

Over the last three decades, biotechnology has evolved into a new scientific technological paradigm (Nelson and Winter, 1982; Dosi, 1988) that has spurred a large number of new science-based dedicated biotech firms who are responsible for the development and commercialization of numerous biotech innovations (Audretsch and Stephan, 1996; McKelvey, 1996a; Zucker *et al.*, 1998; Zucker and Darby, 2001; Powell *et al.*, 2002; Mangematin *et al.*, 2003; Autant-Bernard *et al.*, 2006; Wang *et al.*, 2012).

These firms differ radically from other high-tech firms, as they face highly risky R&D activities due to the technological uncertainty linked to the multi-disciplinary character of the technologies involved (Arora and Gambardella, 1990; Powell *et al.*, 1996). From the outset, biotech firms were mainly focused on research science-based activities and not really on new marketable products (Pisano, 2006). They were creating new science and new technologies outside, or often in conjunction with, universities, with the strategic aim of immediately profiting from the new knowledge developed, both throughout the market for technology (Arora *et al.*, 2001), selling and/or licensing patents or by offering the new start-up they had created to the stock market or to venture capitalists (via IPO and PE). Usually, new biotech firms created during the 1980s lacked the traditional managerial functions necessary for the development, marketing and commercialization of new products; therefore, from the outset, they built strong relationships with potential final users of the new knowledge and technologies created within the industrial, agricultural (white and green biotech) and life sciences sectors (red biotech).

Several studies have documented that the strategic collaborations established by biotech firms were a relevant issue in terms of the new configuration of the industry sector (Baum *et al.*, 2000; Rothaermel and Deeds, 2004, 2006). The relevance of complementary assets (Teece, 1986) between old pharma and new biotech firms in alliance formation was underlined by many authors, because incumbents, allied with new entrants, may benefit from the new biotech knowledge brought about by the new firms who possessed the specialized assets necessary to commercialize the new technology (Rothaermel, 2001; Rothaermel and Deeds, 2004). Thus, despite the presence of 'technological discontinuities', both existing pharma firms and new biotech firms have integrated the new techniques into existing industrial practice. The key to survival for old pharma firms has been a combination of integration with biotech competencies and establishing a dense network of relationships with in-house R&D, new biotech firms and star scientists working in universities (Audretsch and Stephan, 1996; McKelvey, 1996b).

Overall, the growing number of biotech-pharma alliances at the industry level, with their effect on the symbiotic co-existence of old incumbents and new biotech firms, has in some ways blocked the Schumpeterian process of 'creative destruction'. In other words, the biotech industry has emerged without any turbulence, incumbents exiting or shakeouts (on the concept of shakeouts, see: Klepper, 1996; Christensen, 1997; Bonaccorsi and Giuri, 2000). Therefore, in the first phase of the evolution of the biotech trajectory (in the 1980s), the persistence of the industry structure largely stemmed from the competence-enhancing effects of new technologies on existing pharmaceutical firms' capabilities to deal with, and finance, the complex research pipeline of clinical trials of new drugs, profiting from their experienced commercial capabilities (Tushman and Anderson, 1986). During the 1980s and 1990s some large pharma firms entered into a process of mega mergers and business concentrations; therefore, incumbent exit was not dependent on the new revolutionary technology brought about by biotech, but was more explained by a tendency toward an oligopolistic configuration of the industry (Galambos and Sturchio, 1998; Lazonick and Tulum, 2011; Comanor and Scherer, 2013).

Incumbents introduced enhanced learning processes, which enabled them to adapt over time (McKelvey, 1998). This implied a systematic division of labour and a greater industry specialization along the firms' value chains between biotech firms performing the most risky and technologically advanced R&D in genomic issues, DNA recombinant technologies and tissue engineering, and large pharma firms who were more involved in licensed acquisitions and market commercialization (Pisano, 1991). However, the emphasis on the existence of a stable vertical relationship between pharma and biotech firms may represent an incomplete picture of the industry's evolution: this view suffers from being a static picture. Industry structure is not stable since capabilities, investments and underlying technologies evolve (Utterback and Abernathy, 1975). In fact, biotech partnering strategies evolved over time, becoming more and more heterogeneous. In this chapter we analyse how, as a result of the technology evolution, biotech firms' partnering strategies have evolved during the 'maturing' phase of their discovering new science into developing a number of horizontal relationships – defined here as bio-to-bio alliances – with some central 'biotech actors'. These actors represent a clearly distinctive new market niche formed by firms that, over time, have developed some internal organizational capabilities in applying the new science to novel products and biotech treatments and following the path of new personalized medicines. However, in the last decade a tremendous flow of merger and acquisitions (M&As), perpetrated by large pharma firms, has undermined this novel emerging biotech niche. A previously open model of innovation (Chesbrough, 2003), with a distinct duality between biotech and pharma organizations, is being reconverted into a closed one, characterized by the dominance of a hierarchical control of the entire 'discovering' value chain. This chapter analyses the emergence of the biotech niche through the lens of firm creation, as well as alliances and M&As. Its main contribution is of an empirical nature, leading to questions about the traditional division of labour embodied in alliances between dedicated biotech firms and Big Pharmas (BP) (large pharmaceutical companies), the former specializing in research and innovation activities located upstream in the biotech value chain and the latter holding as incumbents the critical complementary resources necessary for the development of new drugs, clinical trials and commercial activities. Although the question of the division of labour between dedicated biotech firms and BP is not a recent one (it was already at the core of Pisano's (1991) paper), recent data are lacking. Such data are very interesting now, since the passing of time makes it possible to study the evolution of the phenomenon. On a more theoretical viewpoint, this chapter establishes the connection between an evolutionary view 'à la Nelson and Winter' and the technological alliances and M&A approach (Teece, 1992; Gulati, 1999; Grant and Baden-Fuller, 2004; De Man and Duysters, 2005).

We established three primary findings. First, there is not a simple division of labour between pharma and biotech firms, rather the division encompasses more actors and more recombinative types of alliances. This division of labour was clearly important in the nascent phase of the biotech niche, but it was very soon followed by a more heterogeneous and recombinative approach toward a plurality of alliance partner selection. Second, in the last few decades the largest biotech firms have become 'poles of alliances' in comparison to the old traditional BP firms and an emergent new biotech niche has been created. Third, incumbents – BP firms – did not follow the alternative of internally absorbing the new 'disruptive' biotech technologies (moving quickly toward the new technological paradigm, transforming their R&D laboratories and their research focus, as has been demonstrated by examples from all the large pharma firms), neither were they displaced from the market (as shown in the industry model evolution by Klepper (1996)). Rather, they used their established oligopolistic power to rapidly acquire these new competitors – which over time had been able to grow from being R&D laboratories into 'real' functioning innovative firms—integrating them into a diverse industrial conglomerate complex, whose overlapping, multilevel borders define the nascent biopharma filière.

On the whole, worldwide, red biotech remains a small and distinct subset (estimated by Rader (2008) to be about 15 per cent) of the biopharmaceutical industry, whether considered in terms of products, R&D, companies, revenue or other parameters. For example, worldwide annual biopharmaceutical revenues in 2008, using the broad biotechnology definition, were about $100 billion, compared with about $650 billion for all pharmaceuticals. The worldwide annual sales of vaccines and blood products were less than $15 billion, comparable to that of sales of the leading pharmaceutical, Lipitor (atorvastatin calcium; Pfizer, New York).

However, the sales of biopharmaceuticals relative to drugs and all pharmaceuticals have been growing in the last few years and, by 2012 (Rader, 2013), they had reached a value of about $165 billion (the sales of vaccines and blood products were about $110 billion). Today BP are not primarily concerned with small-molecule drugs, but they are investing their R&D budget heavily in the development of biopharmaceuticals.

In order to delineate the evolutionary pattern of biotech firms and their portfolio alliances (Wassmer, 2010) we used and compared the two most worldwide complete and informative databases: Bioscan and Medtrack (Schilling, 2009). Bioscan covers mainly the biotech sector, while Medtrack is a larger database that includes information for the pharma sector as well. All information relative to the analysis of M&A was extracted by Medtrack. We assembled a dataset of 530 US and 237 EU biotech firms and 4,695 alliance agreements (3,282 deriving from the US sample and 1,413 from the EU sample).

This chapter is organized according to some specific research questions and is followed by a literature review and a presentation of the empirical results supporting our arguments. The next section includes a brief literature review on the division of labour hypothesis. This is followed by the presentation of some empirical findings on biotech firm creation and a short history of the main companies reflecting the emergence of the biotech niche. The following section begins with a literature review concerning alliances in biotech. In this section we discuss the hypothesis of an existing heterogeneity of alliances, which implies the overcoming of the fixed division of labour between pharma and biotech firms. Empirical support is provided through the elaboration of a novel dataset based on Medtrack. The following section begins with a literature review on M&As in biotech. The extent of the phenomenon of M&A is shown in line with the analysis of the evolution of the biotech niche, which has now evolved into a larger integrated parallel knowledge complex constituting the biopharmaceutical filière.

Disruptive technologies and the emergence of new niches

Technological change in an industry is generally characterized by long periods of incremental change, punctuated by 'discontinuous' radical progress (Nelson and Winter, 1977; Mokyr, 1990). As argued by Schumpeter (1942), the introduction of radical innovations in the economic system activates a process of 'creative destruction', leading to the disruption of industry structure and turbulence and to a flow of firms entering and exiting (Buenstorf et al., 2013). The emergence of a breakthrough technology (Utterback and Abernathy, 1975; Abernathy and Utterback, 1978; Utterback 1994) often equates with firm creation or diversification, either through entering an existing industry or constituting an entirely new industry. Technology life cycle theories (Tushman and Anderson, 1986; Anderson and Tushman, 1990) suggest that the exploration of competing technological trajectories within a highly uncertain and turbulent environment affects incumbents' displacement. As technology matures, the industrial structure by which knowledge is generated and the spatial organizations of scientific and economic activities change as a result of a process of technological consolidation around a dominant design (Abernathy and Utterback, 1978; Utterback, 1994). Technology becomes more specific, the number of entries declines and firms focus on the most promising research avenues. At the level of industry, this leads to more market-based relations: competition among firms intensifies and industry shakeouts may occur (Klepper, 1996; Christensen, 1997). But displacement does not always occur. Accordingly, Tripsas (1997), unraveling the process of creative destruction in the typesetter industry, discovered that incumbents were displaced in only one of the main three technological shifts. She shed light on the interaction of factors such as the level of investment, the existence of highly technical capabilities among incumbents and the influence of complementary assets (distribution channels, service networks and so on) that allowed old firms to absorb the new radical technological paradigms. This is clearly consistent with the evolutionary theory of the firm (Nelson and Winter, 1982; Witt, 1992; Metcalfe, 1998; Dosi *et al.*, 2000; Zollo and Winter, 2002; Dopfer, 2005) where the two alternatives (market displacement of the incumbents or new entry of novel organizations giving rise to the 'speciation' of a new niche) still co-exist. On the one hand, several studies have highlighted the mechanisms of adaptation and the strategic renewal of the incumbent firms' routines as crucial elements in maintaining market position (Delacroix and Carroll, 1983; Carroll, 1985; Carroll and Swaminathan, 1992; Teece *et al.*, 1994; Foster, 1997; Gavetti and Levinthal, 2000; Lavie and Rosenkopf, 2006). On the other hand, the emerging of a new sector, with a Schumpeterian swarming of new firms into the market and the creation of entirely new organizations, appears to many to be nothing other than the quintessential 'law of movement' of capitalism (Schumpeter, 1934). Levinthal (1998) and Adner and Levinthal (2000, 2002) have shown that the emergence of new technologies is often linked to the speciation of technologies into a new niche. This niche is perceived as stable or persistently growing thanks to the contemporaneous improvements of the technology that, with time, may penetrate other niches. At the theoretical level, the identification of the evolutionary patterns of industries has oscillated between two very radical alternatives: displacement (the Schumpeterian gale of creative disruption) or adaptation (Nelson and Winter, 1982; Zollo and Winter, 2002) or a combination of both depending on the sector and other endogenous characteristics of the organizations (Tripsas, 1997). In contrast, researchers studying the evolution of the biotech sector have implicitly presented, but not much discussed, a third model based on the co-existence of old mature organizations (incumbents) bearing old technology with new, recently founded firms bearing new scientific knowledge necessary for the development of new flows of innovation. Therefore, they have highlighted that, in the early stages of new business development, when the internalization of technologies is risky due to technological and market uncertainty, alliances between incumbents (established pharmaceutical firms) and new firms (biotech firms) create a new model of innovation with a specific division of the innovative labour (Arora and Gambardella, 1994; Garnsey and Long, 2008; Gambardella and McGahan, 2010). Furthermore, others have stressed the interactive model of new knowledge creation between old pharma firms and new biotech organizations (Powell *et al.*, 1996), which allows incumbents to persist and new firms to enter the market. We will take this theoretical perspective to analyse the emergence of the biotech niche, looking at the implications of biotech firms' partnering strategies with pharma and how they evolve over time. In particular, we challenge the theoretical hypothesis of the stability of the 'co-existence' of incumbents and new firms, maintaining that what appeared early on as the emergence of a new stable model with the co-habitation of the two types of firms, has recently resulted in systematic 'integrative' hostile acquisitions of the new entrants by the larger, dominant pharma firms.

If the origin of pharma firms derives from the modern process of drug discovery emanating in the chemical research developed at the end of the nineteenth century, then the first technological discontinuity in the industry was characterized by the emergence of the biotech trajectory rooted in the discovery of the technique of recombinant DNA (r-DNA) made by Cohen and Boyer in 1973 on the basis of Watson, Crick and Franklin's hypothesis concerning the double-helix model of DNA. This new scientific development gave rise to the second discontinuity – a new knowledge regime far removed from the old one and mainly dominated by synthetic and organic chemistry. In the 1980s the first biotechnology firms started entering the pharmaceuticals market (Gambardella, 1995; Galambos and Sturchio, 1998; Henderson *et al.*, 1999; Audretsch, 2001; Lee, 2003; Quéré, 2003; Gottinger and Umali, 2008). The third discontinuity was related to the so-called genomics revolution in the 2000s, characterized by the spread of gene sequencing activity and the rise of bioinformatics.

The development of the biotech niche started at the end of the 1970s when the first biotech firms were created. In the US these were pure science-based start-ups or spin-offs from universities and in Europe they were a small group of pharma firms which adopted the new revolutionary technology from the outset for producing biotech drugs made from complex biological processes, which are an alternative modality to the less expensive small-molecule drugs produced via chemical synthesis.

In the US Genentech (founded in 1976), Genzyme (founded in 1981) and AMGen (founded in 1980) were the first *de novo* (start-up) entrants (Tushman and Anderson, 1986) in the emerging biotech niche.

In order to identify the evolution of the biotech niche in our research design, we utilized one of the most comprehensive databases (Bioscan),[1] which provides detailed information on the biotech sector[2] and individual data for each firm. The database covers the period 1900–2006. Classification of organizations/companies as biotech (or not) can be more complex than classifying products and technologies. Some biopharmaceutical companies, for example Biogen, AMGen and Genzyme, also develop, manufacture and market synthetic drugs. The reverse is also true: many large international drug companies like Hoffmann-La Roche, Merck, Pfizer and others, are also involved in biopharmaceuticals. Also, few biopharmaceuticals can be attributed to a single company. Different companies often deserve credit for research, development, manufacturing and marketing.

Thus, when considering some economic parameters such as total industry sales, employment, etc. it would be better to refer to the sales of each individual product; however, this would be impossible. It is important to consider this, because biotechnology business clearly includes all pharmaceuticals produced from biotech-like (small, R&D intensive) life science companies, plus all biopharmaceutical products manufactured and distributed by BP firms. As we will discuss in the following pages, large pharma firms have not been able to absorb the new technological paradigm into their prevailing research methods, but they have activated a flow of defensive and 'hostile' acquisitions (of patents and firms) to launch a novel technological trajectory.

Articles in the major business and financial periodicals often apply the term 'biopharmaceutical' (and biotechnology) to products and companies without any real biotechnology involvement. The terms appear where it would be more appropriate to use emerging, R&D intensive, biotech-like, start-up, new or small-molecule. Misuse is very common. Often, anything that appears high-tech and involves pharmaceuticals (or life sciences), particularly if it is about small companies, is described as biopharmaceutical (and/or biotech). Thus, hundreds of small drug discovery and related service companies that have no involvement in or use of biotechnologies are called biopharmaceutical. Similarly, BP are often included. For example, as argued by (Rader, 2007b), the BioSpace Glossary defines a biopharmaceutical company as: 'involved in research of new drugs as well as the manufacturing, marketing and distribution of pharmaceutical products'. Similarly, the NASDAQ Biotechnology Index includes small biotechnology and small pharmaceutical companies. But clearly, as a whole, the pharmaceutical industry has not morphed into the biotech industry. Biotech firms and pharma drug producers (technologies, R&D activities, companies and subsectors) can be readily distinguished: technologies, products and their methods of production (biological or chemical), and not the firms' sizes, define the industry. From our Bioscan database, for each year starting from 1975, we have plotted the number of newly created biotech firms (see Figure 1.1). Data refers to the net number of entries (entries minus exits), i.e. the number of new active companies per year, discounted by the number of firms that have implemented an exit strategy from the market.

The growth of the biotech niche is significant for all of the 1980s and it accelerates through the 1990s. In about two decades more than 1,000 newly created firms entered and survived within the market. The maximum rate of birth and survival is reached in 2001. After 2001 the biotech niche experienced a phase of 'maturity' and consolidation and entries decelerated. By the end of 2006 the biotech niche appears to be made up of 1,567 biotech firms (declaring at the end of 2006, respectively, 667,674 employees, including scientists and researchers).

The formation of the biotech niche is the result of three distinct processes: first, old pharma firms or medical producers (born before 1975) transformed their characteristic activity, shifting their research toward the new biotech science and

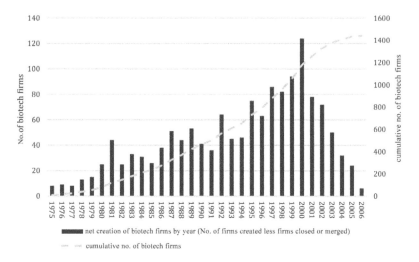

Figure 1.1 The emergence of the biotech niche (1975–2006)

Source: Authors' elaboration on data from Bioscan.

its related technologies (we called these firms *de alio* biotechs – diversification away from another market, but mainly pharma); second, new start-up biotechs were created *de novo* by university scientists and new entrepreneurs; and third, among the new start-ups we also find new independent biotech units created after 1975 by other pharma or biomedical firms. Considering the various countries, the US niche emerges as the most dynamic 'core'. Interestingly, a significant number of new firms entered the market as *de alio* entrants, born between 1912 and 1974. In our database we found 73 US firms, some of which are now important firms leading the markets in bio-instruments, bio-software, reagents, testing and bio-diagnosis services, for example, Allergan (producing an antihistamine to treat allergic conjunctivitis) and Élan (therapies in neurodegenerative and autoimmune diseases; Élan merged with Perrigo in 2013) now listed among the most important US biotech firms. A significant growth of entries characterized the period 1975–1990 (our database lists 346 new biotech companies). But the 'explosion' of the biotech niche occurred in the subsequent period, 1991–2006, when we can observe a huge inflow of 717 new entries. These newly created biotech companies remained of relatively small size, around 50–200 employees. Only a few firms expanded their activities and employment rapidly, other than the first founders (in 2007 Genentech reached 9,800 employees, AMGen 20,000 employees and Genzyme 12,950 employees). We find the suppliers of specialized machinery, diagnostic tools and software among the largest firms, for example Plexis Biosciences, Applera Corp-Applied Biosystems and Applera Corp-Celera Genomics[3]; these latter two are included among the Fortune 500 firms. Looking at the firms established during the 1990s, 2 became quite large reaching about

1,000 employees: Millennium (created in 1993) and Chiron Vision (created in 1995). During the 1990s the scientific success of biotech science also triggered the large pharmas to enter the sector. The US niche attracted the interests of the Swiss company, Roche, that spun off in the US two important, independent firms of significant size (with about 10,000 employees in 2006): the Roche Molecular Systems (created in 1991), which manufactures and supplies diagnostic and blood screening tests based on its polymerase chain reaction technologies, and Roche Biosciences (created in 1995). Abbott created its biotech branch in 2003: Abbott Molecular. A few other small pharmaceutical firms spun off new biotech firms, invading the new niche but they were all of small size and did not grow very much. The transformation of the US biotech technological paradigm caused strategy problems and a stand-off in the largest traditional pharma. As we will discuss in the next section, the slow shift toward new technologies has mainly declined in favour of building a large network of strategic alliances for the purposes of research.

As is shown in Table 1.1, while the number of biotech firms between 1975 and 2006 grew from 126 to 1,442 (creating 340,000 new jobs) the number of pharma firms only doubled, but the new pharma firms were responsible for the net creation of 810,623 new jobs. In fact, the biotech niche, even in the years of maximum expansion, never reached the growth figures characterizing the old pharma industry. In many cases biotech technologies remained at an explorative phase and pharma firms continued to supply the market with traditional products, including blockbusters and small-molecule drugs still based on the old methods of production. At the end of the period analysed in our Bioscan database we could identify an international population of 217 pharma firms (at the end of 2006 and declaring 2,240,621 employees, a figure which is 4 times larger than the total employment created by the biotech firms (at the end of 2006 and declaring 667,674)).

In Europe the first developments in biotech technology were pushed forward by lateral entry from other sectors (mainly pharma), constituting at that time the *de alio* group. Among the pioneers we find the Swiss[4] multinational pharma, Serono, (with about 5,000 employees in 2006), which was founded in Rome, Italy, by Cesare Serono in 1906, but whose headquarters were moved to Switzerland in 1977.[5]

In Switzerland we also find two important and large pharma (with about 90,000 employees each) that were very soon involved in biotech research: Hoffmann-La Roche and Novartis.

The largest European *de alio* biotech is the Danish company, Novo Nordisk, which since its start has focused its research on biological issues and fermentation activities. This firm is continually expanding its activities and also its employment (from 21,000 in 2007 to 37,000[6] in 2012). Novo Nordisk specializes in diabetes and haemophilia care, and growth and hormone replacement therapies. It was created in 1989 following the merger of two old pharma firms, Novo and Nordisk (founded during the 1920s), for the production of a then revolutionary new drug, insulin, extracted from the pancreas of cows, which had just been discovered by two Canadian scientists. The most important European biotech cluster is located in

Table 1.1 Accumulated number of pharma and biotech firms in the period 1900–2006 in the world and total employment registered (as at 31 December 2006)

| 1900–1974 | | | | 1975–2006 | | | | 1900–2006 | | | |
| Pharma | | Biotech | | Pharma | | Biotech | | Pharma | | Biotech | |
Number of firms (traditional pharma)	Total employment	Number of firms (de alio transformation)	Total employment	Number of firms	Total employment	Number of firms	Total employment	Number of firms	Total employment	Number of firms	Total employment
116	1,429,998	126	159,598	100	810,623	1,442	508,876	216	2,240,621	1,568	668,474

Source: Authors' elaboration on data from Bioscan.

the Medicon valley in the cross-national Øresund region, which spans the greater Copenhagen area and the Lund-Malmö area in the province of Scania in Southern Sweden. The biotech niche emerged gradually in that area starting from the early 1990s. According to MVA (2006), there are about 130 dedicated biotech firms, 70 pharmaceutical and 130 biomedical companies, plus a wide range of universities and medical centres such as the Karolinska Institute.

In the UK we find the *de alio* case of Allergy Therapeutics (with about 400 employees in 2006), a pharma firm founded in 1934 and focused on allergy and immunotherapy, plus four important *de novo* leaders emerging during 1980s. They were: Celltech Group (acquired by UCB, a Belgian drug maker, in 2004); Chiroscience Group (specialized in enzymatix hotbed technologies, acquired by Celltech Group in 1999); Mundipharma International Holdings (which opened up in the Cambridge Science Park in 1980 and has been acquired by a German firm); and Shire Pharmaceuticals[7] (with about 3,000 employees in 2006). Many UK small start-ups were created during the 1990s inside the numerous scientific parks created *ad hoc*, such as the famous Cambridge Science Park. Two major UK pharma are involved in biotech research: AstraZeneca (a biopharmaceutical company that was formed in 1999 through the merger of the Swedish firm, Astra, and the British firm, Zeneca) and GlaxoSmithKline (a group formed in the early 2000s following the merger of Glaxo and SmithKline Beecham that at the time began to move into the biotech industry). GlaxoSmithKline divided thousands of its researchers into groups and gave them their own budgets to manage. The changes helped bring some new products to market (Whalen, 2010). In France biotech research includes ancient traditions, starting with the important discoveries of Pasteur. Analysing Bioscan, we observe that the biotech industry was formed by about 10 *de alio* firms that were founded before 1975 and moved their research rapidly into the newly emerging biotech sector, plus about 50 newly created biotech start-ups. Among the former we find Fournier Pharma (with about 3,440 employees in 2006 and acquired in 2006 by Solvay and again in 2011 by the US laboratories, Abbott); Galderma (with 2,300 employees in 2006); and the French bioMérieux (actually the Institut Mérieux, born in 1897, changed its name in 1974). In 1994 bioMérieux acquired Transgene, a true French-dedicated biotechnology firm born in 1979 (today with 270 employees). If we consider the start-ups born after 1975 that became quite large biotech firms (with about 1,000 to 5,000 employees), we find only two: bioMérieux (specializing in tools for laboratory testing, industrial microbiological and in vitro analyses) and LFB (a public organization (it was a public laboratory and is now owned by the state) focused on therapeutic proteins and plasma-derived medicinal products). The typical size of the other French biotech companies is, like in the US, 100 to 150 employees. In France a significant group of pharma firms is now starting to be involved in biotech research, such as the large pharma Sanofi-Aventis, its independent unit Sanofi Pasteur and Ceva veterinary.[8]

In Germany the most important biotech research activities were launched in the past by major pharma and chemical firms that were formed at the end of the nineteenth century and during the 1920s, such as Merck, Schering, Bayer Health

Care Diagnostics Division, Byk Gulden Lomberg, Sandoz and Altana (acquired by the Norwegian Nycomed Group in January 2007 and in turn acquired by the Japanese Takeda Pharmaceutical in September 2011). The German launch into the biotech industry occurred during the 1990s and in the first years of the 2000s, when nearly 40 new start-ups were created thanks to innovative regional policies dedicated to the biotech sector. This favoured the emergence of leading bioregions. Important biotech companies were created, such as Evotech (born in 1995 and with 90 employees by 2006); Lion Biotechnologies (born in 1997 and with 180 employees by 2006); Epigenomics (born in 1998 and with 150 employees by 2006); and Affirmed Therapeutics (born in 2000 and with 2,600 employees by 2006).

In Italy the biotech sector was characterized by a long-lasting structural weakness (Orsenigo, 2001), only partially overcome by the lateral entry of other life sciences firms stemming from applied activities (Belussi and Sedita, 2013). However, a limited group of small pharma firms (Menarini, Zambon, Recordati, Chiesi and Fidia) soon started in the 1980s to make significant investments into biotech R&D. A small niche emerged at the end of the 1990s and during the 2000s with university or R&D spin-offs (among them Siena Biotech with 120 employees in 2006; Bio3 Research with 6 employees in 2006; Gentium with 60 employees in 2006; and Bioxell with 63 employees in 2006).

During the 2000s the biotech niche reached a phase of 'maturity' and the cumulative number of biotech firms existing in the market took an inverse U-shaped form (see Figure 1.1, dotted line). During the initial phase biotech firms were tiny organizations, mainly science-based structures devoted to the activity of exploring new technologies and methodologies, which were mainly related to the 'proof of the concept' and to the targeting of new drugs for the cure of rare diseases. They earned profits by selling idiosyncratic knowledge or patents to other firms. By the end of the 1990s and during the 2000s they became market-based, 'productive' value creation organizations, able to benefit from the business of introducing new products into the market. Thus, after initially entering as pure 'research-based' organizations, placed in a non-competitive division of labour with the pharma firms, they started to slowly grow in their niche by concentrating on specific new biopharmaceutical therapeutic products.

Table 1.2, which refers to the situation at the end of 2006, corroborates this perspective, looking at the product and work-in-progress portfolios of biotech firms in relation to the variegate world of pharma firms. Considering the 126 *de alio* biotech firms born before 1975, only in 8 cases did we find that firms did not yet have marketable products in their pipeline. In contrast, the majority (86) of old biotech firms are active in the market and at the same time they have a number of products in the pipeline. The remaining 29 biotech firms terminated their research pipeline and sell their products directly into the market. The biotech niche consolidated its structure during the boom period of 1975–2006. Out of the total of 1,441 firms considered, only 480 do not declare a product as being sold in the market. More than half (759) of the population of biotech firms has developed a productive capability downstream from their research value chain. The radical

Table 1.2 A typology of pharma and biotech firms, and the accumulated number of pharma and biotech products in the period 1900–2006 in the world (as at 31 December 2006)

1900–1974				1975–2006				1900–2006					
Biotech				*Biotech*				*Pharma*			*Biotech*		
Firms with only product in the pipeline	Firms with products in the pipeline and in the markets	Firms with only product in the markets	Total number of firms	Firms with only product in the pipeline	Firms with products in the pipeline and in the markets	Firms with only product in the markets	Total number of firms	Number of firms	Number of products in the market	Number of products in the pipeline	Number of firms	Number of products in the market	Number of products in the pipeline
8	89	29	126	481	759	201	1,441	216	11,042	1,342	1,568	11,755	6,586

Source: Authors' elaboration on data from Bioscan.

novel creativity that biotech firms have brought into the health system is clearly visible if we confront the number of newly created products attributed to pharma and biotech firms. At the end of 2006 the number of products commercialized by the biotech firms was slightly superior (11,755) to the number of products commercialized by the pharma firms (11,042). On the one side, despite the large number of biopharmaceutical products inserted into the market, the biotech niche was struggling to survive after the internet financial bubble, which reduced the flows of financial support provided to biotech firms by IPOs and venture capitalists. On the other side, biotech firms intensively maximized their recourse to heterogeneous partner alliance in order to consolidate their innovative trajectory, based on knowledge recombination, parallel path search strategies, platform exploration and increased knowledge variety[9] (Krafft, 2014).

Partner alliances supporting the emergence of the bioniche

Since the beginning of the biotech revolution in science, biotech firms have developed strong alliances with pharmaceutical firms in a model of open innovation that resembles the typical 'open innovation model' described by Chesbrough (2003). Allying with well-known pharmaceutical firms was considered useful for acquiring resources, boosting a firm's reputation and building credibility (Dollinger *et al.*, 1997; Hagedoorn and Roijakkers, 2002; Niosi, 2003; Tyebjee and Hardin, 2004). From the pharmaceutical firms' perspective, allying with biotech firms was beneficial for integrating external knowledge, developing absorptive capacity (Cohen and Levinthal, 1990) and exploiting technological spill-overs for the purpose of commercialization (Kale *et al.*, 2002; McKelvey *et al.*, 2004). The alliance between biotech firms and pharma firms could also be justified by the need to find sufficient different partners in order to acquire new knowledge (Greis *et al.*, 1995, Tyebjee and Hardin, 2004; Lane and Probert, 2007), but not so varied as to become 'uninterested' and 'incommunicable'. Thus, partners are more interested if they are 'complementary' close in terms of knowledge specialization, but placed at an average degree of knowledge distance (Nooteboom *et al.*, 2007).

Mowery *et al.* (1998) found that pharmaceutical and biotechnology firms that draw from the same knowledge base (proxied by patent cross-citations and patent common citations), were more likely to partner up and create better-performing alliances. In addition, Lane and Lubatkin (1998), examining the role of absorptive capacity, showed that closeness in basic knowledge helped the partners to operate together more effectively. Persistent alliance strategies are common in innovation-active firms (Bederbos *et al.*, 2012).

In addition to fostering alliances with pharma firms, we expect that biotech firms may have also pursued alliances with public research organizations (PRO). At the beginning of the biotech revolution, in order to explore several competing technology trajectories and decrease the risks of following the wrong path, knowledge production required interactive learning with multiple sources of inspiration (Stuart *et al.*, 2007). Close ties with research organizations (generally co-located) can encourage face-to-face knowledge creation, experimentation, sharing of tacit knowledge and a wider process of exploration. Proximity and co-location support the creation of local networks, where a positive 'Marshallian atmosphere' facilitates the exploration of cutting-edge technology trajectories (Boschma and Frenken, 2010; Boschma, 2005; Frenken and Boschma, 2007). We also observed the emergence of truly co-located biotech dynamic economic areas, characterized both by dense, local social interaction and knowledge circulation and by strong interregional and international connections with outside knowledge sources and partners (Chiesa and Chiaroni, 2005).

Consequently, the development of biotech has revealed itself to be of a 'local' nature since knowledge is highly context-specific and dependent on specific aspects embedded in the local environment (Nelson and Winter, 1982). This is supported by the fact that the complexities of the global business environment and the lack of familiarity between alliance partners located in different countries, may produce a higher risk of opportunism in international alliances than in domestic or local alliances (McCutchen *et al.*, 2004; Anand and Khanna, 2000; Coombs *et al.*, 2006). As technology matured, this view started to be challenged by other perspectives that also maintained the importance of non-local knowledge flows (Al-Laham and Souitairs, 2008). Over time, non-local knowledge flows may alleviate some negative effects that biotech firms might suffer based on organizational inertia and on the risk of becoming trapped along old technological paths (lock-in effect). Accordingly, to avoid path dependency (Arthur, 1994) and eventually the liability of senescence (Hannan *et al.*, 2007), we could expect that international alliances play an important role. Instead of being trapped in only one type of relationship, we could hypothesize that biotech firms' partnering strategies, once tightly vertically integrated, will also be characterized by an increasing degree of horizontal alliances (bio-to-bio). This could allow biotech firms to overcome the pharmaceuticals' bargaining power (Milgrom and Roberts, 1992) and reach the final market autonomously. Another reason to ally with other biotech firms is that this might lessen the risk of knowledge leakage (as opposed to firms with complementary capabilities).[10] To the extent that both parties are similar, they may perceive that they can work together more successfully and manage more effectively the integration of competences and skills necessary in alliances in order to orchestrate a network able to create value (Weisenfeld *et al.*, 2001; Sabatier *et al.*, 2012). In our perspective, these emerging partnership strategies have generated a potential turbulence in the industrial structure and, consequently, a biotech niche has emerged affecting the stability of the industry structure. Therefore, over time, biotech firms started to exhibit novel capabilities in downstream activities (clinical trials, product approval, production and marketing), thus competing with old pharmaceutical firms (Rothman and Kraft, 2006).

An important element favouring the consolidation of the biotech niche is linked to the extended network of alliances that biotech firms were able to develop during the early years, not only playing the function of being an external R&D laboratory for pharma firms but using their portfolio of alliances to consolidate their knowledge recombination (and application: Weitzman, 1998) and their complementary productive marketing capabilities. Networks of biotech firms, venture capital firms, lead user, large corporations and research institutions thus became critical aspects in the dynamics of the biotechnology niche.

In order to update our database, we use another important archive, Medtrack,[11] which is focused not only on the biotech industry but on the entire life sciences sector. We selected Medtrack because it maps in a precise and simple way the alliance category (whether the alliance is related to a product or to a technology), the type of agreement (research, development, licensing, marketing, distribution, funding, etc.) and, especially, allows us to track alliance formation over time. In our analysis we selected only the firms belonging to the aggregate population of US and European biotech firms and only firms having at least one agreement (they represent on average about 75 per cent of the total population of firms). We selected all agreements where a biotech firm was either a 'source' or a 'target'. We concentrated our analysis only on those agreements related to finance, R&D and licensing and excluded marketing and distribution agreements. We collected a total number of 6,513 R&D alliances (4,357 deriving from the US firms and 2,156 from the European firms, associated with 998 biotech firms).[12]

The average biotechnology firm in our analysis has entered into 6.51 alliances: 1.75 with other biotech firms, 2.65 with other pharma firms, 1.59 with PRO and 0.52 with 'other' firms. The average firm has 376 employees and is about 19 years old.

A Pareto distribution of the alliance networks characterizes this industry, but if we also consider the top 100 best-performing companies (in terms of the number of agreements/deals), we can observe the phenomenon of the long tail[13] (Anderson, 2006; Andriani and McKelvey, 2009). This phenomenon deviates from the characteristic Gaussian-based 'average' of the 'normal' statistics and the situation appears to be polarized between a few dominant actors (in terms of number of agreements) and a wide variety of new entrants, which add up to a large number of agreements dispersed among numerous agents.

Figures 1.2, 1.3 and 1.4 allow us to discuss the importance of partnering strategies implemented by our biotech firms and to deal with the theoretical analytical framework discussed. Our analysis reveals that certainly the typology of alliances between pharma and biotech firms plays a focal role for the entire period, explaining the development of the knowledge pipeline and innovation within the bio-pharmaceutical filière. However, we can hypothesize that a strong and exclusive division of labour between biotech and pharma firms was occurring only at a very early stage (discussed extensively in the literature, but not very much evidenced by our data, which suffers from a certain level of incompleteness in the coverage of the dynamics of the 1970s and early 1980s). The analysis of Figures 1.2 and 1.3 suggests that, in the 1990s, biotech firms were already choosing a very heterogeneous alliance portfolio, allying not only with pharma but also with PRO, with other biotech firms and with firms belonging to other industrial sectors.

This process is particularly evident in the pattern of the US firms illustrated by Figure 1.3. In Europe (Figure 1.4) biotech firms did not resort like in the US to a wide heterogeneous plot of alliances.

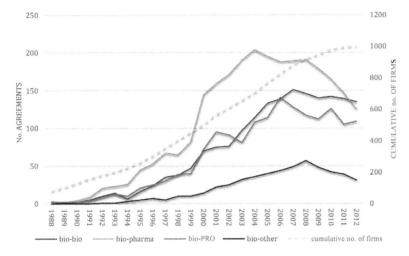

Figure 1.2 Total alliances of biotech companies (only finance, R&D and licensing) by year and cumulative number of companies (1988–2012)

Source: Authors' elaboration on data from Medtrack.

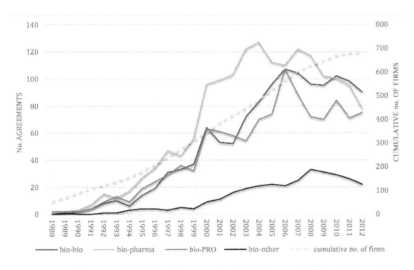

Figure 1.3 Alliances of US biotech companies (only finance, R&D and licensing) by year (1988–2012)

Source: Authors' elaboration on data from Medtrack.

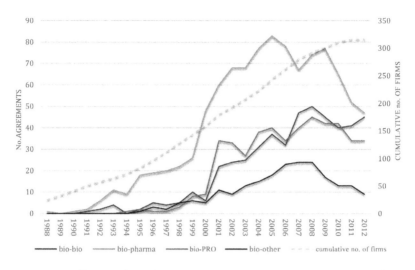

Figure 1.4 Alliances of EU biotech companies (only finance, R&D and licensing) by
year (1988–2012)

Source: Authors' elaboration on data from Medtrack.

The selected strategy of choosing a prevalent alliance with pharma firms can
be considered in this case to be a factor of weakness and not strength: in other
words, demonstrating the consequences of an initially retarded development in
the European context where the biotech niche suffered in many countries as a
result of inferior institutional support (Belussi and Sedita, 2013). As illustrated
in Figure 1.2, the number of bio-to-pharma alliances reached a peak in the period
1999–2004, at the start of the so-called genomic revolution. Figure 1.3 for the US
and Figure 1.4 for Europe exhibit a clear-cut inverted U-shaped curve.

After 2004 (Figure 1.2), the agreements with incumbent pharma firms lose
their attraction and we observe both in the US (Figure 1.3) and in Europe
(Figure 1.4) a stable decline in their absolute number. By the mid-2000s we witnessed (especially in the US, Figure 1.3) a new wave of resurgence in bio-to-bio
and bio-to-PRO alliances.

To conclude, it is interesting to note here that, once we consider the number
of bio-to-bio and bio-to-PRO agreements added together, the cumulative value
of this new aggregated category tends to be overwhelmingly dominant from the
early 2000s onwards. These empirical elaborations support strongly the hypothesis of the end of a simple division of labour. Our data show that the symbiotic
and unilateral relationships described by prior literature as 'fragile' biotech and
'strong' incumbent pharma firms (Rothaermel, 2001; Rothaermel and Hill, 2005)
tended over time to be weakened, because the largest biotech firms, especially
during the 2000s, were attracting a large number of alliances and, in general,
biotech firms tended to deal with multiple actors. Increasingly, biotech companies

are gaining more power because they are transforming themselves into fully integrated biopharmaceutical companies. Some of the deals with pharma firms in the past have involved large upfront payments and milestone commitments (Kang and Afuah, 2010). Biotech firms tend to structure deals that give them higher ownership levels and more long-term involvements with their pharma partners, with deals including profit sharing, co-development and co-promotion (Mudhar, 2006). As the biotechnology niche is maturing, larger biotech is also able to support smaller biotech alliances, forming alliances at early stages of product development and building more collaborative relationships based on co-licensing and co-development (Fisken and Rutherford, 2002).

In Figure 1.5 we have plotted the distribution of the aggregate number of agreements of the top bio and pharma organizations (bio and pharma firms, but including also PROs), ranking from the highest number of agreements being signed by each individual organization to the lowest and considering the entire period 1970–2006. Our universe of considered organizations is divided into five categories (bio, pharma, biomedical, PRO and other sectors). In this picture we observe the striking emergence of large biotech hubs (coloured in black) that can be considered alternative 'poles of alliances' aggregations, in comparison with the old traditional BP (coloured in red).

Our analysis underlines the growth of large biotech firms that are slowly occupying the market power that, in the past, was exclusively exercised by the traditional incumbent pharma firms. Figure 1.5 shows that, among the most important actors dealing with alliance management, there are newly created biotech firms (like Chiron Corp, AMGen, Genentech, Affymetrix, Biogen, Incyte,

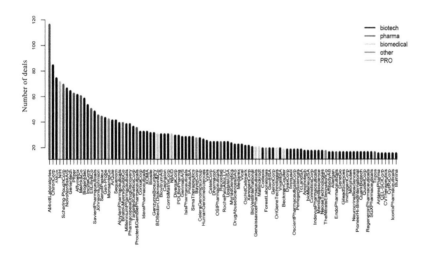

Figure 1.5 Distribution of agreements by number of cumulative agreements in the top 100 organizations (1970–2006)

Source: Authors' elaboration on data from Bioscan.

Gen-Probe, ArQule, Sequenom, Millennium and Genzyme) and *de alio* bio-tech (Novo Nordisk), as well as important pharma incumbents that have moved their research in the last decade toward the new scientific field of research (like Abbott Laboratories, Schering-Plough Corp (merged in 2009 with Merck), Pfizer, Merck, Eli Lilly, Johnson & Johnson and Sanofi Pasteur). Two important US PROs emerged at the core of the biotech alliance network (coloured in blue): the National Institute of Health (NIH) and the National Institute of Allergy and Infectious Diseases (NIAID). Among the firms that come from other sectors (coloured in pink), we find two important multinationals, like Monsanto (involved in agricultural-based biotech) and the chemical firm, Bayer, which has long since extended its activities to pharma. Firms belonging to the bio-medical sector, the sector that produces mainly health machinery and biomedical instruments (coloured in green) show only marginal activity in biotech alliances. However, in Figure 1.5 we can identify three important companies: Beckton, Dickinson and Company,[14] Genaissance Pharmaceuticals,[15] and Mallinckrodt Pharmaceuticals.[16]

The organizational reactions of incumbents to potential threats represented by the emergence of red bioniche was the activation of a flow of M&A

Acquisitions and alliances are two pillars of growth strategy. In a certain way they can be treated as alternative mechanisms for attaining the same goal. But the two strategies differ in many ways: acquisition deals are competitive, based on market prices and risky; alliances are cooperative, negotiated and not so risky (Dyer *et al.*, 2004).

In the literature, the formation of alliances has been interpreted as a substitution of a more concentrated and verticalized governance. However, in some specific cases acquisitions are a more appropriate form, which supersede the benefit of alliances, particularly as a complete and satisfactory mechanism of knowledge exploration and exploitation. For instance, licensing agreements on knowledge sharing are becoming so complex to manage that firms might jump directly from a possible contractual governance (the so-called 'market for technology') to a verticalized solution in which full possession of all the new knowledge jointly created is guaranteed by the legal asset's possession (acquisition). On the other hand, if blind acquisitions are risky and hazardous because of a lack of information completeness regarding the acquired firm, the 'best strategy' implemented by a potential 'acquiring firm' would be to test and better evaluate the technological capability of a partner or the future market of the newly created products by initially building an *ex ante* technology alliance (i.e. risk-controlled acquisition through *ex ante* alliance). Thus, alliances could be considered a gateway mechanism for acquisition (Wang and Zajac, 2007).

Academic literature has widely examined the motivations related to acquisition decisions both at firm and management level (Hayward and Hambrick, 1997; Mittra, 2007). From the firm-level perspective, the most common and evident drivers include growth and scale advantages, i.e. economies of scale and scope (Walter and Barney, 1990), financial synergies (Slusky and Caves, 1991), improved bargaining power, the elimination of overlaps and the utilization of complementary assets (Trautwein, 1990). It is in fact clear, for instance, that M&As might allow acquirers to expand their product pipeline and market share or increase their bargaining power, as a result of size growth as well as rapid access to those complementary resources and knowledge that are useful to sustain their competitive advantage.

More recently, the resource-based theory of the firm and the theory of dynamic capabilities have inspired several studies (Rumelt, 1984; Barney, 1991; Nelson, 1991; Wernerfelt, 1995) that have emphasized how, in order to generate and sustain a competitive advantage with respect to other companies, firms rely heavily on unique and innovative capabilities, i.e. specific expertise and competences related to the development and introduction of new processes and products (Hagedoorn and Duysters, 2002a). Such capabilities might be either endogenous or exogenous (Capron and Anand, 2007). Moreover, as already pointed out, knowledge is often tacit, especially in technological and knowledge intensive contexts, and is thus difficult to transfer from one firm to another (Larsson *et al.*, 1998). Hence, M&As might allow companies to internalize the required (external) knowledge, thereby avoiding the high transaction costs that generally characterize the transmission of tacit knowhow (Pisano, 1991; Bresman *et al.*, 1999). Even if alliances have been found to be generally superior to M&As in generating innovation (De Man and Duysters, 2005), then looking at the theoretical reasons for success and failure of alliances versus M&As, it is the 'indigestibility' argument that is the most distinctive reason. M&As between similar companies do better in terms of innovation than M&As between unrelated companies. In addition, when the process of acquisition and integration runs smoothly, the innovative performance is higher as well. A well-developed post-merger integration process, therefore, could enhance innovation, because the integration of different techniques applied by individual companies might improve the ability to manage innovation and thus R&D productivity, or lower costs. Furthermore, the combination of complementary knowledge might lead to the development of new technologies or products, which would not be individually produced by each partner (Gerpott, 1995). This might have a double repercussion on innovation, i.e. a growth in both its speed and nature.

Despite several motivations accounting for M&A, difficulties arise once we try to explain the trend that has historically characterized the flow of M&As in our economy (Danzon *et al.*, 2007). Several scholars have suggested that M&As took place in periods of change due to such factors as technological advances or deregulation, which are often industry specific and not at all positive, because they may create excess capacity or other inefficiencies (e.g. Hall, 1999; Andrade *et al.*, 2001). Scholars have identified different forms of M&A, among which horizontal, vertical and unrelated M&As. Horizontal M&As involve companies that are closely related as to the products or services they produce; vertical M&As engage companies that had a potential or existing buyer-seller relationship prior to the M&A; unrelated or conglomerate M&As concern companies that are unrelated in terms of the product market in which they are active (Hagedoorn and Duysters, 2002b).

With reference to our research into the biopharmaceutical industry, a high rate of M&A activity has occurred that began in the 1980s (Maybeck and Bains, 2006). Horizontal acquisitions, i.e. pharma-pharma M&As, have been explained by claims of economies of scale and scope due to the research-intensive nature of the industry, whereas market power purposes seem to be improbable because of the already high level of concentration existing in the industry (Danzon *et al.*, 2007). A further possible explanation of large pharmaceutical horizontal M&As might be provided by the excess capacity resulting from patent expirations and gaps in the firm's pipeline and the atypically large role played by patents in the industry (Hall, 1999; Danzon *et al.*, 2007). Another type of horizontal M&A is the biotech-biotech. In the last decade the acquisition of biotech companies has not been simply limited to acquisitions by big incumbents, rather large biotech companies such as AMGen and Gilead Sciences have acquired smaller biotech firms to gain access to complementary technologies, products and markets. In some ways these companies are replacing the role played by the old pharmaceutical companies.

Vertical acquisitions, in particular pharmaceutical acquisitions of biotech companies, were mainly for asset-specific reasons and the possibility of accessing and exploiting for commercial purposes knowledge, technologies and innovations developed by biotech companies (Danzon *et al.*, 2007).

Through M&As pharmaceutical firms gain access to external sources of innovation (Arora and Gambardella, 1990; Hitt *et al.*, 1996; Graebner, 2004), develop and extend their resources and capabilities (Vermeulen and Barkema, 2001; Uhlenbruck *et al.*, 2006) and overcome local search boundaries (Rosenkopf and Nerkar, 2001; Rosenkopf and Almeida, 2003). Thus, in knowledge intensive industries M&As enable pharmaceutical firms to respond to the increasing demand for rapid technological change both in terms of product-related and process-related technologies (Hagedoorn and Duysters, 2002a; Makri *et al.*, 2010).

Data collected on M&As support our claims that alliances could be considered a gateway mechanism for acquisitions and that the biotechnological niche is merging into a broader area: the integrated parallel knowledge complex of the biopharmaceutical filière. The intensification of M&As dates back to the 1990s and 2000s, with a delay in respect of the selection of strategic alliances (Figure 1.2).

Since 1997 the number of M&As has followed a growing, but irregular, pattern. We can observe a stabilization between the years 2008–2011, followed by a significant deceleration in 2012 as a result of both the economic crisis on the one hand and the slowdown in the birth of new biotech firms on the other.

In Figure 1.6 acquisitions (in red) account for 95 per cent of M&As, while only 5 per cent are mergers (in blue). This indicates that acquirers prefer to maintain their independence and structure rather than creating a new entity from the original ones, as in the acquisition of Genentech by Roche that occurred in 2009 at a cost of about $47 billion.[17]

Further confirmation of a general dissolution of the biotech niche within the broader sector of biopharma industry is shown in Figure 1.7.

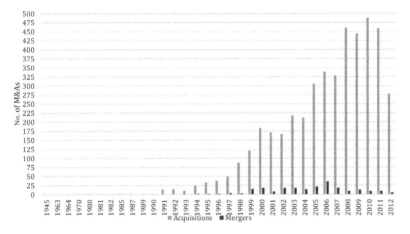

Figure 1.6 M&As in the biopharmaceutical industry per year in the world (1945–2012)

Source: Authors' elaboration on data from Medtrack.

Elaborating further from Figure 1.5, we checked if a biotech firm had been involved in at least one M&A. Figure 1.7 shows that the best-performing biotech companies (in terms of number of upstream alliances: finance, R&D and licensing) have been heavily involved in the process of M&A.[18] Biotechnological firms, highlighted in orange in Figure 1.7, represent companies that have been involved in at least one major M&A conducted in the period 2000–2012 by a pharmaceutical company or by companies coming from 'other sectors' (such as chemical).

This process has particularly affected the 'bulk of the distribution', where nowadays only three *de novo* independent biotech firms remain (AMGen, Affymetrix and Biogen Idec), while Novo Nordisk has been able to maintain its independence in this period. Moreover, the famous Genentech (the first biotech company) was acquired by the Swiss global pharma, Hoffmann-La Roche; Genzyme was acquired in 2011 by the French pharma, Sanofi-Aventis, for about $20 billion[19]; and Chiron was acquired by the Swiss pharma, Novartis, in 2006 for about $6 billion.[20] In the sample of the top 100 firms examined, composed of 76 biotech, 14 pharma and 10 different other organizations that have realized upstream alliances (finance, R&D and licenses), we found that almost 50 per cent of *de novo* biotech companies have been involved in M&A processes with large international players (36 out of 76).

It seems clear why large incumbents are buying the best-performing biotech companies. These companies have a higher rate of innovation in comparison with pharma. In addition, their research laboratories are involved in promising blockbuster drugs (anti-cancer, genetic therapy, tissue engineering and so on). In order to create value for the acquirer, encourage innovative capabilities

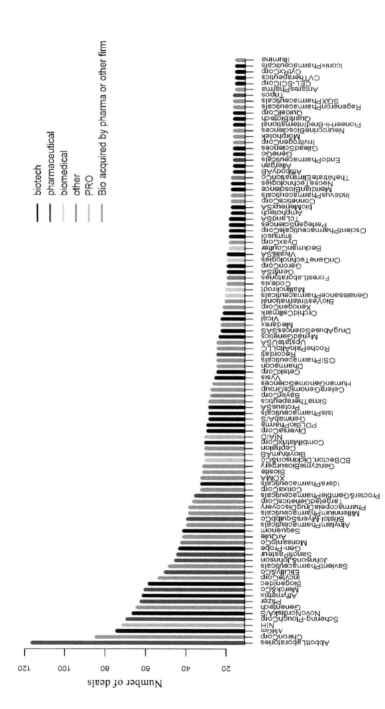

Figure 1.7 Distribution of the top 100 organizations by number of alliances and M&A processes (1970–2006)

Source: Authors' elaboration on data from Bioscan.

and generate innovations, the knowledge acquired through acquisition must be integrated (Larsson and Finkelstein, 1999; Capron and Pistre, 2002; Al-Laham *et al.*, 2010). The complexity of knowledge behind the biotechnological products makes it far more difficult to be absorbed than the new knowledge developed in other types of science (Schweitzer, 2005) where a linear accumulation takes place, as in computer or chip components and where products have modular design (Bower, 2001; Al-Laham *et al.*, 2010). Thus, the challenge and the gamble of the next decade will be to see if the great creativity and innovative potential of the biotech companies acquired could be integrated into the large incumbents. Within the biopharma filière, alliances were clearly transitory instruments (Kogut, 1991; Duysters and De Man, 2003) for surviving in a turbulent industry crossed by a new technology trajectory and a gateway to acquisition for large, dominant pharma firms. We do not explain this process in terms of innovation performance, given the fact that all the relevant literature existing on this topic has confirmed that alliances outperform M&As in terms of innovation performance, rather we explain it as a structural process leading to an organizational stabilization of the 'industry' when it becomes more mature. As has been observed (Comanor and Scherer, 2013), this process in future per se will not alleviate large pharma firms from the historical decline of productivity. On the contrary, the increased concentration brought on by recent mergers may well contribute to a further decline in the rate of innovation being, in other words, a self-defeating strategy that perhaps may make industry outcomes worse in the future. The pharmaceutical industry and the BPs have not simply 'converged' or morphed into a biopharmaceutical industry, as stated by Ernst & Young (2000), where a 'rebranding' approach seems to be the popular view. The underlying source of the pharmaceutical industry's products, R&D, technologies and revenues remains primarily chemical, with the industry dominated by drugs at all levels. Depending on the criteria used, in the US about 15–20 per cent of pharmaceutical products, sales and R&D involve new biopharmaceuticals (Rader, 2007b). If only a small proportion of large pharmaceutical companies are heavily involved in biopharmaceuticals and they have one or more internally developed and/or manufactured product(s) thanks to the enormous flows of acquisitions organized in the last decade, then only a few BP companies in the future will be providing the older biopharmaceuticals, primarily vaccines and plasma proteins (Rader, 2007b). Among the most active BPs in biopharmaceuticals, most of the novel bio products commercialized have been licensed in or acquired and few companies have themselves developed or manufactured more than just one or at most a small number of biopharmaceuticals (Rader, 2008). However, this picture is fast moving. Looking at the majority of 2012 approvals by the Food and Drug Administration (FDA) in the US (Rader, 2013), we see that ten of the total approvals, representing 56 per cent of the total number, involve large BP companies as manufacturer, US marketer and/or parent company (which includes Teva, the world's largest generic drug company).

It is not just a matter of access to new knowledge (with the typical tool implemented through strategic alliances), but of a 'dominant' acquisition of the new knowledge created by biotech firms (and not necessarily integrated with that of the acquiring company).

Conclusions

The entry of biotech firms focused on new scientific discoveries coming from the research laboratories of universities has given rise to a novel evolutionary market niche, where firms compete and cooperate with the old incumbents and where numerous biotech firms have now developed relevant commercial capabilities. The biotech industry is characterized nowadays by a large complex network of alliances, by an open-ended process of competition among different business models and market niches and by a still-undetermined and uncertain path of co-opetition and co-evolution.

In this study we have examined the emergence of the biotech niche adopting an evolutionary perspective. We have built on prior work that has identified the emerging of a new industry by looking at the start-up of new firms. Moreover, we have discussed the various benefits of strategic alliances in biotechnology, including access to the complementary assets possessed by incumbent pharmaceutical firms. Our underlying idea was that partnership strategies evolved as biotechnology matured, supporting and consolidating the biotech firms and, thus, the growth of an entire new biotech niche. Accordingly, in the second phase of the maturity of the industry, biotech firms also started to exhibit superior capabilities in downstream activities (clinical trials, product approval, production and marketing), which enabled them to compete with the old pharmaceutical firms. As a result of this process, biotech firms' partnering strategies, once tightly vertically integrated, also became organized within horizontal strategic alliances in terms of biotech-biotech alliances.

An important segment of large biotech firms emerged, catalysing a growing number of alliances. The advantages of the old incumbent in terms of commercial capabilities and use of 'accumulated experience and knowledge' (Pavitt, 1998; Baron *et al.*, 1999, 2001), vanished. Biotech firms, for a while, have overcome the liability of newness. However, soon after the emergence of a new biotech niche (contrasting, cooperating and competing with the old pharma industry), we saw the reaction of the pharma firms in terms of a growing number of M&As. Our results displace the idyllic view of the bio and pharma niches evolving separately and they also displace the image of a wind of creative destruction forcing the exit of old pharma incumbents. In reality, the reply to the new technological revolution was articulated along different strategies, among which we encountered four different situations. The first is the quick transformation of pharma born before 1975 to biotech science, as Serono and Novo Nordisk (with the formation of a *de alio* niche of new biotech firms). The second is the entry into the biotech niche by large pharma through the creation of biotech spin-offs, such as Roche and Abbott. The third is the growing number of upstream biopharma alliances, which involve particularly large pharma like Abbott Laboratories, Schering-Plough Corp (merged in 2009 with Merck),

Pfizer, Merck, Eli Lilly, Johnson & Johnson and Sanofi Pasteur. The fourth is the large flow of M&As that has created new integrated groups (Bowman and Ward, 2011), with a potential threat to the existence of the biotech niche as an independent industry (such as Roche, Sanofi-Aventis, Novartis, Pfizer, Johnson & Johnson, Eli Lilly, GlaxoSmithKline, AstraZeneca, Merck Serono and Abbott Laboratories).

Large-scale M&As have become the expansion strategy of the pharma firms and they have contributed nearly two-thirds of sales growth over the period 1995–2014. This is in line with the recent pharmaceutical trends of reducing internal R&D, increasing the licensing of early clinical stage drug candidates and buying promising biotech firms (Giniatullina *et al.*, 2013).

This characterizes a discontinuity in the model of open innovation (Chesbrough, 2003), with a fixed and clear-cut division of 'innovative labour' (Bianchi *et al.*, 2011). Many established incumbent large pharma firms have survived the biotech discontinuity (on this issue of technological discontinuity see: Abernathy and Clark, 1985; Levinthal, 1992), not just through a process of knowledge absorption, highlighted for instance by the huge number of pharma holders of DNA patents (like GlaxoSmithKline, Roche, Wyeth, Novartis, Merck and Pfizer, as shown by Hopkins *et al.*, 2008: 9) but through a process of organizational integration (Witt, 2000; Mittra and Williams, 2007), which has changed their technological identity (Zucker and Darby, 1997). Overall, our study indicates the evanescent dissolution of the red biotech niche into the integrated parallel knowledge system of a new biopharmaceutical filière.

Acknowledgements

Support from the ICaTSEM project (Institutional Changes and Trajectories of Socioeconomic Development Models of the EU 7th Framework program) is acknowledged.

Notes

1 Bioscan, which is published by American Health Consultants, provides one of the most comprehensive, publicly available directories covering the global biotechnology industry. The data contained in Bioscan are cumulative (each subsequent issue includes the information of all prior versions). It has been used in a number of prior studies to also track alliance formation over time (cf. Powell *et al.*, 1996; Lane and Lubatkin, 1998; Rothaermel, 2001; Rothaermel and Deeds, 2004; Rothaermel and Boeker, 2008; Schilling, 2009).

2 We paid particular attention to the definition of the biotech sector. We included here all of the companies that have developed biotech technologies and that can be characterized as biotech firms. Thus, we did not follow the official Standard Industrial Classification criteria that often include some biotech companies in the pharmaceutical sector or the self-definition used by the firms. In the Bioscan records analysed some important data regarding the characteristics of the firms were incomplete. After the troublesome work of correction and revision, we gathered all of the missing information through internet

searching using the company websites. We checked the database for accuracy and found that it underestimates the presence of small firms (fewer than 50 employees) both in the biotech and the pharma sectors. For this reason, we followed the thoughts of Rader (2007a: 28) on the correct terminology (and related taxonomy and classification) to be applied to describe any industry. The 'new biotechnology' industry, more commonly in Europe, restricts the term to genetically engineered products (recombinant proteins and monoclonal antibodies), while within the US industry the biopharmaceutical industry refers to pharmaceuticals that are inherently biological in nature due to their manu-facture using live organisms (biotechnology). Sometimes the 'biotech business' view considers biopharmaceutical products (and companies and industry) as being those involving anything pharmaceutical (including small-molecule drugs) associated with smaller, biotech-like companies or that seem to be or can be portrayed as high-tech. Not unusually, the 'pharma business' view considers all pharmaceuticals (and com-panies and industry) to now be biopharmaceutical. In this chapter we adopted the fol-low definition of 'biotech products': those pharmaceuticals that are manufactured by biotechnology methods. This includes not just recombinant proteins and monoclonal antibodies but also vaccines, blood and plasma products, non-recombinant proteins and cultured cellular and tissue products. Biotech technologies can be applied both to process and products. It is very complex here to take into account the definitions and the role played by the regulating agencies in different countries. Actually in the US, some biogenerics or biosimilars (broadly definable as generic biopharmaceutical-related) have been approved by the FDA as generic drugs, including most peptide hor-mones (e.g. insulin, somatropin and calcitonin). See the case cited by Rader (2007a) of the approval of Omnitrope (recombinant E. coli-expressed somatropin) from Sandoz/ Novartis as a generic drug (a follow-on protein version of Genotropin from Pfizer). In contrast, the EU has approved Omnitrope and another recombinant E. coli-expressed somatropin (Valtropin) under its new biosimilar regulations, based on comparisons with Genotropin and Humatrope (from Eli Lilly), respectively.

In conclusion, a working definition of a biopharmaceutical company (Rader, 2007b: 43) is one which considers the company primarily business (determined as majority of revenue, activity and so on) involved in the: 'research, development, manufacturing and/or marketing of biotechnology-based pharmaceutical products or surrogates, including gene and protein sequences. This definition may be broadened to include companies primarily involved with related supplies and services—culture media, bioreactors, assays and analytical services and facilities design. Thus is would include companies primarily involved in bioinformatics, genomics, proteomics and so on, including drug (non-biological molecule) design companies that are substantially using recombinant proteins, nucleotide sequences, or other biological molecules or technologies. It excludes companies primarily involved with non-biological chemical/ drug technologies, including novel chemistries for screening or development of small-molecule drugs', and obviously, it excludes companies producing pharmaceuticals based on chemical technologies.

3   It was in 2006 that Celera Genomics was spun-off from Applera. During 1998, Celera, together with the assistance of The Institute for Genomic Research, sequenced an entire organism's genome for the first time (Haemophilus influenzae bacterium). This dis-covery occurred at nearly the same time as the public project, Human Genome Project, announced to the world that they had sequenced an organism's genome. Celera's work was done at a fraction of the cost of the public project: approximately $300 million of private funding versus about $3 billion of taxpayers' money. Due to the public

debate on open science, Celera was obliged to disclose its information on the genome sequencing without profiting much from their discovery. Celera was later acquired by Quest Diagnostics in 2011.

4 In Switzerland the other important organization in biotech is Syngenta, a world-leading agri-business committed to sustainable agriculture through innovative research and technology.

5 It was the new owner, Bertarelli, which moved the company to Switzerland in 1977, for strategic and financial reasons. During the 1980s the firm became a multinational biotech being also based in the US and specializing in the areas of neurology (for the treatment of multiple sclerosis), infertility and dermatology. A key step in its development was the discovery of extracting urinary gonadotropins, allowing the company to become a leader in fertility treatments (with Pergonal).

6 http://www.novonordisk.com/ (accessed 26 November 2013).

7 The corporate headquarters and major operations base are located in Basingstoke, Hampshire, England. Other major offices are located in the US in Wayne, Pennsylvania and Cambridge, Massachusetts. In addition, Shire owns a manufacturing site in Lexington, Massachusetts and San Diego, California. In 2008, in reaction to new taxation measures announced by the Labour Party on the treatment of royalties on patents, the company moved its tax domicile to Dublin, Ireland. Effected through the creation of a new holding company in St Helier, Jersey in the Channel Islands, it will pay reduced tax on global earnings, where royalties on patents lodged in Ireland are tax free. http://en.wikipedia.org/wiki/Shire_plc (accessed 25 November 2013).

8 Originally known as Sanofi Santé Nutritional Animale, a subsidiary of Sanofi-Aventis, the management conducted the first of three leveraged buy-outs in 1999 and launched Ceva Santé Animale. The latest leveraged management buy-out was completed in 2007. Since 2000, Ceva has acquired 19 companies. Available at: http://www.ceva.com/Who-are-we (accessed 25 November 2013).

9 Contrasting this view, Nesta and Saviotti (2005) found that knowledge diversity was driving innovation in biotechnology in the 1980s, whereas knowledge integration was a more important determinant of innovative activity in the 1990s. They stressed that knowledge integration – expressed as a measure of the coherence of the technologies a firm holds – became an increasingly important determinant of the market value of biotech firms from the early 1990s onwards. They argued that this development signalled the start of an exploitation stage in the technology that followed a long-lasting phase of knowledge exploration (Nesta and Saviotti, 2006). Malerba and Orsenigo (1997) also highlighted that, before the 1980s, pharma firms were characterized by a kind of 'random screening' behaviour as the techniques typical of organic chemistry did not allow for targeted search, while the advent of r-DNA made possible a process of 'guided drug discovery' that represented a more effective way to screen compounds. In fact, Audretsch (2001) noted that from the late 1980s large experienced pharmaceutical firms replaced their broad learning strategies of the exploration phase with a more focused approach targeting specific technologies and applications. In addition to this, Quéré (2003) found that the epoch of r-DNA alliance among biotech and pharma firms was characterized by links occurring mostly in areas of intra-diseases, while in the epoch of genomics the higher degree of complexity of the knowledge base and the general purpose nature of the knowledge base promoted links occurring across different disease areas. This aspect will be further discussed in Chapter 9.

10 After a juridical dispute in the US involving Serostim, for which it was condemned to pay a €700 million penalty, Serono was sold in 2006 for €10.6 billion to Merck KGaA.

11 Medtrack provides a comprehensive view of the biopharmaceutical business pan-orama, by offering insights into pharmaceutical pipelines, sales, epidemiology, patents and deals along with detailed profiles of 23,000 companies. Medtrack is developed and published by Citeline, the world's leading authority on pharmaceutical clinical trials, collecting data from 20,000 unique sources and providing information on more than 2,300 indicators and 100,000 products. Various authors in previous works employed Medtrack to identify their samples (for instance, Diestre and Rajagopalan, 2012).

12 Our population referred to all firms with at least one alliance registered on Medtrack, in particular 681 US firms and 317 European firms located in a selected number of countries: Great Britain (58), France (46), Denmark (38), Sweden (43), Germany (64), Switzerland (32), Italy (15) and Spain (21). Clearly the same firms could be entered into more than one agreement. Agreements with multiple scopes (i.e. finance and licensing) were counted only once.

13 The log-log plot indicates a long-tailed Paretian rank/frequency rather than a 'normal' Gaussian distribution. In a Gaussian distribution, data points are assumed to be inde-pendent-additive. These events generate normal distributions, which sit at the heart of modern statistics. When events are interdependent and/or interactive, normality in distributions is not the norm.

14 Manufactures and sells medical devices, instrument systems and reagents.

15 Leader in applying population genomics and informatics for the development of per-sonalized medicines using mass array technologies.

16 Based in Dublin but with US headquarters, produces and sells imaging agents, contrast products and radio-pharmaceuticals.

17 www.nytimes.com/2009/03/13/ . . . /13drugs.html (accessed 28 November 2013).

18 Medtrack, company sites and financial news were used to collect data about the M&A processes.

19 online.wsj.com/ . . . /SB10001424052748703373404 (accessed 28 November 2013).

20 www.wikinvest.com (accessed 28 November 2013).

References

Abernathy W., Utterback J., 1978. Patterns of industrial innovation. *Technology Review*, 80(7): 41–47.

Abernathy W., Clark K., 1985. Innovation: Mapping the winds of creative destruction. *Research Policy*, 14(1): 3–22.

Adner R., Levinthal D. A., 2000. Technology speciation and the path of emerging tech-nologies, in Day G., Schoemaker P., Gunther R. E., (eds), *Wharton on Emerging Technologies*, John Wiley & Sons, New York.

Adner R., Levinthal D. A., 2002. The emergence of emerging technologies. *California Management Review*, 45(1): 50–66.

Al-Laham A., Souitairs V., 2008. Network embeddedness and new-venture internation-alization: Analyzing international linkages in the German biotech industry. *Journal of Business Venturing*, 23(5): 567–586.

Al-Laham A., Schweizer L., Amburgey T. L., 2010. Dating before marriage? Analyzing the influence of pre-acquisition experience and target familiarity on acquisition suc-cess in the "M&A as R&D" type of acquisition. *Scandinavian Journal of Management*, 26(1): 25–37.

Anand B., Khanna T., 2000. Do firms learn to create value? The case of alliances. *Strategic Management Journal*, 21(3): 295–315.

Anderson C., 2006. *The Long Tail: Why the Future of Business is Selling Less of More,* Hyperion, New York, NY.

Anderson P., Tushman M. L., 1990. Technological discontinuities and dominant designs: A cyclical model of technological change. *Administrative Science Quarterly*, 35(4): 604–633.

Andrade G., Mitchell M., Stafford E., 2001. *New Evidence and Perspectives on Mergers.* Working Paper No. 01-070, Harvard Business School, Cambridge MA. Available at: http://papers.ssrn.com/sol3/papers.cfm?abstract_id=269313 (accessed 20 February 2013).

Andriani P., McKelvey B., 2009. From Gaussian to Paretian thinking. Causes and implications of power laws in organizations. *Organization Science*, 20(6): 1053–1071.

Arora A., Gambardella A., 1990. Complementarity and external linkages: The strategies of the large firms in biotechnology. *The Journal of Industrial Economics*, 38(4): 361–379.

Arora A., Gambardella A., 1994. The changing technology of technological change: General and abstract knowledge and the division of innovative labour. *Research Policy*, 23(5): 523–532.

Arora A., Fosfuri A., Gambardella A., 2001. Markets for technology and their implications for corporate strategy. *Industrial and Corporate Change*, 10(2): 419–451.

Arthur B., 1994. *Increasing Returns and Path Dependence in the Economy*, University of Michigan Press, Ann Arbor, MI.

Audretsch D. B., 2001. The role of small firms in US biotechnology clusters. *Small Business Economics*, 17(1–2): 3–15.

Audretsch D. B., Stephan P. E., 1996. Company-scientist locational links: The case of biotechnology. *The American Economic Review*, 86(3): 641–652.

Autant-Bernard C., Mangematin V., Massard N., 2006. Creation of biotech SMEs in France. *Business Economics*, 26(2): 173–187.

Barney J., 1991. Firm resources and sustained competitive advantage. *Journal of Management*, 17(1): 99–120.

Baron J. N., Hannan M. T., Burton M. D., 1999. Building the iron cage: Determinants of managerial intensity in the early years of organizations. *American Sociological Review*, 64(8): 527–547.

Baron J. N., Hannan M. T., Burton M. D., 2001. Labor pains: Change in organizational models and employee turnover in young, high-tech firms. *American Journal of Sociology*, 106(4): 960–1012.

Baum J., Calabrese T., Silverman B., 2000. Don't go it alone: Alliance network composition and startups' performance in Canadian biotechnology. *Strategic Management Journal*, 21(3): 267–294.

Bederbos R., Gilsing V., Lokshin B., 2012. Persistence of, and interrelation between, horizontal and vertical technology alliances. *Journal of Management*, 38(6): 1812–1834.

Belussi F., Sedita S., 2013. Going alone: The "entrepreneurial-growth model" in the life science industry in Italy. *European Planning Studies*, 23(1): 188–210.

Bianchi M., Cavaliere A., Chiaroni D., Frattini F., Chiesa V., 2011. Organisational modes for open innovation in the bio-pharmaceutical industry: An exploratory analysis. *Technovation*, 31(1): 22–33.

Bonaccorsi A., Giuri P., 2000. When shakeout doesn't occur. The evolution of the turboprop engine industry. *Research Policy*, 29(7): 847–870.

Boschma R., (2005). Proximity and innovation: A critical assessment. *Regional Studies*, 39(1): 61–74.

Boschma R., Frenken K., 2010. The spatial evolution of innovative networks: A proximity perspective, in Boschma R., Martin R., (eds), *The Handbook of Evolutionary Economic Geography*, Edward Elgar, Cheltenham, UK.

Bower J. L., 2001. Not all M&As are alike – and that matters. *Harvard Business Review*, 79(2): 93–101.

Bowman J., Ward J., 2011. *Global Biotechnology Industry*. Available at: www.kelley.indiana.edu (accessed 3 March 2013).

Bresman H., Birkinshaw J., Nobel R., 1999. Knowledge transfer in international acquisitions. *Journal of International Business Studies*, 30(4): 439–462.

Buenstorf G., Cantner U., Hanusch H., Hutter M., Lorenz H. W., Rahmeyer F., 2013. Editorial: The two sides of innovation, in *The Two Sides of Innovation*, Springer International Publishing, New York, pp. 1–7.

Capron L., Pistre N., 2002. When do acquirers earn abnormal returns? *Strategic Management Journal*, 23(9): 781–794.

Capron L., Anand J., 2007. Acquisition-based dynamic capabilities, in Helfat C. E., Finkelstein S., Mitchell M., Peteraf M. A., Singh H., Teece D. J., Winter S. G., (eds), *Dynamic capabilities. Understanding strategic change in organizations*, Blackwell, Oxford, UK.

Carroll G. R., 1985. Concentration and specialization: Dynamics of niche width in populations or organizations. *American Journal of Sociology*, 90(6): 1262–1283.

Carroll G. R., Swaminathan A., 1992. The organizational ecology of strategic groups in the American brewing industry from 1975 to 1990. *Industrial and Corporate Change*, 1(1): 65–97.

Chesbrough H., 2003. The era of open innovation. *The MIT Sloan Management Review*, 127(3): 34–41.

Chiesa V., Chiaroni D., (eds), 2005. *Industrial Clusters in Biotech*, Imperial College Press, London, UK.

Christensen C., 1997. *The Innovator's Dilemma. When New Technologies Cause Great Firms to Fail*, Harvard Business School Press, Cambridge, MA.

Cohen W., Levinthal D., 1990. Absorptive capacity: A new perspective on learning and innovation. *Administrative Science Quarterly*, 35(1): 128–152.

Comanor W., Scherer F. M., 2013. Mergers and innovation in the pharmaceutical industry. *Journal of Health Economics*, 32(1): 106–113.

Coombs J., Mudambi R., Deeds D., 2006. An examination of the investments in U.S. biotechnology firms by foreign and domestic corporate partners. *Journal of Business Venturing*, 21(4): 405–428.

Danzon P. M., Epstein A., Nicholson S., 2007. Mergers and acquisitions in the pharmaceutical and biotech industries. *Managerial and Decision Economics*, 28(4–5): 307–328.

Delacroix J., Carroll G. R., 1983. Organizational foundings: An ecological study of the newspaper industries of Argentina and Ireland. *Administrative Science Quarterly*, 28(2): 274–291.

De Man A.-P., Duysters G., 2005. Collaboration and innovation: A review of the effects of mergers, acquisitions and alliances on innovation. *Technovation*, 25(12): 1377–1387.

Diestre L., Rajagopalan N., 2012. Are all 'sharks' dangerous? New biotechnology ventures and partner selection in R&D alliances. *Strategic Management Journal*, 33(10): 1115–1134.

Dollinger M. J., Golden P. A., Saxton T., 1997. The effect of reputation on the decision to joint venture. *Strategic Management Journal*, 18(2): 127–140.

Dopfer K., 2005. *The Evolutionary Foundation of Economics*, Cambridge University Press, Cambridge, UK.

Dosi G., 1988. Sources, procedures, and microeconomic effects of innovation. *Journal of Economic Literature*, 26(3): 1120–1171.

Dosi G., Nelson R., Winter S., (eds), 2000. *The Nature and Dynamics of Organizational Capabilities*, Oxford University Press, New York, NY.

Duysters G., De Man A., 2003. Transitory alliances: An instrument for surviving turbulent industries? *R&D Management*, 33(1): 49–58.

Dyer J. H., Kale P., Singh H., 2004. When to ally and when to acquire. *Harvard Business Review*, 82(7–8): 109–115.

Ernst & Young, 2000. *Convergence: Biotechnology Industry Report, Millennium Edition*. Ernst & Young, New York, NY.

Fisken J., Rutherford J., 2002. Business models and investment trends in the biotech industry in Europe. *Journal of Commercial Biotechnology*, 8(3): 191–199.

Foster J., 1997. The analytical foundations of evolutionary economics: From biological analogy to economic self-organization. *Structural Change and Economic Dynamics*, 8(4): 427–451.

Frenken K., Boschma R., 2007. A theoretical framework for evolutionary economic geography: Industrial dynamics and urban growth as a branching process. *Journal of Economic Geography*, 7(5): 635–649.

Galambos L., Sturchio J. L., 1998. Pharmaceutical firms and the transition to biotechnology: A study in strategic innovation. *Business History Review*, 72(2): 250–278.

Gambardella A., 1995. *Science and Innovation in the US Pharmaceutical Industry*, Cambridge University Press, Cambridge, UK.

Gambardella A., McGahan A., 2010. Business-model innovation: General purpose technologies and their implications for industry structure. *Long Range Planning*, 43(2–3): 262–271.

Garnsey E., Long Y. Y., 2008. Combining resource-based and evolutionary theory to explain the genesis of bionetworks. *Industry and Innovation*, 15(6): 669–686.

Gavetti G., Levinthal D. A., 2000. Looking forward and looking backward: Cognitive and experiential search. *Administrative Science Quarterly*, 45(1): 113–137.

Gerpott T. J., 1995. Successful integration of R&D functions after acquisitions: An exploratory empirical study. *R&D Management*, 25(2): 161–178.

Graebner M. E., 2004. Momentum and serendipity: How acquired leaders create value in the integration of technology firms. *Strategic Management Journal*, 25(8-9): 751–777.

Giniatullina A., Boorsma M., Mulder G. J., Van Deventer S., 2013. Building for big pharma. *Nature Biotechnology*, 31(4): 284–287.

Gottinger H.-W., Umali C. L., 2008. The evolution of the pharmaceutical-biotechnology industry. *Business History*, 50(5): 583–601.

Grant R., Baden-Fuller C., 2004. A knowledge accessing theory of strategic alliances. *Journal of Management Studies*, 41(1): 61–84.

Greis N. P., Dibner M. D., Bean A. S., 1995. External partnering as a response to innovation barriers and global competition in biotechnology. *Research Policy*, 24(4): 609–630.

Gulati R., 1999. Network location and learning: The influence of network resources and firm capabilities on alliance formation. *Strategic Management Journal*, 20(5): 397–420.

Hagedoorn J., Roijakkers N., 2002. Small entrepreneurial firms and large companies in inter-firm R&D networks – The international biotechnology industry, in Hitt M., Ireland R., Camp S., Sexton D., (eds), *Strategic Entrepreneurship: Creating a New Mindset*, Blackwell, Oxford, UK.

Hagedoorn J., Duysters G., 2002a. External sources of innovative capabilities: The preference for strategic alliances or mergers and acquisitions. *Journal of Management Studies*, 39(2): 167–188.

Hagedoorn J., Duysters G., 2002b. The effect of mergers and acquisitions on the technological performance of companies in a high-tech environment. *Technology Analysis & Strategic Management*, 14(1): 67–85.

Hall B. H., 1999. *Mergers and R&D Revisited: Prepared for the Quasi-Experimental Methods Symposium,* Econometrics Laboratory, UC Berkeley, CA.

Hannan M. T., Pólos L., Carroll G. R., 2007. *Logics of Organization Theory: Audiences, Codes, and Ecologies,* Princeton University Press, NJ.

Hayward M. L., Hambrick D. C., 1997. Explaining the premiums paid for large acquisitions: Evidence of CEO hubris. *Administrative Science Quarterly*, 42(1):103–127.

Henderson R., Pisano G. P., Orsenigo L., 1999. The pharmaceutical industry and the revolution in molecular biology: Interactions among scientific, institutional, and organizational change, in Mowery D., Nelson R., (eds), *Sources of Industrial Leadership: Studies of Seven Industries,* Cambridge University Press, Cambridge, UK.

Hitt M. A., Hoskisson R. E., Johnson R. A., Moesel D. D., 1996. The market for corporate control and firm innovation. *Academy of Management Journal*, 39(5): 1084–1119.

Hopkins M. M., Martin P., Nightingale P., Kraft A., 2008. *Living with Dinosaurs: Genomics and the Industrial Dynamics of the Pharmaceutical Industry,* paper presented at the Druid conference, Copenhagen, Denmark, 20–27 June. Available at: http://www2.druid.dk/conferences/viewpaper.php (accessed 9 December 2013).

Kale P., Dyer J. H., Singh H., 2002. Alliance capability, stock market response, and long-term alliance success: The role of alliance function. *Strategic Management Journal*, 23(8): 747–767.

Kang J., Afuah A., 2010. Profiting from innovations: The role of new game strategies in the case of Lipitor of the US pharmaceutical industry. *R&D Management*, 40(2): 124–137.

Klepper S., 1996. Entry, exit, growth, and innovation over the product life cycle. *The American Economic Review*, 86(3): 562–583.

Kogut B., 1991. Joint ventures and the option to expand and acquire. *Management Science*, 37(1): 19–33.

Krafft J., 2014. Knowledge characteristics and the dynamics of technological alliances in pharmaceuticals. *Journal of Evolutionary Economics*, 24(3): 587–622.

Lane C., Probert J., 2007. The external sourcing of technological knowledge by US pharmaceutical knowledge: Strategic goals and inter-organisational relationships. *Industry and Innovation*, 14(1): 5–25.

Lane P. J., Lubatkin M., 1998. Relative absorptive capacity and interorganizational learning. *Strategic Management Journal*, 19(5): 461–477.

Larsson R., Finkelstein S., 1999. Integrating strategic, organizational, and human resource perspectives on mergers and acquisitions: A case survey of synergy realization. *Organization Science*, 10(1): 1–26.

Larsson R., Bengtsson L., Henriksson K., Sparks J., 1998. The interorganizational learning dilemma: Collective knowledge development in strategic alliances. *Organization Science*, 9(3): 285–305.

Lavie D., Rosenkopf R., 2006. Balancing exploration and exploitation in alliance formation. *Academy of Management Journal*, 49(4): 797–818.

Lazonick W., Tulum Ö., 2011. US biopharmaceutical finance and the sustainability of the biotech business model. *Research Policy*, 40(9): 1170–1187.

Lee J., 2003. Innovation and strategic divergence: An empirical study of the U.S. pharmaceutical industry from 1920 to 1960. *Management Science*, 49(2): 143–159.

Levinthal D., 1998. The slow pace of rapid technological change: Gradualism and punctuation in technological change. *Industrial and Corporate Change*, 7(2): 217–247.

Levinthal D., 1992. Surviving Schumpeterian environments: An evolutionary perspective. *Industrial and Corporate Change*, 1(3): 427–443.

Makri M., Hitt M. A., Lane P. J., 2010. Complementary technologies, knowledge relatedness, and invention outcomes in high technology mergers and acquisitions. *Strategic Management Journal*, 31(6): 602–628.

Malerba F., Orsenigo L., 1997. Technological regimes and sectoral patterns of innovative activities. *Industrial and Corporate Change*, 6(1): 83–116.

Mangematin V., Lemarié S., Boissin J.-P., Catherine D., Corolleur F., Coronini R., Trommetter M., 2003. Development of SMEs and heterogeneity of trajectories: The case of biotechnology in France. *Research Policy*, 32(4): 621–638.

Maybeck V., Bains W., 2006. Small companies mergers: Good for whom? *Nature Biotechnology*, 24(11): 1343–1348.

McCutchen W. W., Swamidass, P. M., Teng, B., 2004. R&D risk-taking in strategic alliances: New explanations for R&D alliances in the biopharmaceutical industry. *Management International Review*, 44(1): 53–67.

McKelvey M., 1996a. *Evolutionary Innovations – The Business of Biotechnology*, Oxford University Press, Oxford, UK.

McKelvey M., 1996b. Discontinuities in genetic engineering for pharmaceuticals? firms jumps and lock-in in systems of innovation. *Technology Analysis & Strategic management*, 8(2): 107–116.

McKelvey M., 1998. Evolutionary innovations: Learning, entrepreneurship and the dynamics of the firm. *Journal of Evolutionary Economics*, 8(2): 57–75.

McKelvey M., Orsenigo L., Pammolli F., 2004. Pharmaceuticals analyzed through the lens of a sectoral innovation, in Malerba F., (ed.), *Sectoral System of Innovation*, Cambridge, Cambridge University Press, UK, pp. 73–120.

Metcalfe S., 1998. *Evolutionary Economics and Creative Destruction*, Routledge, London, UK.

Milgrom P., Roberts J., 1992. *Economics, Organization, and Management*, Prentice Hall, New York, NY.

Mittra J., 2007. Life science innovation and the restructuring of the pharmaceutical industry: Merger, acquisition and strategic alliance behaviour of large firms. *Technology Analysis & Strategic Management*, 19(3): 279–301.

Mittra J., Williams R., 2007. Evolution of the life science industries. *Technology Analysis & Strategic Management*, 19(3): 251–255.

Mokyr J., 1990. Punctuated equilibria and technological progress. *The American Economic Review*, 80(2): 350–354.

Mowery D. C., Oxley J. E., Silverman B. S., 1998. Technological overlap and inter-firm cooperation: Implications for the resource-based view of the firm. *Research Policy*, 27(5): 507–523.

Mudhar P., 2006. Spotlight pharma-biotech alliances. *Pharmaceutical Technology Europe*, 18(6): 18–22.

MVA, 2006. *Medicon Valley Academy Annual Report 2006*, Lund and Copenhagen Medicon Valley Academy Press, Lund, Denmark.

Nelson R. R., 1991. Why do firms differ, and how does it matter? *Strategic Management Journal*, 12(2): 61–74.

Nelson R. R., Winter S. G., 1977. In search of a useful theory of innovation, in *Innovation, Economic Change and Technology Policies*, Birkhäuser, Basel, Switzerland, pp. 215–245.

Nelson R. R., Winter S. G., 1982. *An Evolutionary Theory of Economic Change*, Belknap Press, Cambridge, MA.

Nesta L., Saviotti P. P., 2005. Coherence of the knowledge base and the firm's innovative performance: Evidence from the US pharmaceutical industry. *Journal of Industrial Economics*, 53(1): 123–142.

Nesta L., Saviotti P. P., 2006. Firm knowledge and market value in biotechnology. *Industrial and Corporate Change*, 15(4): 625–652.

Nooteboom B., Vanhaverbeke W., Duysters G., Gilsing V., Van den Oord A., 2007. Optimal cognitive distance and absorptive capacity. *Research Policy*, 36(7): 1016–1034.

Niosi J., 2003. Alliances are not enough explaining rapid growth in biotechnology firms. *Research Policy*, 32(5): 737–750.

Orsenigo L., 2001. The (failed) development of the biotechnology cluster in Lombardy. *Small Business Economics*, 17(1): 77–92.

Pavitt K., 1998. Technologies, products and organization in the innovating firm: What Adam Smith tells us and Joseph Schumpeter doesn't. *Industrial and Corporate Change*, 7(3): 433–452.

Pisano G. P., 1991. The governance of innovation: Vertical integration and collaborative arrangements in the biotechnology industry. *Research Policy*, 20(3): 237–249.

Pisano G. P., 2006. *Science Business: The Promise, the Reality, and the Future of Biotech*, Harvard Business School Press, Cambridge, MA.

Powell W. W., Koput K. W., Smith-Doerr L., 1996. Interorganizational collaboration and the locus of innovation: Networks of learning in biotechnology. *Administrative Science Quarterly*, 41(1): 116–145.

Powell W. W., Koput K. W., Bowie J. I., Smith-Doerr L., 2002. The spatial clustering of science and capital: Accounting for biotech firm–venture capital relationships. *Regional Studies*, 36(3): 291–305.

Quéré M., 2003. Knowledge dynamics: Biotechnology's incursions into the pharmaceutical industry. *Industry and Innovation*, 10(3): 255–273.

Rader R. A., 2007a. What is a biopharmaceutical? Part 1: (Bio)technology-based definitions. *BioExecutive International*, 1(2), March: 60–65. Available at: www.biopharma.com/terminology.html (accessed 26 February 2013).

Rader R. A., 2007b. What is a biopharmaceutical? Part 2: Company and industry definitions. *BioExecutive International*, 1(3), May: 42–49. Available at: www.biopharma.com/terminology.html (accessed 26 February 2013).

Rader R. A., 2008. (Re)defining biopharmaceutical. *Nature Biotechnology*, 26(7): 743–751.

Rader R. A., 2013. FDA Biopharmaceutical product approvals and trends in 2012. *BioProcess International*, 11(3): 18–26.

Rosenkopf L., Nerkar A., 2001. Beyond local search: Boundary-spanning, exploration, and impact in the optical disc industry. *Strategic Management Journal*, 22(4): 287–306.

Rosenkopf L., Almeida P., 2003. Overcoming local search through alliances and mobility. *Management Science*, 49(6): 751–766.

Rothaermel F. T., 2001. Incumbent's advantage through exploiting complementary assets via interfirm cooperation. *Strategic Management Journal*, 22(6–7): 687–699.

Rothaermel F. T., Deeds D. L., 2004. Exploration and exploitation alliances in biotechnology: A system of new product development. *Strategic Management Journal*, 25(3): 201–221.

Rothaermel F. T., Hill W., 2005. Technological discontinuities and complementary assets: A longitudinal study of industry and firm performance. *Organization Science*, 16(1): 52–70.

Rothaermel F. T., Deeds D. L., 2006. Alliance type, alliance experience and alliance management capability in high-technology ventures. *Journal of Business Venturing*, 21(4): 429–460.

Rothaermel F. T., Boeker W., 2008. Old technology meets new technology: Complementarities, similarities, and alliance formation. *Strategic Management Journal*, 29(1): 47–77.

Rothman H., Kraft A., 2006. Downstream and into deep biology: Evolving business models in 'top tier' genomics companies. *Journal of Commercial Biotechnology*, 12(2): 86–98.

Rumelt R. P., 1984. Toward a strategic theory of the firm, in Lamb R., (ed.), *Competitive Strategic Management*. Prentice Hall, Englewood Cliffs, New Jersey, pp. 556–570.

Sabatier V., Kennard A., Mangematin V., 2012. When technological discontinuities and disruptive business models challenge dominant industry logics. Inside the drug industry. *Technological Forecasting and Social Change*, 79(5): 949–962.

Schilling M., 2009. Understanding alliance data. *Strategic Management Journal*, 30(3): 233–260.

Schumpeter J. A., 1934. *The Theory of Economic Development*, Harvard University Press, Cambridge, MA. (Oxford University Press, New York, NY, 1961.) First published in German, 1912.

Schumpeter J. A., 1942. *Capitalism, Socialism and Democracy*, Harper and Brothers (Harper Colophon edition, 1976), New York, NY.

Schweitzer L., 2005. Organizational integration of acquired biotechnology companies into pharmaceutical companies: The need for a hybrid approach. *Academy of Management Journal*, 48(6): 1051–1074.

Slusky A. R., Caves R. E., 1991. Synergy, agency, and the determinants of premia paid in mergers. *The Journal of Industrial Economics*, 39(3): 277–296.

Stuart T. E., Ozdemir S. Z., Ding W. W., 2007. Vertical alliance networks: The case of university-biotechnology-pharmaceutical alliances chains. *Research Policy*, 36(4): 477–498.

Teece D. J., 1986. Profiting from technological innovation: Implications for integration, collaboration, licensing, and public policy. *Research Policy*, 15(6): 285–305.

Teece D. J., 1992. Competition, cooperation and innovation: Organizational arrangements for regimes of rapid changes. *Journal of Economic Behavior and Organization*, 18(1): 1–25.

Teece D. J., Rumelt R. P., Dosi G., Winter S., 1994. Understanding corporate coherence: Theory and evidence. *Journal of Economic Behavior and Organization*, 23(1): 1–30.

Trautwein F., 1990. Merger motives and merger prescriptions. *Strategic Management Journal*, 11(4): 283–295.

Tripsas M., 1997. Unraveling the process of creative destruction: Complementary assets and firm survival in the typesetter industry. *Strategic Management Journal*, 18(Summer Special Issue): 119–142.

Tushman M. L., Anderson P., 1986. Technological discontinuities and organizational environments. *Administrative Science Quarterly*, 31(3): 439–465.

Tyebjee T., Hardin J., 2004. Biotech-pharma alliances: Strategies, structures, and financing. *Journal of Commercial Biotechnology*, 10(4): 329–339.

Uhlenbruck K., Hitt M. A., Semadeni M., 2006. Market value effects of acquisitions involving internet firms: A resource-based analysis. *Strategic Management Journal*, 27(10): 899–913.

Utterback J., 1994. *Mastering the Dynamics of Innovation*. Harvard Business School Press, Cambridge, MA.

Utterback J., Abernathy W., 1975. A dynamic model of process and product innovation. *Omega*, 3(6): 639–656.

Vermeulen F., Barkema H., 2001. Learning through acquisitions. *Academy of Management Journal*, 44(3): 457–476.

Walter G. A., Barney J. B., 1990. Research notes and communications management objectives in mergers and acquisitions. *Strategic Management Journal*, 11(1): 79–86.

Wang J. H. A., Chen T. Y. B., Tsai C. J., 2012. In search of an innovative state: The development of the biopharmaceutical industry in Taiwan, South Korea and China. *Development and Change*, 43(2): 481–503.

Wang L., Zajac E. J., 2007. Alliance or acquisition? A dyadic perspective on interfirm resource combinations. *Strategic Management Journal*, 28(13), 1291–1317.

Wassmer U., 2010. Alliances portfolios: A review and research agenda. *Journal of Management*, 36(1): 141–171.

Weisenfeld U., Reeves J. C., Hunck-Meiswinkel A., 2001. Technology management collaboration profile: Virtual companies and industrial platforms in high-tech biotechnology industries. *R&D Management*, 31(1): 91–100.

Weitzman M. L., 1998. Recombinant growth. *Quarterly Journal of Economics*, 113(2): 331–360.

Wernerfelt B., 1995. The resource-based view of the firm: Ten years after. *Strategic Management Journal*, 16(3): 171–174.

Whalen J., 2010. Glaxo tries biotech model to spur drug innovations, *Wall Street Journal*. Available at: http://online.wsj.com/news/articles/ SB1000142405274870456920457532 8580921136768 (accessed 3 March 2013).

Witt U., 1992. Evolutionary concepts in economics. *Eastern Economic Journal*, 18(4): 405–419.

Witt U., 2000. Changing cognitive frames – changing organisational forms: An entrepreneurial theory of organisational development. *Industrial and Corporate Change*, 9(4): 733–755.

Zollo M., Winter S., 2002. Deliberate learning and the evolution of dynamic capabilities. *Organization Science*, 13(3): 339–351.

Zucker L. G., Darby M. R., 1997. Present at the biotechnological revolution: Transformation of technological identity for a large incumbent pharmaceutical firm. *Research Policy*, 26(4–5): 429–446.

Zucker L. G., Darby M. R., 2001. Capturing technological opportunity via Japan's star scientists: Evidence from Japanese firms' biotech patents and products. *Journal of Technology Transfer*, 26(1–2): 37–58.

Zucker L. G., Darby M. R., Brewer M. B., 1998. Intellectual human capital and the birth of U.S. biotechnology enterprises. *The American Economic Review*, 88(1): 290–306.

2 Innovation in US metropolitan areas

The role of global connectivity

Kristin Brandl, Marcelo Cano Kollmann, Hongryol Cha, Izzet Darendeli, T. J. Hannigan, Ahreum Lee, Seojin Kim, Vittoria Giada Scalera, Alessandra Perri, Robert D. Hamilton III and Ram Mudambi

Introduction

Multinational enterprises (MNEs) create superior value by leveraging intangible assets, such as R&D, across borders (Mudambi, 2008). The process of leveraging entails accessing and sourcing knowledge from different locales and recombining it with the knowledge the MNE already possesses to create new knowledge (Almeida, 1996; Cantwell and Santangelo, 2000; Awate *et al.*, 2015). However, there is an established literature which suggests that, while it is easier for MNEs to source and recombine codified knowledge, the process of leveraging tacit knowledge is much more challenging. As a result, these earlier studies suggest that MNEs' search for tacit knowledge takes place in spatial proximity, often within local home country clusters (Jaffe *et al.*, 1993; Cantwell and Janne, 1999; Patel and Vega, 1999).

Studies have confirmed that MNEs take advantage of various agglomeration related externalities such as local buzz and rapid diffusion (Bathelt *et al.*, 2004) and are more inclined to source tacit knowledge locally. On the other hand, there is growing empirical evidence that suggests that MNEs are increasingly sourcing knowledge from geographically distant locations, in spite of all the challenges involved (Gittelman, 2007). This often requires MNEs to be part of globally distributed innovation networks that absorb, create and manage geographically dispersed knowledge from 'knowledge hot-spots' (Bathelt *et al.*, 2004) or 'centres of excellence' (Bartlett and Ghoshal, 1989; Cantwell and Janne, 1999), since knowledge creation across such geographically distant clusters occurs through the formation of global pipelines (Bathelt *et al.*, 2004) and depends on distinct inter-personal, organizational and institutional linkages (Lorenzen and Mudambi, 2013). As local and global knowledge sourcing are becoming complements in the innovation strategies of successful firms (Bathelt *et al.*, 2004; Gittelman, 2007), MNEs must become orchestrators of local and global flows of knowledge (Lorenzen, 2004).

Not only is the knowledge sourcing behaviour of MNEs changing but the locations from which MNEs seek knowledge are changing as well. Emerging country clusters and location peripheral regions of advanced economies are growing in importance and striving to become innovation hubs in the global knowledge network. Recent studies show that, in addition to their low-cost advantages, these locations can serve as novel repositories of knowledge for advanced countries MNEs (AMNEs) (Contractor *et al.*, 2010; D'Agostino *et al.*, 2013; Mudambi and Santangelo, 2015). Furthermore, the national innovation systems of emerging countries develop over time and these locations create innovative actors of their own (Athreye and Cantwell, 2007; Lewin *et al.*, 2009); there is a growing literature on emerging country MNEs' (EMNEs) efforts to catch up with AMNEs and become dominant in the relevant innovation ecosystems (Von Zedtwitz, 2006; Awate *et al.*, 2012).

Although firms and firm strategies are central to the evolution of the knowledge connections between locations, the literature is rather silent on providing a theoretical foundation and empirical evidence on how different knowledge sourcing patterns emerge and change (Iammarino and McCann, 2013). While studies have documented the importance of knowledge networks in geographic and technology space, be it through the lens of the individual firm, the MNE network or the location (Jacobs, 1969; Delgado *et al.*, 2014), the longitudinal process through which a sea change in the innovation activities emerges has not been explicitly examined.

In particular, objective metrics calibrating the true extent of the bimodal knowledge sourcing efforts are scarce: current country level 'innovation score' data (Economist Intelligence Unit, 2009) tend to focus on the location of knowledge-creating activities and ignore linkages. However, as MNEs 'fine slice' their global value chain activities and locate them around the world (Mudambi, 2008), the resulting entry of new emerging economy locations into global innovation systems does not necessarily reflect a reduction in the importance of traditional locations like the US In other words, the firms that are the linchpins of knowledge networks, the key orchestrators of knowledge flows and are positioned atop the inventor-assignee dynamic may be revealed by studying and disaggregating global value chains. Developing an understanding of knowledge networks may, therefore, shed light on differences between shifts in the location of activities and shifts in the location of value creation or value appropriation (Dedrick *et al.*, 2009; OECD, 2011). Analysing these dynamic changes requires the researcher to focus on the notion of connectivity that remains underexplored in the literature.

The iBEGIN Knowledge Maps Project explores such mechanisms of knowledge spillovers into and from clusters, the intra- and inter-connection of firms, locations and their innovation activities and how the disaggregation of the value chain into ever more specialized activities – 'fine slicing' (Mudambi, 2008) – introduced mobility and flexibility into knowledge sourcing patterns. Our project aims to analyse the firm and individual inventor networks of major US metro areas by examining patent data, specifically inventor co-location, to enhance our process-based understanding of the international connectivity of the innovative activity.

Using patents from the US Patent and Trademark Office (USPTO), we generate knowledge maps for the 917 Core-Based Statistical Areas (CBSAs) designated by the US Office of Management and Budget (OMB). Analysing trends in city-level innovative activity over a 35-year period allows us to highlight findings with powerful implications to both the policymakers and MNE managers. The core research questions relating to knowledge networks that we seek to address are:

1 How do different policy, industrial and firm-specific factors impact the global connectivity of local and regional innovation?
2 How these factors moderate the production of local knowledge?

Our initial results indicate that until 1990, there was a reasonably good correlation between population size and inventor numbers; the top four inventing CBSAs were the biggest metros – New York, Los Angeles, Chicago and Philadelphia, but from 1990 onwards there was a sea change in terms of population and innovative activity. The connectedness to global networks became more important as the 'Silicon Valley' CBSAs of San Jose and San Francisco emerged (1991–1992), followed by Boston (1993–1994) and Seattle (1999–2000). Of the traditional large metros, only Los Angeles was able to maintain some degree of comparability with these new innovative hubs. These trends suggest that innovative activity is an interdependent world consisting of foreign inventors, local firms, MNEs, subsidiaries and institutions, and the global connectivity is the key to retaining and enhancing the local innovation systems.

Data and methods

Patent data from the USPTO affords scholars an opportunity to analyse large tranches of innovation data, including the classification of the invention, the location of inventors and the ownership of the intellectual property created in the invention. The challenges involved in the collection of patent data are well documented and have been alleviated by the creation of publicly accessible databases, such as that of the National Bureau of Economic Research (NBER) (Hall *et al.*, 2001). More recently, research teams have sought to disambiguate inventor data in an effort to fully map the knowledge creation networks of individuals. One such project is the Harvard Patent Network Dataverse (DVN), a product of the Harvard Business School and the Harvard Institute of Quantitative Social Science (Lai *et al.*, 2013). The DVN work draws on both raw data from the USPTO and processed data from the NBER set to create a disambiguated set of patent inventor observations from 1975 through to 2010 (Lai *et al.*, 2013). While the goal of the DVN work was to be able to trace inventor mobility over time, it does offer scholars the benefit of a parsed and complete set of USPTO patents covering a 35-year period. The full database contains information on over 9.1 million patent inventors, with a single data file containing more than 1.3 gigabytes of information (Lai *et al.*, 2013).

While the existence of a publicly available patent dataset represents a valuable first step for innovation scholars, there remains the core issue of identifying, extracting and analysing important subsets of information. In the case of the Temple Knowledge Maps Project, data on *specific* CBSAs are extracted in order to conduct meaningful analyses. This involves building new databases by matching locations in the DVN patent database with CBSA boundaries, as defined by the US OMB. There are numerous location markers in the DVN patent inventor records and we have used zip codes to identify inventors located in the CBSAs of interest to our study. However, we must be able to identify *all* inventors on a given patent, not just those located in our CBSAs. As a result, we must then match patent numbers to all CBSA-based inventors. This generates a list of patents with at least one inventor located in the CBSA of interest.

The CBSA subset of data is then cross-tabulated to the patent unit of analysis: a step that allows us to analyse the locational network of inventors. For example, the co-inventor network on patent number 8457013 reports that seven inventors are distributed in the Philadelphia and China. A corresponding analysis of the patent's assignee, Metrologic Instruments (based in Blackwood, New Jersey) shows that R&D is undertaken at firm-owned locations in the US and China. On an aggregate level, our study takes CBSA patents and constructs measures of international inventor connectedness. That is to say, to what degree do inventors based in a particular city collaborate internationally? Taking the location analysis further, we leverage the latitude and longitude coordinates to generate full maps of innovative activity and collaboration in both space and time.

The trajectory of this research allow us to mine the large scale DVN database to identify all CBSA-relevant patents spanning 35 years. This creates a panel dataset of computed measures, such as an inventor geographic dispersion index and the proportion of CBSA patents with *any* connectedness. Furthermore, using the CBSA-level data to generate geographic maps of innovative activity allows us to track the development of innovative clusters over time and identity some of the drivers of collaborative innovation.

Preliminary findings

In the following section we present an overview of the main trends highlighted by the preliminary analysis of the innovation activities of the top 35 CBSAs. After the description of the distribution and evolution of the US innovative activity, we present a short overview of the innovation trends of the Philadelphia CBSA.

US innovative activity

Figure 2.1 shows the changing locations of US innovative activity during the period 1975–2010. During around 1990, the data emphasize that population size and inventor numbers were strongly correlated. More specifically, the top four inventing CBSAs were the biggest metros – New York, Los Angeles, Chicago

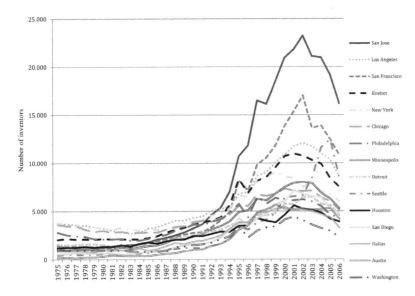

Figure 2.1 Number of inventors in the top 15 CBSAs (sorted by application date, 1975–2006)

Source: Authors' elaboration

and Philadelphia. However, from 1990 onwards, there was a sea change and the Silicon Valley CBSAs started to play the predominant role among the most innovative US cities. San Jose and San Francisco took off first (1991–1992), followed by Boston (1993–1994) and Seattle (1999–2000). After this shift, only Los Angeles of the traditional large metros was able to maintain some degree of comparability with these new innovative hubs.[1]

The picture is made even clearer by examining the share of total innovative activity in the major innovating CBSAs. In Figure 2.2 it is possible to observe that the shares of the big metros like New York, Chicago and Philadelphia fall continuously. Only Los Angeles and Boston are able to maintain a stable share. Meanwhile, the shares of the Silicon Valley CBSAs rise steadily, along with those of San Diego, Austin and Seattle. With respect to innovative productivity, Seattle, San Jose, San Francisco and Boston appear to be the most productive US cities in terms of US-based inventors, also showing the highest growth trend.

Even with its large base of innovative activity Silicon Valley still shows only the 4th fastest growth over the period. Figure 2.3 demonstrates that Austin experienced the fastest growth, followed by Seattle and Portland. In general, the innovation growth is occurring in the South and West and the highest growth rate in the traditional industrial heartlands of the Midwest and the North is registered by Minneapolis at 11th. Finally, California has the highest number of CBSAs showing fast innovation growth (three of the top ten).

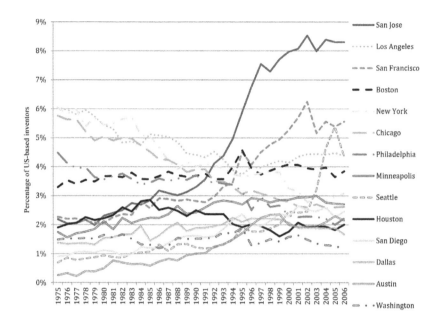

Figure 2.2 Percentage of US-based inventors in the top 15 CBSAs (sorted by application date, 1975–2006)

Source: Authors' elaboration.

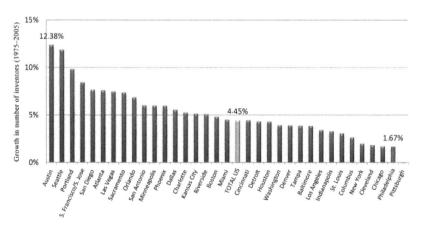

Figure 2.3 Growth in number of inventors in the top 35 CBSAs (CAGR, sorted by application date, 1975–2005)

Source: Authors' elaboration.

Innovation in the Philadelphia area

Figure 2.4 highlights the high connectedness of Philadelphia-based patents. In fact, during the 1986–2007 period the percentage of internationally connected patents in the Philadelphia area was consistently higher than the national average. The good news is that Philadelphia-based innovation shows growth trend in terms of connectedness and the pace is faster than that of the US

Looking at the geographical dispersion of inventors, we see that from 1986 onwards Philadelphia-based patents were much more internationally connected than the US-based patents overall. This finding suggests that the co-inventors of patents with at least one inventor located in Philadelphia area were more geographically distributed than the co-inventors of patents with all non-US- or all US-based inventors (see Figure 2.5). The United Kingdom, Germany and Canada represented the top three locations of foreign co-inventors, as shown in Figure 2.6. However, from 2004 onwards the number of Chinese co-inventors increased dramatically and, although in the following years the growing trend was not stable, China still maintains its role of major innovative partner with Philadelphia.

A representative example of innovative connectedness between Philadelphia and China is Metrologic Instruments. The company, founded in 1968 by Carl Harry Knowles, represents the lion's share of the Philadelphia CBSA connectedness to China (13 per cent of the inventors of its patents are located in China). Metrologic initially specialized in instructional laser kits and, in 1975, it became the world's first producer of hand-held bar code scanners that today are used in retailing, healthcare, postal services, logistics services and many other industry verticals. The international expansion of Metrologic drove the company to set up

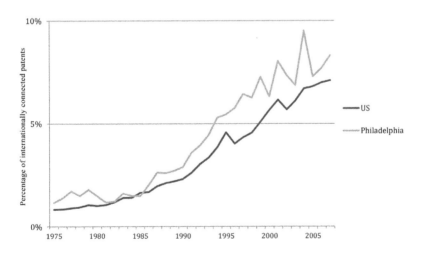

Figure 2.4 Percentage of internationally connected patents: comparison between US- and Philadelphia-based patents (sorted by application date, 1975–2007)

Source: Authors' elaboration.

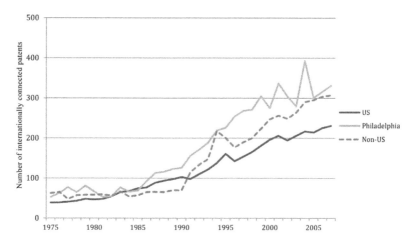

Figure 2.5 Geographical dispersion of inventors: comparison between US-, Philadelphia- and non-US-based patents (sorted by application date, 1975–2007)

Source: Authors' elaboration.

a manufacturing and R&D center in Suzhou, China, in 1998. Ten years later it was acquired by Honeywell and today it possesses 446 patents (3,189 inventors) and over 100 pending. Among its 'star scientists' we include the founder, Carl Harry Knowles (354 patents), Xiaoxun Zhu (208 patents) and Thomas Amundsen (131 patents). Collectively, the first five inventors are represented on 95.7 per cent

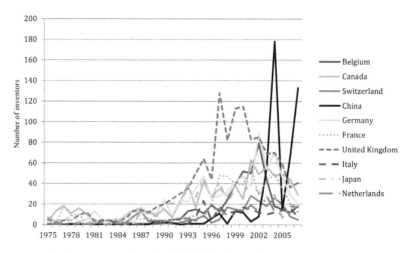

Figure 2.6 Top ten locations of Philadelphia-based inventors (sorted by application date, 1975–2007)

Source: Authors' elaboration.

of Metrologic's patents. Removing Knowles (to control for owner-bias), the remaining four inventors still account for 72.9 per cent of Metrologic's patents.

Although there is good news related to the high geographical dispersion of Philadelphia-based innovation, Figure 2.7 points out that the share of Philadelphia-based patents as a percentage of US patents presents a negative trend and from 2000 onwards it fell dramatically below 3 per cent (expect for 2002). In total, Philadelphia's share of US innovative activity has dropped by half in 35 years. This undesirable path should be probably linked to the considerable reduction in the number of patents in the traditional core industries for the Philadelphia area, such as chemical, drugs and medical. In fact, these manufacturing industries have historically represented the main sources of local innovation and from 2001 they showed a declining path, which is particularly severe in the case of drugs and medical (Figure 2.8).

Conclusion

Prior studies show that the ability to create value from knowledge necessitates a wide-mouth funnel in knowledge inflow with access to broader and deeper knowledge bases, along with the capability to integrate diverse knowledge sets. It also requires the ability to balance between in-house and external knowledge sourcing and to choose which projects to pursue and which ones to terminate. In-house knowledge sourcing is important since complex innovations require spatial concentration (Jaffe *et al.*, 1993) and external knowledge sourcing is important in order to source knowledge from other knowledge bases and clusters that will provide the necessary understanding of the current, complementary and emerging technological domains for new recombinations (Brusoni *et al.*, 2001).

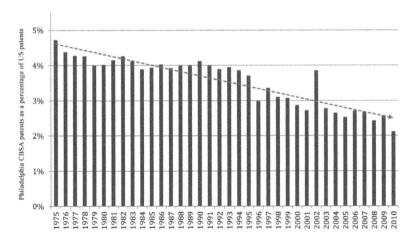

Figure 2.7 Philadelphia CBSA patents as a percentage of US patents (sorted by application date, 1975–2010)

Source: Authors' elaboration.

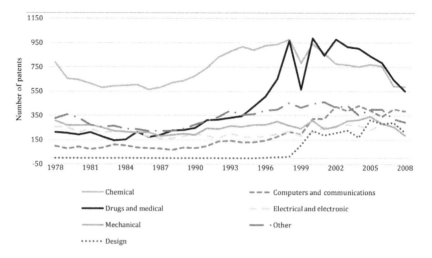

Figure 2.8 Primary technology category of Philadelphia-based patents (sorted by estimated grant date, 1978–2008)

Source: Authors' elaboration.

On the other hand, innovation is a collaborative process since different parties (universities, firms, government and R&D institutions) are increasingly becoming involved in the development funnel leading to innovation. In today's world, successful innovations are the result of collaborations that occur between both co-located as well as distant pairs of actors. Hence, connectivity is as important as an effective knowledge sourcing.

Connectivity between locations provides the basis for the existence of such knowledge sourcing and collaborative relationships. To the extent that locations and firms represent the nodes in a network, the connections between them represent the edges (Beugelsdijk *et al.*, 2010). Bathelt *et al.* (2004) have referred to the edges as pipelines between clusters and analyse them as mechanisms through which connectivity is established in the first place. Lorenzen and Mudambi (2013) argue that connectivity is a diverse and wider concept, so that organizational pipelines must be supplemented to include personal relationships as well.

The nature of the connectivity between firms and locations may ultimately impact the nature of the resulting innovation (Lorenzen and Mudambi, 2013). Several have warned against the lock-in of domestic actors working only with small numbers of global links (Humphrey and Schmitz, 2002; Narula, 2002). Gereffi (1999) shows that connectivity can change local clusters' linkages and help them escape from lock-in. The globalization of innovation and the strategies adopted by the MNEs to leverage globally distributed knowledge, have created an interdependent world, in which 'local' and 'global' need to coexist. Hence global connectivity is the key to retaining and enhancing local innovation systems, especially now that MNEs increasingly locate innovative activities worldwide. However, the current literature does not provide explicit empirical analysis of such connectivity and the literature has yet to fully explore the nature of these connections, particularly through the lens of specific technologies, locations or firms. With this in mind, we made use of knowledge maps to represent the largely tacit connections of inventor networks in the iBEGIN Project. This provided us with an intertemporal picture of the precise nature of the dependence and linkages of a location to other locations, industries and individuals.

Our empirical results tell of a processional story of rising and declining locations among the 917 CBSAs in the US in terms of their innovative activity between 1975 and 2010. While prior studies considered that characteristics of locations and actors involved in innovation are tightly interconnected, with disaggregation of activities through 'fine slicing' of the value chain connectivity provides flexibility in the innovation process. Similarly, we observe that while some of the CBSAs lacked agglomeration benefits to start with, international connectivity compensated for these weaknesses and proved to be vital in sustaining their level of innovative activity. In the early period (before 1990), our results confirm the positive and strong correlation between the population of the location and its innovative output. However, from 1990 onwards, we observe that this relationship weakened by the emergence of new innovative hubs such as Silicon Valley with relatively smaller population sizes. The biggest, older CBSAs (New York, Los Angeles and Chicago) exhibit lower per capita innovation rates compared to the newer hubs of Silicon Valley and Boston.

While the period through 1990 was marked with a low level of connectedness, so that innovation had a predominantly local focus. Thus, inventor numbers tracked population size. During the later period after 1990, the extent of connectedness rose so that innovation output was a function both of local specialized resources as well as orchestrating entities like universities and multinational firms that could recombine these with complementary resources from the region and from around the globe. These results confirm the complementary role of external connections during the evolution, and the health of, innovative clusters.

Recent studies have also started to stress the importance of personal ties and pipelines in addition to intra-firm, inter-firm and other institutional linkages in collaborations (Saxenian, 1996; Bathelt *et al.*, 2004; Lorenzen and Mudambi, 2013). These connections and pipelines provide 'organized proximity' to the knowledge residing in the distant locale (Saxenian, 1996). Our empirical analysis shows how these pipelines emerge and develop over time. From a macro perspective, we provide evidence of how CBSA innovative clusters have evolved through the knowledge networks that nourish them. While domestic connectedness seems to be largely driven by proximity (Riverside–Los Angeles; Sacramento–Silicon Valley; Baltimore–DC; Akron–Cleveland), international connectivity arose as a result of personal linkages and pipelines. As the case of Metrologic showed, a relatively small number of individuals can spark the connectivity among firms and locations and also have a disproportionate effect on a local innovation system.

Lastly, our analysis provides evidence of the changing dynamics related to the diversification versus specialization of innovation clusters. We find that over time, older CBSAs generally become more technologically diversified while newer CBSAs become more specialized. Furthermore, we observe two patterns that are very distinct from each other in Silicon Valley: San Francisco becomes more technologically diversified and behaves like an 'older' CBSA (e.g. Detroit and Cleveland), while San Jose becomes more specialized and behaves like a 'newer' CBSA (e.g. Austin, Portland and Seattle). Therefore, we provide evidence for externalities related to both specialization (Marshall, 1920) and diversity (Jacobs, 1969).

From the perspective of policymakers, our analysis suggests that sustaining a cluster's comparative innovative output over time requires careful choices about balancing internal density and external dispersion of connectivity. It is through these well-thought out choices that local innovative actors can establish and maintain connections to the 'centres of excellence' to ensure a constant rejuvenation of ideas. Hence, central and local authorities should take necessary steps to provide an environment supporting both hard (electronic networks, airline connections, road and rail) as well as soft (orchestrating actors like universities and immigrant diasporas) assets for the connectivity of the regions.

Note

1 The DVN database runs through 2010 and is sorted by application date. This induces 'right truncation' in the data, i.e. many patents applied for in 2005 and 2006 have not yet been granted by 2010. This is why the curves slope downwards toward the end of the graphed period.

References

Almeida P., 1996. Knowledge sourcing by foreign multinationals: Patent citation analysis in the U.S. semiconductor industry. *Strategic Management Journal*, 17(Special Issue: Knowledge and the Firm): 155–165.

Athreye S., Cantwell J., 2007. Creating competition? Globalisation and the emergence of new technology producers. *Research Policy*, 36(2): 209–226.

Awate S., Larsen M. M., Mudambi R., 2012. EMNE catch up strategies in the wind turbine industry: Is there a trade-off between output and innovation capabilities? *Global Strategy Journal*, 2(3): 205–223.

Awate S., Larsen M. M., Mudambi R., 2015. Accessing vs. sourcing knowledge: A comparative study of R&D internationalization between emerging and advanced economy firms. *Journal of International Business Studies*, forthcoming.

Bartlett C., Ghoshal S., 1989. *Managing across Borders: The Transnational Solution*, Harvard Business School Press, Cambridge, MA.

Bathelt H., Malmberg A., Maskell P., 2004. Clusters and knowledge: Local buzz, global pipelines and the process of knowledge creation. *Progress in Human Geography*, 28(1): 31–56.

Beugelsdijk S., McCann P., Mudambi R., 2010. Place, space and organization: Economic geography and the multinational enterprise. *Journal of Economic Geography*, 10(4): 485–493.

Brusoni S., Prencipe A., Pavitt K., 2001. Knowledge specialization, organizational coupling, and the boundaries of the firm: Why do firms know more than they make? *Administrative Sciences Quarterly*, 46(4): 597–621.

Cantwell J., Janne O., 1999. Technological globalisation and innovative centres: The role of corporate technological leadership and locational hierarchy. *Research Policy*, 28(2–3): 119–144.

Cantwell J., Santangelo G., 2000. Capitalism, profits and innovation in the new techno-economic paradigm. *Journal of Evolutionary Economics*, 10(1): 131–157.

Contractor F. J., Kumar V., Kundu S. K., Pedersen T., 2010. Reconceptualizing the firm in a world of outsourcing and offshoring: The organizational and geographical relocation of high-value company functions. *Journal of Management Studies*, 47(8): 1417–1433.

D'Agostino L., Laursen K., Santangelo G., 2013. The impact of R&D offshoring on the home knowledge production of OECD investing regions. *Journal of Economic Geography*, 13(1): 145–175.

Dedrick J., Kraemer K. L., Linden G., 2009. Who profits from innovation in global value chains? A study of the iPod and notebook PCs. *Industrial and Corporate Change*, 19(4): 81–116.

Delgado M., Porter M., Stern S., 2014. Clusters and entrepreneurship. *Journal of Economic Geography*, 10(4): 495–518.

Economist Intelligence Unit, 2009. *A New Ranking of the World's Most Innovative Countries*, Economist Intelligence Unit Report, April. Available at: http://graphics.eiu. com/PDF/Cisco_Innovation_Complete.pdf (accessed 15 September 2014).

Gereffi G., 1999. International trade and industrial upgrading in the apparel commodity chain. *Journal of International Economics*, 48(1): 37–70.

Gittelman M., 2007. Does geography matter for science-based firms? Epistemic communities and the geography of research and patenting in biotechnology. *Organization Science*, 18(4): 724–741.

Hall B. H., Jaffe A., Trajtenberg M., 2001. *NBER Patent Citations Data File: Lessons, Insights and Methodological Tools*. Working Paper No. 8498, National Bureau of Economic Research, Cambridge, MA.

Humphrey J., Schmitz H., 2002. How does insertion in global value chains affect upgrading in industrial clusters? *Regional Studies*, 36(9): 1017–1027.

Iammarino S., McCann P., 2013. *Multinationals and Economic Geography*, Edward Elgar, Cheltenham, UK.

Jacobs J., 1969. *The Economy of Cities*, The Vintage Press, New York, NY.

Jaffe A., Trajtenberg M., Henderson R., 1993. Geographic localization of knowledge spillovers as evidenced by patent citations. *Quarterly Journal of Economics*, 108(3): 577–598.

Lai R., D'Amour A., Yu A., Sun Y., Fleming L., 2013. *Disambiguation and Co-authorship Networks of the U.S. Patent Inventor Database (1975–2010)*. Available at: http://hdl. handle.net/1902.1/15705 UNF:5:RqsI3LsQEYLHkkg5jG/jRg==theHarvard Dataverse Network [Distributor] V5 [Version] (accessed 17 September 2014).

Lewin A., Massini S., Peeters C., 2009. Why are companies offshoring innovation? The emerging global race of talent. *Journal of International Business Strategy*, 40(6): 901–925.

Lorenzen M., 2004. Knowledge and geography. *Industry and Innovation*, 12(4): 399–407.
Lorenzen M., Mudambi R., 2013. Clusters, connectivity and catch-up: Bollywood and Bangalore in the global economy. *Journal of Economic Geography*, 13(3): 501–534.
Marshall A., 1920. *Principles of Economics*, Macmillan, London, UK.
Mudambi R., 2008. Location, control and innovation in knowledge-intensive industries. *Journal of Economic Geography*, 8(5): 699–725.
Mudambi R., Santangelo G., 2015. From shallow resource pools to emerging clusters: The role of MNE subsidiaries in peripheral areas. *Regional Studies*, forthcoming.
Narula R., 2002. Innovation systems and 'inertia' in R&D location: Norwegian firms and the role of systemic lock-in. *Research Policy*, 31(5): 795–816.
OECD, 2011. *Global Value Chains: Preliminary Evidence and Policy Issues*, DSTI/IND(2011)3, OECD, Paris, France. Available at: http://www.oecd.org/industry/ind/47945400.pdf (accessed 20 September 2014).
Patel P., Vega M., 1999. Patterns of internationalisation of corporate technology: Location vs. home country advantages. *Research Policy*, 28(2–3): 145–155.
Saxenian A., 1996. *Regional Advantage: Culture and Competition in Silicon Valley and Route 128*, Harvard University Press, Boston, MA.
Von Zedtwitz M., 2006. International R&D strategies of TNCs from developing countries: The case of China, in UNCTAD, (ed.), *Globalization of R&D and Developing Countries. Proceedings of an Expert Meeting*, United Nations, New York and Geneva.

3 Competition and cooperation in entrepreneurial ecosystems

A lifecycle analysis of a Canadian ICT ecosystem

*Anna Minà, Giovanni Battista Dagnino
and Soumaya Ben Letaifa*

Introduction

The term ecosystem draws on the Greek ('οιχος' = environment and 'συστημα' = system) and means 'home system'. Hence, ecosystem refers to the biological community of interacting organisms and their physical context (Willis, 1997). In the last two decades, the concept of ecosystem has progressively gained importance in management research as well (Mars *et al.*, 2012). Scholars have borrowed the term ecosystem from biology to portray a context based on: 'the community of organizations, institutions, and individuals that impact the enterprise and the enterprise's customers and suppliers' (Teece, 2007: 1325; Gueguen and Isckia, 2009; Mars *et al.*, 2012).

Ecosystems are networks in continuous interactions (Gummesson, 2008) that are capable of generating the ecosystem's life, growth and transformation (Ben Letaifa, 2014). The literature suggests that we should understand how ecosystems shape cooperative and competitive relationships between firms and, consequently, the evolution of the ecosystem (Zahra and Nambisan, 2011, 2012; Kapoor and Lee, 2013). At the same time, however, the extant literature has largely overlooked investigating the ecosystem as an *unfolding* phenomenon. Actually, most studies have taken a pretty static view of the ecosystem by focusing on the firms operating in the ecosystem and on their interdependence with complementors (Brandenburger and Nalebuff, 1996), rather than detecting the environmental dynamics in which such interorganizational networks emerge and evolve. There is, in fact, little understanding of how successful entrepreneurial ecosystems come into being and evolve (Feldman and Braunerhjelm, 2004; Mason and Brown, 2014). Past studies have investigated either the influence of a specific core firm on the losses and survival of its complementors and complementors' providers (Pierce, 2009) or how the opportunities and challenges faced by innovators that belong to an ecosystem are able to influence the focal firm's performance (Adner and Kapoor, 2010). Similarly, they have detected how the differences in the way ecosystem firms are organized, as regards complementary activities, impinge on their decisions to invest in new technologies within the business ecosystem (Kapoor and Lee, 2013).

Accordingly, a vantage perspective to study an ecosystem from a more dynamic or evolutionary perspective is to examine the ecosystem evolution along its *lifecycle*. Since: 'creating, shaping, navigating, and exploiting business ecosystems requires entrepreneurial insight, coupled with strategic thinking' (Zahra and Nambisan, 2012: 219), in this study we unambiguously recognize the relevance of understanding the evolution of entrepreneurial ecosystems and will, therefore, focus our attention on these *entrepreneurial* ecosystems (Isenberg, 2010; Krueger, 2012a, 2012b). This chapter therefore aims to detect and explain the entrepreneurial ecosystem lifecycle process by means of a *longitudinal* perspective that spans over time and waves of change.

At the conceptual level, to this end we draw on Moore's (1993) evolutionary stages of a business ecosystem's model to trace the path of an ecosystem's evolution. We consider the *interplay* between cooperation and competition as antecedents of each phase of the ecosystem lifecycle. The purpose of this chapter is, therefore, to understand how competitive and cooperative behaviours emerging among the ecosystem players contribute to the evolution of the entrepreneurial ecosystem as a whole.

At the empirical level we have selected a specific intriguing case, i.e. the case of a Canadian ICT ecosystem located close to the city of Montreal in the decade from 1999 to 2009. By leveraging on multiple data sources available, the case at hand allows us to categorize clearly how the sequence of developing stages in which higher/lower cooperation and competition among entrepreneurs has shaped the various phases of the ecosystem lifecycle.

Given the relative novelty of ecosystem research in strategy and entrepreneurship (Adner and Kapoor, 2010; Zahra and Nambisan, 2012; Kapoor and Lee, 2013), this study contributes to previous investigations in two main ways. First, since entrepreneurial ecosystems' literature stresses that firms are engaged in complex multilevel interactions that combine both competition and cooperation in the value creation phase (Lado *et al.*, 1997), we extend our understanding of competitive and cooperative behaviours and their interplay (i.e. coopetitive behaviour) along the entire entrepreneurial ecosystem's lifecycle. Second, by applying the lifecycle model to the empirical context of an entrepreneurial ecosystem, the study contributes in that it permits us to single out and delineate the characteristic traits of entrepreneurial ecosystems in each phase of development and, therefore, how they evolve over time, i.e. the so-called 'ecosystem evolutionary lifecycle'.

The next section of this chapter builds on the theoretical background of the study. We discuss the levels of analysis and the actors in a business ecosystem, introduce the characteristic traits of entrepreneurial ecosystems and discuss the cooperative, competitive and coopetitive nature of the relationships emerging within entrepreneurial ecosystems. The following section discusses the main methodological features of this study, which is followed by a portrayal of the sequential stages of the Canadian ICT entrepreneurial ecosystem and shows how the interplay between competitive and cooperative challenges shapes its evolutionary lifecycle. The final section discusses the results of the study, presents the key conclusions and gathers the key implications of our findings for future theoretical and empirical research.

Theoretical background

The concept of a business ecosystem emerged essentially in the early 1990s to describe the relationships between various players in a business environment. In 1993 James Moore coined the expression 'business ecosystem' to refer to the: 'economic community supported by a foundation of interacting organizations and individuals' (Moore, 1993: 76). Drawing on biological ecosystems, business ecosystems are composed of groups of firms that interact and share dependencies to create *products*, to develop *technologies* and create *value* (Moore, 1996; Zahra and Nambisan, 2012).

Business ecosystems include lead producers, market customers, rival firms and other interested parties that benefit from the web of connections between actors and products that is greater than in traditional business designs. Accordingly, they represent *meta-organizational* structures that are characterized, on the one hand, by heterogeneous sets of resources, competences and deployments leading to innovations. On the other hand, these structures are epitomized by homogeneous actors that interact with the aim of gaining and sustaining a competitive advantage at the ecosystem level (Moore, 1993, 1996; Iansiti and Levien, 2004a, 2004b; Adner and Kapoor, 2010).

In this vein: 'globalization of markets and industry generate powerful forces towards, on the one hand, increasing homogeneity and, on the other hand, opening new markets and cultures, towards increasing heterogeneity. These two countervailing trends cross through business ecosystems' (Corallo *et al.*, 2007: xxi). The main idea underlining the emergence of a business ecosystem is that technological, product and strategic changes by a single firm have widespread implications for firm performance and survival (Teece, 2007; Pierce, 2009).

Levels of analysis and actors of business ecosystems

Since several actors, such as complementors, suppliers and buyers are embedded in the environment in which firms operate, environmental characteristics affect profoundly their performance (Teece, 2010). Firms should not be conceived as single members of a specific industry, but: 'as a part of a business ecosystem that crosses a variety of industries' (Moore, 1993: 76). Therefore, firms in an ecosystem cannot take into consideration, as happened in the past, merely their own core markets and core operations, neither can they focus uniquely on their ability to create more value than their competitors. Such a traditional approach would, in fact, make firms blind to understanding the developments that are occurring 'outside their core'. According to this stream, it is important to consider the *context* in which firms operate (Adner and Kapoor, 2010; Kapoor and Lee, 2013) as well as the network of strategic interdependence among industry players that are generated (Zahra and Nambisan, 2012; Kapoor and Lee, 2013; Dagnino *et al.* 2015).

Figure 3.1 reports the illustration of a business ecosystem that reveals three main levels of interaction: (1) core business; (2) enlarged enterprise; and (3) ecosystem (Moore, 1993). The core business includes direct suppliers, core competences and distribution channels. Level two encompasses the enlarged enterprise, including suppliers of suppliers, direct customers and their customers, standards bodies and suppliers of complementary products and services. Level three of the ecosystem includes all the peripheral actors as well (Ben Letaifa, 2014).

More specifically, Iansiti and Levien (2004b) have explored the different roles that different organizations play in an ecosystem. In their model the organizations involved in the business ecosystem can be: (1) keystones; (2) dominators; (3) niche players; and (4) hub landlords.

Keystone players are the actors that are in charge of improving the general success of the ecosystem. They are central hubs through which most of the connections between actors take place. On one hand they: 'create value and increase ecosystem productivity by connecting network participants to one another or by making the creation of new products by third parties more efficient' (Iansiti and Levien, 2004a: 74). On the other hand, they share rare and valuable resources and knowledge for activating innovation processes within the business ecosystem. Consequently, keystones are simply the most powerful actors in the ecosystems who take advantage of their influence over the other players, even though they do not necessarily have to be the biggest firm in the network.

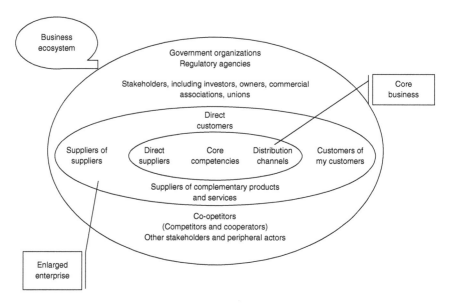

Figure 3.1 The business ecosystem

Source: Adapted from Moore (1996: 27) and Ben Letaifa (2014).

Dominators exploit their position by appropriating the value created or taking over the system, i.e. they are indicated as *value* dominators or *physical* dominators, respectively. While the former indirectly affect the system by appropriating the value the other firms of the ecosystem have generated, the latter directly influence the system by governing a large proportion of the network (Iansiti and Levien, 2004a: 75).

Niche players make up the biggest portion of the ecosystem in terms of value creation and innovation by differentiating from the other members of the network, although they have the least influence over it. Finally *hub landlords* provide: 'little new value to its network' (Iansiti and Levien, 2004a: 74), making the ecosystem unstable.

From the business ecosystem to the entrepreneurial ecosystem

Within a business ecosystem firms produce: 'goods and services of value to customers, who are themselves members of the ecosystem' (Moore, 1996: 29). Therefore, they are frequently typified by some entrepreneurial orientation (Lumpkin and Dess, 2001; Alvarez and Barney, 2010). The continuous exchanges occurring between entrepreneurial leaders and firms push towards permanent change and innovation that, together, shape the evolution of the entrepreneurial ecosystems (Van de Ven, 1993; Spilling, 1996; Neck and Meyer, 2004).

Entrepreneurial ecosystems refer to the amount of environmental variables (tangible and intangible) and interactive players (e.g. organizations and institutions) that coexist and reciprocally interact in a geographically defined area (Gnyawali and Fogel, 1994; Fogel, 2001; Iansiti and Levien, 2004a, 2004b; Cohen, 2006). Any entrepreneurial ecosystem displays a set of: 'individual elements – such as leadership, culture, capital markets, and open-minded customers – that combine in complex ways' (Isenberg, 2010: 3).

In one sense firms with entrepreneurial insights are capable of: 'adapting and transforming themselves as the forces of competition change', as well as to: 'simultaneously creating and discovering opportunities, while creatively and profitably exploiting other opportunities' (Zahra and Nambisan, 2012: 219). Consequently, the entrepreneurial ecosystem implies the emergence of both opportunity-seeking and advantage-seeking behaviours that, in turn, allow firms to obtain superior rents in the ecosystem (Hitt *et al.*, 2011). In this way, they are able to contribute to the wealth and evolution of the ecosystem per se.

In another sense the entrepreneurial ecosystem offers a highly flavoured and interacting environment for firms to win opportunities for entrepreneurs to emerge. Government leaders and other institutions (e.g. universities, research centres and professional support services such as lawyers, accountants and banks) play an important role in shaping a supporting environment for entrepreneurship to emerge (Spilling, 1996; Isenberg, 2010). For instance, they can attract external stakeholders (such as new entrepreneurs and investors) and provide rules of interaction that generate opportunities for collaboration between firms (Carlsson and Stankiewicz, 1991; Neck and Meyer, 2004; Cohen, 2006).

Characteristics features of entrepreneurial ecosystems

As mentioned above, by exploiting the entrepreneurial opportunities emerging within the entrepreneurial ecosystem firms are able to achieve competitive advantages and create value for them and for the ecosystem as a whole. The members of any entrepreneurial ecosystem depend on each other and: 'like biological species', they: 'share their fate with each other' (Iansiti and Levien, 2004a: 69). The repeated interactions with all the members contribute to business success, making the ecosystem healthy and helping it to flourish over time.

Iansiti and Levien (2004a) identify three main factors that allow the success of an ecosystem: (1) productivity; (2) robustness; and (3) niche creation (Iansiti and Levien, 2004a). *Productivity* refers to the ecosystem's: 'ability to consistently transform technology and other raw materials of innovation into lower costs and new products' (Iansiti and Levien, 2004a: 72).

Robustness implies that an entrepreneurial ecosystem should be able to manage the uncertainties and unpredictable events that might significantly affect its evolution (Larson, 1992). If an ecosystem is robust, firms are more likely to predict such uncertainties and react properly to them. The competitive advantage of the firms embedded in the ecosystem supports and ensures that the ecosystem remains robust for all its members. Furthermore, a robust ecosystem allows members to take opportunities as well as grow and gain a competitive advantage. This condition explains why a good measure of the robustness of an ecosystem is: 'the survival rates of ecosystem members, either over time or relative to comparable ecosystems' (Iansiti and Levien, 2004a: 73).

An entrepreneurial ecosystem should take into consideration the possibility of growing a niche of valuable new functions in order to grow in diversity (Iansiti and Levien, 2004a: 73). Diversity is a relevant condition driving firms to explore and develop innovative activities by adopting new technologies as well as enhancing new products and businesses.

Relationships within entrepreneurial ecosystems

While mainstream strategy studies have traditionally assumed that firms compete mainly for capturing value (Porter, 1980; Schmalensee, 1985; Dierickx and Cool, 1989; Barney, 1991; Peteraf, 1993) or, alternatively, cooperate to integrate heterogeneous resources, skills and capabilities in the value creation phase (Contractor and Lorange, 1988; Dyer and Singh, 1998), in entrepreneurial ecosystems we typically observe the interplay of cooperation and competition (Moore, 1996; Adner and Kapoor, 2010; Kapoor and Lee, 2013).

Scholars have acknowledged that cooperation and competition between and among firms frequently occur *simultaneously* (Bidault et al., 1992; Garud, 1994; Das and Teng, 2000; Dussauge et al., 2000; Park et al., 2014), while others have labelled the interplay of cooperation and competition as *coopetition* (Brandenburger and Nalebuff, 1996; Bengtsson and Kock, 2000; Gnyawali and Park, 2009, 2011; Rai, 2013). Under coopetition firms are engaged in a win-win game with variable end results, meaning that they compete and cooperate for the creation of value, whereas they might compete in the value appropriation phase. Coopetition explains how cooperating with complementors can make the 'pie bigger' rather than competing fiercely over a fixed pie (Brandenburger and Nalebuff, 1996; Dagnino, 2009; Gnyawali and Park, 2011).

We can confirm that entrepreneurial ecosystems are characterized by *coopetition* (Ben Letaifa, 2014), and therefore firms usually interact – either purposefully or unintentionally – to bring forth their offerings via a product or service to the marketplace. Firms in such ecosystems may be separated as regards ownerships; however, they are strictly interwoven and work: 'cooperatively and competitively to support new products, satisfy customer needs, and eventually incorporate the next round of innovations' (Moore, 1993: 76).

Methods

As we have reported above, through repeated interaction firms coevolve their knowledge and capabilities as well as: 'tend[ing] to align themselves' (Moore, 1996: 27). By doing so, they cooperate and contribute to the competitive advantage of the entrepreneurial ecosystem as a whole and compete in order to get most of the value created (Brandenburger and Nalebuff, 1996; Ritala, 2012). In such a way, each firm's fate is directly related to the other actors of the ecosystem as they closely coopete to thrive and prosper. On this basis, this chapter explores how the interplay of competition and cooperation shape the evolution of the entrepreneurial ecosystem's lifecycle.

Since the inner nature of our research is explorative, it implies a fine-grained investigation that is typically adopted in qualitative analysis (Yin, 2011). In this study we therefore develop an indepth longitudinal case study (Eisenhardt, 1989; Yin, 2011) of a specific entrepreneurial ecosystem. We shall cease discussing theoretical sampling so as to justify the decision we took to select a single case study (Eisenhardt, 1989; Heugens and Mol, 2005; Gibbert *et al.*, 2008).

Theoretical sampling

We have decided to adopt and inspect a Canadian ICT ecosystem based in Montreal, Quebec, over a period of ten years from 1999 to 2009. Three main reasons justify the choice of this entrepreneurial ecosystem. First, the Canadian ICT ecosystem taken into account presents all the characteristic traits of an entrepreneurial ecosystem that, in turn, leads to the emergence of both opportunity-seeking and advantage-seeking behaviours. In fact, the Canadian ICT ecosystem was initially formed by involving more than 100 firms (both big and small), partly because of Quebec Government funding coupled with private funding. The ecosystem basically engaged all of the key players in the Canadian ICT industry who were destined for rapid growth. Second, the Canadian ICT ecosystem studied exhibits an intriguing ten-year life cycle (1999–2009) that we were able to study closely in its entirety and, to our knowledge, for the first time ever. In such a way, we were able to perform an indepth analysis of all the evolutionary phases of the ecosystem, exactly from its dawn to termination. Third, through studying the emergence of competitive and cooperative thrusts among the key players of the Canadian entrepreneurial ecosystem, the inspection of this case allows us to detect how the interplay between competition and cooperation has contributed to shaping, in specific ways, the various phases of the ecosystem lifecycle.

Data sources

To develop our study, we used both primary and secondary data sources. First, we conducted over 40 interviews with 35 ecosystem leaders, such as CEOs, vice-presidents and public decision makers of the entrepreneurial ecosystem. Most of them have covered such positions for more than two decades (also in other contexts). In studying the Canadian ICT ecosystem, we dug into multiple sources of data that were thoroughly juxtaposed and decoded via a triangulation of facts (Jick, 1979). Accordingly, the interviews aimed at triangulating data sources by targeting multiple positions in the ecosystems, i.e. telecommunications' carriers, network equipment manufacturers, content providers, niche suppliers, financial angels, associations, public institutes for innovation and universities (see Table 3.1). While the nationality of the universities, carriers, financial angels and niche suppliers' institutes and associations of the entrepreneurial ecosystem was essentially Canadian, most of the network equipment manufacturers were either American or European. The interviews were semi-structured and lasted two hours on average. All of them have been recorded and transcribed. The questions posed

Table 3.1 Types of interfirm relationships

	Competition	*Cooperation*	*Coopetition*
Agent interests in the value creation processes	Conflicting interests	Fully converging interests	Partially converging interests
Type of game	Win-lose game	Balanced positive sum game	Balanced but variable positive sum game
Key Variable	Market power, competing resource and competence endowments, innovation	Complementary resource and competence endowments deployed for the benefit of both agents	Competing and complementary resource and competence endowments deployed for partially convergent objectives

Source: Authors' elaboration.

to the managers aimed at understanding: (1) the reasons underlying the emergence of the Canadian ICT ecosystem, specifically the interviews were aimed at exploring the 'why' and 'how' of the creation and evolution of the ICT ecosystem; and (2) how cooperative and competitive relationships emerge and evolve among the players of the ecosystem. The verbatim records resulting from the interviews helped to understand the whole lifecycle of the ecosystem, starting from its creation until its dissolution. One of the authors of this chapter spent about ten months interviewing key leaders in the ecosystem and complemented the interviews' data with a range of non-participative observations of five innovation meetings and several secondary documents. In so doing we were eventually able to cease the opportunity to grasp the evolution of the entrepreneurial ecosystem as a whole.

Temporal bracketing

The Canadian ICT ecosystem studied had a lifespan of ten years (1999–2009) (see Table 3.2). According to Moore: 'every business ecosystem develops in four distinct stages: birth, expansion, leadership, and self-renewal – or, if not self-renewal, death. In reality, of course, the evolutionary stages blur, and the managerial challenges of one stage often crop up in another' (Moore: 1993: 76).

We collected the data starting in 2007 and ending in 2009, during the ecosystem's dissolution phase. We therefore frame the temporal evolution of the

Table 3.2 Canadian ICT ecosystem's respondents' profiles

Type of organization	Number of organizations	Respondents' positions	Number of interviews
Carriers	2	Vice-president	4
		Associate director	4
Network equipment manufacturers	3	Vice-president	2
		Director	4
Content providers	2	Vice-president	2
Niche suppliers	5	CEOs	5
Public institutes	2	President	2
		Innovation Senior Advisor	2
		Senior economists	2
Financial angels	2	CEOs	2
Associations	1	CEO	1
Universities	4	Partnership chairman	2
		Professors	6
Total	**21**		**38**

Source: Adapted by Ben Letaifa.

ecosystem and partition the decade under investigation (1999–2009) into four main phases (i.e. phase I: 1999; phase II: 1999–2004; phase III: 2005–2008; and phase IV: 2008–2009). This division was based on the four crucial situations that the Canadian ICT ecosystem showed: start, coexistence of competition and cooperation, prevalence of competition over cooperation and dissolution. The reasons underlying the choice of our temporal bracketing research strategy are related to the continuity of the activities within each phase and the discontinuities of actions between the phases (Langley and Truax, 1994; Langley, 1999). Furthermore, by adopting the temporal bracketing strategy, we can confirm that we are in the favourable position of being able to perform cross-case comparisons, thereby increasing the external validity of this study.

In 1999 the Canadian ICT ecosystem was built in order to help members to reciprocally interact and foster cooperation between them. From 1999 to 2004 each member of the ecosystem agreed to co-create the ecosystem by launching a state-of-the-art technological infrastructure and identifying key projects that were important to initiate the process. Starting in 2005, various ecosystem members began to fight with each other with the aim of maximizing their own strategic supremacy within the ecosystem, as well as minimizing the influence of the other 'rival' members. From 2008 stiff competition among members started to surface along with the emergence of new environmental conditions and innovation outside the ecosystem, which put the survival of the Canadian ICT ecosystem at serious risk and eventually led to its dissolution in 2009.

Analysis of the case

In this section we draw from Moore's four-phase model of evolution of the business ecosystem to interpret the Canadian ICT ecosystem's lifecycle. Specifically, we illustrate the evolution of the ecosystem that is characterized, in each phase, by the: 'complex interplay between competitive and cooperative business strategies' (Moore, 1993: 76). Departing from Ben Letaifa (2014) analysis of the same ecosystem that was targeted to grasp the value creation and capture the dynamics within the ecosystem, we have been able to present an alternative explanation as to how the ecosystem's founders and members interpreted and managed their competitive-cooperative relationships over time. We pinpoint the four relevant phases that truly correspond to a progression in the levels of explanation, in which higher/lower cooperation or competition among actors allows the development of the ICT ecosystem lifecycle.

Phase I: 1999. Birth of the entrepreneurial Canadian ICT ecosystem

As anticipated, the Canadian ICT ecosystem started in 1999. To support this initiative, the Quebec Government provided half of the financial founding, while the members of the Canadian ICT ecosystem provided the other half. Since each player contributed according to its size, the carriers that held a strong oligopoly vantage position in the Canadian telecommunications (ICT) market were the primary contributors (Ben Letaifa, 2014). The key leaders were either the founders of the ecosystem who funded and decided on every project (i.e. carriers, network equipment manufacturers, public institutes, government), or the key members who participated in the value creation process (e.g. financial angels, universities, associations, niche suppliers, etc.).

The creation of the Canadian ICT ecosystem was based on the premise that members would engage in *high cooperation* with each other, to conjointly develop new products and services as well as new technologies. Therefore, the ecosystem's cooperative challenge was to shape an intensely cooperating environment in which members could share resources and their deployments with each other within the ecosystem (Adner and Kapoor, 2010). The initial competitive challenges required that firms were able to exploit the opportunities outspreading from operating in an entrepreneurial ecosystem by maintaining some kind of autonomy from it.

Phase II: 1999–2004. Expansion of the entrepreneurial Canadian ICT ecosystem

From 1999 to 2004, the Canadian ecosystems members agreed to co-create the ecosystem by launching a state-of-the-art technological infrastructure and identifying key projects that were important to start it going. The main purpose was to create an environment in which all members would intensely cooperate with each other in order to be competitive: 'against other ecosystems to control strategic markets' (Moore, 1993: 79). Therefore, the cooperative challenges were to instill a change in the founders' mindsets, in terms of developing full commitment of the players that had to share resources and knowledge to create innovations within the ecosystem (Ben Letaifa, 2014). The competitive challenges still remained in that players attempted to be able to exploit the opportunities stemming from the ecosystem and win more value than other members.

Phase III: 2004–2008. Leadership (and competition) in the entrepreneurial Canadian ICT ecosystem

As reported earlier, building the Canadian ICT ecosystem implied a significant change in the founders' mindsets towards full cooperation between players. In this regard, the cooperative challenges were related to developing a convincing vision of the ecosystem, so as to make members support it and improve the overall quality level of the ecosystem as a whole. However, although the actors had initially declared their full commitment and willingness to build the ecosystem and reciprocally interact, it actually resulted in their being unable to shift from a competitive approach to a truly coopetitive one. Once the ecosystem had reached a stage of maturity and it was possible to reap profits from innovations, actors started experimenting with a sort of *competitive race* between them with the aim of becoming the leader of the ecosystem, rather than: 'working [both] cooperatively and competitively' (Moore, 1993: 76). Therefore, this could have resulted in the Canadian ICT ecosystem becoming a leader over the other ICT ecosystems in the country.

Instead of meticulously pursuing the superior shared interests of the ecosystem, starting in 2004 various ecosystem members began looking to maximize their own interests over the other actors. As emerged clearly from the pool of interviews performed, the ecosystem's players never managed to focus on full cooperation, while they had previously declared that cooperation was a non-eliminable requisite condition for the emergence of the ecosystem as a whole.

Phase IV: 2008–2009. Dissolution of the entrepreneurial Canadian ICT ecosystem

Starting in 2008, ecosystem members initiated to act in a merely opportunistic fashion (Williamson, 1985) and to use the ecosystem as the context through which to exploit the opportunities to *systematically* compete more aggressively with each other. Each player within the Canadian ICT ecosystem began aiming at improving their own private interests at the expense of other members (Park and Russo, 1996; Khanna *et al.*, 1998) by capturing the resources and knowledge emerging within the ecosystem and: 'applying them to its own operations' (Khanna *et al.*, 1998: 195). This was proved by the higher ratio of private interests over common interests, as well as by the higher opportunistic behaviour of ecosystem firms to achieve competitive advantage independently vis-à-vis the other ecosystem members. In fact, while the ecosystem members were supposed to cooperate with each other, they conceived the ecosystem as the means through which they could achieve primarily (although not uniquely) their own interests. They declared their approach to the ecosystem's relationships considering that 'there are no equal cooperators' among them and that members 'are very strong in the strategic game'. Therefore, since members operated in the same environment, they were willing to exploit the ecosystem by absorbing the resources, capabilities and knowledge of the other members (Park and Russo, 1996). Within this high-rivalry context, understandably the emergence of a condition in which cooperation and coopetition could coexist turned out to be impossible in the Canadian ICT ecosystem. This condition inevitably circumvented the development of common projects and eventually led to the ecosystem's dissolution (see Table 3.3).

Contribution and conclusion

On the basis of the indepth study into the intriguing case of a Canadian ICT ecosystem, this chapter advances a couple of significant contributions to acknowledged ecosystem studies in strategy and entrepreneurship (Adner and Kapoor, 2010; Zahra and Nambisan, 2012; Kapoor and Lee, 2013). First, by applying Moore's (1993) lifecycle model to the key context of a specific entrepreneurial ecosystem along the decade of its operation (1999–2009), this study is able to delineate the characteristic traits of each of the four phases of development of

Table 3.3 Evolutionary phases of the Canadian ICT ecosystem: competitive and cooperative challenges

Time	Phase	Cooperative challenges	Competitive challenges
1999	Birth	Foster cooperation among members of the ecosystem to develop innovations	Exploit the opportunities outspreadingfrom being part of the entrepreneurial ecosystem
1999–2004	Expansion	Change the mindset of the members of the ecosystem and work with all of them to share existing resources and knowledge, as well as develop new ideas	Maximizing members' individual position within the ecosystem
2004–2008	Leadership	Work together to make the ecosystem a leadervis-à-vis other ICT ecosystems	Developing a competitive race among the firms of the ecosystem so as to reap more advantage over rivals
2008–2009	Dissolution	Put members' efforts into saving existing ecosystem, developing common projects (not occurring completely)	Maximizing the benefits arising from participating in the ecosystem

Source: Authors' elaboration.

an entrepreneurial ecosystem: birth, expansion, leadership and dissolution, or the '*ecosystem evolutionary lifecycle*'.

This condition may be enlightening for at least two reasons: first and foremost, since we have been exposed for the first time to the advantage of being able to observe an entrepreneurial ecosystem along its entire lifecycle, we can purport that, by doing so, we have been able to retrace how the ecosystem evolved over the entire period of its existence (the decade 1999–2009). This confirms the high degree of internal validity of our research. Second, while we are perfectly aware that the study of a single case always brings some generalizability problems (Yin, 2011), since each ecosystem usually emerges under a unique set of conditions and circumstances (Mason and Brown, 2014), we can also add that the investigation of the entire ecosystem's lifecycle is a *critical* condition in applying a conceptual model or framework that may allow extending the application of our results to other entrepreneurial ecosystems. For this reason we hope that additional research, when applied to other cases following our detection of the lifecycle of the Canadian ICT entrepreneurial ecosystem, will check for the external validity and replication of our findings.

Second, since the entrepreneurial ecosystems' literature underscores that firms are engaged in complex multilevel interactions that combine and recombine competitive and cooperative thrusts in the value creation phase (Lado *et al.*, 1997), by applying Moore's (1993) model to the Canadian ICT ecosystem we have been able to broaden our appreciation of unfolding competitive and cooperative behaviours and their interplay (i.e. coopetitive behaviour) along the entire entrepreneurial ecosystem's lifecycle (i.e. the so-called '*ecosystem coopetitive relationships*'). This condition offers some appealing insights into the entrepreneurial ecosystem literature in that, while we acknowledge that extant studies have approached the discovery and analysis of entrepreneurial ecosystems specifically by focusing on the regulators and geography (Ben Letaifa and Rabeau, 2013; Vogel, 2013), we have taken another pathway by concentrating our attention on ecosystem firms that presented some degree of entrepreneurial orientation (Isenberg, 2011) in approaching the dynamics of ecosystem competitive, cooperative and coopetitive behaviours.

Last but not least, since our study goes from the birth to the termination of the Canadian ecosystem and while we have uncovered the motives underlying ecosystem termination, we recognize that we have fallen short by not inspecting what happened after the termination, in particular to see if there was an attempt to rebuild and relaunch the ecosystem. For this reason, it seems interesting to try to understand what occurred in the aftermath of the Canadian ICT ecosystem extinction. Since we know that one of the key growth drivers of entrepreneurial ecosystems is the process of '*entrepreneurial recycling*' (Bahrami and Evans, 1997; Mason and Harrison, 2006), it would be appealing to examine whether (or not) this process of ecosystem relaunching actually occurred. Entrepreneurs who have built successful firms typically leave their firms soon after it has been sold, but they usually remain involved in the cluster, reinvesting their wealth and experience to create additional entrepreneurial activities (Mason and Brown, 2014). Further studies may wish to detect the existence of the entrepreneurial recycling hypothesis in the case of the Canadian ICT ecosystem.

References

Adner R., Kapoor R., 2010. Value creation in innovation ecosystems: How the structure of technological interdependence affects firm performance in new technology generations. *Strategic Management Journal*, 31(3): 306–333.

Alvarez S. A., Barney J. B., 2010. Entrepreneurship and epistemology: The philosophical underpinnings of the study of entrepreneurial opportunities. *Academy of Management Annals*, 4(1): 557–583.

Bahrami H., Evans S., 1997. Flexible re-cycling and high-technology entrepreneurship. *California Management Review*, 37(3): 62–89.

Barney J., 1991. Firm resources and sustained competitive advantage. *Journal of Management*, 17(1): 99–120.

Ben Letaifa S., 2014. The uneasy transition from supply chains to ecosystems: The value-creation/value-capture dilemma. *Management Decision*, 52(2): 278–295.

Ben Letaifa S., Rabeau Y., 2013. Too close to collaborate? How geographic proximity could impede entrepreneurship and innovation. *Journal of Business Research*, 66(10): 2071–2078.

Bengtsson M., Kock S., 2000. "Coopetition" in business networks – to cooperate and compete simultaneously. *Industrial Marketing Management*, 29(5): 411–426.

Bidault F., Laurent P., Segla C., 1992. Competitive and cooperative strategies in engineering services. *Long Range Planning*, 25(3): 43–49.

Brandenburger A. M., Nalebuff B. J., 1996. *Co-opetition*, HarperBusiness, London, UK.

Carlsson, B., Stankiewicz, R., (1991). On the nature, function and composition of technological systems. *Journal of Evolutionary Economics*, 1(2): 93–118.

Cohen B., 2006. Sustainable valley entrepreneurial ecosystems. *Business Strategy and the Environment*, 15(1): 1–14.

Contractor F. J., Lorange P., 1988. Competition vs. cooperation: A benefit/cost framework for choosing between fully-owned investments and cooperative relationships. *Management International Review*, 28(4): 5–18.

Corallo A., Passiante G., Prencipe A., (eds), 2007. *The Digital Business Ecosystem*, Edward Elgar, Cheltenham, UK.

Dagnino G. B., 2009. Coopetition strategy: A new kind of interfirm dynamics for value creation, in Dagnino G. B., Rocco E., (eds), *Coopetition Strategy: Theory, Experiments and Cases*, Routledge, London, UK.

Dagnino G. B., Levanti G., Minà A., Picone P. M., 2015. Interorganizational network and innovation: A bibliometric study and proposed research agenda. *Journal of Business and Industrial Marketing*, forthcoming.

Das T. K., Teng B. S., 2000. A resource-based theory of strategic alliances. *Journal of Management*, 26(1): 31–61.

Dierickx I., Cool K., 1989. Asset stock accumulation and sustainability of competitive advantage. *Management Science*, 35(12): 1504–1511.

Dussauge P., Garrette B., Mitchell W., 2000. Learning from competing partners: Outcomes and durations of scale and link alliances in Europe, North America and Asia. *Strategic Management Journal*, 21(2): 99–126.

Dyer J. H., Singh H., 1998. The relational view: Cooperative strategy and sources of interorganizational competitive advantage. *Academy of Management Review*, 23(4): 660–679.

Eisenhardt K. M., 1989. Building theories from case study research. *Academy of Management Review*, 14(4): 532–550.

Feldman M., Braunerhjelm P., 2004. The genesis of industrial clusters, in Braunerhjelm P., Feldman M., (eds), *Cluster Genesis: Technology-Based Industrial Development*, Oxford University Press, Oxford, UK, pp. 1–15.

Fogel G., 2001. An analysis of entrepreneurial environment and enterprise development in Hungary. *Journal of Small Business Management*, 39(1): 103–109.

Garud R., 1994. Cooperative and competitive behaviors during the process of creative destruction. *Research Policy*, 23(4): 385–394.

Gibbert M., Ruigrok W., Wicki B., 2008. What passes as a rigorous case study? *Strategic Management Journal*, 29(13): 1465–1474.

Gnyawali D. R., Fogel D., 1994. Environments for entrepreneurship development: Key dimensions and research implications. *Entrepreneurship Theory and Practice*, 18: 43–63.

Gnyawali D. R., Park B. J. R., 2009. Co-opetition and technological innovation in small and medium-sized enterprises: A multilevel conceptual model. *Journal of Small Business Management*, 47(3): 308–330.

Gnyawali D. R., Park B. J. R., 2011. Co-opetition between giants: Collaboration with competitors for technological innovation. *Research Policy*, 40(5): 650–663.

Gueguen G., Isckia T., 2009. The borders of mobile handset ecosystems: Is coopetition inevitable? In Hesselman C., Giannelli C., (eds), *Mobileware 2009 Workshops*, *Lecture Notes of the ICST*, 12, 45–54.

Gummesson E., 2008. Extending the service-dominant logic: From customer centricity to balanced centricity. *Academy of Marketing Science Journal*, 36(1):15.

Heugens P., Mol M. J., 2005. So you call that research? Mending methodological biases in strategy and organization departments of top business schools. *Strategic Organization*, 3(1): 117–128.

Hitt M. A., Ireland R. D., Sirmon D. G., Trahms C. A., 2011. Strategic entrepreneurship: Creating value for individuals, organizations, and society. *Academy of Management Perspectives*, 25(2): 57–75.

Iansiti M., Levien R., 2004a. Strategy as ecology. *Harvard Business Review*, 82(3): 68.

Iansiti M., Levien R., 2004b. *The Keystone Advantage*, Harvard Business School Press, Cambridge, MA.

Isenberg D. J., 2010. How to start an entrepreneurial revolution. *Harvard Business Review*, 88(6): 40–50.

Isenberg D. J., 2011. *The Entrepreneurship Ecosystem Strategy as a New Paradigm for Economy Policy: Principles for Cultivating Entrepreneurship*, Babson Entrepreneurship Ecosystem Project, Babson College, Babson Park, MA.

Jick T. D., 1979. Mixing qualitative and quantitative methods: Triangulation in action. *Administrative Science Quarterly*, 24(4): 602–611.

Kapoor R., Lee J. M., 2013. Coordinating and competing in ecosystems: How organizational forms shape new technology investments. *Strategic Management Journal*, 34(3): 274–296.

Khanna T., Gulati R., Nohria N., 1998. The dynamics of learning alliances: Competition, cooperation, and relative scope. *Strategic Management Journal*, 19(3): 193–210.

Krueger N. F., 2012a. *Candidates Guide to Growing a More Entrepreneurial Economy*, available at SSRN, 2098094. Available at: http://papers.ssrn.com/sol3/papers.cfm?abstract_id=2098094 (accessed 15 October 2014).

Krueger N. F., 2012b. *Markers of a Healthy Entrepreneurial Ecosystem*, available at SSRN, 2056182. Available at: http://papers.ssrn.com/sol3/papers.cfm?abstract_id=2056182 (accessed 18 October 2014).

Lado A. A., Boyd N. G., Hanlon S. C., 1997. Competition, cooperation, and the search for economic rents: A syncretic model. *Academy of Management Review*, 22(1): 110–141.

Langley A., 1999. Strategies for theorizing from process data. *Academy of Management Review*, 24(4): 691.

Langley A., Truax J., 1994. A process study of new technology adoption in smaller manufacturing firms. *Journal of Management Studies*, 31(5): 619–652.

Larson A., 1992. Network dyads in entrepreneurial settings: A study of the governance of exchange relationships. *Administrative Science Quarterly*, 37(1): 76–104.

Lumpkin G. T., Dess G. G., 2001. Linking two dimensions of entrepreneurial orientation to firm performance: The moderating role of environment and industry life cycle. *Journal of Business Venturing*, 16(5): 429–451.

Mars M. M., Bronstein J. L., Lusch R. F., 2012. The value of a metaphor: Organizations and ecosystems. *Organizational Dynamics*, 41(4): 271–280.

Mason C. M., Harrison R. T., 2006. After the exit: Acquisitions, entrepreneurial recycling. *Regional Studies*, 40(1): 55–73.

Mason C. M., Brown R., 2014. *Entrepreneurial Ecosystems and Growth Oriented Entrepreneurship*, Presentation to OECD LEED, Programme workshop on entrepreneurial ecosystems and growth-oriented entrepreneurship, The Hague, 7 November. (Final Version, January 2014). Available at: http://www.oecd.org/cfe/leed/entrepreneurial-ecosystems.pdf (accessed 7 October 2014).

Moore J. F., 1993. Predators and prey: A new ecology of competition. *Harvard Business Review*, 71(3): 75–86.

Moore J. F., 1996. *The Death of Competition: Leadership & Strategy in the Age of Business Ecosystems*, HarperBusiness, New York, NY.

Neck H., Meyer G., 2004. An entrepreneurial system view of new venture creation. *Journal of Small Business Management*, 42(2): 190–208.

Park B. J. R., Srivastava M. K., Gnyawali D. R., 2014. Walking the tight rope of coopetition: Impact of competition and cooperation intensities and balance on firm innovation performance. *Industrial Marketing Management*, 43(2): 210–221.

Park S. H., Russo M. V., 1996. When competition eclipses cooperation: An event history analysis of joint venture failure. *Management Science*, 42(6): 875–890.

Peteraf M. A., 1993. The cornerstones of competitive advantage: A resource-based view. *Strategic Management Journal*, 14(3): 179–191.

Pierce L., 2009. Big losses in ecosystem niches: How core firm decisions drive complementary product shakeouts. *Strategic Management Journal*, 30(3): 323–347.

Porter M. E., 1980. *Competitive Advantage*, The Free Press, New York, NY.

Rai R. K., 2015. A co-opetition-based approach to value creation in interfirm alliances construction of a measure and examination of its psychometric properties. *Journal of Management*, forthcoming.

Ritala P., 2012. Coopetition strategy – when is it successful? Empirical evidence on innovation and market performance. *British Journal of Management*, 23(3): 307–324.

Schmalensee R., 1985. Do markets differ much? *The American Economic Review*, 75(3): 341–351.

Spilling O. R., 1996. The entrepreneurial system: On entrepreneurship in the context of a mega-event. *Journal of Business Research*, 36(1): 91–103.

Teece D. J., 2007. Explicating dynamic capabilities: The nature and microfoundations of (sustainable) enterprise performance. *Strategic Management Journal*, 28(13): 1319–1350.

Teece D. J., 2010. Alfred Chandler and "capabilities" theories of strategy and management. *Industrial and Corporate Change*, 19(2): 297–316.

Van de Ven H., 1993. The development of an infrastructure for entrepreneurship. *Journal of Business Venturing*, 8(3): 211–230.

Vogel P., 2013. *Building and Assessing Entrepreneurial Ecosystems*, Presentation to OECD LEED, Programme workshop on entrepreneurial ecosystems and growth-oriented entrepreneurship, The Hague, 7 November. Available at: http://www.oecd.org/cfe/leed/entrepreneurial-ecosystems.pdf (accessed 7 October 2014).

Williamson O. E., 1985. *The Economic Institutions of Capitalism*, Simon and Schuster, New York, NY.

Willis A. J., 1997. The ecosystem: An evolving concept viewed historically. *Functional Ecology*, 11(2): 268–271.

Yin R., 2011. *Case Study Research: Design and Methods*, Sage Publishing, Beverly Hills, CA.

Zahra S. A., Nambisan S., 2011. Entrepreneurship in global innovation ecosystems. *AMS Review*, 1(1): 4–17.

Zahra S. A., Nambisan S., 2012. Entrepreneurship and strategic thinking in business ecosystems. *Business Horizons*, 55(3): 219–229.

Part II
Alliances and innovation

4 Partnering strategies in biotech firms

A longitudinal perspective

Daniela Baglieri, Fiorenza Belussi and Luigi Orsi

Introduction

A large number of previous works have focused on alliances (Arora and Gambardella, 1990) in biotechnology, because dedicated biotechnology firms (DBFs), created as startups from university research, formed a new emerging industrial niche that can be seen as an: 'unusual case of competence destruction' (Powell *et al.*, 1996: 124). Upstream and downstream alliances were the key sources of exploring new research avenues and exploiting valuable and patentable knowledge in the marketplace.[1] More precisely, agreements with universities tended to be focused on more basic research objectives, whereas those with large, 'established' pharmaceutical (pharma) firms were more product-specific (Rothaermel and Deeds, 2006). Powell *et al.* (1996) deserve the credit for having discussed the important role played by biotech alliances, as the real 'locus of innovation' within an 'open model' (Chesbrough, 2003) of biotech research, where the recombination of new knowledge and particularly the discovery of cutting-edge molecular knowledge, reside within the 'network' of interorganizational relations. Established pharma firms appear to be, in these analyses, crucial key partners for the survival and growth of the new DBFs (Gerde and Mahto, 2004), even if in the literature numerous other aspects have emerged as relevant: the starting conditions and competitive context (Barney and Zajac, 1994), the characteristics of the founding team (Zucker *et al.*, 1998), the main strategic decisions adopted (Cooper, 1998) and the geographical environment (Powell, 1999).

Several main advantages have been pinpointed by those researchers who have produced important empirical works on this issue. Even if the DBFs are knowledgeable enough to perform their R&D activities quite independently, allying with well-known pharma firms may allow them to: (1) find financial support in a world where markets appear to be inefficient structures for financing innovation (Audretsch and Feldman, 2005; Lazonick and Tulum, 2011; Hopkins *et al.*, 2013); (2) provide access to complementary assets (Pisano, 1990, 1991); (3) activate formal and informal processes of knowledge transfer and learning (Mowery *et al.*, 1996; Veugelers, 1997; Shenkar and Li, 1999; Norman, 2002); (4) create competitive advantage (Dyer and Singh, 1998); and (5) build a reputational mechanism (Baum and Oliver, 1991; Stuart *et al.*, 1999) that allows DBFs to increase their relational capital. Therefore, we can arrive at the conclusion that firms' strategic alliances are important and can influence firms' capabilities, as well as others' perceptions of their capabilities. There is no doubt that pharma firms are key partners for DBFs, but their importance has probably been overestimated and we are in complete disagreement with Hagedoorn and Roijakkers (2002), who have calculated that bio-pharma alliances are so popular as to account for up to 80% of all alliances observed in this industry.

The previously mentioned 'cooperative view' may be opposed to a more competitive view of alliances. Many alliances are characterized by co-opetition dynamics, i.e. partners collaborate and compete simultaneously (Lado *et al.*, 1997; Oliver, 2001, 2004; Quintana-Garcıa and Benavides-Velasco, 2004). Cooperation in strategic alliances may help partners to specialize in core business and gain access to certain resources that the firm does not own but are necessary for developing a specific activity. On the other hand, competition is needed to keep the creative tension within organizations. A syncretism between competition and cooperation might not be disruptive per se: it may foster greater knowledge seeking and a higher capacity to innovate than if cooperation and competition were both strategies pursued separately. Firms can cooperate, sharing and pooling together specific internal capabilities in some areas, but they may strongly compete in others. In each distinguishable niche, or subsector, organizations compete over the use of resources, as has been highlighted by researchers following a population ecology perspective (Hannan and Freeman, 1977; Foster, 1997; Volberda and Lewin, 2003). Thus, in this context, we can hypothesize that conflicts may emerge between old incumbents and novel DBFs for the sharing of the new knowledge created through alliances. In other words, the clear-cut division of labour envisaged in the literature in the past could be considered as only a transitory feature of the sector, not destined to last any longer. As observed by Stuart *et al.* (2007), although:

> [j]ust a handful of biotechnology companies have become fully integrated across all stages of the drug development process (e.g. Amgen, Genentech, Genzyme, Biogen Idec), many have migrated part of the way down the value chain by investing the surpluses from past alliances and external financing rounds in the development of a broader suite of capabilities. In turn, as biotechnology firms extend their internal scope to incorporate more downstream functions, they become less dependent on downstream alliance partners at the early stages of the drug development process. (Stuart *et al.*, 2007: 483)

In a mature stage of the development of biotech technologies, DBFs prosper not only if they are able to create alliances with large corporations that will provide financial resources (as well as manufacturing, marketing and regulatory expertise), learning and reputation but also if they become involved with a network of other agents, such as other DBFs, venture capital firms, public research organizations (PROs) and other industrial firms, which help them to establish a new industry niche. We can also hypothesize that, as the number of direct linkages with partners increases, more knowledge will be transferred and accessed. Thus, following Ahuja (2000) and Zahra *et al.* (2000), we can presume that this will increase the DBFs' innovative capacity, impacting positively on their innovative output.

We will try to demonstrate in this chapter the assumption that DBFs' partnering strategies are more complex than the 'classical' symbiotic relationship portrait revealed in prior work (Hagedoorn, 1993; Hagedoorn and Schakenraad, 1994; Liebeskind *et al.*, 1996; Helfat, 1997; George *et al.*, 2001). DBFs might choose their strategic alliance partners by considering both value creation and rent appropriation issues. In this vein, allying with established pharmaceutical firms might increase the risk of knowledge leakage; therefore, allying with other biotech firms may be perceived as less risky. We test these hypotheses on a sample of US and EU biotechnology firms. We establish four primary findings to explain the innovative output deriving from DBF alliances: (1) biotech-biotech alliances matter; (2) better innovative performance is realised by biotech firms with a composite alliances portfolio, including both bio-pharma and bio-bio agreements; (3) considering the typology of alliances, a path dependency behaviour emerges; and (4) if we look at the spatial dimension of alliances, there are clear-cut differences between US and EU biotech firms. We believe these findings may enrich the growing body of work on strategic alliances and provide new insights for strategic entrepreneurship.

Theory and hypotheses

Partnering strategies and bargaining power

Partnering strategies analysis in biotech is a well-established field of research (Teece, 1992; Hagedoorn, 1993, 1996; Greis *et al.*, 1995; Kogut, 1998). This literature has tried to understand the motives that lead firms to cooperate in their innovative efforts. Hagedoorn (1993), in his overview, establishes three main factors: technological complementarities, reduction of the innovation time-span and market access to the new technologies. These motives that underline the formation of strategic technological partnerships clearly differ from those related to partnerships based on cost-economizing operations that are more associated with the control of standard transaction costs. Biotech firms present a compelling and straightforward logic for entering into alliances, particularly considering the need to explore the new fields of knowledge related to RNA recombination, bioinformatics, small drugs' development and genomics. As is well known, the full exploitation of this knowledge, i.e. a novel therapeutic drug, is a time-consuming process, surrounded by a high level of uncertainty and failure, which develops following a ten-year pipeline of various clinical phases (Inkpen, 1998). Rothaermel (2001) found evidence of the importance of complementary assets in alliance formation between new and incumbent firms, given that new entrant biotech firms may benefit from allying with incumbents that possess the specialized complementary assets necessary to commercialize the new technology.

But strategic alliances are inherently incomplete contracts in which the property rights associated with alliance output may not be well defined (Clarke-Hill *et al.*, 2003). As a result, collaborators risk opportunistic exploitation by their partners, including leaking proprietary knowledge to partners or losing control of important assets (Hamel, 1991; Das and Teng, 1996; Inkpen and Beamish, 1997; Baum *et al.*, 2000). Within an alliance agreement, firms may adopt a pure, competitive behaviour and then the risk of a 'learning race' emerges, once they start looking for a maximum absorption of distinctive competencies from their partner, trying to protect their own core resources and capabilities (Khanna *et al.*, 1998; Kale *et al.*, 2000). Established firms might be particularly aggressive in allying with a new biotech, enjoying their greater bargaining power (Kale *et al.*, 2002). New biotech firms may have no choice but to enter into alliances with large pharmaceutical firms if they need market access, because for them forward integration is unfeasible in the short term due to a lack of the necessary resources (Rothaermel and Deeds, 2004).

Thus, we set the two following hypotheses that led us to predict that:

Hypothesis 1:   *Other things being equal, biotech firms are likely to choose pharmaceutical firms as partners rather than other biotech firms in order to increase their innovative performance.*

Hypothesis 2:   *Other things being equal, biotech firms are likely to choose other biotech firms as partners rather than pharmaceutical firms in order to increase their innovative performance.*

Partnering strategies and portfolio analysis

Although a focus on complementary assets represents a fruitful line of inquiry for a deeper understanding of the formation of alliances within the bio-pharma industry, such a perspective potentially ignores how firms overcome the uncertainties associated with such partnerships (Kale *et al.*, 2000). In fact, DBFs are usually the weaker bargaining partner, since they capture only a proportion – very often, the minority – of the rents generated by any future sales of valuable knowledge emerging from the alliance. To realise a successful outcome from each strategic alliance, DBFs need to overcome both the coordination costs and the potential opportunism of their partners (Milgrom and Roberts, 1992). Strategic alliances typically represent a 'co-opetition' framework, where an inherent tension exists between cooperative and competitive behaviour (Khanna *et al.*, 1998). For this reason, on the one hand, it can be hypothesized that DBFs with no prior alliance experience are likely to enter into partnering with firms that they feel are similar to them, avoiding the more powerful large pharma firms. Thus, they may prefer to ally with other biotech firms. As argued by Mowery *et al.* (1998), firms with similar technological capabilities (proxied by patent cross-citation and patent common citations) are more likely first, to form an alliance, and second, to create a better-performing alliance. Lane and Lubatkin (1998) also confirmed this trend.

They found that similarities in basic knowledge and organizational practices helped the partners to operate together more effectively, increasing knowledge value creation. However, on the other hand, allying with pharmaceutical firms may offer access to complementary capabilities (expertise in or access to managing clinical trials, marketing and distribution) and better opportunities to access global markets.

The tendency to ally with a specific partner typology may lead to the emergence of path dependencies, whereby: 'a firm's previous investments and its repertoire of routines (its "history") constrain its future behaviour' (Teece *et al.*, 1994: 17). Path dependence in DBFs' alliances could emerge because inertia facilitates routine-based experiential learning. Specifically, we assume that DBFs' routines represent a persistent pattern of behaviour based on past experience (Nelson and Winter, 1982) that is: 'the outcome of trial and error learning and the selection and retention of prior behaviours' (Gavetti and Levinthal, 2000: 113). Hence, DBFs' accumulated alliances experience reinforces established routines within each domain (Lavie and Rosenkopf, 2006) and inertia may occur in partner selection, affecting alliance propensity. By continuously allying with a homogeneous group of partners, however, DBFs can develop a narrow absorptive capacity, while firms that have accumulated experience with a heterogeneous group of partners can develop a broad absorptive capacity for interacting and exchanging knowledge with characteristically distinct partners. This led us to predict that:

Hypothesis 3a: *Other things being equal, biotech firms are more likely to choose as a partner in their portfolio another biotech in order to increase their innovative performance.*

Hypothesis 3b: *Other things being equal, biotech firms are more likely to choose as a partner in their portfolio a pharma firm in order to increase their innovative performance.*

Hypothesis 3c: *Other things being equal, biotech firms are more likely to choose as a partner in their portfolio a heterogeneous firm in order to increase their innovative performance.*

The geographical context of partnering strategies

According to Niosi (2003), knowledge-intensive products are characterized by increasing returns to scale: they have high upfront costs (from R&D and marketing) and rapidly-declining production costs per unit (Arthur, 1994; Niosi, 2000). Accessing global markets is the best way to maximize returns on a knowledge-intensive product. In addition, it may be worthwhile to ally with multinational firms in order to gain access to a broad set of experiences with diverse partners (Anand and Khanna, 2000) that allow entrepreneurial firms to develop a truly international experience (Hoang and Rothaermel, 2005). In contrast, biotech clusters have been portrayed in the literature as a clear example of the positive effect of co-location, which is responsible, in specific locations, for having activated many proximity-driven synergies (Powell *et al.*, 2002; Coenen *et al.*, 2004). Some authors have also proposed a novel approach within this literature, emphasising a kind of dual perspective to interpret cluster dynamics: local synergies must work together with the intention of building external linkages (Fontes, 2005; Waxel and Malmberg, 2007; Belussi *et al.*, 2010; Ter Wal, 2014). In addition to these factors, the complexities of the global business environment and the lack of familiarity between alliance partners who are located in different countries may produce a higher perceived risk of opportunism in international alliances than in domestic alliances (McCutchen *et al.*, 2004). Following a rent appropriation rationale, we can test the following dual-paired hypotheses:

Hypothesis 4:   *Other things being equal, biotech firms are more likely to choose international rather than domestic firms as partners.*
Hypothesis 5:   *Other things being equal, biotech firms are more likely to choose domestic rather than international firms as partners.*

Methods

The data to test the hypotheses proposed here are found in a sample of biotech firms listed in Bioscan that have entered into, at least, one agreement/alliance. We limited the sampling of our firms to 530 US firms and 237 EU firms located in Italy, France, Denmark and Sweden. We covered the period 1973–2006. These firms are typically DBFs engaged in the research, development and commercialization of therapeutics. We selected the entire universe of firms listed in Bioscan created in those years and that were active on 31 December 2006. This process yielded a sample of 767 biotechnology firms and 4,694 alliance agreements (3,281 deriving from the US sample and 1,413 from the EU sample). In the next step, we obtained each firm's alliance history. Bioscan lists detailed qualitative information about each of the firms' alliances, such as the focal firm's partners, the month and year when the alliance was established and what area of the industry value chain it covers (research, drug discovery, development, clinical trials, FDA regulatory process, marketing and sales). All agreements were codified on the basis of their content using the following schema: 1=funding (105), 2=research (1,145), 3=development (1,031), 4=technology transfer (100), 5=licensing (1,214), 6=marketing and communication (557), 7=distribution (244), 8=production (222), 9=services and equipment (76). We also collected information regarding the companies with which the 'Bioscan firms' have reached an agreement (size of the firm, age and sector of activity). Thus, we scanned the websites of about 2,000 firms. We reclassified the sectors of activity of our companies and biotech organizations, dividing our sample into four subsectors: biotech, pharmaceutical, others (biomedical, health and servicing, chemical sector, applied engineering, etc.) and PROs. Thus, we measured alliance networks comprehensively, considering horizontal alliances with other biotechnology firms, vertical-downstream alliances with pharmaceutical, chemical and marketing firms, and vertical-upstream alliances with universities, research institutes, government laboratories, hospitals and industry associations. Data presented[2] are also related to the analysis of firms' alliance portfolios. In order to simplify the analysis of each individual firm alliances' portfolio, we have also aggregated alliances into three subsectors: bio, pharma and others. Hence, we created the category of firms that have in their portfolio only alliances: (a) with bio and others (row 18); (b) with pharma and others – but not bio (row 19); (c) with all – bio, pharma and others (row 20); and (d) with neither bio nor pharma, but only with others (row 20). We classified the type of agreement and type of organization that signed the agreement with our 767 biotech firms (pharma: 868; biotech: 1,648; PRO: 675 and firms belonging to other sectors: 433). We paid particular attention to the definition of the biotech sector. We include here all the companies that have developed biotech technologies and that can be characterized as a DBF. Thus, we did not follow the official Standard Industrial Classification criterion that often includes some biotech companies in the pharmaceutical sector. In the Bioscan records analysed, some important data regarding the characteristics of the firms were incomplete. After some time-consuming work of correction and revision, we gathered all the missing information through internet searching, using the company websites. Extensive effort was required to ascertain the necessary information to run our econometric tests (size of the firm, age and location). Only in a few cases were we obliged to exclude from our analysis those companies or agreements which we did not have sufficient information on to be able to classify them. Some analyses presented are general and refer to the entire population of DBFs included in the Bioscan database. In order to better distinguish the relational strategy adopted by the DBFs in partner selection, we divided our archive into two sets of data, separating the US and European firms.

Model specifications

Descriptive statistics and correlations are presented in Table 4.1 (US) and Table 4.4 (EU). They show that independent variables are weakly correlated with one another. Consequently, the risk of multicollinearity does not appear to be very relevant. However, Table 4.1 shows that some independent variables, particularly among the types of agreement, are correlated with one another. Consequently, multicollinearity diagnostics were examined. We explicitly assessed potential multicollinearity in all models and found that the variance inflation factors were well below the suggested cut-off point of 10 (Kleinbaum *et al.*, 1988) with the exception of model 8 (Tables 4.2 and 4.3), where we have two independent variables slightly beyond the threshold of 10 (bio agreements and national agreements).

The dependent variable, number of patents (or number of products in the pipeline), is a count variable taking on discrete non-negative integer values, including zero, so a Poisson or a negative binomial specification is recommended. We applied the following specification of a Poisson regression model to test our hypotheses (Greene, 1997):

Table 4.1 Descriptive statistics *and Pearson's correlation coefficients (US biotech firms)*

Variables	sample	mean	S.D.	min	max	1	2	3	4	5	6
1 Patents	530	117.323	315.324	0	3536	1.000					
2 Products (3+4)	530	12.230	52.365	0	1007	0.098	1.000				
3 Pipeline products	530	4.264	4.860	0	50	0.310	0.153	1.000			
4 Products on the market	530	7.966	51.844	0	1000	0.070	0.996	0.061	1.000		
5 Agreements	530	6.191	7.209	1	68	0.485	0.067	0.304	0.040	1.000	
6 Bio-bio agreements	530	2.787	4.485	0	47	0.506	0.098	0.304	0.071	0.883	1.000
7 Bio-pharma agreements	530	1.523	2.438	0	20	0.357	0.024	0.219	0.004	0.688	0.468
8 Bio-PRO agreements	530	1.132	2.107	0	16	0.030	−0.026	0.090	−0.034	0.404	0.116
9 Bio-other sectors agreements	530	0.749	1.368	0	10	0.216	0.030	0.073	0.023	0.526	0.362
10 Local agreements	530	0.917	1.884	0	19	0.395	0.071	0.221	0.051	0.637	0.671
11 National agreements	530	3.379	4.424	0	37	0.421	0.021	0.304	−0.008	0.895	0.752
12 International agreements	530	1.894	2.708	0	22	0.330	0.097	0.158	0.083	0.757	0.656
13 Size	530	380.292	1421.530	1	20000	0.507	0.163	0.291	0.137	0.382	0.432
14 Age	530	17.106	8.620	5	40	0.224	0.194	0.084	0.188	0.166	0.139
15 History	530	1992	7.281	1980	2005	−0.201	−0.177	−0.122	−0.167	−0.211	−0.172
16 Time to first agreement	530	7.115	6.168	0	26	0.110	0.192	0.057	0.188	−0.047	0.004
17 Ownership	530	0.504	0.500	0	1	0.163	0.015	0.265	−0.009	0.256	0.188
18 Bio and others – excluding pharma agreements	530	0.358	0.480	0	1	−0.038	−0.033	−0.072	−0.026	−0.196	−0.009
19 Pharma and others – excluding bio agreements	530	0.125	0.330	0	1	−0.076	−0.040	−0.091	−0.031	−0.170	−0.235
20 All agreements	530	0.360	0.481	0	1	0.180	0.083	0.220	0.064	0.483	0.372
21 Neither bio nor pharma agreements	530	0.157	0.364	0	1	−0.118	−0.031	−0.112	−0.021	−0.225	−0.266

7	8	9	10	11	12	13	14	15	16	17	18	19	20	21
1.000														
0.052	1.000													
0.229	0.116	1.000												
0.270	0.243	0.299	1.000											
0.634	0.439	0.445	0.396	1.000										
0.608	0.189	0.466	0.352	0.472	1.000									
0.144	0.074	0.227	0.392	0.298	0.259	1.000								
0.053	0.086	0.190	0.092	0.140	0.148	0.291	1.000							
−0.083	−0.114	−0.226	−0.116	−0.183	−0.182	−0.280	−0.955	1.000						
−0.108	−0.044	−0.003	−0.032	−0.065	0.003	0.190	0.714	−0.711	1.000					
0.241	0.105	0.144	0.099	0.253	0.200	0.157	0.215	−0.232	0.149	1.000				
−0.464	−0.073	−0.061	−0.065	−0.167	−0.203	0.001	−0.065	0.084	0.045	−0.132	1.000			
0.104	−0.119	−0.131	−0.156	−0.166	−0.074	−0.037	−0.090	0.113	−0.042	−0.014	−0.282	1.000		
0.596	0.078	0.144	0.231	0.420	0.437	0.083	0.107	−0.136	−0.082	0.195	−0.561	−0.283	1.000	
−0.269	0.101	0.011	−0.078	−0.185	−0.242	−0.077	0.027	−0.035	0.086	−0.071	−0.322	−0.163	−0.323	1.000

Table 4.2 Determinants of patents' estimates for a Poisson regression model (530 observations, US firms)

Variables	Model 1		Model 2		Model 3		Model 4	
	Coeff.	Std. err	Coeff.	Std. err	Coeff.	Std. err	Coeff.	Std. err
Intercept	1.374 ***	0.028	1.123 ***	0.029	1.387 ***	0.029	1.308 ***	0.029
Agreements	0.027 ***	0.000					0.028 ***	0.000
Bio-bio agreements			0.018 ***	0.001				
Bio-pharma agreements			0.093 ***	0.001				
Bio-PRO agreements			−0.013 ***	0.002				
Bio-other sectors agreements			−0.036 ***	0.003				
Local agreements					0.006 ***	0.001		
National agreements					0.054 ***	0.001		
International agreements					0.000	0.001		
Size	0.424 ***	0.003	0.438 ***	0.003	0.422 ***	0.003	0.419 ***	0.003
Age	0.353 ***	0.012	0.424 ***	0.012	0.323 ***	0.012	0.364 ***	0.012
Time to first agreement	−0.017 ***	0.001	−0.016 ***	0.001	−0.010 ***	0.001	−0.018 ***	0.001
Ownership (dummy)	0.142 ***	0.010	0.065 ***	0.010	0.112 ***	0.010	0.163 ***	0.010
Bio and others – excluding pharma agreements (dummy)							0.142 ***	0.009
Pharma and others – excluding bio agreements (dummy)								
All (dummy)								
Neither bio nor pharma agreements								
AIC	81990		78034		80546		81768	
Pseudo R squared	0.503		0.528		0.512		0.504	

Significant codes: *p<0.1; **p<0.05; ***p<0.001<

Model 5		Model 6		Model 7		Model 8	
Coeff.	Std. err	Coeff.	Std. err	Coeff.	Std. err	Coeff.	Std. err
1.486 ***	0.029	1.374 ***	0.028	1.513 ***	0.028	0.844 ***	0.034
0.026 ***	0.000	0.023 ***	0.000	0.026 ***	0.000		
						0.026 ***	0.002
						0.063 ***	0.002
						−0.062 ***	0.003
						−0.042 ***	0.003
						0.059 ***	0.003
						0.053 ***	0.002
						−0.004 **	0.001
0.424 ***	0.003	0.427 ***	0.003	0.408 ***	0.003	0.412 ***	0.003
0.322 ***	0.012	0.310 ***	0.012	0.348 ***	0.012	0.360 ***	0.013
−0.015 ***	0.001	−0.012 ***	0.001	−0.013 ***	0.001	−0.006 ***	0.001
0.150 ***	0.010	0.112 ***	0.010	0.138 ***	0.010	0.084 ***	0.010
						0.717 ***	0.019
−0.416 ***	0.018					0.539 ***	0.018
		0.243 ***	0.010			0.548 ***	0.019
				−0.771 ***	0.020	−0.103 ***	0.026
81368		81370		80225		74179	
0.507		0.507		0.514		0.552	

Table 4.3 Determinants of patents' estimates for a Poisson regression model in small firms with fewer than 50 employees (220 observations, US firms)

Variables	Model 1		Model 2		Model 3		Model 4	
	Coeff.	*Std. err*	*Coeff.*	*Std. err*	*Coeff.*	*Std. err*	*Coeff.*	*Std. err*
Intercept	1.420 ***	0.110	1.140 ***	0.113	1.349 ***	0.109	1.431 ***	0.114
Agreements	0.042 ***	0.004					0.042 ***	0.004
Bio-bio agreements			0.078 ***	0.006				
Bio-pharma agreements			0.154 ***	0.009				
Bio-PRO agreements			−0.056 ***	0.007				
Bio-other sectors agreements			−0.043 ***	0.012				
Local agreements					0.150 ***	0.013		
National agreements					−0.002 ***	0.005		
International agreements					0.087	0.006		
Size	0.265 ***	0.021	0.201 ***	0.021	0.291 ***	0.021	0.265 ***	0.021
Age	0.171 ***	0.043	0.372 ***	0.045	0.155 ***	0.042	0.168 ***	0.043
Time to first agreement	0.049 ***	0.003	0.041 ***	0.003	0.052 ***	0.003	0.049 ***	0.003
Ownership (dummy)	0.266 ***	0.029	0.211 ***	0.031	0.234 ***	0.030	0.265 ***	0.029
Bio and others – excluding pharma agreements (dummy)							−0.011 ***	0.029
Pharma and others – excluding bio agreements (dummy)								
All (dummy)								
Neither bio nor pharma agreements								
AIC	5676		5262		5506		5678	
Pseudo R squared	0.280		0.345		0.307		0.280	

Significant codes: *$p<0.1$; **$p<0.05$; ***$p<0.001$

Model 5		Model 6		Model 7		Model 8	
Coeff.	Std. err	Coeff.	Std. err	Coeff.	Std. err	Coeff.	Std. err
1.509 ***	0.111	1.631 ***	0.112	1.432 ***	0.110	0.871 ***	0.126
0.040 ***	0.004	0.022 ***	0.004	0.033 ***	0.004		
						0.035 ***	0.009
						0.194 ***	0.012
						−0.057 ***	0.012
						−0.069 ***	0.014
						0.130 ***	0.016
						−0.003 ***	0.011
						0.275 **	0.021
0.267 ***	0.021	0.223 ***	0.021	0.241 ***	0.021	0.223 ***	0.021
0.146 ***	0.043	0.118 ***	0.043	0.236 ***	0.043	0.299 ***	0.047
0.049 ***	0.003	0.052 ***	0.003	0.048 ***	0.003	0.045 ***	0.003
0.275 ***	0.029	0.233 ***	0.030	0.244 ***	0.029	0.188 ***	0.031
						0.319 ***	0.062
−0.237 ***	0.046					0.340 ***	0.057
		0.398 ***	0.033			0.480 ***	0.058
				−0.291 ***	0.037	−0.324 ***	0.037
5650		5535		5615		5105	
0.284		0.302		0.290		0.370	

Table 4.4 Descriptive statistics and Pearson's correlation coefficients (EU biotech firms)

Variable	sample	mean	S.D.	min	max	1	2	3	4	5	6
1 Patents	237	67.316	95.530	1	462	1.000					
2 Products (3+4)	237	7.281	9.053	1	61	0.311	1.000				
3 Pipeline products	237	4.333	3.602	0	13	0.269	0.611	1.000			
4 Products on the market	237	2.947	7.422	0	50	0.248	0.923	0.260	1.000		
5 Agreements	237	5.965	6.245	1	27	0.136	0.066	0.228	−0.030	1.000	
6 Bio-bio agreements	237	2.982	3.926	0	23	0.340	0.197	0.410	0.042	0.678	1.000
7 Bio-pharma agreements	237	1.053	1.736	0	8	0.150	−0.037	0.106	−0.097	0.423	0.296
8 Bio-PRO agreements	237	1.316	3.129	0	19	−0.199	−0.118	−0.052	−0.118	0.584	−0.036
9 Bio-other sectors agreements	237	0.614	2.102	0	14	−0.060	0.035	−0.096	0.089	0.486	−0.044
10 Local agreements	237	1.526	2.508	0	10	0.018	−0.044	0.024	−0.066	0.620	0.044
11 National agreements	237	2.158	3.458	0	17	0.109	0.019	0.194	−0.071	0.783	0.745
12 International agreements	237	2.281	2.590	0	11	0.163	0.178	0.269	0.086	0.765	0.598
13 Size	237	344.474	948.811	1	5300	0.284	0.743	0.229	0.795	−0.019	0.065
14 Age	237	14.667	9.773	5	40	0.184	0.558	0.247	0.560	−0.120	−0.094
15 History	237	1996	6.489	1980	2005	−0.196	−0.263	−0.167	−0.240	0.135	0.137
16 Time to first agreement	237	6.053	6.365	0	25	0.191	0.284	0.171	0.264	−0.288	−0.151
17 Ownership	237	0.228	0.423	0	1	0.116	0.272	0.301	0.186	0.057	0.153
18 Bio and others – excluding pharma agreements	237	0.491	0.504	0	1	0.023	−0.042	−0.052	−0.026	−0.397	−0.077
19 Pharma and others – excluding bio agreements	237	0.070	0.258	0	1	−0.020	−0.146	−0.141	−0.110	−0.132	−0.211
20 All (dummy)	237	0.351	0.481	0	1	0.098	0.186	0.251	0.105	0.396	0.334
21 Neither bio nor pharma agreements (dummy)	237	0.088	0.285	0	1	−0.188	−0.106	−0.203	−0.032	0.152	−0.238

7	8	9	10	11	12	13	14	15	16	17	18	19	20	21
1.000														
−0.066	1.000													
−0.024	0.366	1.000												
0.211	0.723	0.510	1.000											
0.287	0.218	0.375	0.157	1.000										
0.434	0.416	0.178	0.318	0.402	1.000									
−0.087	−0.105	0.051	−0.054	−0.043	0.065	1.000								
−0.046	−0.071	−0.037	−0.036	−0.170	−0.028	0.661	1.000							
0.042	0.018	0.083	0.009	0.196	0.055	−0.397	−0.889	1.000						
−0.134	−0.201	−0.164	−0.163	−0.288	−0.153	0.460	0.820	−0.857	1.000					
0.056	−0.096	−0.020	−0.098	0.097	0.103	0.107	0.269	−0.252	0.267	1.000				
−0.601	−0.236	−0.188	−0.279	−0.271	−0.326	0.076	−0.006	−0.037	0.153	−0.116	1.000			
0.311	−0.117	−0.081	−0.169	−0.113	−0.003	−0.083	−0.040	0.010	−0.046	0.014	−0.270	1.000		
0.576	0.044	0.013	0.199	0.331	0.321	0.029	0.078	−0.009	−0.088	0.126	−0.722	−0.202	1.000	
−0.190	0.448	0.385	0.309	0.022	0.039	−0.109	−0.085	0.071	−0.081	−0.021	−0.305	−0.085	−0.228	1.00(

$$E\left(PAT_i\Big/X_i\right) = e^{\beta X_i}$$

where PAT_i is the number of patents by firm i and X_i is a vector of regressors containing the independent and control variables described above, so the logarithm of the response variable is linked to a linear function of explanatory variables. In other words, the Poisson regression model expresses the log outcome rate as a linear function of a set of predictors (Christensen, 1997). To obtain consistent and robust standard errors that are corrected for over-dispersion, we employed a general linear model (GLM) estimation technique using R 2.12.1 (Gourieroux *et al.*, 1984).

Variables

Dependent variables

We used three proxies linked to the firms' innovative capability: the number of family patents and the number of products (which are further separated into: (a) products already commercialized and (b) products related to different stages of development and still inserted in the innovation pipeline (Phases I–II and III). We found that the patent indicator, which, as known, represents the most reliable information on the innovative performance of the firm, is also the indicator connected with the higher stability and coherence of the regression model (see Appendix 4.1). The informative source for the patent data was the QPat archive. We included here all patents registered in the period 1995–2010. Information on products in the market and in the pipeline was collected by reading the Bioscan archive and transforming the descriptive notes included for each firm into cardinal numbers. We tried to solve the fundamental problem of potential endogeneity inserted in our data using the patent lag variable (retarding at five years the 'productivity' of the alliance and excluding firms that had only signed alliances before the 1990s, for which we did not collect any patents). Thus, we were able to answer the question: Do alliances enhance performance or are alliances spuriously correlated with performance because superior firms are better able to secure alliances? Our study design and the empirical models elaborated can control for much of the unobserved heterogeneity underlying this criticism (e.g. lagged performance), enabling us to interpret our results with greater confidence (Jacobson, 1990).

Independent variables

Number of agreements: this variable is an indicator of the portfolio strategies pursued by biotech firms. Entering into an agreement enables DBFs to increase their innovation capability and to commercialize property rights stemming from research. The number of agreements was deduced by Bioscan. It is known that this represents the most important information collected by the database, which also registers the date and content of the alliance, and the name and location of the partner involved. Information on the type of agreements was codified into nine categories related to the innovative stage of the value chain (from finance to R&D, up to marketing) and by the type of organization involved. Thus, we categorised the agreements as bio-bio, bio-pharma, bio-PRO and bio-other sectors.

We also distinguished agreements in relation to the localisation of the partner as follows: (1) local agreements: licensing agreements with partners located in the same state; (2) national agreements: licensing agreements with partners located in the same nation (US for American firms); and (3) international agreements: agreements with partners located outside the national borders. The variable 'time to the first agreement' indicates the time lag existing from the foundation of the firm to the date of the first agreement signed by the organization. This variable shows the propensity to build early research alliances. In other words, it configures a particular attitude of the firm to open its boundaries through searching for novel alliances.

We also focused our attention on the alliances' portfolio. We organized biotech firms into four groups: (1) those that articulate their alliance strategy excluding pharma firms (thus, that have in their portfolio only bio-bio alliances or alliances with PRO and other sectors firms); (2) bio and others – excluding pharma agreements (dummy); (3) biotech firms that only make alliances with pharma (and/or with PRO and other sectors), excluding other biotech firms; and (4) pharma and others – excluding bio agreements. Finally, we created another category, one of 'mixed firms', which includes firms that choose to make alliances with both pharma and bio firms (also including PRO or/and firms of other sectors). This latter group is defined here as 'all'. Finally, there is the category of firms that did not sign alliances either with bio or with pharma, but have only agreements with PRO and with firms belonging to other sectors.

Control variables

We incorporated control variables that may impact on the innovative firms' performance in entering agreements. We controlled for time to first agreement, firm ownership, age (history) and firm size (size is proxied by the number of employees). This information refers to the latest available data published on the firm's website or to the data reported in the Bioscan archive.

Estimation model

We ran a Poisson analysis on the data collected, dividing our firms into two samples corresponding to the US and European firms. The hypothesis that we tested is that there is a systematic difference in repeated engagements in strategic alliance between the US and EU samples.

Results

Tables 4.1 (US) and 4.4 (EU) present the summary statistics and correlations among the variables. The average biotechnology firm in the US (EU) has entered into 6.2 (6.0) alliances: 2.8 (3.0) with other biotech firms, 1.5 (1.0) with other pharma firms, 1.1 (1.3) with PRO, and 0.8 (0.6) with firms belonging to other sectors. The average biotech firm in the US (EU) has 380 (344) employees and is about 17 (15) years old. As we can see, no structural differences have emerged until now from the two data sets. But US firms demonstrate, as expected, a very high innovation performance in comparison with EU biotech, both measuring innovation with the indicator of patents (117 vs. 67) or products, 12 vs. 7. However, if we consider the average number of products in the pipeline (4 vs. 4) again, the differences vanish between the two samples, confirming the recent take-off of the European biotech industry (Ernst & Young, 2012). As we expected, bio-bio alliances appear to be the dominant type of agreement in the two samples, corresponding to about half of the total number of agreements signed by the biotech firms in the two continents.

In Figures 4.1 to 4.4 the US and EU data are presented in an aggregated form (the two samples display a very similar trend). We elaborated time-series data showing the type of partnership over time in absolute numbers (Figure 4.1); the relative evolution of agreements over time in the various categories, considering each year (Figure 4.2); the evolution of agreements over time, distinguishing national and international types in absolute numbers (Figure 4.3); and the relative evolution of agreements over time, distinguishing national and international agreements and considering each year as a percentage (Figure 4.4).

The relevance of the bio-bio category has increased since 1994 for the dynamics of partnerships (Figure 4.1). A clear acceleration in the rate of bio-bio agreements

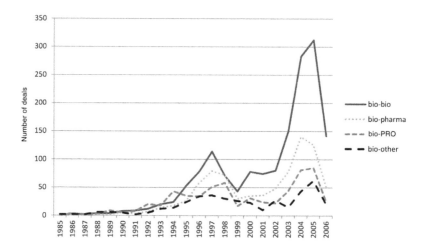

Figure 4.1 DBF partnering strategies over time in the various categories

Source: Authors' elaboration on data from Bioscan.

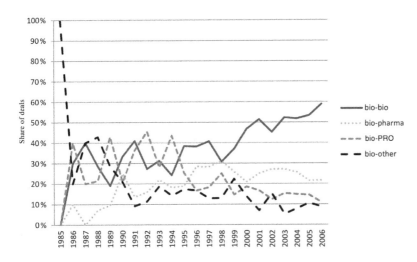

Figure 4.2 Evolution of agreements over time in the various categories in the various years (each year = 100%)

Source: Authors' elaboration on data from Bioscan.

has also occurred in the last period considered (2000–2006), when biotech firms started to explore the new genomic science. Measuring the distribution of the typology of agreements in each year (Figure 4.2), we observe since 1994 the declining role of the weight of the bio-PRO typology. Upstream alliances with universities and other research institutions were clearly more important at an

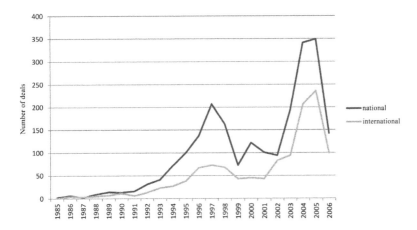

Figure 4.3 Evolution of agreements over time distinguishing national and international types

Source: Authors' elaboration on data from Bioscan.

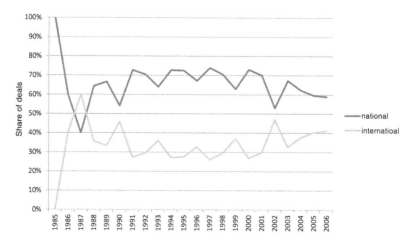

Figure 4.4 Evolution of agreements over time distinguishing national and international types as a percentage in the various years (each year = 100%)

Source: Authors' elaboration on data from Bioscan.

initial stage of knowledge exploration, when basic science was still at the core of leading scientific discoveries, and mainly developed in public institutions and with public financial support. The important presence of international agreements (Figure 4.3) characterizes the entire period examined. The involvement of foreign partners (Figure 4.4) allows us to observe that they do not represent just the final path of a discovering pipeline, when biotech firms had to commercialize their innovations, but rather a persistent modality in which specialized international capabilities are continuously recombined with local or national research.

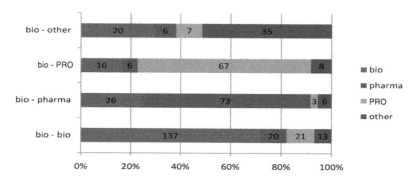

Figure 4.5 Type of partnership after the first agreement – second agreement is reported in the rows – all types of agreements (1–9) are included

Source: Authors' elaboration on data from Bioscan.

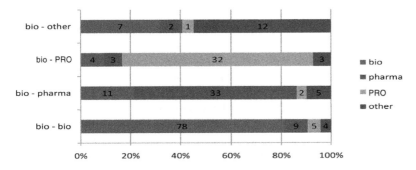

Figure 4.6 Type of partnership after the first agreement – only agreement types 1–4 (research)

Source: Authors' elaboration on data from Bioscan.

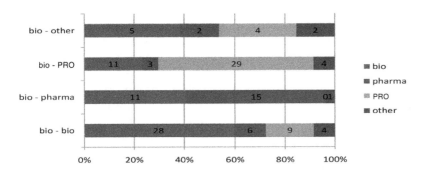

Figure 4.7 Type of partnership after the first agreement – only agreement type 5 (licences)

Source: Authors' elaboration on data from Bioscan.

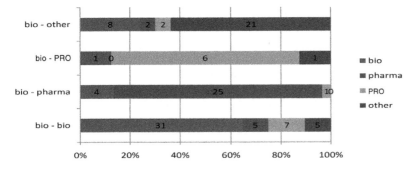

Figure 4.8 Type of partnership after the first agreement – only agreement types 6–9 (marketing and distribution)

Source: Authors' elaboration on data from Bioscan.

An interesting elaboration is regarding the propensity of biotech firms to rep-licate alliances with the same partner with which they have already signed an agreement. In Figures 4.5 to 4.8 we focused our attention on the first two agree-ments signed by the biotech firms (excluding from the analysis those firms with incomplete data and firms with only one agreement), distinguishing all agree-ments: only research agreements (1–4 typology), only licensing (5 typology) and only marketing and distribution (6–9 typology). As shown in the Figures, there is significant path dependence in alliance-building in all the categories considered. We can see, for instance, in Figure 4.5 that out of the 191 firms that have signed a bio-bio agreement, 137 have signed a subsequent bio-bio agreement. The same happened for the other types of alliance.

However, the type of data collected does not allow us to better understand the motivations that have pushed biotech firms to replicate partner selection, be they related to learning effect, better control of risks or expectations of higher rewards potentially realised.

The econometric analysis presented in Tables 4.2 and 4.3 for US and 4.5 for EU firms allows us to discuss the effect of partnering strategies, implemented by biotech firms in the US and the EU, on innovation performance. Detailed analy-ses on small firms (with fewer than 50 employees) are provided only for the US sample, as the number of observations on EU small firms in the Bioscan archive are too limited.

Model 1 represents the base model with all the control variables included. This model highlights some considerations. First, it confirms the importance of firm size in boosting the innovative performance of the biotech firms both for the US (large and small firms) and the EU sample. Strictly related to the size of the company, the type of ownership also shows a positive impact on innovative per-formance. Moreover, listed companies that are larger and have a more structured organization, find it easier to achieve higher levels of innovative performance in terms of patents. The age of the firm shows some controversial results. In the case of US firms, age is positively related to the number of patents of the companies (see Tables 4.2 and 4.3), while for European biotech firms it would seem that the younger the firms, the more productive they are in terms of the breadth of the pat-ent portfolio (Table 4.5). Finally, as expected, a positive association between the number of agreements and innovation activity emerges from our data, both for the US and EU sample, confirming the results of Inkpen (1998). The coefficient in the two cases is both positive and significant (model 1).

Once we distinguish the type of agreement, the patenting activity of the firms emerges as positively and significantly correlated with alliances only for the bio-bio and bio-pharma alliances (model 2). In contrast, alliances with PROs and with firms of other sectors are significant, but they hold a negative sign in the US (or are not significant for the EU firms, as shown in Table 4.5). This supports the view that alliances with PROs are too exploratory in terms of knowledge crea-tion and they do not generate results that can be appropriated through patent-ing. In contrast, and probably for opposite reasons, alliances with firms of other sectors are too applicative and contribute little to the inventive activity of firms.

Thus, both *Hypothesis 1* and *Hypothesis 2* are confirmed. This also confirms some results obtained by Baum *et al.* (2000) and Quintana-Garcia and Benavides-Velasco (2004) in which cooperation with competitors (co-opetition) played a positive role. Also, *Hypothesis 1* that placed under scrutiny the behaviour of very small DBFs (with fewer than 50 employees) was confirmed. US small biotech firms followed the same pattern as larger firms.

Let us now discuss the impact of biotech firms' portfolios on innovation activity (rows 18–20). In the US biotech firms that have developed exclusive alliances with pharmas (model 5) emerged with a significant and negative sign. The coefficient for alliance with a pharma in row 19 is negative and statistically significant ($\beta = -0.280$, $p<0.001$). This suggests that, in exclusive alliances with pharmas, DBFs tend to be expropriated by their innovative capabilities, being unable to properly defend their power over intellectual property rights (IPRs) or suffering from an incapacity to stop knowledge leakages. *Hypothesis 3b* did not find any confirmation. In contrast, in the US sample, biotech firms that have developed exclusive alliances with other biotech firms (model 4) could benefit from a positive impact on their innovative performance. The sign here is significant and positive ($\beta = 0.142$, $p<0.001$). Thus, *Hypothesis 3a* is fully confirmed. Our data also support *Hypothesis 3c*, that establishes the existence of a positive impact on firms that possess a heterogeneous (row 20 for all agreements) alliances' portfolio, including pharma and biotech firms (model 6). The sign here is not only significant and positive but the value of the parameter is particularly high ($\beta = 0.243$, $p<0.001$). These econometric estimations draw attention to the fact that the best strategy for biotech firms is to enter into a large portfolio of multiple types of alliance (all). Heterogeneous alliances are connected to various sources and types of knowledge and they highly support the innovative activity of biotech firms, allowing them, at the same time, to escape from too close and too exclusive relationships with dominant pharma firms.

This does not lead us to deny the issue of complementary assets. Instead, it teaches us how biotech firms can tackle this need: through a heterogeneous portfolio of alliances instead of an exclusive bio-pharma relationship.

In the EU (Table 4.5) our econometric estimations find a less clear-cut result: the old model of the synergic division of labour between biotech and pharma firms seems to be still alive. In Table 4.5 we can observe that firstly, exclusive relationships with pharma firms do not lead to a negative sign, as in the case of the US biotech, but to a positive and relatively significant parameter ($\beta = 0.216$, $p<0.05$); and secondly, that exclusive alliances with biotechs do not emerge as positive, as in the US case ($\beta = 0.093$, $p<0.1$). Thus, in the case of the European biotech firms, Hypothesis 3a was weakly supported and *Hypothesis 3b* was confirmed.

Hypothesis 4 and *Hypothesis 5* look at the performance of alliances from a geographical angle, considering the localisation of the partners (model 3). In the US sample (Table 4.2), local and national (federal) alliances matter ($\beta = 0.006$, $p<0.001$; $\beta = 0.054$, $p<0.001$), while international alliances emerged as not significant. Thus, while *Hypothesis 5* was confirmed, we have to reject *Hypothesis 4*. Model 3 also provides interesting clues for understanding the strategic behaviour

Table 4.5 Determinants of patents' estimates for a Poisson regression model (237 observations, EU firms)

Variables	Model 1		Model 2		Model 3		Model 4	
	Coeff.	*Std. err.*	*Coeff.*	*Std. err.*	*Coeff.*	*Std. err.*	*Coeff.*	*Std. err.*
Intercept	3.455 ***	0.115	3.103 ***	0.128	3.732 ***	0.116	3.320 ***	0.131
Agreements	0.009 ***	0.003					0.012 ***	0.003
Bio–bio agreements			0.028 ***	0.004				
Bio–pharma agreements			0.059 ***	0.010				
Bio–PRO agreements			−0.213 ***	0.015				
Bio–other agreements			0.001	0.018				
Local agreements					−0.045 ***	0.008		
National agreements					−0.029 ***	0.005		
International agreements					0.052 ***	0.007		
Size	0.473 ***	0.013	0.381 ***	0.015	0.508 ***	0.014	0.466 ***	0.014
Age	−0.619 ***	0.063	−0.276 ***	0.071	−0.845 ***	0.068	−0.574 ***	0.066
Time to first agreement	0.008 *	0.004	−0.001	0.004	0.015 ***	0.004	0.005	0.004
Ownership (dummy)	0.239 ***	0.041	0.142 ***	0.043	0.315 ***	0.043	0.244 ***	0.041
Bio and others – excluding pharma agreements (dummy)							0.093 *	0.042
Pharma and others – excluding bio agreements (dummy)								
All (dummy)								
Neither bio nor pharma agreements (dummy)								
AIC	35914		31616		35101		35886	
Pseudo R squared	0.373		0.456		0.389		0.374	

Significant codes: *p<0.1; **p<0.05; ***p<0.001

Model 5			Model 6			Model 7			Model 8		
Coeff.		Std. err.	Coeff.		Std. err.	Coeff.		Std. err.	Coeff.		Std. err.
3.442	***	0.116	3.447	***	0.116	3.388	***	0.116	3.746	***	0.176
0.010	***	0.003	0.010	***	0.003	0.014	***	0.003			
									0.077	***	0.008
									−0.013		0.016
									−0.270	***	0.020
									−0.046	*	0.021
									−0.016	***	0.012
									−0.062	***	0.013
									0.064	***	0.012
0.478	***	0.014	0.473	***	0.013	0.434	***	0.014	0.398	***	0.016
−0.636	***	0.064	−0.614	***	0.064	−0.515	***	0.065	−0.498	***	0.078
0.009	*	0.004	0.007	*	0.004	0.006	*	0.004	0.009	*	0.005
0.238	***	0.042	0.241	***	0.042	0.200	***	0.042	0.256	***	0.044
									0.663	***	0.171
0.216	**	0.068							0.374	***	0.081
			−0.020		0.042				−0.396	***	0.095
						−1.104	***	0.147	−0.354	***	0.072
35840			35932			35147			28070		
0.375			0.373			0.388			0.526		

of small biotech firms (with fewer than 50 employees). In terms of innovative performance, they appear to benefit more from local and international than from national (federal) alliances.

In Europe (Table 4.5), in contrast, only international alliances ($\beta = 0.052$, $p<0.001$) matter and play a positive role in the inventive activity of biotech firms. Thus, only *Hypothesis 5* was confirmed while *Hypothesis 4* was rejected. In the 'mature' and more developed US biotech clusters, 'clustering externalities' exert a certain influence, while in Europe biotech clusters are still in an embryonic stage and firms base their innovative strategies, sourcing knowledge and access to complementary capabilities mainly through partnering with international actors.

Discussion and conclusions

Biotech firms are an important component of high technology industries. Their consolidation can contribute to the growth of the economy. Many studies have attempted to identify the factors that determine their innovative performance, focusing in particular on the issue of strategic alliances (Hagedoorn, 1993, 1996; Greis *et al.*, 1995; Powell *et al.*, 1996; Kogut, 1998; Arora and Gambardella, 2000; Rothaermel and Deeds, 2004, 2006; Pisano, 2006).

Biotech firms appear quite adept at performing internal R&D activity. However, to successfully develop and apply new knowledge for the introduction of novel products (and therapies) to the market, they need to be allying vertically (upstream and downstream) and horizontally (with other biotech partners). Alliances might help biotech firms to find financial support, access complementary assets, activate learning and develop new capabilities. This chapter contributes to the extant literature by examining how alliances, and alliances' portfolios, have supported the innovative performance of biotech firms in the US and Europe. Our analyses are based on the elaboration of a unique and very important source: the Bioscan database, which is considered one of the best archives for the documentation of the development of this industry in the US and Europe. While many studies (for instance Baum *et al.*, 2000; Quintana-Garcia and Benavides-Velasco, 2004; Gay and Dousset, 2005; Stuart *et al.*, 2007) limit themselves to analysing a single country or continent (typically in the US case), we extend our analysis to include both the US and a group of European countries, sampling 530 US and 237 EU firms, including 4,695 alliance agreements (3,282 from the US sample and 1,413 from the EU sample). We cover a long period for the analysis of alliances (1973–2006) and a more limited period (1990–2010) for the analysis of their impact on the innovative performance of firms (using a five-year lag time). Thus, we have built a solid and reliable database to test our hypotheses and to find results that, until now, had not been satisfactorily empirically documented.

In this study we examined *who partners with whom*. The central idea was that partnering strategies evolve as the industry matures. Accordingly, agreements can be conceived both as knowledge creation tools and also as a rent appropriation mechanism, where weak partners struggle to protect their core assets. Alliance formations have a cooperative (knowledge and learning) and a competitive rationale (rent capture). Following this line of inquiry, we prove the hypothesis that pharmaceutical firms are not the exclusive partner for exploiting biotech firms' market opportunities. Although complementary assets owned by pharmaceutical firms are crucial to sustaining the commercialization of products under development, biotech firms may perceive these relationships as risky for their control over property rights. Accordingly, bio-pharma relationships neither comprehensively demonstrate the way in which biotech firms form and further develop alliances, nor indicate how the division of innovative labour works among new and incumbent firms.

Our findings highlight that both biotech and pharma are crucial partners in alliances. But there is an increasing number of bio-bio alliances and this calls for a more fine-grained understanding of the evolution of the biotech industry. The importance of bio-bio alliances has also recently been confirmed by the Bioassociate Industry Blog (2013). If we analyse the top 2013 global deals reported regarding licensing, co-development, collaboration and general partnership, we can calculate a total deal value of about $32 billion, of which about 50% represents 26 deals involving a bio-bio transaction.

We argue here that the most strategic partnering option for biotech firms may be the formation of heterogeneous alliances, where biotech firms lessen the risk of knowledge leakage, disputes and litigation over the control of IPRs.

The industrial dynamics that we have explored among the partnering strategies of biotech firms have also evidenced in Chapter 1 a large reorganization of the industry, with mergers and acquisitions (M&As) and the entry of new organizations (Bowman and Ward, 2011).

Many biotech firms have become major industry players, entering directly into the commercial channels previously managed only by large pharma firms and some have become niche players, operating in specific pharmaceutical products or in platform technologies. But in recent years, as we calculated in Chapter 1, at least 40 biotech firms have been acquired by pharmas. The most significant acquisitions of the last few years in the bio-pharma sector were Pfizer buying Wyeth, Merck buying Schering-Plough, Roche buying Genentech, Sanofi-Aventis buying Genzyme and AstraZeneca buying MedImmune.

It is important now to summarise the key findings as our work reached some important conclusions from three directions. The first is that, in contrast to common wisdom, and considering the impact on the biotech firms' performance, the role of bio-bio alliances appears crucial. Thus, bio-bio alliances matter. The number of bio-bio alliances is associated with firms' innovation performance (also, as would be expected, the number of bio-pharma alliances), but having an exclusive portfolio of alliances with pharmas reduces the probability of patenting activity. The best strategic option signalled by our analyses for biotech firms, in partnering strategy, is building a heterogeneous mix of alliances, including both pharma and biotech firms.

Second, US biotech firms gained more productivity (patents) from local and national alliances than from international alliances, while for the recently founded European firms the influence of international agreements is higher. As regards the US biotech firms, this underlines the role of local agglomeration already discussed by Coombs *et al.* (2006).

Third, within the biotech sector, an evolutionary trend is visible and an important segment of large biotech firms is now emerging that appear to catalyse a growing number of alliances with heterogeneous partners, involving vertical and horizontal alliances (Dunlap-Hinkler *et al.*, 2010) and encompassing more actors and more recombinative processes. It is perhaps too soon to evaluate in depth the consequences that this phenomenon will provoke within the competitive race of DBFs in relation to the dominant power of the large, old incumbents. Perhaps a new path to profits in biotech is emerging: taking the acquisition exit (Behnke and Hültenschmidt, 2007).

Appendix 4.1

Note: Table 4A.1 begins overleaf.

Table 4A.1 Determinants of pipeline products estimates for a Poisson regression model (530 observations, US firms)

Variables	Model 1 Coeff.	Std. err.	Model 2 Coeff.	Std. err.	Model 3 Coeff.	Std. err.	Model 4 Coeff.	Std. err.
Intercept	1.021 ***	0.142	0.937 ***	0.144	1.072 ***	0.143	1.047 ***	0.145
Patents	0.001 ***	0.000	0.001 ***	0.000	0.001 ***	0.000	0.001 ***	0.000
Agreements	0.011 ***	0.003					0.011 ***	0.003
Bio-bio agreements			0.017 ***	0.005				
Bio-pharma agreements			0.015 *	0.009				
Bio-PRO agreements			0.031 ***	0.009				
Bio-other sectors agreements			−0.057 ***	0.017				
Local agreements					0.019 *	0.010		
National agreements					0.031 ***	0.005		
International agreements					−0.029 ***	0.009		
Size	0.087 ***	0.016	0.092 ***	0.016	0.090 ***	0.016	0.088 ***	0.016
Age	−0.140 *	0.060	−0.110 *	0.061	−0.171 **	0.061	−0.145 *	0.060
Time to first agreement	0.004	0.005	0.002	0.005	0.007	0.005	0.004	0.005
Ownership (dummy)	0.461 ***	0.048	0.455 ***	0.048	0.454 ***	0.048	0.457 ***	0.048
Bio and others – excluding pharma agreements (dummy)							−0.039	0.047
Pharma and others – excluding bio agreements (dummy)								
All (dummy)								
Neither bio nor pharma agreements (dummy)								
AIC	3320.6		3306.2		3296.1		3321.9	
Pseudo R squared	0.174		0.183		0.187		0.174	

Significant codes: *p<0.1; **p<0.05; ***p<0.001

Model 5		Model 6		Model 7		Model 8	
Coeff.	Std. err.	Coeff.	Std. err.	Coeff.	Std. err.	Coeff.	Std. err.
1.117 ***	0.144	1.108 ***	0.144	1.063 ***	0.142	1.052 ***	0.163
0.001 ***	0.000	0.001 ***	0.000	0.001 ***	0.000	0.001 ***	0.000
0.010 ***	0.003	0.005 *	0.003	0.010 ***	0.003		
						0.029 **	0.010
						0.045 **	0.014
						−0.019	0.014
						−0.073 ***	0.018
						0.048 **	0.016
						0.058 ***	0.012
						−0.102 ***	0.013
0.091 ***	0.016	0.084 ***	0.016	0.081 ***	0.016	0.086 ***	0.016
−0.170 **	0.061	−0.209 ***	0.061	−0.137 *	0.060	−0.231 ***	0.065
0.004	0.005	0.009 *	0.005	0.005	0.005	0.011 *	0.005
0.466 ***	0.048	0.439 ***	0.048	0.459 ***	0.048	0.442 ***	0.048
						−0.004	0.100
−0.280 ***	0.075					−0.421 ***	0.082
		0.290 ***	0.049			0.153 *	0.087
				−0.1952 **	0.0693	−0.378 *	0.091
32861.6		3288.6		3314.3		3250.7	
0.187		0.189		0.178		0.212	

Table 4A.2 Determinants of pipeline products estimates for a Poisson regression model (237 observations, EU firms)

Variables	Model 1		Model 2		Model 3		Model 4	
	Coeff.	*Std. err.*	*Coeff.*	*Std. err.*	*Coeff.*	*Std. err.*	*Coeff.*	*Std. err.*
Intercept	0.767 *	0.457	0.326	0.480	0.800 *	0.465	0.665	0.504
Patents	0.001	0.001	0.000	0.001	0.000	0.001	0.001	0.001
Agreements	0.022 *	0.011					0.024 *	0.012
Bio–bio agreements			0.047 **	0.016				
Bio–pharma agreements			−0.013	0.041				
Bio–PRO agreements			0.017	0.025				
Bio–other agreements			−0.065	0.048				
Local agreements					0.009	0.029		
National agreements					0.005	0.020		
International agreements					0.054 *	0.027		
Size	0.133 *	0.059	0.106 *	0.063	0.143 *	0.063	0.128 *	0.060
Age	−0.085	0.240	0.186	0.257	−0.116	0.256	−0.053	0.248
Time to first agreement	0.007	0.016	−0.006	0.017	0.007	0.016	0.006	0.017
Ownership (dummy)	0.393 **	0.147	0.326 *	0.151	0.392 *	0.153	0.400 **	0.147
Bio and others – excluding pharma agreements (dummy)							0.075	0.152
Pharma and others – excluding bio agreements (dummy)								
All (dummy)								
Neither bio nor pharma agreements (dummy)								
AIC	323.900		321.850		326.150		325.660	
Pseudo R squared	0.194		0.236		0.203		0.195	

Significant codes: *p<0.1; **p<0.05; ***p<0.001

Model 5		Model 6		Model 7		Model 8	
Coeff.	Std. err.	Coeff.	Std. err.	Coeff.	Std. err.	Coeff.	Std. err.
0.775 *	0.450	0.812 *	0.454	0.675	0.463	0.284	0.628
0.001	0.001	0.001	0.001	0.001	0.001	0.000	0.001
0.020 *	0.011	0.017	0.012	0.029 *	0.012		
						0.085 **	0.033
						−0.025	0.066
						0.027	0.043
						−0.043	0.062
						0.009	0.054
						−0.054	0.042
						0.064 *	0.025
0.127 *	0.059	0.125 *	0.060	0.080	0.065	0.106	0.068
−0.058	0.237	−0.114	0.240	0.043	0.248	0.102	0.259
0.005	0.016	0.011	0.016	0.007	0.016	−0.004	0.017
0.402 **	0.147	0.370 *	0.148	0.362 *	0.148	0.339 *	0.152
						−0.133	0.540
−0.487	0.327					0.416	0.368
		0.203	0.147			0.199	0.418
				−0.683 *	0.354	−0.542 *	0.372
325.720		322.550		325.150		324.650	
0.198		0.234		0.213		0.197	

Notes

1 Support from the ICaTSEM project (Institutional Changes and Trajectories of Socioeconomic Development Models of the EU 7th Framework program) is acknowledged.
2 The use of different database highlights (e.g. Bioscan and Medtrack databases) some structural differences in the configuration of the alliances' typology among firms. Bioscan is more focused on biotech firms; thus it contains a greater number of bio-bio alliances than Medtrack, which has a more generalized data set.

References

Ahuja G., 2000. Collaborative networks, structural holes, and innovation: A longitudinal study. *Administrative Science Quarterly*, 45(3): 425–455.
Anand B., Khanna, T., 2000. Do firms learn to create value? The case of alliances. *Strategic Management Journal*, 21(3): 295–315.
Arora A., Gambardella A., 1990. Complementarity and external linkages: The strategies of the large firms in biotechnology. *The Journal of Industrial Economics*, 38(4): 361–379.
Arthur B., (ed.), 1994. *Increasing Returns and Path Dependence in the Economy*, University of Michigan Press, Ann Arbor, MI.
Audretsch D., Feldman M., 2005. Small-firm strategic research partnerships: The case of biotechnology. *Technology Analysis & Strategic Management*, 15(2): 273–288.
Barney J., Zajac E., 1994. Competitive organizational behavior: Toward an organizationally-based theory of competitive advantage. *Strategic Management Journal*, 15(5): 5–9.
Baum J., Oliver C., 1991. Institutional linkages and organizational mortality. *Administrative Science Quarterly*, 36(2): 187–218.
Baum J., Calabrese T., Silverman B., 2000. Don't go it alone: Alliance network composition and startups' performance in Canadian biotechnology. *Strategic Management Journal*, 21(3): 267–294.
Behnke N., Hültenschmidt N., 2007. *Journal of Commercial Biotechnology*, 78(2): 78–85.
Belussi, F., Sammarra, A., Sedita, S. R., 2010. Learning at the boundaries in an 'Open Regional Innovation System': A focus on firms' innovation strategies in the Emilia Romagna life science industry. *Research Policy*, 39(6): 710–721.
Bioassociate Industry Blog, 2013. *Biotech & Pharma 2013 Licensing & Partnering Activity Review: Diminishing Upfronts, Increasing Platform Licenses Indicate Stronger Risk Aversion among Big Pharma*. Available at: http://bio-associate.blogspot.com.au/2014/01/biotech-pharma-2013-licensing.html (accessed 24 October 2014).
Bioscan, 1985–2006. *The Worldwide Biotech Industry Reporting Service*, American Health Consulting, Atlanta, GA.
Bowman J., Ward J., 2011. *Global Biotechnology Industry*. Available at: www.kelley.indiana.edu (accessed 3 March 2013).
Chesbrough H., 2003. The era of open innovation. *The MIT Sloan Management Review*, 127(3): 34–41.
Christensen R., 1997. *Log-Linear Models and Logistic Regression*, Springer Verlag, New York, NY.
Clarke-Hill C., Li H., Davies B., 2003. The paradox of co-operation and competition in strategic alliances: Towards a multi-paradigm approach. *Management Research News*, 26(1): 1–20.

Coenen L., Moodysson J., Asheim B., 2004. Nodes, networks and proximities: On the knowledge dynamics of the Medicon Valley biotech cluster. *European Planning Studies*, 12(7): 1003–1018.

Coombs J., Mudambi R., Deeds D., 2006. An examination of the investments in U.S. biotechnology firms by foreign and domestic corporate partners. *Journal of Business Venturing*, 21(4): 405–428.

Cooper R. G., 1998. *Product Leadership*, Perseus, Reading, UK.

Das T. K., Teng B. S., 1996. Risk types and inter-firm alliance structures. *Journal of Management Studies*, 33(6): 827–843.

Dunlap-Hinkler D., Kotabe M., Mudambi R., 2010. A story of breakthrough versus incremental innovation: Corporate entrepreneurship in the global pharmaceutical industry. *Strategic Entrepreneurship Journal*, 4: 106–127.

Dyer J. H., Singh H., 1998. The relational view: Cooperative strategy and sources of interorganizational competitive advantage. *Academy of Management Review*, 23(4): 660–679.

Ernst & Young, 2012. *Beyond Borders: Global Biotechnology Report 2012*. Available at: http://www.ey.com/GL/en/Industries/Life-Sciences/Beyond-borders—global-biotech nology-report-2012 (accessed 24 October 2014).

Fontes M., 2005. Distant networking: The knowledge acquisition strategies of 'out-cluster' biotechnology firms. *European Planning Studies*, 13(6): 899–920.

Foster J., 1997. The analytical foundations of evolutionary economics: From biological analogy to economic self-organization. *Structural Change and Economic Dynamics*, 8(4): 427–451.

Gavetti G., Levinthal D. A., 2000. Looking forward and looking backward: Cognitive and experiential search. *Administrative Science Quarterly*, 45(1): 113–137.

Gay B., Dousset B., 2005. Innovation and network structural dynamics: Study of the alliance network of a major sector of the biotechnology industry. *Research Policy*, 34(10): 1457–1475.

George G., Zahra S. A., Wheatley K. K., Khan R., 2001. The effects of alliance portfolio characteristics and absorptive capacity on performance: A study of biotechnology firms. *Journal of High Technology Management Research*, 12(2): 205–226.

Gerde V., Mahto R., 2004. Disruptive technology and interdependence: The relationships of BioMEMS technology and pharmaceutical firms. *Journal of High Technology Management Research*, 15(1): 73–89.

Gourieroux C., Monfort A., Trognon C., 1984. Pseudo-maximum likelihood methods: Application to Poisson models. *Econometrica*, 42(3): 701–720.

Greene W. H., 1997. *Econometric Analysis*, Prentice Hall, Upper Saddle River, NY.

Greis N. P., Dibner M. D., Bean A. S., 1995. External partnering as a response to innovation barriers and global competition in biotechnology. *Research Policy*, 24(4): 609–630.

Hagedoorn J., 1993. Understanding the rationale of strategic technology partnering: Interorganizational modes of cooperation and sectoral differences. *Strategic Management Journal*, 14(5): 371–385.

Hagedoorn J., 1996. Trends and patterns in strategic technology partnering since the early seventies. *Review of Industrial Organization*, 11(5): 601–616.

Hagedoorn, J., Schakenraad J., 1994. The effect of strategic technology alliances on company performance. *Strategic Management Journal*, 15(4): 291–309.

Hagedoorn J., Roijakkers N., 2002. Small entrepreneurial firms and large companies in inter-firm R&D networks – The international biotechnology industry, in Hitt M., Ireland R., Camp S., Sexton D., (eds), *Strategic Entrepreneurship: Creating a New Mindset*, Blackwell, Oxford, UK.

Hamel G., 1991. Competition for competence and interpartner learning within international strategic alliances. *Strategic Management Journal*, 12(S1): 83–103.

Hannan T., Freeman J., 1977. The population ecology of organization. *American Journal of Sociology, 82(5): 929–964.*

Helfat C., 1997. Know-how and asset complementarity and dynamic capability accumulation: The case of R&D. *Strategic Management Journal*, 18(5): 339–360.

Hoang H., Rothaermel F. T., 2005. The effect of general and partner-specific alliance experience on joint R&D project performance. *Academy of Management Journal*, 48(2): 332–345.

Hopkins M., Crane P., Nightingale P., Baden-Fuller C., 2013. Buying big into biotech: Scale, financing, and the industrial dynamics of UK biotech, 1980–2009. *Industrial and Corporate Change*, 22(4): 903–952.

Inkpen A., 1998. Learning, Knowledge Acquisition, and Strategic Alliances. *European Management Journal*, 16(2): 223–229.

Inkpen A., Beamish P. W., 1997. Knowledge, bargaining power, and the instability of international joint ventures. *Academy of Management Review*, 22(1): 177–202.

Jacobson R., 1990. Unobservable effects and business performance. *Marketing Science*, 9(1): 74–85.

Kale P., Singh H., Perlmutter H., 2000. Learning and protection of proprietary assets in strategic alliances: Building relational capital. *Strategic Management Journal*, 21(3): 217–237.

Kale P., Dyer J. H., Singh H., 2002. Alliance capability, stock market response, and long-term alliance success: The role of alliance function. *Strategic Management Journal*, 23(8): 747–767.

Khanna T., Gulati R., Nohria N., 1998. The dynamics of learning alliances: Competition, cooperation, and relative scope. *Strategic Management Journal*, 19: 193–210.

Kleinbaum D. G., Kupper L. L., Muller K. E., 1988. *Applied Regression Analysis and Other Multivariate Methods*, 2nd edition, PWS-Kent, Boston, MA.

Kogut B., 1998. Joint ventures: Theoretical and empirical perspectives. *Strategic Management Journal*, 9(4): 319–332.

Lado A. A., Boyd N. G., Hanlon S. C., 1997. Competition, cooperation, and the search for economic rents: A syncretic model. *Academy of Management Review*, 22(1): 110–141.

Lane P. J., Lubatkin M., 1998. Relative absorptive capacity and interorganizational learning. *Strategic Management Journal*, 19(5): 461–477.

Lavie D., Rosenkopf R., 2006. Balancing exploration and exploitation in alliance formation. *Academy of Management Journal*, 49(4): 797–818.

Lazonick W., Tulum Ö., 2011. US biopharmaceutical finance and the sustainability of the biotech business model. *Research Policy*, 40(9): 1170–1187.

Liebeskind J., Oliver A., Zucker L., Brewer M., 1996. Social networks, learning, and flexibility: Sourcing scientific knowledge in new biotechnology firms. *Organization Science*, 7(4): 783–831.

McCutchen W. W., Swamidass P. M., Teng B., 2004. R&D risk-taking in strategic alliances: New explanations for R&D alliances in the biopharmaceutical industry. *Management International Review*, 44(1): 53–67.

Milgrom P., Roberts J., 1992. *Economics, Organization, and Management*, Prentice Hall, New York, NY.

Mowery D. C., Oxley J. E., Silverman B. S., 1996. Strategic alliances and interfirm knowledge transfer. *Strategic Management Journal*, 17(S2): 77–91.

Mowery D. C., Oxley J. E., Silverman B. S., 1998. Technological overlap and inter-firm cooperation: Implications for the resource-based view of the firm. *Research Policy*, 27(5): 507–523.

Nelson R., Winter S., 1982. *An Evolutionary Theory of Economic Change*, Belknap Press, Cambridge, MA.

Niosi J., 2000. *Explaining Rapid Growth in Canadian Biotechnology Firms*, The Science and Technology Redesign Project, Statistics Canada, Ottawa, Canada. Available at: http://publications.gc.ca/site/eng/96319/publication.html (accessed 20 October 2014).

Niosi J., 2003. Alliances are not enough explaining rapid growth in biotechnology firms. *Research Policy*, 32(5): 737–750.

Norman P., 2002. Protecting knowledge in strategic alliances. Resource and relational characteristics. *Journal of High Technology Management Research*, 13(2):177–202.

Oliver A. L., 2001. Strategic alliances and the learning life-cycle of biotechnology firms. *Organization Studies*, 22(3): 467–489.

Oliver A. L., 2004. On the duality of competition and collaboration: Network-based knowledge relations in the biotechnology industry. *Scandinavian Journal of Management*, 20(1):151–171.

Pisano G. P., 1990. The R&D boundaries of the firm: An empirical analysis. *Administrative Science Quarterly*, 35(1): 153–176.

Pisano G. P., 1991. The governance of innovation: Vertical integration and collaborative arrangements in the biotechnology industry. *Research Policy*, 20(3): 237–249.

Pisano G. P., 2006. *Science Business: The Promise, the Reality, and the Future of Biotech*, Harvard Business School Press, Cambridge, MA.

Powell W., 1999. The social construction of an organizational field: The case of biotechnology. *International Journal of Biotechnology*, 1(1): 42–66.

Powell W., Koput, K., Smith-Doerr, L., 1996. Interorganizational collaboration and the locus of innovation: Networks of learning in biotechnology. *Administrative Science Quarterly*, 41(1): 116–145.

Powell W, Koput K., Bowie J., Smith-Doerr L., 2002. The spatial clustering of science and capital: Accounting for biotech firm–venture capital relationships. *Regional Studies*, 36(3): 291–305.

Quintana-Garcia C., Benavides-Velasco C., 2004. Cooperation, competition, and innovative capability: A panel data of European dedicated biotechnology firms. *Technovation*, 24(12): 927–938.

Rothaermel F. T., 2001. Incumbent's advantage through exploiting complementary assets via interfirm cooperation. *Strategic Management Journal*, 22(6–7): 687–699.

Rothaermel F. T., Deeds D. L., 2004, Exploration and exploitation alliances in biotechnology: A system of new product development. *Strategic Management Journal*, 25(3): 201–221.

Rothaermel F. T., Deeds D. L., 2006. Alliance type, alliance experience and alliance management capability in high-technology ventures. *Journal of Business Venturing*, 21(4): 429–460.

Shenkar O., Li J., 1999. Knowledge search in international cooperative ventures. *Organization Science*, 10(2): 134–143.

Stuart T. E., Hoang H., Hybels R. C., 1999. Interorganizational endorsements and the performance of entrepreneurial ventures. *Administrative Science Quarterly*, 44(2): 315–349.

Stuart T. E., Ozdemir S. Z., Ding W. W., 2007. Vertical alliance networks: The case of university-biotechnology-pharmaceutical alliance chains. *Research Policy*, 36(4): 477–498.

Teece D., 1992. Competition, cooperation and innovation: Organizational arrangements for regimes of rapid changes. *Journal of Economic Behavior and Organization*, 18(1): 1–25.

Teece, D., Rumelt R. P., Dosi G., Winter S., 1994. Understanding corporate coherence: Theory and evidence. *Journal of Economic Behavior and Organization*, 23(1): 1–30.

Ter Wal A., 2014. The dynamics of the inventor network in German biotechnology: Geographic proximity versus triadic closure. *Journal of Economic Geography*, 14(3): 589–620.

Veugelers R., 1997. Internal R&D expenditures and external technology sourcing. *Research Policy*, 26(3): 303–315.

Volberda H. W., Lewin A. Y., 2003. Co-evolutionary dynamics within and between firms: From evolution to co-evolution. *Journal of Management Studies*, 40(8): 2111–2136.

Waxel A., Malmberg A., 2007. What is global and what is local in knowledge-generating interaction? The case of the biotech cluster in Uppsala, Sweden. *European Planning Studies*, 19(2): 137–159.

Zahra S. A., Ireland R. D., Hitt M. A., 2000. International expansion by new venture firms: International diversity, mode of market entry, technological learning and performance. *Academy of Management Journal*, 43(5): 925–950.

Zucker L. G., Darby M. R., Brewer M. B., 1998. Intellectual human capital and the birth of US biotechnology enterprises. *The American Economic Review*, 88(1): 290–306.

5 Management of the collaboration network of Italian biotech firms

Do firms experience a diminishing return from alliances?

Luigi Orsi and Fiorenza Belussi

Introduction

Previous research has shown that strategic alliances allow firms to improve the speed of patenting (Shan *et al.*, 1994), the timing of innovation (George *et al.*, 2002; Kelley and Rice, 2002) and the speed of initial public offering (Stuart *et al.*, 1999), and improve stock values (DeCarolis and Deeds, 1999) and export sales (Leiblein and Reuer, 2004). According to the resource based view (RBV), firms must define their competitive strategies, focusing on their core competencies. The strategic resources are those which are rare, non-imitable and non-substitutable. The central feature of the RBV approach is that the heterogeneity of resources is a necessary, but not sufficient, condition. Often firms cannot afford the acquisition of needed resources, but these may be found through the social relations of the entrepreneur (Alvarez and Barney, 2002) or borrowed through strategic alliances (Ahuja and Katila, 2001). Some researchers have shown that the experience of alliance with the same partner, over time, has a positive effect on the performance of subsequent alliances between these actors (Zollo *et al.*, 2002) and that firms are reluctant to change their solid alliances (Reuer *et al.*, 2002). Biotechnology companies are based on a complex knowledge base, which is not just derived from biology or molecular chemistry but also from bioinformatics and nanotechnology. Biotech companies generally do not yet have products on the market. In order to attract investors they need to signal their value through their patent portfolio. Our research examines the impact of strategic alliances on production pipelines, as for instance in Rothaermel and Deeds (2006), by looking at a sample of 97 pure Italian biotech companies.

The management of strategic alliances

Strategic alliances are voluntary agreements between independent enterprises that allow them to obtain new technology. Allied firms can capture complementary resources to develop and market new products and technologies and, to date, these have become an important tool for the success of high-tech ventures. Alliances have two important advantages: first, they relieve the firm from developing the full range of complementary resources and skills required for innovation, marketing and commercialization; second, they favour the rapid commercialization of innovation.

The main consideration, in relation to licensing, is with regard to the reliability and skills of the licensee – in particular, its capacity to apply the knowledge contained in the patent. The ability to manage a strategic alliance is built by the firms over time and requires coded routines and specific strategies, as well as tacit knowledge. The ability to manage alliances can become a competitive advantage for a company (Schoonhoven *et al.*, 1990; Barney, 1991; Godfrey and Hill, 1995; Powell *et al.*, 1996; Dyer and Singh, 1998; Alvarez and Busenitz, 2001; Alvarez and Barney, 2002; Ireland *et al.*, 2002). The ability to manage multiple alliances simultaneously is related to firms' performance (Rothaermel and Deeds, 2006). The management of alliances is complex due to the uncertainties and difficulties involved in project development; therefore, it is not surprising that some partnerships do not follow firms' expectations (Kogut, 1989; Teece *et al.*, 1997). Alliances are characterized by complexity (denoted by the number of technologies, people and routines) and ambiguity (lack of understanding of logical links between knowledge and the desired result of a commercial product), as well as tacitness (Reed and DeFillippi, 1990).

Alliances with universities and other research institutions, namely those based on research and development (upstream alliances), are characterized by high uncertainty. They involve the transfer of tacit knowledge and require the creation of new scientific knowledge, i.e. new for both partners. However, despite the higher uncertainty, upstream alliances might generate the new ideas that support the creation of new drugs. Alliances for the marketing of the product (downstream alliances) are concentrated on the complementarity of the partners' knowledge. Typically, contract research biotech firms need experienced partners for the commercialization and further development and testing of their products in the pipeline. The alliance portfolio is very important for firms because the choice of partners can avoid knowledge lock-in effects and help the firms to enter quickly into new areas.

In alliances for licensing, biotech firms sell their technology (or products in the pipeline) to other organizations. Instead of profiting from their products, firms gain advantages from the selling of their knowledge. Companies must find a balance in their number of alliances, because a too limited number reduces the new knowledge access, while too many alliances challenge the ability of the firm to manage them. An excessive number of alliances can produce negative effects related to mismanagement problems.

Rothaermel and Deeds (2006), studying a sample of biotech firms, have found that the relationship between the total number of alliances and the development of new products is an inverted U-shaped relationship that exists independently of each type of agreement. Thus, an important hypothesis to verify is if we can extend the results obtained in that case, using an American sample of firms, to other realities, such as that of the Italian biotech sector.

Therefore, our analysis will try to understand: first, if there is a diminishing return from alliances in terms of the new number of products created (in the pipeline and on the market); second, if different types of alliance are associated with different levels of productivity where, in particular, those stipulated for research and development (upstream alliances) are more productive than those regarding the marketing and commercial issues (downstream alliances); third, if for Italian biotech firms it is not just the importance of the number of alliances but also their relative position in the network (structural hole approach according to Burt, 1992).

Methodology

The sample

The biotech industry in Italy is made up of 394 companies. Italy ranks as the third European country in terms of the number of pure biotech companies (248) that concentrate their activity in biotech's core business (Assobiotech, 2012). Only about half of the sample can be defined as exclusively 'red biotech', i.e. working in the area of health therapeutics. We select a sample of 97 companies, for which the international database, Medtrack, provides information about the alliances registered and the development of new products (also in pipelines). Data refer to the Medtrack archive for the period 1995–2006. Our sample covers about 90 per cent of Italian biotech firms having developed at least one alliance and it is, thus, very representative for the Italian case.

Dependent variables

The variable *products in pipelines and on the market* was measured by summing the products in development and products on the market. The use of information on pipelines is advantageous, because some companies do not have any products approved or sold on the market.

Independent variables

Companies also compete in the field of building high capacities for management through a great number of alliances. This variable was measured by counting the total number of alliances that a company is able to manage simultaneously, in particular by evaluating the point, known as the point of diminishing returns, when the addition of a new alliance is detrimental to business performance when measured in terms of new products. Thus, the total number of alliances has been collected. Alliances were distinguished by type: partnership with universities and other research institutions (upstream), partnerships for product development and marketing (downstream) and partnerships with firms for licences.

Upstream alliances might be expected to have a stronger effect on performance because their content is more scientific and requires more skills in transferring the new knowledge into new products. Thus, we hypothesize that the point of diminishing returns will be reached in the long term, after concluding several alliances. In contrast, those stipulated for commercial purposes (downstream alliances) might have regard to the licence of an already existing product or the technology already used in an approved drug. The same is true for licensing. We can suggest here that network dynamics can affect the productivity of firms; thus, some network centrality measures were used as independent variables. They include total degree (the total number of other nodes to which a node is connected), betweenness (nodes which occur on many short paths between other nodes have higher betweenness than those that do not) and closeness measures (nodes which are 'shallow' to the other nodes tend to have short geodesic distances to other nodes within the network and, thus, higher closeness). Closeness is preferred in centrality analysis to the mean shortest-path length, as it gives higher values to more central nodes and it is, therefore, usually positively associated with other measures, such as total degree. Betweenness is different, because it measures the capacity to be a bridge between dissimilar groups in the network. In other words, betweenness is a measure used to describe the importance of the node in the network, according to the shortest path, and closeness is a measure used to describe how close the node is to other nodes.

We proxied a biotechnology firm's alliance experience by its alliance years, which is the cumulative sum of the alliance duration for each of the firm's alliances (Rothaermel and Deeds, 2006). We included other indicators: considering the level of innovativeness (using the cumulative number of family patents), the typology of alliance (considering if the biotech firm was the originator actor – source – or the partner), if the alliance was on product, on technology or miscellaneous and if the company was a target (or a source) of a merger and acquisition (M&A). In addition, we also considered the ownership of the company (i.e. whether it is a public company, a subsidiary or a spin-off from university). We also scrutinized the issue of internationalization, measured by the number of international agreements. The indicator 'technological diversity' measures the technological diversity of the partners of the alliance by looking at the product dimension and considering the 12 classes of products used by Medtrack (it was normalized from 0 and 1).

Lastly, we took into account the localization of the company. To simplify the interpretation of the results, variables have been standardized and the dependent variable – number of new products – takes non-negative integers, including zero.

To test the hypotheses we used the Poisson regression model. Control variables considered were: the age of the firm, year of foundation and size of the enterprise (using as a variable the number of employees because start-ups especially have not yet acquired a positive income during their first years).

$$E(NPD_i/X_i) = e^{\beta X_x}$$

Here NPD_i corresponds to the number of new products of each company and X_i is the vector of regressors, which include the independent and control variables.

Results

Tables 5.1 and 5.2 show the averages, standard deviations and correlations. As can be seen from the results shown in Table 5.1, the biotechnology companies part of our sample have, on average, a foundation year in 1994, have developed on average three products, have registered six international patents and have a number of employees equal to 78. Of these companies 3 per cent are public (97 per cent are private), 21 per cent are represented by subsidiaries (79 per cent

Table 5.1 Descriptives

Variables	Mean	S.D.	Min	Max	Sum	Count
New product development	2.856	6.958	0	40	277	97
Year of foundation	1994	16.112	1919	2009		97
Firm size	78.639	182.866	4	1,500	7,628	97
Firm age	17.742	16.112	3	93	1,721	97
Firm innovativeness	6.381	13.393	0	115	619	97
Ownership (public = 1)	0.031	0.174	0	1	3	97
Subsidiary (yes = 1)	0.216	0.414	0	1	21	97
Technological diversity	1.804	1.178	1	7	175	97
University spin off (yes = 1)	0.175	0.382	0	1	17	97
Geographical position (north = 1)	0.557	0.499	0	1	54	97
Total alliances	1.474	3.416	0	19	143	97
Source of alliances	0.680	1.912	0	11	66	97
Partner of alliances	0.794	2.010	0	11	77	97
Alliances on product	0.691	1.822	0	8	67	97
Alliances on technology	0.371	1.034	0	7	36	97
Miscellaneous alliances	0.412	1.560	0	11	40	97
Upstream alliances	0.876	2.736	0	16	85	97
Downstream alliances	0.928	2.088	0	12	90	97
Licensing agreement	0.567	1.554	0	9	55	97
International alliances	1.206	2.776	0	15	117	97
Alliances experience	9.299	23.409	0	121	902	97
M&A target	0.103	0.489	0	3	10	97
M&A source	0	0	0	0	0	97
M&A dummy (yes = 1)	0.062	0.242	0	1	6	97

Source: Authors'elaboration.

Table 5.2 Pearson's correlation matrix

	Variables	1	2	3	4	5	6	7	8	9
1	New product development	1								
2	Year of foundation	0.018	1							
3	Firm size	0.296	−0.076	1						
4	Firm age	−0.018	−1.000	0.076	1					
5	Firm innovativeness	0.635	0.055	0.252	−0.055	1				
6	Ownership (dummy)	0.331	0.045	−0.025	−0.045	0.299	1			
7	Subsidiary (dummy)	0.116	−0.012	0.294	0.012	0.244	−0.094	1		
8	Technological diversity	−0.038	−0.053	0.198	0.053	−0.039	0.030	0.109	1	
9	University spin off (dummy)	−0.030	0.277	−0.136	−0.277	−0.025	0.231	−0.111	0.193	1
10	Geographical position (dummy)	−0.049	0.051	0.026	−0.051	0.060	0.159	0.116	0.152	0.029
11	Total alliances	0.517	0.125	0.149	−0.125	0.535	0.431	0.044	−0.075	0.015
12	Source of alliances	0.511	0.129	0.093	−0.129	0.517	0.625	−0.043	−0.014	0.092
13	Partner of alliances	0.392	0.090	0.165	−0.090	0.418	0.138	0.117	−0.114	−0.061
14	Alliances on product	0.731	0.103	0.288	−0.103	0.645	0.490	0.103	−0.072	0.004
15	Alliances on technology	0.173	0.095	−0.006	−0.095	0.126	0.109	−0.141	0.018	0.018
16	Miscellaneous alliances	0.163	0.091	−0.006	−0.091	0.336	0.298	0.070	−0.092	0.017
17	Upstream alliances	0.482	0.114	0.180	−0.114	0.541	0.336	0.097	−0.121	−0.049
18	Downstream alliances	0.528	0.118	0.132	−0.118	0.569	0.580	0.006	−0.019	0.081
19	Licensing agreement	0.260	0.104	0.045	−0.104	0.356	0.320	0.050	−0.104	0.024
20	International alliances	0.471	0.127	0.154	−0.127	0.504	0.310	0.079	−0.074	−0.015
21	Alliances experience	0.460	0.106	0.117	−0.106	0.503	0.415	0.065	−0.083	0.003
22	M&A target	0.271	0.031	0.143	−0.031	0.259	0.329	0.197	−0.109	−0.098
23	M&A dummy	0.296	0.025	0.177	−0.025	0.224	0.201	0.177	−0.103	−0.118
24	Betweenness centrality	0.341	0.088	0.092	−0.088	0.374	0.189	−0.018	−0.101	−0.052
25	Closeness centrality	0.389	0.035	0.100	−0.035	0.422	0.267	0.036	−0.008	−0.068

Source: Authors'elaboration.

10	11	12	13	14	15	16	17	18	19	20	21	22	23	24	25
1															
0.125	1														
0.156	0.864	1													
0.064	0.878	0.517	1												
0.100	0.825	0.856	0.588	1											
−0.001	0.646	0.487	0.634	0.321	1										
0.157	0.798	0.569	0.815	0.427	0.376	1									
0.112	0.908	0.719	0.859	0.753	0.598	0.713	1								
0.139	0.905	0.873	0.706	0.824	0.427	0.735	0.691	1							
0.139	0.897	0.682	0.875	0.567	0.568	0.925	0.808	0.799	1						
0.097	0.964	0.737	0.937	0.764	0.648	0.789	0.920	0.827	0.902	1					
0.132	0.976	0.803	0.894	0.757	0.565	0.879	0.871	0.899	0.930	0.953	1				
0.061	0.438	0.247	0.509	0.363	−0.056	0.572	0.453	0.466	0.580	0.490	0.522	1			
−0.029	0.493	0.268	0.583	0.422	0.115	0.511	0.546	0.442	0.570	0.585	0.537	0.825	1		
0.067	0.861	0.700	0.798	0.609	0.726	0.693	0.910	0.609	0.770	0.833	0.825	0.189	0.347	1	
0.107	0.637	0.541	0.567	0.562	0.508	0.401	0.496	0.641	0.542	0.634	0.610	0.344	0.388	0.401	1

are independent firms) and 17 per cent of them originated as academic spin-offs. Considering the location, 55 per cent of firms are located geographically in the northern part of Italy. The 97 companies studied (Table 5.1) have organized a total of 143 alliances. On average, each firm has realized about one and a half alliances and nearly all of these were international alliances (1.206). They can be further distinguished into upstream alliances (research and development) with a frequency of 0.876, licensing with a frequency of 0.567 and downstream alliances (new product development and marketing) with a frequency of 0.928. Alliances were more frequent for products (0.691) than for technology (0.371). The average experience was 9 years, with a deviation from 0 to 121 years (calculated as the sum of years of total alliances of a firm). About 10 per cent of the firms involved in an alliance have been the target of an M&A.

In Table 5.2 we find some high correlations between variables, so we control for the possibility of multi-collinearity risk. We explicitly assessed potential multi-collinearity in all models and found that the variance inflation factors (VIFs) were well below the suggested cut-off point of ten (Kleinbaum *et al.*, 1988).

Tables 5.3 and 5.4 contain the results of the regression to test the hypotheses that we have formulated. Model 1 is the basic model, containing only the control of the dependent variables, while the other models are an improvement on the former. Firms' productivity, in terms of number of products already in the market or in the pipelines, was associated with size, patenting activity (firm innovativeness) and ownership (being a public company), but not with age (the variable is not significant) or with the fact of being localized in the north of Italy (the variable is significant, but with a negative sign). Model 2 evaluates the impact of the experience in profiting from collaborations. Experience in alliances, measured by the number of years, appears to influence positively the productive performance of firms. The impact of the total number of alliances is considered in model 3. As we can see from Table 5.3 the result obtained is particularly significant: the coefficient is high, positive and the p value is <0.001. Model 4 considers the position of the firms (being the firm originating, not the alliance). It is significant in both cases. Thus, the positive effect on the productivity of firms is not only realized by the originators of the alliances but by all partners. Model 5 looks at the typology of the alliance, taking into account the objectives of the partnership (i.e. agreements on product, or technology or miscellaneous). As expected, product alliances show a higher association with the number of new products. While the resulting values for the first two cases are positive (collaborations on product or technology) and significant (p <0.001), for the other kind of collaborations – miscellaneous – the outcome is negative. Models 6 to 8 examine the effects of each type of alliance on the productivity of firms. Downstream alliances come out as the more productive type of alliance; however, the difference from the other two typologies is not very large. In any case, the relationship is both significant and positive in all cases (p <0.001). Looking at the squared variable, we can prove that the relationship between the number of alliances of firms and the development of new products is an inverted U-shaped curve and this relationship holds regardless of any type of alliance: for upstream alliances, licensing and downstream alliances.

Model 9 verifies the role of M&A operations that emerge here as a positive determinant of firms' productivity. The results for each individual type of agreement remain robust and significant, even in model 11, which assesses simultaneously all types of alliance.

We determined in Figure 5.1 the point of diminishing returns for each type of alliance weighted on the number of new products developed. Licensing reaches its inflection point faster (after an average of six alliances) than the other types of agreements: downstream (after seven alliances) and upstream (after ten alliances). If we compare our results with other similar research analyses (Rothaermel and Deeds, 2006) based on a different country (US), it emerges that Italian biotech firms are more productive through using upstream alliances, whereas US biotech firms, which represent a more mature niche, benefit more from downstream alliances. This underlines the fact that Italian biotech firms, within alliances, are playing the role of technology sellers, while US biotech firms are the buyers that use the newly acquired (or co-developed) knowledge for new therapeutic drugs.

From model 10 we can also infer that the relative position of the focus firm within the portfolio alliances matters. Highest values of betweenness centrality and closeness centrality are associated with more productive firms. A network analysis was subsequently conducted. Figure 5.2 depicts the core graph on which the more connected firms are mapped.

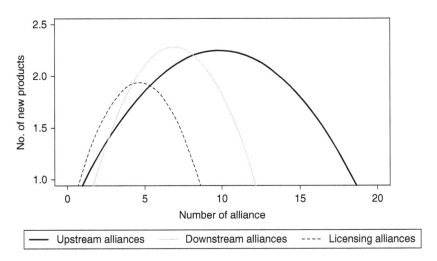

Figure 5.1 Effects of alliance types on the relationship between strategic alliances and new product development

Source: Authors' elaboration.

Table 5.3 Determinants of new product development estimates for a Poisson regression model (97 observations, models 1–6)

Variables	Model 1		Model 2		Model 3		Model 4		Model 5		Model 6	
	Coeff.	Std. err.	Coeff.	Std. err.	Coeff.	Std. err.	Coeff.	Std. err.	Coeff.	Std. err.	Coeff.	Std. err.
(Intercept)	0.534 ***	0.088	0.407 ***	0.095	0.271 **	0.102	0.394 ***	0.096	0.279 **	0.102	0.510 ***	0.087
Firm size	0.323 ***	0.053	0.281 ***	0.052	0.094	0.073	0.238 ***	0.054	0.190 *	0.113	0.224 ***	0.061
Firm age	0.053	0.067	0.121 *	0.068	0.256 ***	0.069	0.149 *	0.067	0.240 ***	0.070	0.114 *	0.067
Firm innovativeness	0.347 ***	0.030	0.290 ***	0.030	0.161 ***	0.033	0.242 ***	0.033	0.180 ***	0.035	0.226 ***	0.035
Ownership (dummy)	0.407 ***	0.039	0.296 ***	0.042	0.081 *	0.047	0.261 ***	0.050	0.222 ***	0.049	0.224 ***	0.053
Subsidiary (dummy)	0.009	0.078	0.007	0.078	−0.065	0.085	0.082	0.081	0.063	0.089	−0.091	0.095
Technological diversity	−0.147	0.101	0.049	0.100	0.087	0.096	0.071	0.099	0.018	0.113	0.020	0.099
University spin off (dummy)	−0.088	0.084	−0.115	0.087	−0.086	0.087	−0.132	0.090	−0.164 *	0.098	−0.050	0.086
Geographical position (dummy)	−0.554 ***	0.086	−0.624 ***	0.088	−0.521 ***	0.091	−0.622 ***	0.088	−0.484 ***	0.089	−0.545 ***	0.085
Alliances experience			0.397 ***	0.048								
Total alliances					2.000 ***	0.198						
(Alliances)^2					−1.441 ***	0.187						
Source of alliances							0.308 ***	0.072				
Partner of alliances							0.223 ***	0.052				
Product alliances									0.769 ***	0.078		
Technology alliances									0.231 ***	0.053		

Miscellaneous alliances				−0.377 *** 0.082	
Upstream alliances					0.900 *** 0.223
(Upstream alliances)^2					−0.594 ** 0.207
Downstream alliances					
(Downstream. alliances)^2					
Licensing agreement					
(Licensing agreement)^2					
International alliances					
M&A target (dummy)					
Betweenness centrality					
Closeness centrality					
Aic	701.82	649.61	570.23	639.37	558.82	671.95
Chi square	259.00	140.20	25.50	78.00	43.90	51.10
Adjusted R square	0.38	0.44	0.52	0.45	0.54	0.42
Highest VIF	0.99	0.96	3.78	0.93	1.23	4.77

Significant codes: *p<0.1; **p<0.05; ***p<0.001

Source: Authors' elaboration.

Table 5.4 Determinants of new product development estimates for a Poisson regression model (97 observations, models 7–11)

Variables	Model 7		Model 8		Model 9		Model 10		Model 11	
	Coeff.	Std. err.	Coeff.	Std. err	Coeff.	Std. err.	Coeff.	Std. Err.	Coeff.	Std. err.
(Intercept)	0.320 **	0.099	0.497 ***	0.089	0.415 ***	0.095	0.320 **	0.101	0.229 *	0.107
Firm size	0.154 *	0.063	0.269 ***	0.055	0.276 ***	0.053	0.299 ***	0.056	0.139 *	0.084
Firm age	0.235 ***	0.070	0.107	0.068	0.127	0.068	0.170 *	0.072	0.221 **	0.074
Firm innovativeness	0.166 ***	0.034	0.316 ***	0.030	0.286 ***	0.031	0.224 ***	0.032	0.129 *	0.059
Ownership (dummy)	0.221 ***	0.042	0.233 ***	0.048	0.302 ***	0.042	0.292 ***	0.041	0.321 ***	0.070
Subsidiary (dummy)	0.137 *	0.081	-0.004	0.080	0.011	0.078	0.070	0.082	0.229 *	0.097
Technological diversity	0.042	0.096	-0.021	0.099	0.043	0.100	-0.027	0.096	-0.146	0.117
University spin off (dummy)	0.024	0.086	-0.092	0.083	-0.101	0.089	0.020	0.086	-0.259 *	0.131
Geographical position (dummy)	-0.546 ***	0.088	-0.521 ***	0.086	-0.606 ***	0.092	-0.580 ***	0.085	-0.446 ***	0.098
Alliances.experience					0.313 *	0.136				
Alliances										
(Alliances)^2										
Source of alliances										
Partner of alliances										

	Model 1	Model 2	Model 3	Model 4	Model 5
Product alliances					
Technology alliances					
Miscellaneous alliances					
Upstream alliances	1.392 *** 0.134				0.669 * 0.331
(Upstream alliances)^2	-0.868 *** 0.116				-2.151 *** 0.528
Downstream alliances					0.982 *** 0.246
(Downstream alliances)^2					-0.790 *** 0.176
Licensing agreement		0.916 *** 0.188			0.439 0.290
(Licensing agreement)^2		-0.718 *** 0.198			-0.712 ** 0.218
International alliances			0.082 0.124		
M&A target (dummy)			0.171 *** 0.045		0.114 * 0.076
Betweenness centrality				0.586 ** 0.044	1.765 *** 0.354
Closeness centrality				0.129 *** 0.084	0.059 * 0.133
Aic	591.53	676.45	690.61	628.24	558.41
Chi square	46.90	129.90	229.70	97.30	23.10
Adjusted R square	0.50	0.41	0.40	0.46	0.55
Highest VIF	1.73	3.78	0.93	0.89	4.58

Significant codes: *p<0.1; **p<0.05; ***p<0.001

Source: Authors' elaboration.

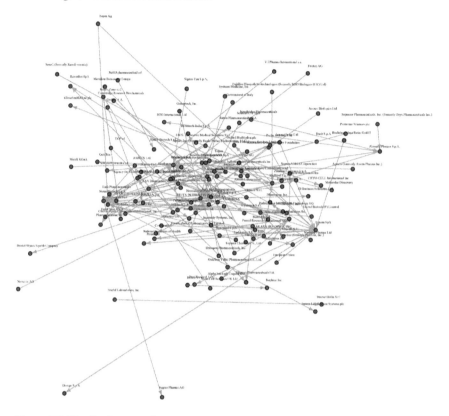

Figure 5.2 The firm's network

Source: Authors' elaboration.

Discussion and conclusions

Scholars have suggested that firms differ systematically in their ability to manage internal resources and external alliances (Hagedoorn, 1993; Shan *et al.*, 1994; Dacin *et al.*, 1997; Chang, 2008). If, in general, alliances play a positive role in increasing the competitiveness of firms (Dutta and Weiss, 1997; Chiesa and Manzini, 1998; Doz and Hamel, 1998; Gulati, 1998; Stuart *et al.*, 1999), firms might experience a diminishing return from alliances (Rothaermel and Deeds, 2006).

Our research has examined the impact of strategic alliances on the production pipelines regarding an Italian sample of biotech firms. The performance of 97 Italian biotech firms was tested. Our sample covers about 90 per cent of Italian biotech firms that have developed at least one alliance and it is very representative of the universe (Sorrentino, 2009). A common problem in research on strategic management is the fact that management skills tend to be unobservable (Godfrey and Hill, 1995).

In this chapter we have focused on observable aspects of management, as in Draulans *et al.* (2003), Rothaermel and Deeds (2006) and Kale and Singh (2009).

We have tested the hypotheses of the existence of an inverted U-shaped curve in the relationship between the number of alliances and the firm's performance (number of products in the market and in the pipeline). This means that there is a kind of 'optimal number' of alliances that biotech firms can manage. In this sense our results confirm those researches conducted on larger US samples. However, in the case of Italy, the main result is that the most important association found was the one with upstream (and not with downstream) alliances. In fact, it appears that the Italian biotech firms are more effective in doing research than they are in marketing technologies. Several others factors came out as significant in determining the productivity of alliances, for example patenting, experience, size of the firm, ownership (being a public company) and network centrality in the existing alliance portfolio. In contrast, and differently from what we expected, being a university spin-off did not increase the probability of higher productivity in alliances.

References

Ahuja G., Katila R., 2001. Technological acquisitions and the innovation performance of acquiring firms: A longitudinal study. *Strategic Management Journal*, 22(3): 197–220.

Alvarez S. A., Busenitz L. W., 2001. The entrepreneurship of resource-based theory. *Journal of Management*, 27(6): 755–775.

Alvarez S. A., Barney J. B., 2002. Resource-based theory and the entrepreneurial firm, in Hitt M. A., Ireland R. D., Camp S. M., Sexton D. L., (eds), *Strategic Entrepreneurship. Creating a New Mindset*, Blackwell, Oxford, UK, pp. 89–105.

Assobiotech, 2012. *Rapporto sulle Biotecnologie in Italia*, BiotechInItaly. Available at: http://www.biotechinitaly.com/Allegati/download_rapporto.pdf (accessed 15 September 2014).

Barney J., 1991. Firm resources and sustained competitive advantage. *Journal of Management*, 17(1): 99–120.

Burt R., 1992. *Structural Holes*, Harvard University Press, Cambridge, MA.

Chang K., 2008. The strategic alliance of the biotechnology firm. *Applied Economics*, 40(23): 3089–3100.

Chiesa V., Manzini R., 1998. Organizing for technological collaborations: A managerial perspective. *R&D Management*, 28(3): 199–212.

Dacin M. T., Hitt M. A., Levitas E., 1997. Selecting partners for successful international alliances: Examination of US and Korean firms. *Journal of World Business*, 32(1): 3–16.

DeCarolis D. M., Deeds D. I., 1999. The impact of stocks and flows of organizational knowledge on firm performance: An empirical investigation of the biotechnology industry. *Strategic Management Journal*, 20(4): 953–968.

Doz Y. L., Hamel G., 1998. *Alliance Advantage. The Art of Creating Value through Partnering*, Harvard Business School Press, Cambridge, MA.

Draulans J., De Man A. P., Volberda H. W., 2003. Building alliance capability: Management techniques for superior alliance performance. *Long Range Planning*, 36(2): 151–166.

Dutta S., Weiss A. M., 1997. The relationship between a firm's level of technological innovativeness and its pattern of partnership agreements. *Management Science*, 43(March): 343–356.

Dyer J. H., Singh H., 1998. The relational view: Cooperative strategy and sources of interorganizational competitive advantage. *Academy of Management Review*, 23(4): 660–679.

George G., Zahra S. A., Wood D. R., 2002. The effects of business-university alliances on innovative output and financial performance: A study of publicly traded biotechnology companies. *Journal of Business Venturing*, 17(6): 577–609.

Godfrey P. C., Hill C. W. L., 1995. The problem of unobservables in strategic management research. *Strategic Management Journal*, 16(7): 519–533.

Gulati R., 1998. Alliances and networks. *Strategic Management Journal*, 19(4): 293–317.

Hagedoorn J., 1993. Understanding the rationale of strategic technology partnering: Interorganizational modes of cooperation and sectoral differences. *Strategic Management Journal*, 14(5): 371–385.

Ireland R. D., Hitt M. A., Vaidyanath D., 2002. Alliance management as a source of competitive advantage. *Journal of Management*, 28(3): 413–446.

Kale P., Singh H., 2009. Managing strategic alliances: What do we know now, and where do we go from here? *Academy of Management Perspective*, 23(3): 45–62.

Kelley D. J., Rice M. P., 2002. Advantage beyond founding. Strategic use of technologies. *Journal of Business Venturing*, 17(1): 41–57.

Kleinbaum D. G., Kupper L. L., Muller K. E., 1988. *Applied Regression Analysis and Other Multivariate Methods*, 2nd edition, PWS-Kent, Boston, MA.

Kogut B., 1989. The stability of joint ventures: Reciprocity and competitive rivalry. *Journal of Industrial Economics*, 38(3): 183–198.

Leiblein M. J., Reuer J. J., 2004. Building a foreign sales base: The roles of capabilities and alliances for entrepreneurial firms. *Journal of Business Venturing*, 19(2): 258–307.

Powell W. W., Koput K. W., Smith-Doerr L., 1996. Interorganizational collaboration and the locus of innovation: Networks of learning in biotechnology. *Administrative Science Quarterly*, 41(1): 116–145.

Reed R., DeFillippi R. J., 1990. Causal ambiguity, barriers to imitation, and sustainable competitive advantage. *Academy of Management Review*, 15(1): 88–102.

Reuer J. J., Zollo M., Singh H., 2002. Post-formation dynamics in strategic alliances. *Strategic Management Journal*, 23(2): 135–141.

Rothaermel F. T., Deeds D. L., 2006. Alliance type, alliance experience and alliance management capability in high-technology ventures. *Journal of Business Venturing*, 21(4): 429–460.

Schoonhoven C. B., Eisenhardt K. M., Lyman K., 1990. Speeding products to markets: Waiting time to first product introduction in new firms. *Administrative Science Quarterly*, 35(1): 177–207.

Shan W., Walker G., Kogut B., 1994. Interfirm cooperation and startup innovation in the biotechnology industry. *Strategic Management Journal*, 15(5): 387–394.

Sorrentino M., 2009. *Le Imprese Biotech Italiane. Strategie e Performance*, edizioni Il Mulino, Bologna, Italy.

Stuart T. E., Hoang H., Hybels R. C., 1999. Interorganizational endorsements and the performance of entrepreneurial ventures. *Administrative Science Quarterly*, 44(2): 315–349.

Teece D. J., Pisano G., Shuen A., 1997. Dynamic capabilities and strategic management. *Strategic Management Journal*, 18(7): 509–533.

Zollo M., Reuer J. J., Singh H., 2002. Interorganizational routines and performance in strategic alliances. *Organization Science*, 13(6): 701–713.

6 Which alliance partners become attractive targets for acquisitions in biotech?

Prior experience versus relational capabilities

Daniela Baglieri, Fiorenza Belussi and Luigi Orsi

Introduction

In the literature, it is well acknowledged that a firm's knowledge base can grow through a series of knowledge-enhancing investments over time or through acquiring external knowledge capabilities (Cohen and Levinthal, 1989; Huber, 1991; Ahuja and Katila, 2001).

However, the rapid changes in technology and the need for continuous innovation in high-technology industries, have often stimulated firms to increase their resources and capabilities through strategic alliances (Pisano, 1989; Parkhe, 1993; Hagedoorn and Duysters, 2002; Capron and Mitchell, 2009) and mergers and acquisitions (M&As) (Uhlenbruck *et al.*, 2006; Makri *et al.*, 2010). M&As occur when independent companies combine their operations into a novel entity, both merging more or less equal companies or obtaining majority ownership in another company (Hagedoorn and Duysters, 2002). For instance, Hitt *et al.* (1996) found that firms that acquire another organization with a high level of technological intensity increase their organizational learning, while Villalonga and McGahan (2005) found that the likelihood of a firm choosing acquisition, among other forms of collaboration, is higher when the technological potential partner possesses crucial resources. High-tech acquisitions are able to capture real value from the deal (Chaudhuri and Tabrizi, 1999).

Over the last few decades in particular, the phenomenon of acquisitions has intensified in the biotech and pharma industry as a means of acquiring external knowledge useful for innovation. As described in Chapter 1, technological integration between RNA technologies (and genomics) with more traditional methods to discover new therapeutic drugs with small molecule research and the shortening of product cycle times were all factors stimulating industry consolidation via M&A. For instance, in 2012 the total value of M&As involving US and European biotech companies increased 9 per cent from the previous year – setting aside 2011's big mergers, i.e. Sanofi/Genzyme and Gilead/Pharmasset (Ernst and Young, 2013).

While post-acquisition performance research has been growing in the last decade (Moeller *et al.*, 2004; De Man and Duysters, 2005; Makri *et al.*, 2010), research on pre-acquisition motivations has been scant, with a few exceptions. By analysing the US computer industry, Yang and Zhiang (2011) found that explorative learning and relative embeddedness in alliance networks both interact to drive subsequent acquisitions of alliance partners. Bruyaka and Durand (2012), focusing on a sample of French biotech alliance portfolios, revealed that possessing valuable resources in terms of international patents increases the probability of firms being acquired, whereas high levels of diversity in terms of partner types decreases this probability, pointing out that possessing diverse resources does not guarantee that synergies will be realized. Another line of research has been devoted to obtaining a deeper understanding of the impact of prior alliance in post-acquisition performance in terms of patenting speed (Al-Laham *et al.*, 2010) and firms' survival (Powell *et al.*, 1996; Baum *et al.*, 2000; Silverman and Baum, 2002; Bruyaka and Durand, 2012).

In our theoretical setting, pre-acquisition motivations are studied. First, we have postulated here that the size of the target alliance portfolio might influence the acquisition, because it can increase the capability to both manage and orchestrate resources from different partners. Second, we have argued that, in biotech settings, acquiring firms can better benefit from target alliance portfolio diversity, because the access to heterogeneous knowledge is expected to enhance their innovative capabilities. Third, we explored the role of prior alliance experience. Kale *et al.* (2000) argue that it allows the acquirer to check the strategic and organizational fit, providing a glimpse of the target's firm-specific resources and opening up the possibility of selecting, evaluating and integrating them (Porrini, 2004; Capron and Mitchell, 2009; Yang and Zhiang, 2011). At the same time, prior alliance experience enables partners to build a mutual trust, which positively affects the post-acquisition integration performance (Lubatkin, 1983; Fowler and Schmidt, 1989; Singh and Zollo, 1998; Haleblian and Finkelstein, 1999; Hayward, 2002).[1] These observations could lead us to hypothesize that those strategic alliances and acquisitions are in practice not substituting mechanisms, rather that acquisitions often follow strategic alliances (Folta and Miller, 2002; Dyer *et al.* 2004; Porrini, 2004; Zollo and Reuer, 2010; Al-Laham *et al.*, 2010; Yang and Zhiang, 2011; Bruyaka and Durand, 2012).

The aim of this chapter is to bridge those analyses that have primarily relied on the study of strategic alliances' performances (Rothaermel and Boeker, 2008) across the field of research on the role of network embeddedness in influencing the innovative performance of firms, following the interesting approach to exploration and exploitation provided by Gilsing *et al.* (2008) and Yang and Zhiang (2011) and applying it to the theoretical setting of the M&A research in the biotech industry. This appears to be an interesting, and not yet developed, path of research. Analysing data regarding 316 US biotech firms, which were involved in alliance strategy, we looked at the acquisition pattern. We discovered that the number of existing alliances (relational capabilities) positively affects the likelihood of being acquired and that being involved in alliances with dissimilar technological partners increases this probability, while prior target alliance experience with the acquirer, differently from what is hypothesized, resulted in not being significant. Our study sheds new light on the alliance and acquisition literature, contributing to clarify some important aspects.

On the one hand, while large pharmas have often acquired prior alliance partners, in the biotech industry as a whole, prior alliance experience does not generally increase the likelihood of being acquired. On the other hand, a key insight is that acquirers not only target a specific firm and its innovative capability (measured by the number of family patents owned, as found in some studies), or, alternatively, measured by what we have called here product innovation experience (related to the number of products in the pipeline and on the market), but also its relational capabilities, measured by the whole alliance's portfolio. Finally, we found that targets with a high level of centrality, and betweenness centrality, had a higher attractiveness.

The chapter is organized as follows: in the next two sections we present the theoretical framework of our study. First, the development of the hypotheses is discussed. In the following three sections we provide a description of the methodology used and a discussion of the results. In the final section we present some limitations of our study, as well as some brief implications for further research.

Theory and hypotheses

The role of prior experience in alliances as a prerequisite of acquisition

Several factors can favour a firm's strategy based on the acquisition of another firm with which a mutual technological agreement was established in the past. Through acquiring an alliance partner, firms can reduce the risk of wrong selection and facilitate knowledge integration (Hennart, 1988). Although the subsequent integration can be riddled with organizational inertia (Barkema and Vermeulen, 1998), acquisition is an ideal mechanism to fully absorb the knowledge produced by an external partner and to solve the issue of alliance instability and litigation on property rights (Inkpen and Beamish, 1997). In fact, information asymmetry and opportunism can inhibit market-mediated resource transactions (Williamson, 1995) and the cost of using the market increases as resources become more firm-specific and complex. This explains why, in the last decade, the biotech industry has been witness to a significant flow of acquisitions, both between pharma and biotech and among the same segments of the biotech firms. A question immediately rises. Are alliances becoming an incomplete mechanism for knowledge exploration and exploitation? Licensing and R&D agreements are becoming so complex that partners are forced to opt for full possession of the knowledge assets through acquisition in order to properly use the new scientific knowledge created in the alliance. However, blind acquisitions are risky and hazardous, because there is always a certain degree of information incompleteness regarding the acquired firm. In this setting, we can hypothesize that the acquiring firm will accumulate during the time that the alliance exists, enough knowledge and information about the partner to the point where they decide whether or not to fully integrate them into the activity of the acquiring firm, using an appropriate post-acquisition integration approach for their specific situation (Schweizer, 2005; Puranam *et al.*, 2006).

In other words, alliances can be used as a screening tactic for acquisitions (e.g. Balakrishnan and Koza, 1993; Nanda and Williamson, 1995). However, quite surprisingly, Schoenberg (2001) found that an organization's ability to transfer knowledge after the acquisition consistently falls short of expectations. If the pre-acquisition collaboration and experience in managing the alliance enables firms to build mutual respect, trust and a similar working culture, the two firms have a higher probability of becoming the object of an M&A only if the acquisition process brings more advantages, in comparison with the previous status of being mere allies (Al-Laham *et al.*, 2010). If the alliance status still remains an ideal position when firms need to recombine their knowledge and capability to further jointly invest in research and product development, or for the execution of specific tasks, acquisition allows a full integration and a better absorption of knowledge.

Why firms prefer acquisition to alliance

Prior research has not distinguished the advantages of acquisition over alliance: acquisitions and strategic alliances have been viewed as the two pillars of growth strategy that allow firms to overcome their lack of knowledge, reducing R&D costs and increasing the number of potential products in the pipeline (Ahuja and Katila, 2001; Ranft and Lord, 2002).

The two strategies differ in many ways: acquisition deals are competitive, based on market prices and are risky; alliances are cooperative, negotiated and not as risky (Dyer *et al.*, 2004). Companies habitually deploy acquisitions to increase scale or cut costs and use partnerships to enter new markets and customer segments and absorb or create new knowledge. Dyer *et al.* (2004) have argued that most companies simply do not compare the two strategies before picking one. Consequently, they take over firms they should have collaborated with and ally with those they should have bought, making a great number of both acquisitions and alliances.

Accordingly, they are largely seen as similar but alternative mechanisms (Wang and Zajac, 2007), although, in some specific cases, acquisitions have been perceived as a more complete and satisfactory mechanism of knowledge exploitation and integration. For instance, firms entering into technology licensing agreements to jointly develop new products might perceive a high risk of knowledge leakage. Thus, they might prefer acquisition to better control the new knowledge jointly created (Inkpen and Beamish, 1997). Therefore, firms use M&A to acquire resources and skills difficult to produce internally or through strategic alliances (Capron *et al.*, 1998; Moeller *et al.*, 2004).

Previous literature has examined firm (and management) motivations underlying acquisition decisions (Hayward and Hambrick, 1997). The most frequently cited are growth and related scale-advantages (Walter and Barney, 1990), financial synergies (Slusky and Caves, 1991), improved bargaining power of managers (Schildt and Laamanen, 2006) and the elimination of overlaps and utilization of complementary assets (Trautwein, 1990). Failures in value creation have also been studied in numerous empirical works (e.g. Slusky and Caves, 1991; Hayward and Hambrick, 1997). Proprietary assets have the advantage of being a better way to replicate firms' internal routines (Nelson and Winter, 1982), to reproduce local 'organizing principles' (Kogut, 1991) and to tap into existing external local networks through their own subsidiary (Jaffe *et al.*, 1993). Thus, acquisitions can be considered an important external source of knowledge in order to foster innovation (Arora and Gambardella, 1990; Hitt *et al.*, 1996). Taken as a whole, acquisition often remains the dominant choice compared to strategic alliances (Lippman and Rumelt, 1982). Al-Laham *et al.* (2010) found that firms often consider acquisitions after a period of 'dating', emphasizing the fact that a complementary perspective is, in high-tech settings, more pertinent.

Blind acquisitions are perceived as risky and hazardous, however, due to information asymmetry and information incompleteness. Firms may, therefore, decide to enter into cooperative agreements to gather information about partners up to the point when they decide, or not, to fully integrate them (Schweizer, 2005; Puranam *et al.*, 2006). As argued by Dyer and Singh (1998), when firms acquire alliance partners, they may increase their absorptive capacity, inducing an effective knowledge transference across interfirm boundaries, which allows them to overcome the issue of imitability of capabilities (Lippman and Rumelt, 1982). Thus, more generally, under which conditions will firms resort to acquisitions? While the characteristics, benefits and needs of the acquiring firms have been deeply investigated, little research has been devoted to study the conditions under which biotech firms become an attractive target. Hence:

Hypothesis 1:   *The likelihood of acquisition is higher for firms with prior alliance experience with the acquiree than for firms having a general alliance experience.*

Knowledge acquisition through alliances

Several contributions have demonstrated that firms with a significant number of alliances learn to create more value as they accumulate experience (Fiol and Lyles, 1985; Simonin, 1997; Child and Yan, 1999; Anand and Khanna, 2000; Rothaermel and Deeds, 2004). This learning positively influences the firm's rate of patenting or the introduction of new products on the market and, consequently, their stock market value (Shan *et al.*, 1994; Deeds and Hill, 1996; Anand and Khanna, 2000; Sampson, 2002; Al-Laham *et al.*, 2010). Strategic alliances play an essential role in transferring knowledge, specifically tacit knowledge, being the potential source of firm-level competitive advantage (Kogut and Zander, 1993, 1996). In the literature, it is assumed that the more a firm is involved in creating a network of alliances, the more it will be able to manage them, because over time it accumulates crucial experience in managing them. In many studies the ability to manage alliances is also measured as the number of alliances or as the years of experience, i.e. the number of years in which a company has been involved in alliances (Rothaermel and Deeds, 2006). Therefore, considering alliance experience as a function of the accumulated number of alliances signed by a biotech firm, we can assume that acquirers will target experienced firms; thus firms are involved in a larger network of alliances. We therefore derive the following hypotheses:

Hypothesis 2a: *The relational capabilities of the target firm (measured as the number of alliances) will have a positive effect on the likelihood of being acquired.*

Hypothesis 2b: *The relational capabilities of the target firm (distinguished in upstream and downstream alliances) will have a positive effect on the likelihood of being acquired.*

However, successful management of interorganizational agreements is difficult to achieve. Negative outcomes or failures might be attributed to a variety of factors: lack of strategic fit in terms of complementary resources (Harrigan, 1985); lack of organizational fit (Levitt and March, 1988) in terms of compatible organizational cultures, decision-making processes and systems (Kale *et al.*, 2000); lack of trust (Arino and de la Torre, 1998); inappropriate choice of governance structure (Hennart, 1988; Zajac and Olsen, 1993); and inability to manage conflict (Doz and Hamel, 1998). Thus, if in order to avoid negative outcomes or failures firms must build long-term experience in managing alliances (Rothaermel and Deeds, 2006), the ability to manage alliances beyond a certain number will decline, due to the effect of 'congestion'. When firms are inserted in a too dense alliance network, they suffer from a higher probability of falling into a competence trap. Fixed, established routines and procedures, based on a set of past experiences (Hoang and Rothaermel, 2010), may lead firms to concentrate only on similar tasks, reducing their learning capabilities (Levinthal and March, 1993; Simonin, 1997). Consequently, we assume that:

Hypothesis 3:   *The likelihood of being acquired is a parabolic, inverted U-shaped function of the relational capabilities of the target firm.*

Product innovation experience and acquisitions

In the context of our study, where acquisitions require substantial financial investment, the existence of innovative capabilities (patents)[2] is no longer sufficient to qualify a biotech firm as an attractive target for an M&A. Strategic technology alliances involving licensing agreements could, for instance, be a good substitution.

The knowledge acquired through patents or R&D alliances must be integrated with a variety of other, different competences before being transformed into a successful new drug (Henderson and Cockburn, 1996; Macher and Boerner, 2006).

Thus, for firms the right signal might be not only the patenting activity but also the real number of products inserted in the final pipeline or the number of products already commercialized (Zirger, 1997). Regarding this claim, it has been demonstrated that the likelihood (and the speed) of obtaining a new Food and Drug Administration (FDA) approval for a given therapeutic area, depends upon the firm's past experience in developing new drugs (Macher and Boerner, 2006). A firm must possess specific know-how in therapeutic domains (diseases) to extract the full potential and create the greatest value from the new discoveries and, for this reason, it becomes an attractive target for an acquisition (Rothaermel, 2001).

These arguments lead to the following research hypothesis:

Hypothesis 4: *The product development experience of the target firm, measured as the number of products (placed in the pipeline and on the market), will have a positive effect on the likelihood of being acquired.*

In addition, we also argue that strong, 'mature' biotech firms already possessing a large number of products on the market and in their pipeline will not be interested in entering into an acquisition process. Thus, it can be hypothesized that 'mature' biotech firms and very dynamic firms having a vast catalogue with an ample range of new products, will discourage potential acquirers from undertaking any negotiations for acquisition. Consequently, we assume that:

Hypothesis 5: *The likelihood of being acquired is a parabolic, inverted U-shaped function of the product development experience, measured as in Hypothesis 2, of the target firm.*

The 'network effect' in acquisitions

In alliances' portfolio networks focal firms benefit from the various collaborations and from their potential access to the whole alliance network of their partners. A large alliance network may be a useful resource in providing private information related to acquisition opportunities (Haunschild, 1993; Gulati, 1995b, 1999; Dyer and Singh, 1998). It can provide fine-grained information to help companies evaluate potential acquisition targets, thereby increasing the likelihood of acquisition (Pablo, 1994; Coff, 2002). In addition, the intense social interaction existing among network partners can decrease the potential moral hazard related to an acquisition (Dierickx and Koza, 1991). Powell *et al.* (1996) argue that central connectedness shapes a firm's reputation, generates visibility and allows access to new knowledge and resources. A core/periphery network structure is characterized by a cohesive subgroup of core actors and a set of peripheral actors that are loosely connected to the core (Borgatti and Everett, 2000; Cattani and Ferriani, 2008). Central players in a network of alliances are attractive as potential targets.

Hypothesis 6:   *The likelihood of being acquired will be positively correlated to the position of the target firm in its alliances' portfolio network (betweenness centrality and closeness centrality).*

Technological diversity and similarity in alliances

The notion of diversity encompasses two basic dimensions. On the one hand, diversity is associated with the rich typology of agents potentially involved in an alliance; on the other hand, it is connected to the different abilities, competencies and types of knowledge that the members of an alliance possess, which can be measured on a technological map. Competencies or technologies, depending on their content, might be placed in proximity or, in contrast, far away. We refer to this aspect in order to individuate the concept of 'technological distance'(Wuyts *et al.*, 2005) that belongs to the innovation and strategic alliances' literature. By using some appropriate indicators (patents, products, R&D activities), differences in the technological knowledge base possessed by firms within an alliance can be measured.

A low technological distance (knowledge similarity) between alliance participants in strategic technology alliances can be considered an efficient mechanism to foster and exploit the potential for learning and innovation (Hagedoorn, 1993; Powell, 1998; Stuart, 1998; Ahuja, 2000; Rowley *et al.*, 2000; Rosenkopf and Almeida, 2003). However, this assumption has also been criticized (Rosenkopf and Nerkar, 2001; Rosenkopf and Almeida, 2003; Ahuja and Katila, 2004).

Nooteboom (1999, 1992), studying the relationship between the technological distance and innovation performance in alliances, suggested the existence of an inverted U-shaped connection. This means that, up to a certain point, increases in technological distance among partners positively affect learning by interaction and, thus, innovation performance. Divergent perspectives initially stimulate and help the interacting parts to extend their knowledge, allowing them to connect and integrate their original expertise. Nonetheless, when technological distance becomes considerable, this might preclude the mutual understanding needed to utilize opportunities for novel combinations of complementary resources. In other words, although a certain mutual understanding is needed for collaboration and, additionally, familiarity produces trust (Gulati, 1995a) that promotes successful collaborations, too much familiarity may remove the innovative steam needed for collaboration (Nooteboom, 2000). What emerges is the existence of an engaging challenge, i.e. finding partners at a distance large enough to offer variety for innovation, but small enough to enable collaboration so as not to prevent mutual understanding. Hence, it is necessary to identify the so-called 'optimal technological distance' (Wuyts *et al.*, 2005; Nooteboom, 2006, 2000). Specifically, it has been proved that optimal technological distance is lower for exploitation than for exploration, because the latter is orientated towards more radical novel combinations and benefits from a higher distance, whereas the former is more focused on complementary capabilities, i.e. a lower distance can better accommodate it (Nooteboom, 2006; Nooteboom *et al.*, 2007).

In international business literature, technological distance is conceived as a problem to be overcome, mainly by accumulating experience in cross-border collaborations (e.g. Barkema *et al.*, 1997), overly stressing the benefits of homogeneous resources and forgetting the positive effects of dealing with heterogeneous knowledge.

Acquisitions can be used as a way to explore, i.e. develop new areas of technological expertise or exploit, i.e. reinforce existing technological capabilities (March, 1991; Phene *et al.*, 2012). These arguments suggest that knowledge similarities are less likely to contribute to radically new inventions (Fleming, 2001). Capron *et al.* (1998) show how, in technology-intensive industries (such as the biotechnology industry), firms use acquisitions to obtain new knowledge to reconfigure their existing businesses. Hence, if planned carefully, acquisitions can help to overcome some myopia of learning and facilitate exploratory searches (Phene *et al.*, 2012). Consequently, we assume that:

Hypothesis 7:   *The likelihood of being acquired will be positively correlated to the technological similarity in alliances' networks.*

Hypothesis 8a: *The technological similarity in alliances' networks will negatively moderate the positive effect of the relational capabilities, as measured in Hypothesis 1, of the target firm on the likelihood of being acquired.*

Hypothesis 8b: *The technological similarity in alliances' networks will negatively moderate the positive effect of the product development experience, as measured in Hypothesis 2, of the target firm on the likelihood of being acquired.*

Empirical analysis

Data and sample

We obtained data from several sources in three different steps. In the first phase, a complete list of all deals in the biopharmaceutical industry without any filter regarding the type, date, value or country of the deals, was obtained from Bioscan. Many reasons contribute to explain the choice of this source. Bioscan provided qualitative information about each firm, such as its new product development, number of employees, year of foundation, whether the firm is public or private, whether the firm is a subsidiary or independent, etc. Moreover, Bioscan listed detailed information about each firm's alliances, such as the focal firm's partners and the month and year when the alliance was entered into (Rothaermel and Deeds, 2006). Furthermore, it supplied specific data, which were fundamental for the construction of our key measures. To create the sample, we identified all biotechnology active firms listed in the 2006 Bioscan industry directory that have realized at least one agreement and focused on human therapeutic and diagnostic applications – biomaterials and tissue regeneration, blood products, gene therapy, stem cell therapy and vaccines, following a similar selection made by Rothaermel and Boeker (2008).

Thus we picked out the ego-network of alliances for each firm in our sample (an ego-network is composed of the links between the focal firm and its direct partners, and the links among direct partners). We then built a network generated by the sum of the ego-networks and from this we calculated the centrality indices for each focal firm in the sample. We constructed the symmetric matrix for the studied period using the package Igraph in R 3.1.1.[3]

Bioscan provided these data for nearly the whole sample. Nonetheless, we proceeded with a double check of their truthfulness and with the gathering of any missing information. Due to their different levels of detail, three distinct data banks were employed: Amadeus, Orbis[4] and Compustat.[5] First, financial and corporate data about European firms were obtained from Amadeus, which actually contains information on around 19 million companies across Europe. Second, Compustat was used to gather information about non-European listed companies, since it is a database of financial, statistical and market information on active and inactive companies throughout the world. Finally, we employed Orbis, which contains information on both listed and unlisted companies world-wide, with an emphasis on private companies, in order to obtain data on unlisted sampled firms. Additionally, missing data were directly obtained from the official websites of companies.

We obtained a random sample of the US DBF firms (including the universe of the larger ones, such as AMGen, Genentech, Genzyme, Cephalon, Allergan, etc.) recorded in Bioscan and a sample of the European ones located in France, Italy, Denmark, Sweden, the UK and Germany. After cleaning the data we obtained 316 DBFs, of which 283 were US and 33 EU firms (employing about 150,000 workers and representing 70–75 per cent of the entire global industry). We realize that the representativeness of European firms is underestimated, as Bioscan is a US database.

Second, to create a measure of firms' innovativeness, we relied on published patent data available up to 2006 from the QPat database. QPat is Questel/Orbit's internet database providing the searchable full text of world published patents from 1974 to the present day for about 80 countries. For the industrial researcher, QPat offers invaluable competitive intelligence and market knowledge (Lambert, 2004). We preferred the indicator of published data in order to avoid the litigation issues potentially contained in the application patent data.

Although previous works, i.e. Ahuja and Katila (2001), Hagedoorn and Duysters (2002), Makri *et al.* (2010) and Diestre and Rajagopalan (2012) utilized data on patents taken from US databases, we decided to employee QPat for two reasons. First, our major purpose was to analyse a firm's ability to patent and protect its knowledge at a worldwide level and QPat provides extensive coverage with 95 patent authorities. Second, QPat is characterized by a great flexibility, which allowed us to identify and export fundamental data for the construction of our key measures. We also collected M&A information from 2006 to 2012 using the Medtrack database (Diestre and Rajagopalan, 2012). Medtrack is an integrated platform that offers insights into biopharmaceutical pipelines, sales, epidemiology, patents, M&As and more, to give a comprehensive view of the biopharmaceutical business landscape.

Medtrack data cross over 2,300 indications and over 100,000 products. Medtrack houses 23,000 company profiles and compiles data through tens of thousands of public and private resources. We double checked the alliance data provided in Bioscan with information from Medtrack and all of the relevant companies' websites. Only in a few cases were we obliged to exclude from our analysis some companies or the agreements for which we did not have sufficient information to classify them.

Model specifications

The unit of our analysis, as explained in the theory section, is the target firm. Descriptive statistics and correlations are presented in Tables 6.1 and 6.2. All variables were mean centred prior to creating the interaction terms to avoid collinearity problems (Aiken and West, 1991).

Table 6.1 Descriptive statistics

Variables	Mean	S.D.	Min	Max	Count
Passive M&A	0.244	0.430	0	1	316
Alliances experience (number of alliances)	7.465	7.347	1	68	316
Betweenness centrality	251.551	967.123	0	10278.474	316
Closeness centrality	0.012	0.004	0	0.014	316
Upstream alliances exp (1–5 categories)	5.785	6.251	0	52	316
Downstream alliances exp (6–9 categories)	1.693	2.328	0	16	316
Product innovation experience	14.611	66.779	0	1007	316
Pipeline products	4.497	5.117	0	50	316
Product on the market	10.114	66.263	0	1000	316
Technological similarity index	0.339	0.435	0	2.969	316
Size	484.810	1702.997	3	20000	316
Age	17.699	8.960	5	40	316
Ownership (public=1)	0.513	0.501	0	1	316
Innovative performance (number of family patents)	151.810	346.778	0	2535	316
Alliance before M&A	0.038	0.191	0	1	316
International alliances	0.282	0.301	0	1	316

Source: Authors' elaboration.

Table 6.2 Correlation matrix

Variables	1	2	3	4	5	6	7	8	9	10	11	12	13	14	15	16
1 Passive M&A	1.000															
2 Alliances experience	0.173	1.000														
3 Betweenness centrality	0.182	0.505	1.000													
4 Closeness centrality	−0.083	0.186	0.117	1.000												
5 Upstream alliances experience	0.161	0.954	0.499	0.218	1.000											
6 Downstream alliances experience	0.092	0.551	0.259	−0.024	0.305	1.000										
7 Product development experience	0.128	0.019	0.016	−0.004	−0.008	0.079	1.000									
8 Pipeline products	0.150	0.214	0.216	0.094	0.223	0.063	0.139	1.000								
9 Product on the market	0.032	0.003	−0.001	−0.011	−0.025	0.075	0.997	0.063	1.000							
10 Similarity index	−0.140	−0.315	−0.239	−0.162	−0.326	−0.191	−0.124	−0.234	−0.006	1.000						
11 Size	0.051	0.312	0.366	0.039	0.273	0.259	0.132	0.267	0.113	0.220	1.000					
12 Age	−0.012	0.110	0.066	0.017	0.034	0.264	0.203	0.134	0.194	0.071	0.312	1.000				
13 Ownership (public=1)	0.126	0.220	0.085	0.079	0.205	0.152	−0.008	0.260	−0.028	0.171	0.153	0.289	1.000			
14 Innovative performance (family patents)	0.064	0.371	0.364	0.056	0.363	0.188	0.048	0.245	0.029	0.334	0.428	0.224	0.155	1.000		
15 Alliance before M&A (Yes=1)	0.015	0.129	0.080	0.102	0.031	0.074	0.053	0.170	0.012	0.129	0.199	0.021	0.003	0.017	1.000	
16 International alliances	−0.007	0.047	−0.053	0.006	0.003	0.149	0.082	−0.106	0.091	−0.048	0.005	0.063	0.009	−0.042	0.008	1.000

Source: Authors' elaboration.

The correlations show that independent variables are weakly correlated with one another. Consequently, the risk of multicollinearity does not appear to be very relevant. However, Table 6.1 shows that some independent variables, and in particular the relational capabilities, are correlated with one another. Consequently, multicollinearity diagnostics were examined. We undertook some additional tests to detect possible multicollinearity. We regressed each independent variable on all the other independent variables and this test did not indicate multicollinearity. In addition, we used a number of other multicollinearity diagnostics. We explicitly assessed potential multicollinearity in all models and found that the variance inflation factors were well below the suggested cut-off point of ten (Kleinbaum *et al.*, 1988).

The dependent variable, passive M&A, is a dichotomous variable taking on discrete non-negative integer values and assumes a value of zero if the company has not been acquired or has merged with another firm and takes the value of one if the firm has been acquired or merged in the period 2006–2011. The estimation procedure assessed the likelihood that a given firm is the target of an M&A alliance in the selected time window (Rothaermel and Boeker, 2008). As a result of the binary nature of the dependent variable, we estimated the likelihood of M&A alliance formation using a logit model (Diestre and Rajagopalan, 2012).

We applied the following specification of a logistic regression model to test our hypotheses:

$$p = \frac{\exp(Z)}{1 + \exp(Z)}$$

where p is the proportion of occurrences, $Z = \beta\_0 + \beta\_1 \, x\_1 + \ldots + \beta\_k \, x\_k$ and $x\_1 \ldots x\_k$ are the explanatory variables. The inverse relation of the equation is:

$$Z = In\left(\frac{P}{1-p}\right)$$

in other words the natural logarithm of the odd ratio, known as the logit. The logit regression model expresses the log outcome rate as a linear function of a set of predictors (Christensen, 1997).

We ran a logistic regression on the data collected, dividing the analysis into six models. The goodness of the models was controlled through the likelihood ratio and the adjusted R-squared index. Table 6.3 shows the results of the analysis.

Although we had multiple years of data, cross-sectional analysis was preferred for several reasons. First, since many of the independent and control variables varied either very little or not at all over time, a panel data analysis with almost identical explanatory variables would add very little information and increase dependence across residuals. Second, the event that we were studying is sufficiently infrequent that observing every potential M&A on an annual basis would dramatically increase the relative number of zeros over ones in the final sample (Diestre and Rajagopalan, 2012).

Variables

Dependent variables

We used *passive M&A* as a proxy of the firms' capability to grow and finance and access novel technologies through an alternative channel. We found that the M&A indicator, which, as is well known represents one of the most reliable pieces of information on the growth performance of the firm, is also the indicator connected with the higher stability and coherence of the regression model. The informative source for the M&A data was the Medtrack archive. Medtrack is the most comprehensive database of private and public biomedical companies. Business developers and financial professionals use Medtrack to obtain information on pipelines, financials, competitive products, deals, mechanisms of action, partnering, M&A data and patent information on biotech companies and products worldwide. We included here all passive M&As registered in the period 2006–2011. We used a lag variable of five years to control for endogeneity with the independent variables.

Independent variables

We analysed the relational capabilities of the target firm in many ways. We examined each of the measures of alliances' management experience (in different regressions), because each measure has its advantages and disadvantages. The first measure is *alliance experience*, which captures the target firm's ability to manage deals with other firms. Prior literature classifies it as a dynamic capability, which contributes to the achievement of competitive advantage (Teece *et al.*, 1997) by increasing firms' capacity to manage several alliances (Rothaermel and Deeds, 2006). Although believing that a proxy based on the cumulative sum of the alliance duration for each of the firm's alliances, such as that developed by Rothaermel and Deeds (2006), is coherent with the theoretical assumption that at a firm level this kind of experience is accumulated through learning-by-doing over time, we adopted the traditional perspective of counting the number of alliances (Shan *et al.*, 1994; Deeds and Hill, 1996; Anand and Khanna, 2000; Kale *et al.*, 2002; Sampson, 2002; Zollo *et al.*, 2002; Rothaermel and Deeds, 2004; Hoang and Rothaermel, 2005). Particularly, we considered the total number of alliances in the period 1973 to 2006. We then squared the variable in order to test for diminishing marginal returns of alliances on the firms' technological performance. We then divided the number of alliances into *upstream alliances' experience* and *downstream alliances' experience*. Information on the types of agreement was codified into nine categories related to the innovative stage of the value chain. All agreements were codified on the basis of their content using the following schema: 1 = funding, 2 = research, 3 = development, 4 = technology transfer, 5 = licensing, 6 = marketing and communication, 7 = distribution, 8 = production and 9 = services and equipment, i.e. from finance/R&D up to marketing. *R&D alliances' experience* was the cumulative number of deals from 1 to 5 in the period 1973 to 2006, while the *distribution alliances' experience* was the number of deals from 6 to 9.

In order to evaluate the relative position of each focal firm in its alliance portfolio, we elaborated some centrality measures. This allowed us to understand how the firm's position in the network influenced the probability of a merger or an acquisition.

The first measure used is *betweenness centrality*. This is a centrality measure of a node within a network. Nodes that occur on many of the shortest paths between other nodes have higher betweenness than those that do not. Betweenness centrality measures the capacity to be a bridge between dissimilar groups in the network.

The second measure used is *closeness centrality*, which is also a centrality measure of a node within a network. Nodes that are 'shallow' to the other nodes (i.e. those that tend to have short geodesic distances to other nodes within the network) have higher closeness. Closeness is preferred in centrality analysis to mean the shortest path, as it gives higher values to more central nodes and, for this reason, is usually positively associated with other measures such as the absolute number of links.

Betweenness and closeness are also the common measures for centrality analysis. Betweenness is a measure that describes the importance of the node in the network, according to the shortest path. Firms with a high betweenness index are companies acting as a bridge between different clusters and are able to handle information efficiently. Closeness measures how close the firm is to other firms in the alliances' network.

The *similarity index* was constructed starting from more than 100 areas of expertise in the biotech industry contained in the Bioscan database. Subsequently we systematized these areas with the help of an expert biotechnologist and, finally, we mapped the similarities of the biotech firm *a_i* and the firm *b_i* with which it has made an alliance. The index is 0 if there are no similar areas of business and grows when similar areas are encountered. The formula is as follows:

$$similarity\ index_{a_i} = \frac{\Sigma(areas_{a_i} \cap areas_{b_i})}{\Sigma(areas_{a_i} \cup areas_{b_i})} = \frac{\Sigma similarities_{a \cap b}}{\Sigma(areas_{a_i} \cup areas_{b_i})}$$

We assumed that the higher this measure, the more the partners were technologically related. When dealing with multiple deals, we computed the technology similarity for each of the agreements and then calculated an average value.

We identified the number of drugs developed in the past as a proxy for *product development experience* (Ahuja, 2000; Nerkar and Roberts, 2004; Macher and Boerner, 2006). Product development experience was measured by the cumulative number of products the firm had on the market and in the pipeline in the period pre-M&A. The acquirer firms could have a preference for target firms with the strongest resource complementarities, i.e. with the greatest development experience.

We measured innovative performance using the patent data available from the QPat database, counting the number of family patents from the year of each firm's foundation up to 2006.

Control variables

We included control variables that may influence the probability of being acquired. We controlled for firm *'ownership'* by a dummy variable (public = 1, private = 0), *'age'* of the company to capture the firm's experience in the industry, measured by its age since foundation and *'firm size'* in 2006 using the number of employees as a proxy. We preferred this measure to more traditional ones, such as market share, because in this industry many biotechnology firms do not have positive revenues (Rothaermel and Deeds, 2006). We used the family patents count up to 2006 as a proxy linked to the firms' innovative capability: the number of family patents as a proxy for innovativeness was preferred over the absolute number of patents that also count the country of application.

We controlled for whether an acquired company had made an alliance before the acquisition with the acquiring firm ('Alliances before M&A', no = 0, yes = 1). This is a proxy to capture the existence of prior alliance experience with the acquirer. Several authors (Schoenberg, 2001; Schweizer, 2005; Puranam *et al.*, 2006; Al-Laham *et al.*, 2010) found that an organization's ability to transfer knowledge after the acquisition consistently falls short of expectations, but if the two companies know each other due to collaboration in a prior alliance, they should be able to determine the appropriate post-acquisition integration approach.

International alliances are determined by the share of international deals as part of the total number of a firm's deals, according to the localization of the partner.

Results

Table 6.1 presents descriptive statistics for the variables included in the analyses. We tested our hypotheses on a cross-sectional data set encompassing the acquisitions, alliance management experience, development experience, patenting activities and technological similarities in the alliances' network of 316 firms from the biopharmaceutical industry engaged in 77 M&As completed during the period 2006–2011 and 2,359 strategic alliances realized by the sample firms during their existence since the year of their foundation up to 2006 (about 25 per cent of the firms included in our sample).

The average biotech firm was about 17 years old at the time of the beginning of the focal period (2006) and had 484 employees. More specifically, the oldest companies are Allergan and Biocon Elan Corp., founded about 40 years ago and the youngest are Alder Biopharmaceuticals and Cara Therapeutics founded about 5 years ago. The minimum number of employees was recorded by Urogene SA and Aquagene and was equal to 3, while the maximum was 20,000 people employed by AMGen. With reference to the ownership of the firm, 51 per cent of our sample is public while the remaining firms are private. In terms of innovative performance of the biotech firms in our sample, measured in 2006, the average number of family patents owned was about 151 and varied from a minimum of zero to a maximum of 2,535 (Allergan).

The average value of the alliances' management capability, measured in terms of number of alliances before the focal period, was 7.46 and varied between 1 and 68. The average number of upstream agreements was 5.78, while the average number of downstream agreements was 1.69. The average international alliances' experience, measured by the share of international deals in the total number of firm's deals according to the localization of the partner, was 0.28 and varied from 0 to 1. The average number of products in the pipeline and on the market was 14.71, varying from 0 to about 1,000. The average value of similarity index in the alliances' network was 0.33 with a maximum value of 2.97. Surprisingly, only 12 biotech target firms in our sample made an alliance before the M&A with the acquiring firm, so this variable does not seem to be as important in the acquisition process.

All the econometric model results are presented in Table 6.3. Model 1 represents the base model and includes the control variables and the innovative performance of firms. It shows that larger firms ($p < 0.05$) with better innovative performance ($p < 0.01$) who were public ($p < 0.05$) were more likely to be acquired through M&As, suggesting that such biotech firms were perceived as an attractive target by other firms. The *age* of the firm and the *alliances before M&A* results are positive, but not statistically significant, while the variable *internationalization* was negative and not statistically significant. Hence Hypothesis 1 was not supported.

In model 2 we added some proxies for relational capabilities (number of agreement, betweenness score and closeness score) and similarity index. Overall, the incremental variance explained by model 2 over model 1 was significant ($\chi^2 = 13.7$).

More specifically, we found that relational capabilities had a positive and significant effect on the likelihood of M&A (alliances' experience $p < 0.01$, betweenness score $p < 0.001$ and closeness score $p < 0.05$), which supports Hypotheses 2a, 2b and 6, while the effect of the similarity index on the likelihood of being acquired is negative and statistically significant ($p < 0.05$). Thus, Hypothesis 7 does not find confirmation.

In addition, model 3 showed that when dividing the *number of alliances* into *upstream alliances' experience* and *downstream alliances' experience* both variables had a positive and significant effect (upstream alliances' experience $p < 0.001$ and *downstream alliances' experience* $p < 0.05$) on the likelihood of M&A formation, which also supports Hypothesis 2b.

In model 4 we tested Hypothesis 3, but all the proxies used for relational capabilities were insignificant (we reported only the squared number of agreements, but we tested also the betweenness centrality squared and the closeness centrality squared with the same results), so Hypothesis 3 was not supported.

Table 6.3 Results of the logit regression model

Variables	Model 1		Model 2		Model 3	
	Coeff.	*Std. err.*	*Coeff.*	*Std. err.*	*Coeff.*	*Std. err.*
Intecept	−1.586 ***	0.319	−1.689 ***	0.378	1.124 *	0.508
Alliances experience			0.006 **	0.002		
Alliances experience^2						
Upstream alliances exp					0.018 ***	0.001
Downstream alliances exp					0.015 *	0.007
Betweenness centrality			0.001 ***	0.000	0.001 **	0.000
Closeness centrality			0.652 *	0.315	0.601 *	0.297
Product development experience						
Product development experience^2						
Alliances exp*similarity						
Development exp*similarity						
Similarity index			−0.493 *	0.227	−0.521 *	0.219
Innovative performance (family patents)	0.003 **	0.001	0.002 *	0.001	0.002 *	0.001
Size	0.011 *	0.006	0.013	0.011	0.008 *	0.003
Age	0.007	0.016	0.005	0.023	0.003	0.035
Ownership (public=1)	0.566 *	0.280	0.601 *	0.295	0.581 *	0.294
Alliance before M&A (Yes=1)	0.091	0.110	0.102	0.118	0.087	0.126
International alliances	−0.021	0.027	−0.019	0.037	0.012	0.025
Adjusted r squared	0.314		0.296		0.301	
−2 log likelihood	242.4		228.7		225.3	
LR (chi squared)			13.7**		17.1***	
Average VIF	2.745		2.811		2.358	
Max VIF	5.606		5.916		4.935	

Significant codes: *p<0.05; **p<0.01; ***p<0.001
Likelihood ratio (LR) values test for the increment in the overall model fit after including additional variables. All models are compared with model 1.

Source: Authors' elaboration.

Model 4		Model 5		Model 6		Model 7	
Coeff.	Std. err.	Coeff.	Std. err.	Coeff.	Std. err.	Coeff.	Std. err.
−1.059 *	0.521	−1.011 *	0.505	−1.209 *	0.523	−1.119 *	0.507
0.034 *	0.016	0.014 *	0.007	0.015 *	0.007	0.018 *	0.008
−0.007	0.684						
0.001 **	0.000						
6.710 *	3.429						
		0.001 **	0.000	0.061 **	0.020	0.047 **	0.016
				0.003 *	0.001		
						−0.005 *	0.002
						−0.012 **	0.003
−0.533 *	0.227	−0.435 *	0.221	−0.463 *	0.236	−0.564 *	0.228
0.002 *	0.001	0.001 **	0.000	0.001 **	0.000	0.002 **	0.000
0.009	0.014	0.002 *	0.001	0.004 *	0.001	0.002 *	0.001
0.008	0.027	0.011	0.017	0.019	0.039	0.012	0.028
0.595 *	0.293	0.592 *	0.306	0.584 *	0.309	0.587 *	0.308
0.098	0.112	0.109	0.118	0.095	0.136	0.105	0.111
0.023	0.049	0.201	0.489	−0.015	0.195	0.023	0.059
0.278		0.293		0.286		0.328	
227.1		223.9		226.3		223.5	
15.3**		18.5***		16.1**		18.9***	
7.915		2.847		8.277		6.287	
15.734		4.512		16.001		9.585	

Hypothesis 4 is tested in model 5. In support of Hypothesis 4, we found that product development experience (measured as the number of products placed in the pipeline and on the market) had a positive and significant effect ($p < 0.01$) on the likelihood of forming an M&A agreement.

In model 6 we added the squared term of product development experience to test the inverted U-shaped hypothesis on the likelihood of completing an M&A. In this case, the squared term is significant ($p < 0.05$) and positive, so Hypothesis 5 is not confirmed. Targets with a growing number of products are increasingly considered attractive firms for M&A.

We tested the final two hypotheses (Hypotheses 8a and 8b) by adding inter- action terms to model 6. In model 7 the likelihood ratio test showed that the inclusion of these interaction terms significantly improved the model ($\chi^2 = 18.9$). Consistent with Hypotheses 8a and 8b, we found that the interaction between rela- tional capabilities and technological similarity, as well as the interaction between product development experience and technological similarity, were both negative and significant ($p < 0.05$ and $= p < 0.01$ respectively).

Discussion and conclusion

The purpose of this study was to examine which factors make a company more attractive for M&As in the biotech industry, considering its alliance portfolio net- work. We selected a sample of 316 US and European firms.

We examined several factors: (a) the prior alliance experience; (b) innovative performance; (c) the alliance portfolio technological distance (index of similar- ity); and (d) the relational capabilities of the focal firms selected where we include the alliances' experience indicator, together with two indicators of centrality (betweenness and closeness). These latter indicators show the brokerage position of the firms – this is the standard way to calculate the 'structural holes' position à la Burt (1992) – within the whole alliance network and the relative centrality of each firm in the network.

Clearly, partially differentiating from standard network theory, we did not con- sider the whole alliance network of the biotech industry, rather only the segment made up of the sum of the partial alliances' networks deriving from our selected 316 firms, which appear to represent a significant portion of the overall biotech industry (150,000 employees in a total industry estimation of 170,000–200,000).[6] We merged two different research fields: the strategic alliances' approach (Rothaermel and Deeds, 2004), where alliances experience is the focus of the analysis, and the research stream interest in studying the impact of technological distance on alliances' performance (Gilsing *et al.*, 2008), as in Yang and Zhiang (2011) who have studied the drivers of acquisitions of alliance partners in the US computer industry.

Thus, we added to the existing literature an original contribution based on the extension of this theoretical framework to another important high-tech sector.

Consistent with prior studies (e.g. Rothaermel and Boeker, 2008; Diestre and Rajagopalan, 2012), our empirical results show that firms' relational capabilities

(Hypothesis 2a), firms' betweenness and closeness centrality in alliance portfolio (Hypothesis 6) and innovative performance and product development experience (Hypothesis 5) significantly increased the likelihood of being acquired, while the firm's technological relatedness appeared to be not so important (Hypotheses 7).

Surprisingly, we found that prior alliance experience (alliances before M&A) is positive, but not statistically significant regarding the likelihood of being acquired, meaning that having previously worked with a target firm in the biotech sector is not an essential element of the acquisition process. This is because other crucial factors emerged as more important, such as the relational capabilities of the target, its central position within the alliance network and the level of technological dissimilarity of the alliance network.

Considering the relational capabilities of the target firms on the likelihood of being acquired, it should be noted that we measured these capabilities in different ways. The most significant factor that emerged in our regression analysis was not only the high absolute number of alliances but also the level of centrality of the target firms and, in particular, the favourable position of being able to play a positional bridging role in the whole network of alliances (betweenness centrality).

This core connectedness shapes the target's reputation (Dierickx and Koza, 1991; Powell *et al.*, 1996) and knowledge flows. In our work we have also shown that acquirers are significantly more interested in those firms that have developed higher relational capabilities in handling R&D (upstream) alliances than marketing/distribution (downstream) capabilities.

Hypothesis 3 was not confirmed. The characteristics of being a central node within the alliances' network and of possessing high relational capacity and experience were related to the likelihood of being acquired in a linear way. Thus, these variables did not show any 'decreasing return', excluding the existence of the presence of an inverted U-shaped form between the relational capabilities and the probability of being acquired.

Consistently with prior literature, we found that product development experience (measured by the number of products in the pipeline and on the market) had a positive and significant effect on the likelihood of M&As, as found also by Rothaermel and Boeker (2008). Our findings are in line with the hypothesis that pharmaceutical companies or large biotech firms might be interested in the value generated from a rich portfolio of new biotech products, since the market saturation of traditional products is high. The likelihood (and the speed) of obtaining FDA approval depends upon a firm's prior experience in developing new drugs for a given therapeutic area (Macher and Boerner, 2006) and the capacity to reach the market with new products is a key issue for the survival of a company in the biopharmaceutical industry. In fact, our Hypothesis 5 was not supported, because acquiring firms appeared to be increasingly interested in biotech firms with higher levels of experience in product development. This means that when a firm has a great number of products in its pipeline, as well a large number of products on the market, it possesses great value for encouraging a potential acquirer to undertake a negotiation.

Finally, we have evaluated the effects of knowledge similarity within the alliances' networks on the likelihood of being acquired. Prior researches have demonstrated that similarities in knowledge facilitate incremental renewal, while dissimilarity (knowledge heterogeneity) would be more likely to support radical and discontinuous transformations (Agarwal and Helfat, 2009). If Diestre and Rajagopalan (2012) found that technological relatedness had a positive and significant effect on the likelihood of alliance formation, a different discourse emerges in the case of acquisition. Acquiring firms are more interested in heterogeneous and diversified alliances' portfolio networks than in the acquisition of focal firms with technologically similar alliances. This is, in fact, what emerges in our estimations (Hypothesis 7). Actually, too much similarity in the alliances' network also moderates the positive effects of the variable 'relational capabilities' (Hypothesis 8a) and of the variable 'product development experience' (Hypothesis 8b) on the likelihood of M&As. As argued by March (1991), organizational *exploration* is conceived as: 'search, variation, risk taking, experimentation, play, flexibility, discovery, and innovation' (March, 1991). In other words, exploration is linked to the pursuit of new knowledge, the adoption of novel technologies and the creation of products with unknown demand. But these activities are uncertain and often produce negative returns. Thus, the benefits of exploration emerge slowly and in the distant future (Greve, 2007). M&As can be used by firms to select distant knowledge targets (Vermeulen and Barkema, 2001) and capabilities that: 'differ markedly from a firm's existing skills' (Capron and Mitchell, 2009: 298). Here we can conjecture about the M&A strategy being concretely applied by the acquiring firms in terms of choosing and favouring a model of knowledge exploration in contrast to a less preferred selected model of knowledge exploitation.

Limitations and future research

This study presents several limitations. First, we used only a simple dummy variable for measuring the acquisitions. Nonetheless, such acquisitions could themselves vary on many dimensions and reflect many different objectives. Second, the study is conducted with reference to a single industry – biotechnology – so our findings may not be generalized to other industries and competitive settings. Regulatory processes in this industry are time and capital intensive, so acquisitions could also be motivated by institutional factors. Third, our data are censored. We considered only acquisitions at one point in time, at the end of the study period. Future research could try to delineate the evolution of a firm's management capability over time in the development of multiple acquisitions. Fourth, the sampling of our firms included 316 biotech firms, of which 283 were US firms and 33 EU (employing about 150,000 workers and representing the 70–75 per cent of the entire global industry), but we could not collect evidence regarding the determinants of the acquisition process in other countries, such as in developing nations. Finally, our study has a descriptive nature to the extent that we explore partners' selection decisions, but not the consequences of post-acquisition.

Notes

1 Post-integration performance, especially of R&D activities, is a critical stage for the success of acquisition (Larsson and Finkelstein, 1999; Schweiger and Lippert, 2005; Paruchuri *et al.*, 2006).
2 Patents are the typical proxy utilized to measure the innovative performance of a company (Stuart and Podolny, 1996; Ahuja, 2000). Patents are also generally highly correlated with the variable 'new products', but this variable in biotech sectors is not very significant: new products (or new technologies) are not immediately commercialized, because therapeutic new drugs need FDA approval and, during the clinical trials, many new products fail to meet the necessary standards of conformity to health security. Thus, the indicator of patents only partially captures the commercial applicability of the novel invention.
3 R 3.1.1 is a free, open source software environment for statistical computing and graphics.
4 Amadeus and Orbis are both developed and published by Bureau Van Dijk, a leading publisher of company information and business intelligence.
5 Compustat has been published by Standard and Poor's since 1962.
6 See Ernst & Young, 2013. The statistical portal, 2013. *Statistics and Facts About the Biotech Industry*. Available at: http://www.statista.com/topics/1634/biotechnology-industry/ (accessed 29 November 2013).

References

Agarwal R., Helfat C. E., 2009. Strategic renewal of organizations. *Organization Science*, 20(2): 281–293.
Ahuja G., 2000. Collaboration networks, structural holes, and innovation: A longitudinal study. *Administrative Science Quarterly*, 45(3): 425–455.
Ahuja G., Katila R., 2001. Technological acquisitions and the innovation performance of acquiring firms: A longitudinal study. *Strategic Management Journal*, 22(3): 197–220.
Ahuja G., Katila, R., 2004. Where do resources come from? The role of idiosyncratic situations. *Strategic Management Journal*, 25(8–9): 887–907.
Aiken L. S., West S. G., 1991. *Multiple regression: Testing and interpreting interactions*, Sage Publications, Inc, New York, NY.
Al-Laham A., Schweizer L., Amburgey T. L., 2010. Dating before marriage? Analyzing the influence of pre-acquisition experience and target familiarity on acquisition success in the 'M&A as R&D' type of acquisition. *Scandinavian Journal of Management*, 26(1): 25–37.
Anand B., Khanna T., 2000. Do firms learn to create value? The case of alliances. *Strategic Management Journal*, 21(3): 295–315.
Arino A., de la Torre J., 1998. Learning from failure: Towards an evolutionary model of collaborative ventures. *Organization Science*, 9(3): 306–325.
Arora A., Gambardella A., 1990. Complementarity and external linkages: The strategies of the large firms in biotechnology. *Journal of Industrial Economics*, 38(4): 361–379.
Balakrishnan S., Koza M. P., 1993. Information asymmetry, adverse selection and joint-ventures: Theory and evidence. *Journal of Economic Behavior & Organization*, 20(1): 99–117.
Barkema H. G., Vermeulen F., 1998. International expansion through start-up or acquisition: A learning perspective. *Academy of Management Journal*, 41(1): 7–26.

Barkema H. G., Shenkar O., Vermeulen F., Bell J. H., 1997. Working abroad, working with others: How firms learn to operate international joint ventures. *Academy of Management Journal*, 40(2): 426–442.

Baum J., Calabrese T., Silverman B., 2000. Don't go it alone: Alliance network composition and startups' performance in Canadian biotechnology. *Strategic Management Journal*, 21(3): 267–294.

Borgatti S. P., Everett M. G., 2000. Models of core/periphery structures. *Social Networks*, 21(4): 375–395.

Bruyaka O., Durand R., 2012. Sell-off or shut-down? Alliance portfolio diversity and two types of high-tech firms' exit. *Strategic Organization*, 10(7): 7–30.

Burt R., 1992. *Structural Holes*, Harvard University Press, Cambridge, MA.

Capron L., Mitchell W., 2009. Selection capability: How capability gaps and internal social frictions affect internal and strategic renewal. *Organization Science* 20(2): 294–312.

Capron L., Dussauge P., Mitchell W., 1998. Resource redeployment following horizontal acquisitions in Europe and North America, 1988–1992. *Strategic Management Journal*, 19(7): 631–661.

Cattani G., Ferriani S., 2008. A core/periphery perspective on individual creative performance: Social networks and cinematic achievements in the Hollywood film industry. *Organization Science*, 19(6): 824–844.

Chaudhuri S., Tabrizi B., 1999. Capturing the real value in high-tech acquisitions. *Harvard Business Review*, 77(5): 123.

Child J., Yan Y., 1999. Investment and control in international joint ventures: The case of China. *Journal of World Business*, 34(1): 3–15.

Christensen C., 1997. *The Innovator's Dilemma: When New Technologies Cause Great Firms to Fail*, Harvard Business School Press, Cambridge, MA.

Coff R. W., 2002. Human capital, shared expertise, and the likelihood of impasse in corporate acquisitions. *Journal of Management*, 28(1): 107–128.

Cohen W., Levinthal D., 1989. Innovation and learning: The two faces of R&D. *Economic Journal*, 99(397): 569–596.

Deeds D. L., Hill C. W., 1996. Strategic alliances and the rate of new product development: An empirical study of entrepreneurial biotechnology firms. *Journal of Business Venturing*, 11(1): 41–55.

De Man A.-P., Duysters G., 2005. Collaboration and innovation: A review of the effects of mergers, acquisitions and alliances on innovation. *Technovation*, 25(12): 1377–1387.

Dierickx I., Koza M., 1991. Information asymmetries: How not to 'buy a lemon' in negotiating mergers and acquisitions. *European Management Journal*, 9(3): 229–234.

Diestre L., Rajagopalan N., 2012. Are all 'sharks' dangerous? New biotechnology ventures and partner selection in R&D alliances. *Strategic Management Journal*, 33(10): 1115–1134.

Doz Y. L., Hamel G., 1998. *Alliance Advantage: The Art of Creating Value through Partnering*, Harvard Business School Press, Cambridge, MA.

Dyer J. H., Singh H., 1998. The relational view: Cooperative strategy and sources of interorganizational competitive advantage. *Academy of Management Review*, 23(4): 660–679.

Dyer J. H., Kale P., Singh H., 2004. When to ally and when to acquire. *Harvard Business Review*, 82(7–8): 109–115.

Ernst & Young, 2013. *Beyond Borders, Biotechnology Industry Report 2013*. Available at: https//ey.com/beyondborders (accessed 29 November 2013).

Fiol C. M., Lyles M. A., 1985. Organizational learning. *Academy of Management Review*, 10(4): 803–813.

Fleming L., 2001. Recombinant uncertainty in technological search. *Management Science*, 47(1): 117–132.

Folta T. B., Miller K. D., 2002. Real options in equity partnerships. *Strategic Management Journal*, 23(1): 77–88.

Fowler K. L., Schmidt D. R., 1989. Determinants of tender offer post-acquisition financial performance. *Strategic Management Journal*, 10(4): 339–350.

Gilsing V., Nooteboom B., Vanhaverbeke W., Duysters G., Van den Oord A., 2008. Network embeddedness and the exploration of novel technologies: Technological distance, betweenness centrality and density. *Research Policy*, 37(10): 1717–1731.

Greve H. R., 2007. Exploration and exploitation in product innovation. *Industrial and Corporate Change*, 16(5): 945–975.

Gulati R., 1995a. Does familiarity breed trust? The implications of repeated ties for contractual choice in alliances. *Academy of Management Journal*, 38(1): 85–112.

Gulati R., 1995b. Social structure and alliance formation patterns: A longitudinal analysis. *Administrative Science Quarterly*, 40(4): 619–652.

Gulati R., 1999. Network location and learning: The influence of network resources and firm capabilities on alliance formation. *Strategic Management Journal*, 20(5): 397–420.

Hagedoorn J., 1993. Understanding the rationale of strategic technology partnering: Interorganizational modes of cooperation and sectoral differences. *Strategic Management Journal*, 14(5): 371–385.

Hagedoorn J., Duysters, G., 2002. External sources of innovative capabilities: The preference for strategic alliances or mergers and acquisitions. *Journal of Management Studies*, 39(2): 167–188.

Haleblian J., Finkelstein S., 1999. The influence of organizational acquisition experience on acquisition performance: A behavioral learning perspective. *Administrative Science Quarterly*, 44(1): 29–56.

Harrigan K. R., 1985. Vertical integration and corporate strategy. *Academy of Management Journal*, 28(2): 397–425.

Haunschild P. R., 1993. Interorganizational imitation: The impact of interlocks on corporate acquisition activity. *Administrative Science Quarterly*, 38(4): 564–592.

Hayward M. L., 2002. When do firms learn from their acquisition experience? Evidence from 1990 to 1995. *Strategic Management Journal*, 23(1): 21–39.

Hayward M. L., Hambrick D. C., 1997. Explaining the premiums paid for large acquisitions: Evidence of CEO hubris. *Administrative Science Quarterly*, 42(1): 103–127.

Henderson R. M., Cockburn, I. M., 1996. Scale, scope, and spillovers: The determinants of research productivity in drug discovery. *The Rand Journal of Economics*, 27(1): 32–59.

Hennart J. F., 1988. A transaction costs theory of equity joint ventures. *Strategic Management Journal*, 9(4): 361–374.

Hitt M. A., Hoskisson R. E., Johnson R. A., Moesel D. D., 1996. The market for corporate control and firm innovation. *Academy of Management Journal*, 39(5): 1084–1119.

Hoang H., Rothaermel F. T., 2005. The effect of general and partner-specific alliance experience on joint R&D project performance. *Academy of Management Journal*, 48(2): 332–345.

Hoang H., Rothaermel F. T., 2010. Leveraging internal and external experience: Exploration, exploitation, and R&D project performance. *Strategic Management Journal*, 31(7): 734–758.

Huber G. P., 1991. Organizational learning: The contributing processes and the literatures. *Organization Science*, 2(1): 88–115.

Inkpen A. C., Beamish P. W., 1997. Knowledge, bargaining power, and the instability of international joint ventures. *Academy of Management Review*, 22(1): 177–202.

Jaffe A. B., Trajtenberg M., Henderson R., 1993. Geographic localization of knowledge spillovers as evidenced by patent citations. *The Quarterly Journal of Economics*, 108(3): 577–598.

Kale P., Singh H., Perlmutter H., 2000. Learning and protection of proprietary assets in strategic alliances: Building relational capital. *Strategic Management Journal*, 21(5): 217–237.

Kale P., Dyer J. H., Singh H., 2002. Alliance capability, stock market response, and long-term alliance success: The role of the alliance function. *Strategic Management Journal*, 23(8): 747–767.

Kleinbaum D. G., Kupper L. L., Muller K. E., 1988. *Applied Regression Analysis and Other Multivariate Methods*, 2nd edition, PWS-Kent, Boston, MA.

Kogut B., 1991. Joint ventures and the option to expand and acquire. *Management Science*, 37(1): 19–33.

Kogut B., Zander U., 1993. Knowledge of the firm and the evolutionary theory of the multinational corporation. *Journal of International Business Studies*, 24(4): 625–645.

Kogut B., Zander U., 1996. What firms do? Coordination, identity, and learning. *Organization Science*, 7(5): 502–518.

Lambert N., 2004. *Internet Patent Information in the 21st Century: A Comparison of Delphion, Micropatent, and QPAT*, International Chemical Information Conference Exhibition, Annecy, France, 17–20 October, pp. 1–2. CD-ROM resource.

Larsson R., Finkelstein S., 1999. Integrating strategic, organizational, and human resource perspectives on mergers and acquisitions: A case survey of synergy realization. *Organization Science*, 10(1): 1–26.

Levinthal D. A., March J. G., 1993. The myopia of learning. *Strategic Management Journal*, 14(S2): 95–112.

Levitt B., March J. G., 1988. Organizational learning. *Annual Review of Sociology*, 14: 319–340.

Lippman S. A., Rumelt R. P., 1982. Uncertain imitability: An analysis of interfirm differences in efficiency under competition. *The Bell Journal of Economics*, 13(2): 418–438.

Lubatkin M., 1983. Mergers and the performance of the acquiring firm. *Academy of Management Review*, 8(2): 218–225.

Macher J. T., Boerner C. S., 2006. Experience and scale and scope economies: Tradeoffs and performance in development. *Strategic Management Journal*, 27(9): 845–865.

Makri M., Hitt M. A., Lane P. J., 2010. Complementary technologies, knowledge relatedness, and invention outcomes in high technology mergers and acquisitions. *Strategic Management Journal*, 31(6): 602–628.

March J., 1991. Exploration and exploitation in organizational learning. *Organization Science*, 2(1): 71–87.

Moeller S. B., Schlingemann F. P., Stulz R. M., 2004. Firm size and the gains from acquisitions. *Journal of Financial Economics*, 73(2): 201–228.

Nanda A., Williamson P. J., 1995. Use joint ventures to ease the pain of restructuring. *Harvard Business Review*, 73(6): 119.

Nelson R. R., Winter S. G., 1982. *An Evolutionary Theory of Economic Change*. Belknap Press, Cambridge, MA.

Nerkar A., Roberts P. W., 2004. Technological and product-market experience and the success of new product introductions in the pharmaceutical industry. *Strategic Management Journal*, 25(8–9): 779–799.

Nooteboom B., 1992. Towards a dynamic theory of transactions. *Journal of Evolutionary Economics*, 2(4): 281–299.

Nooteboom B., 1999. *Inter-Firm Alliances: Analysis and Design*, Routledge, London, UK.

Nooteboom B., 2000. *Learning and Innovation in Organizations and Economies*, Oxford University Press, Oxford, UK.

Nooteboom B., 2006. *Cognitive Distance in and Between Cops and Firms: Where Do Exploitation and Exploration Take Place, and How Are They Connected?* Paper for DIME workshop on Communities of Practice, Durham, 27–28 October. Available at: https://ideas.repec.org/p/tiu/tiucen/0297da3c-db06-43eb-8d11-231fc43b1e58.html (accessed 25 November 2013).

Nooteboom B., Vanhaverbeke W., Duysters G., Gilsing V., Van den Oord A., 2007. Optimal cognitive distance and absorptive capacity. *Research Policy*, 36(7): 1016–1034.

Pablo A., 1994. Determination of acquisition integration level: A decision-making perspective. *Academy of Management Journal*, 37(4): 803–839.

Parkhe A., 1993. Messy research, methodological predispositions, and theory development in international joint ventures. *Academy of Management Review*, 18(2): 227–268.

Paruchuri S., Nerkar A., Hambrick D. C., 2006. Acquisition integration and productivity losses in the technical core: Disruption of inventors in acquired companies. *Organization Science*, 17(5): 545–562.

Phene A., Tallman S., Almeida P., 2012. When do acquisitions facilitate technological exploration and exploitation? *Journal of Management*, 38(3): 753–783.

Pisano G. P., 1989. Using equity participation to support exchange: Evidence from the biotechnology industry. *Journal of Law, Economics, & Organization*, 5(1): 109–126.

Porrini P., 2004. Can a previous alliance between an acquirer and a target affect acquisition performance? *Journal of Management*, 30(4): 545–562.

Powell W. W., 1998. Learning from collaboration: Knowledge and networks in the biotechnology and pharmaceuticals industries. *California Management Review*, 40(3): 228–240.

Powell W. W., Koput K. W., Smith-Doerr L., 1996. Interorganizational collaboration and the locus of innovation: Networks of learning in biotechnology. *Administrative Science Quarterly*, 41(1): 116–145.

Puranam P., Singh H., Zollo M., 2006. Organizing for innovation: Managing the coordination-autonomy dilemma in technology acquisitions. *Academy of Management Journal*, 49(2): 263–280.

Ranft A. L., Lord M. D., 2002. Acquiring new technologies and capabilities: A grounded model of acquisition implementation. *Organization Science*, 13(4): 420–441.

Rosenkopf L., Nerkar A., 2001. Beyond local search: Boundary-spanning, exploration, and impact in the optical disc industry. *Strategic Management Journal*, 22(4): 287–306.

Rosenkopf L., Almeida P., 2003. Overcoming local search through alliances and mobility. *Management Science*, 49(6): 751–766.

Rothaermel F. T., 2001. Complementary assets, strategic alliances, and the incumbent's advantage: An empirical study of industry and firm effects in the biopharmaceutical industry. *Research Policy*, 30(8): 1235–1251.

Rothaermel F. T., Deeds D. L., 2004. Exploration and exploitation alliances in biotechnology: A system of new product development. *Strategic Management Journal*, 25(3): 201–221.

Rothaermel F. T., Deeds D. L., 2006. Alliance type, alliance experience and alliance management capability in high-technology ventures. *Journal of Business Venturing*, 21(4): 429–460.

Rothaermel F. T., Boeker W., 2008. Old technology meets new technology: Complementarities, similarities, and alliance formation. *Strategic Management Journal*, 29(1): 47–77.

Rowley T., Behrens D., Krackhardt D., 2000. Redundant governance structures: An analysis of structural and relational embeddedness in the steel and semiconductor industries. *Strategic Management Journal*, 21(3): 369–386.

Sampson R., 2002. *Experience, Learning and Collaborative Returns in R&D Alliances*, Working Paper, Stern School of Business, New York University, NY.

Schildt H. A., Laamanen T., 2006. Who buys whom: Information environments and organizational boundary spanning through acquisitions. *Strategic Organization*, 4(2): 111–133.

Schoenberg R., 2001. Knowledge transfer and resource sharing as value creation mechanisms in inbound continental European acquisitions. *Journal of Euromarketing*, 10(4): 99–114.

Schweiger D. M., Lippert R. L., 2005. *The Critical Link in M&A Value Creation. Mergers and Acquisitions: Managing Culture and Human Resources*, Stanford University Press, Stanford, CA.

Schweizer L., 2005. Knowledge transfer and R&D in pharmaceutical companies: A case study. *Journal of Engineering and Technology Management*, 22(4): 315–331.

Shan W., Walker G., Kogut B., 1994. Interfirm cooperation and startup innovation in the biotechnology industry. *Strategic Management Journal*, 15(5): 387–394.

Silverman B. S., Baum J. A., 2002. Alliance-based competitive dynamics. *Academy of Management Journal*, 45(4): 791–806.

Simonin B. L., 1997. The importance of collaborative know-how: An empirical test of the learning organization. *Academy of Management Journal*, 40(5): 1150–1174.

Singh H., Zollo M., 1998. Creating value in post-acquisition integration processes. *The Wharton School Financial Institutions Center*, 98–33.

Slusky A. R., Caves R. E., 1991. Synergy, agency, and the determinants of premia paid in mergers. *The Journal of Industrial Economics*, 39(3): 277–296.

Stuart T. E., 1998. Network positions and propensities to collaborate: An investigation of strategic alliance formation in a high-technology industry. *Administrative Science Quarterly*, 43(3): 668–698.

Stuart T. E., Podolny J. M., 1996. Local search and the evolution of technological capabilities. *Strategic Management Journal*, 17(S1): 21–38.

Teece D. J., Pisano G., Shuen A., 1997. Dynamic capabilities and strategic management. *Strategic Management Journal*, 18(7): 509–533.

Trautwein F., 1990. Merger motives and merger prescriptions. *Strategic Management Journal*, 11(4): 283–295.

Uhlenbruck K., Hitt M. A., Semadeni M., 2006. Market value effects of acquisitions involving internet firms: A resource-based analysis. *Strategic Management Journal*, 27(10): 899–913.

Vermeulen F., Barkema H., 2001. Learning through acquisitions. *Academy of Management Journal*, 44(3): 457–476.

Villalonga B., McGahan A. M., 2005. The choice among acquisitions, alliances, and divestitures. *Strategic Management Journal*, 26(13): 1183–1208.

Walter G. A., Barney J. B., 1990. Research notes and communications management objectives in mergers and acquisitions. *Strategic Management Journal*, 11(1): 79–86.

Wang L., Zajac E. J., 2007. Alliance or acquisition? A dyadic perspective on interfirm resource combinations. *Strategic Management Journal*, 28(13): 1291–1317.

Williamson O. E., 1995. Transaction cost economics and organization theory, in *Organization Theory: From Chester Barnard to the Present and Beyond*, Oxford University Press, Oxford, UK, pp. 207–256.

Wuyts S., Colombo M. G., Dutta S., Nooteboom B., 2005. Empirical tests of optimal cognitive distance. *Journal of Economic Behavior and Organization*, 26(6): 813–840.

Yang H., Zhiang L., 2011. Behind acquisitions of alliance partners: Exploratory learning and network embeddedness. *Academy of Management Journal*, 54(5): 1069–1080.

Zajac E. J., Olsen C. P., 1993. From transaction cost to transactional value analysis: Implications for the study of interorganizational strategies. *Journal of Management Studies*, 30(1): 131–145.

Zirger B. J., 1997. The influence of development experience and product innovativeness on product outcome. *Technology Analysis and Strategic Management*, 9(3): 287–297.

Zollo M., Reuer J. J., 2010. Experience spillovers across corporate development activities. *Organization Science*, 21(6): 1195–1212.

Zollo M., Reuer J. J., Singh H., 2002. Interorganizational routines and performance in strategic alliances. *Organization Science*, 13(6): 701–713.

7 Do acquisitions increase acquirers' innovative performance in the biopharma industry?

An empirical investigation

Maria Francesca Savarese, Fiorenza Belussi, Kristina Rakic and Luigi Orsi

Introduction

The last decade has been characterized by an increasing number of mergers and acquisitions (M&As). This phenomenon, different from the past, has mainly involved knowledge-intensive and high-tech industries, where innovation is the most relevant competitive weapon firms rely on, as opposed to mature industries where competition is based on economies of scale and cost efficiency. Contributions based on the resource-based view of the firms (Barney, 1991; Wernerfelt, 1995) and on the knowledge-based view of the firms (Levitt and March, 1988; Nonaka, 1991; Conner and Prahalad, 1996; Grant, 1996; Cloodt *et al.*, 2006) provide some useful insights to understand this phenomenon.

Through M&A, firms gain access to external sources of innovation (Arora and Gambardella, 1990; Hitt *et al.*, 1996; Graebner and Eisenhardt, 2004), develop and extend their resources and capabilities (Vermeulen and Barkema, 2001; Uhlenbruck *et al.*, 2006) and overcome local searching boundaries (Rosenkopf and Nerkar, 2001; Rosenkopf and Almeida, 2003). Thus, in knowledge-intensive industries M&As enable firms to respond to the increasing demand for rapid technological change both in terms of product-related and process-related technologies (Hagedoorn and Duysters, 2002a; Makri *et al.*, 2010).

Despite their growing popularity, there are still few contributions that look at M&As as strategies to drive firms' innovative performances. Existing studies tend to investigate the impact of M&As on financial performance (e.g. Lindgren, 1982; Shrivastava, 1986; Haspeslagh and Jemison, 1991; Greenwood *et al.*, 1994; Hakanson, 1995) or to explore strategic alliances instead of considering particularly the activity of M&A (e.g. Hagedoorn and Schakenraad, 1994; Rosenkopf and Almeida, 2003; Rothaermel and Deeds, 2004, 2006; Hagedoorn and Wang, 2012). This chapter specifically focuses on M&As and attempts to contribute to the existing literature by providing additional insights to better understand the influence of M&As in boosting firms' innovation performance, utilizing both quantitative (number of family patents) and qualitative measures (number of forward patent citations). Our study uncovers a neglected, yet positive, side of acquisitions: they may sustain the innovative path of the acquirers and foster long-term survival. While in other chapters of the book we have stressed the positive role of entering into a variety of alliances (see Chapters 1, 4, 6 and 8), in the present study we will deal with the analysis of the post-acquisition innovative performance. This study refers to the capacity of the acquiring firm to absorb the acquired firm's knowledge base and to assimilate and transform it into new knowledge for the acquirers. In order to do this, we will look at the number of patents' applications in the post-acquisition period and at the number of forward citations received by those patents from all international inventors.

The research study concerns 151 acquirers in the biopharmaceutical industry that have completed 217 M&As in the period 2001–2005. The dataset integrates data from several sources, such as Medtrack, Orbit-QPat and Orbis.

The structure of the chapter is as follows: the next two sections are devoted to the literature review and theory development. In the fourth part of the chapter we develop our methodology. The fifth part of the chapter is devoted to data analysis and discussion. In the last section we summarize our findings.

Research on acquisitions

Research on acquisitions has typically focused on acquisitions' financial performance or organization integration. This study moves beyond that perspective and analyses the innovative performance of the acquiring firms, both utilizing quantitative (family patents) and qualitative measures (forward patent citations). We argue here that the development of the firm's knowledge base through inhouse investments might be a suboptimal choice in comparison – or a necessary complementary strategy – with a model of open innovation (Chesbrough, 2003) in which firms can discover more quickly, and at a lower price, new avenues of research using other firms' knowledge and the resources openly available. They can also cooperate with suppliers, public institutions or even potential competitors who possess the specific required inputs, or be involved in a process of 'learning by interacting' (Powell et al., 1996). In order to remain competitive and to dismantle involuntary inertial behaviour, firms must have access to and explore similar or complementary knowledge, blending it for fuelling the creative process. But, there is clearly a trade-off between the use of openly available knowledge, or knowledge localized within a firm's network where all actors can contemporarily make use of it, and the individual discovering a unique path of research, based on inhouse proprietary knowledge. Non-shared knowledge and idiosyncratic knowledge, linked to firm-specific capabilities, which are in the exclusive possession of the firm, might carry more value for firms.

Thus, in the high-tech industry, the recourse to acquisition strategy may comply with these two polar opposite needs: (a) the need to find fresh external new knowledge and to follow novel problem-solving solutions already (or in the course of being) discovered by other firms; and (b) the stringent competitive condition of excluding rivals from the access to and sharing of the newly acquired (or previously co-developed) knowledge.

The process of M&A consents to a 'proprietary' use of external knowledge sources (and this is quite different from the activation of a 'lean' orchestration of strategic alliances where co-sharing is an imperative). This makes it more likely that knowledge deriving from the acquired firms will be integrated by the acquiree into its knowledge base, reducing the probability of losing control over its use, or of suffering from leakages.

Although firms can rely on alliance learning, alliances only allow for partial control, while acquisitions afford complete ownership control of assets (Balakrishnan and Koza, 1993; Yin and Shanley, 2008). These two modalities are often interrelated (as discussed in Chapter 6) and both are often used to access external resources (Hagedoorn and Duysters, 2002a; De Man and Duysters, 2005; Zollo and Reuer, 2010). They share some common motivations, such as synergy seeking, but they entail different opportunities, flexibilities and risks. On the one hand, alliances allow a partial involvement, a weaker status over the control of knowledge and a continuous reassessment of partners' contribution, while acquisitions represent a more radical shift and an irreversible strategic choice on new knowledge and resources' appropriation.

Clearly, even if acquisitions serve to revitalize the firm's knowledge pipeline, an important empirical insight of the last decade's literature has underlined that acquisitions bear high costs, usually correlated to the disbursement of a significant sum of money, where sometimes the acquisitions become a burden of additional costs for the acquiring firms, such as a takeover premium. A wide stream of research has studied how acquisitions influence acquiring companies, often stressing some negative aspects. Hitt *et al.* (1996) have argued that acquisitions require funding, time and the attention of top management; thus, this could potentially divert the acquiring firm from internal growth and innovation. Acquisitions demand irreversible financial and managerial commitment and, if the results are unsatisfactory, acquiring firms must disinvest paying high costs (Datta, 1991; Chatterjee *et al.*, 1992). However, firms may also achieve greater market power; they may become able to overcome barriers to entry, or to enter new markets more quickly.

Quantitative and qualitative indicators of innovativeness

A consolidated praxis related to measuring innovation activity in firms is the use of the number of patents registered by an organization in a given period (Griliches and Schmookler, 1963). Patents form a central pathway for capturing the value of intangible assets in a high-tech industry (Cohen *et al.*, 2000). Patents can potentially generate and support earnings through two modalities: first, they can be traded or licensed out and second, they can provide critical protection for core production technologies or products. In patenting, the invention goes through a rigorous and objective verification process as laid down by the regulations. Patenting reduces the level of asymmetric information between inventors and investors and provides collaterals for the company; both are important means of controlling investors' risk.

Patent analysis covers a wide stream of research. However, the proxy of the patent counting suffers from a strong analytical limitation. It is well known that not all patents are the same and the distribution of their value, whatever proxy we can use to evaluate their 'quality' or 'economic value', is highly skewed. Patents usually have a highly skewed value distribution: few patents have a very high economic value, whereas most patents have a low economic value or none at all (Harhoff *et al.*, 2003).

A new avenue of research at the end of the 1990s has been the use of patent citations (Trajtenberg 1990; Narin, 1993; Lanjouw, 1999). This has signified a shift in the literature towards more qualitative estimations of the innovative activity in firms. When a patent is cited by a researcher or technician, it implies that it bears some value for the advancement of the knowledge frontier. As argued by Narin and Olivastro (1988): 'a highly cited patent regards a technical advance of particular relevance'. In turn, patents' citations can be distinguished in forward and backward citations. Citations in the patent document are indications of prior art and refer to the existing body of knowledge. These citations are made by an applicant, but verified (and possibly amended) by the patent examiner. The role of these citations is to limit the scope of protection and indicate which invention is specifically patented. Backward citations position the new invention with respect to previous patents. Citations by other patents (forward citations, influenced clearly by the time lag selected) are considered to reflect the patent's technological significance and applicability as well 'appropriability', i.e. the ability of the inventors to benefit from their inventions (Narin 1993; Trajtenberg *et al.*, 1997).

Recent patent valuation literature relates backward citations to the basicness of an innovation. Citations to previous patents (backward citations) position the new invention within its application area and are linked especially to the 'basicness' of a patent (Trajtenberg *et al.*, 1997). The term 'basicness' refers to such fundamental features as closeness to science and originality and is closely connected to choices and efforts of R&D. Forward citation counts the economic value of an innovation (Trajtenberg, 1990; Albert *et al.*, 1991; Harhoff *et al.*, 2003). Also, Narin *et al.* (1987) used US pharmaceutical forward patents' citations in an attempt to connect patent citations to the financial characteristics of companies; some of the company-specific financial characteristics could be explained by using patent statistics. In the same line of enquiry, Hall *et al.* (2001) used forward patent citation weighted patent counts to estimate the market value of US companies listed on the stock exchange. They found that patent citations could provide a more accurate picture of the company's intangible assets.

Forward patents' citations represent a realized interest of a technology, but data are available only following a substantial time period after the granting of (or the application for) a patent. Most of the forward citations are made by claimants independent of the patent holder and also reflect a realized interest for the cited patent; consequently, the empirical literature (Tuomo *et al.*, 2006) shows a clear association of economic value and technological significance with forward citations. In contrast, backward citations look merely at the past, but they are available immediately online, being part of the granting documentation.

Methodology

The research setting deals with the biopharmaceutical industry for several reasons. First, competition in this industry is knowledge-based (Chang, 2008). Thus, firms' competitiveness largely relies on their dynamic capability (Teece, 2007), social capital and networking (Nahapiet and Ghoshal, 1998) and absorptive capacity (Cohen and Levinthal, 1990). Second, this industry is the outcome of the combination and merging of two complementary sets of competencies. The developments in biotechnology have disrupted upstream R&D competencies in the pharmaceutical industry, but have been competence-preserving in downstream commercialization activities (Powell *et al.*, 1996). Thus, the rise of biotechnology has stimulated firms from the biotechnological and pharmaceutical sectors to enter strategic alliances and M&As in order to complement their respective strengths and weaknesses (e.g. Rothaermel, 2001; Rothaermel and Boeker, 2008; Adegbesan and Higgins, 2011). This is confirmed by the fact that the biopharmaceutical industry has a high frequency of alliances (Hagedoorn, 1993) and has witnessed considerable M&A activity (Goldman Sachs, 2001).

Even if M&As are quite common in the pharmaceutical and biotech industry, many of them have not yet generated benefits (Bower, 2001). There are two main reasons for this: first, acquirers are required to manage the trade-off between the need for integrating acquired biotech companies, in order to absorb and exploit their research and innovative capabilities, and the need to preserve their autonomy. Second, difficulties and negative outcomes arise from organizational and cultural differences existing between biotech and pharma companies. In general, biotech firms are dynamic, lean and effective in fostering innovation, since they are characterized by a low level of hierarchy, open communication and informal organizational structures, flexibility, risk taking inclination and significant participation by employees in the ownership. On the other hand, pharmaceutical companies usually have a formal structure, high levels of hierarchy and slow decision-making processes (Powell *et al.*, 1996). Thus, the biopharmaceutical industry is an appropriate research setting for testing the significance of these aspects on post-M&A technological performance.

Sample and data sources

Our analysis was tested on a cross-sectional dataset of 151 acquirers (mainly in the biopharmaceutical industry) that had completed 217 M&As in the bio industry in the period from 2001 to 2005. We constructed this dataset by integrating data from several sources according to the following procedure.

First, we extracted firms from Medtrack. The following criteria were applied: (a) firms should have completed at least one M&A in the time window of five years (e.g. Ahuja and Katila, 2001; Hagedoorn and Duysters, 2002a; Diestre and Rajagopalan, 2012) between 2001 and 2005; and (b) all firms not involved in technological M&As were excluded (Ahuja and Katila, 2001; Makri *et al.*, 2010). On the basis of these criteria, we identified 229 North American and European acquirers that had completed 404 technological M&As between 2001 and 2005.

Second, we collected data about acquirers' and targets' patenting application activities (number of family patents, number of forward citations and number of licensed patents) from Orbit-QPat. Although previous works, e.g. Ahuja and Katila (2001), Hagedoorn and Duysters (2002b), Makri *et al.* (2010) and Diestre and Rajagopalan (2012) utilized data on patents taken from US databases, we decided to employ Orbit-QPat for at least two reasons. First, our major purpose was to analyse a firm's ability to patent and protect its knowledge at a world-wide level. Orbit-QPat provides extensive coverage with 95 patent authorities. Second, it is characterized by great flexibility, which allowed us to identify and export fundamental data for the construction of our key measures. For each target and acquirer we collected all the patents granted between 1995 and 2011. We excluded all the firms that had not been granted patents between 1995 and 2011. Thus, our sample resulted in 151 acquirers that had completed 217 technological M&As between 2001 and 2005.

Finally, we employed Orbis in order to obtain additional data on listed and unlisted sampled firms.

Research design

We used four variables to characterize firms' pre- and post-M&A technological performances: invention quantity, invention quality, citations per patents and licensed patents. Changes in technological performances were calculated in a window of six years before and after the M&A had been completed. According to Singh (1971) and Buono and Bowditch (1989), it takes an average of five years before acquired organizations are assimilated and the benefits of the M&A emerge. However, according to these studies, acquirers vary considerably in their capacity to assimilate acquired firms. Some companies are able to merge their organizations within one year, whereas others take longer than five years. Furthermore, Pakes and Griliches (1984) suggest that it takes an average of one year before invention through R&D leads to patent applications. Thus, it takes an average of six years before the potential of M&As may be reflected in acquirers' technological performance (Hagedoorn and Duysters, 2002a).

In this chapter some quantitative and qualitative indicators were used to describe the acquirers' modification to their global innovation capacity during the pre- and post-M&A period. Moreover, to operationalize our measures relating to patents, we used the application date as a reference.

The cumulated number of patents – called, as in Makri *et al.* (2010) *invention quantity* – is a measure of firms' technological/invention productivity (Hitt *et al.*, 1996; Mowery *et al.*, 1996; DeCarolis and Deeds, 1999; Malerba and Orsenigo, 1999; Sørensen and Stuart, 2000; Hall *et al.*, 2001), which we based on the number of patents produced by a firm in a given range of time (Griliches, 1998). We operationalized this variable as the sum of patents granted to a firm in the six-year period post M&A. However, our objective was to measure the extent to which M&As contribute to enhancing firms' invention productivity in terms of the number of patents granted. Thus, we calculated the total number of patents the acquirer was granted in the one- to six-year period before the M&A took place. Average values were computed for firms engaged in multiple acquisitions.

The number of forward citations received by the new patents (patent applications) is a measure of the quality of the invention produced by the acquirers, which we call here, as in Makri *et al.* (2010), *invention quality*. This indicator was calculated in the window from one to six years after the M&A date for each patent by summing up all citations cumulated up to 2013, but dividing this cumulated number by the number of years in which the patent was cited (i.e. we created a measure of citations per year for the patents granted post M&A). This measure can be considered a proxy of the quality (technical importance) of invention, because it reflects the ability of a set of patents to support and stimulate future inventions (Trajtenberg, 1990; Makri *et al.*, 2010). Our objective was to measure the extent to which M&As contribute to enhancing firms' invention quality in terms of number of citations. Thus, we compared the total number of citations received by the acquirer patents' applications in the window from one to six years before the M&A date (divided by the number of years from the last year of the six-year window pre M&A to the end of 2013, i.e. we created a measure of citations per year for the patents granted pre M&A) with the post-M&A patent application citations. Average values were computed for firms engaged in multiple acquisitions.

The *citations per patent ratio* was calculated as the ratio between the citations received by the acquirer patents granted in the window from one to six years after the M&A date that was divided by the number of years from the last year of the six-year window to the end of 2013, and the number of patents granted in the six-year window post M&A (i.e. we created a measure of annual citations per patent ratio for the patents granted post M&A). In the same way, we also calculated the annual citations per patent ratio for the patents granted in the six-year window pre M&A. Average values were computed for firms engaged in multiple acquisitions.

Number of licensed patents is a measure of invention performance and, in particular, a proxy of the acquirer strategy related to the open innovation orientation. This measure is operationalized as the number of licenses granted to the acquirer patents applied for in the window from one to six years after the M&A date that was divided by the number of years from the last year of the six-year window to the end of 2013 (i.e. we created a measure of licensing per year for the patents applied for post M&A). In the same way, we also calculated the licenses per year for the patents granted in the six-year window pre M&A. Average values were computed for firms engaged in multiple acquisitions.

Results and discussion

Our sample consists of 60 European (Germany = 14, United Kingdom = 9, Switzerland = 9, Denmark = 5, Ireland = 4, Italy = 4, Netherlands = 4, Sweden = 4, France = 4 and Spain = 3) and 91 North American (US = 81 and Canada = 10) firms. Of the companies in our sample 36 were engaged in multiple M&As during the focal period (e.g. Johnson & Johnson = 7, Pfizer = 7, Abbott Laboratories = 5, Integra Lifesciences = 5, Genzyme Corp. = 4, Agilent Technologies = 4,

Angiotech Inc. = 4 and Cephanlon = 3), while the remaining were involved in only 1 acquisition. The average number of M&As in the focal period was 1.46 and varied from a minimum of 0 to a maximum of 7. The average acquirer firm was about 31 years old at the time of the first M&A in the focal period and had 7,821 employees. More specifically, the oldest company was founded in 1849 (Pfizer Inc.) and the youngest in April 2003 (Bioceros), which suggests that the latter participated in an M&A immediately after it was founded. The minimum number of employees (n = 3) was recorded by Jazz Pharmaceuticals Plc, Nutra Pharma Corporation and Whatman Plc, while the maximum (n = 127,600) was by Johnson & Johnson. Finally, with reference to the status of the acquirers in the sample, i.e. whether they were public or private companies, 101 of them were listed on the stock exchange, while the remaining 51 were unlisted.

In this section we discuss our results: first by analysing them in an aggregate way (all the firms in our sample); second by comparing the results achieved by North American companies and those achieved by European companies; and third, dividing our sample for the typology of the acquiring firms. We have segmented the industry into five types of firm strictly related to their core business: (1) big pharmaceutical companies, which are the leading companies based on sales of prescription medicines, including generic drugs, such as Pfizer, Novartis and Roche; (2) big biotech companies, which are leading companies in terms of sales of human therapeutic and diagnostic applications, such as biomaterials and tissue regeneration, blood products, gene therapy, stem cell therapy, vaccines and bio-diagnostic products, such as Genentech, Genzyme, Chiron and AMGen (Rothaermel and Boeker, 2008); (3) pharma companies, including all the small and medium pharmaceutical firms; (4) biotech companies including all the small and medium biotech firms; and (5) others.

In Table 7.1 we present the aggregate results, including all sampled firms. The results clearly show an increasing trend in the post-M&A period related to both the invention quantity and the invention quality. The number of patents in the six-year window pre M&A is, on average, 221.73, with a minimum value of 0 and a maximum value of 4,915. This compares with an average value in the post-acquisition period of 293.03, with a minimum value of 0 and a maximum value of 5,919. This result is consistent with the literature that perceives acquisition as a tool to improve the innovative performance (measured in terms of invention quantity) of the companies in high-tech environments (Makri *et al.*, 2010). If we look at the data relating to the quality of innovation performance measured in terms of number of citations per year for the patents granted pre and post M&A, we can also say that, in this case, we find an increase in the quality of the patent portfolio of the companies in the post-M&A period. There were 235.7 annual citations on average in the six-year window pre M&A, compared with an average value of 329.26 post M&A. Thus, we can assert that acquiring firms have been able to absorb the technological knowledge from the target company and they can recombine this new knowledge into the internal R&D process that leads to an increase in both the quantity and quality of the patents' portfolio of the acquirer. If we look at the citations per patents ratio we can observe a small decrease in the

Table 7.1 Descriptive statistics on all firms in the sample

Variables	Mean	Median	S.D.	Min	Max	Count
Invention quantity pre M&A	221.73	23.00	614.07	0.00	4915.00	151
Invention quantity post M&A	293.03	39.00	822.41	0.00	5919.00	151
Invention quality pre M&A	235.70	31.92	623.89	0.00	5355.36	151
Invention quality post M&A	329.26	52.50	824.32	0.00	6215.83	151
Citations per patent ratio pre M&A	8.37	6.00	10.59	0.00	105.61	151
Citations per patent ratio post M&A	6.72	5.50	6.64	0.00	56.25	151
Licensing pre M&A	0.16	0.00	0.55	0.00	4.25	151
Licensing post M&A	0.30	0.00	1.09	0.00	7.83	151

Source: Authors' elaboration.

post-M&A period (from 8.37 annual citations per patents pre M&A to 6.72 post M&A). This means that we have a more than proportional increase in the number of patents than in the number of citations. In the sample of all the firms, it seems that, in general, the acquisitions led to an increase in both the invention quantity and invention quality, but it would seem to give priority to a greater invention quantity over invention quality. The last indicator is related to the proxy of the open innovation strategy of the acquiring firms. This measure changes from an average of 0.16 patents licensed in the pre-M&A period to an average value of 0.33 in the post-M&A period, marking a slight improvement. It would seem that, in general, there is a tendency by companies involved in the acquisition process to use open innovation strategies to better withstand the existing strong competition. But, in general, we observe a low level of licensed patents in comparison to the great increase in patenting applications.

In a second step we have distinguished the acquirers, separating the results between the North American and European firms (see Table 7.2). Our analyses highlight the greater ability of the North American companies in the management of the M&A processes and their higher capabilities to internalize and reuse the target technological knowledge base. The average value of invention quantity in post M&A for the North American firms is 398.23 patents, which presents an increasing trend in comparison with the pre-M&A period (269.25 patents). In contrast, the European firms exhibit a decreasing trend (148.60 patents in the pre-M&A period versus 133.47 patents in the post-M&A period). Also, the indicator of invention quality ranked quite highly among the North American firms in comparison with the European ones (434.35 citations per year versus 169.87), even if the trend in invention quality in both continents for the post-M&A period rises. Another interesting result is provided by the greater utilization of the licensing of North American companies (0.42 licensed patents per year) in comparison with European firms (0.12 licensed patents per year), showing the existence of higher technological capabilities associated with a greater use of open innovation strategies. Clearly the European acquirers suffer from an inferior absorptive

Table 7.2 Descriptive statistics divided into US firms and EU firms

	Variables	Mean	Median	S.D.	Min	Max	Count
US	Invention quantity pre M&A	269.95	28.00	713.87	0.00	4915.00	91
	Invention quantity post M&A	398.23	58.00	1012.98	0.00	5919.00	91
	Invention quality pre M&A	299.74	37.75	755.64	0.00	5355.36	91
	Invention quality post M&A	434.35	70.29	1004.72	0.00	6215.83	91
	Citations per patent ratio pre M&A	7.65	6.47	5.16	0.00	27.00	91
	Citations per patent ratio post M&A	6.26	5.46	4.87	0.00	25.62	91
	Licensing pre M&A	0.18	0.00	0.60	0.00	4.25	91
	Licensing post M&A	0.42	0.00	1.35	0.00	7.83	91
EU	Invention quantity pre M&A	148.60	20.00	415.06	0.00	2254.00	60
	Invention quantity post M&A	133.47	23.50	333.59	0.00	1942.00	60
	Invention quality pre M&A	138.56	25.46	320.39	0.00	1671.70	60
	Invention quality post M&A	169.87	25.67	380.54	0.00	2167.20	60
	Citations per patent ratio pre M&A	9.47	5.15	15.56	0.00	105.61	60
	Citations per patent ratio post M&A	7.43	5.55	8.66	0.00	56.25	60
							60
	Licensing pre M&A	0.11	0.00	0.46	0.00	3.33	
	Licensing post M&A	0.12	0.00	0.42	0.00	3.00	60

Source: Authors' elaboration.

capability[1] compared with the North American ones, in terms of their smaller size (the average number of employees of the European firms is 6,680, while the average number of employees of the North American firms is 8,651), their more limited experience in managing strategic alliances (the average number of alliances pre M&A of the European firms is 6.87 compared with 8.85 of the American firms) and their lower capacity to manage M&A processes (the average number acquisitions pre M&A of the European firms is 0.45 compared with 0.57 of the American firms).

In general, our data registered an important improvement in the proxies utilized for capturing the innovative output of firms in that the number of patent applications, the number of patent citations and also the number of patents that were licensed doubled. Thus, M&As produced a positive shift in the inventing capabilities of acquirers. In this context, the lower number of average citations per patent ratio post M&A needs to be correctly interpreted, not just as a diminished value of the patent realized as a result of rapid growth in the number of patents considered in the denominator of the equation in the formula. The productivity of M&A results are far greater for the US sample than for European firms,

Table 7.3 Descriptive statistics divided into big biotech firms, big pharmaceutical firms, biotech firms and pharma firms

	Variables	Mean	Median	S.D.	Min	Max	Count
BIG BIO	Invention quantity pre M&A	454.29	182.00	570.98	33.00	2081.00	17
	Invention quantity post M&A	607.71	207.00	1348.78	23.00	5747.00	17
	Invention quality pre M&A	535.02	307.25	733.14	30.30	3205.17	17
	Invention quality post M&A	626.88	345.60	983.89	11.71	4269.86	17
	Citations per patent ratio pre M&A	6.93	6.51	3.09	2.91	14.64	17
	Citations per patent ratio post M&A	7.84	6.15	5.70	2.55	24.56	17
	Licensing pre M&A	0.32	0.13	0.54	0.00	2.25	17
	Licensing post M&A	0.36	0.20	0.41	0.00	1.20	17
BIG PHARMA	Invention quantity pre M&A	1106.73	958.00	924.75	12.00	2777.00	15
	Invention quantity post M&A	1293.87	1252.00	1001.54	119.00	3059.00	15
	Invention quality pre M&A	1017.17	993.83	753.04	9.11	2545.00	15
	Invention quality post M&A	1462.79	1126.25	1154.76	166.25	4337.67	15
	Citations per patent ratio pre M&A	5.03	4.93	1.09	3.24	6.66	15
	Citations per patent ratio post M&A	5.98	5.85	1.22	3.89	8.95	15
	Licensing pre M&A	1.08	0.50	1.33	0.00	4.25	15
	Licensing post M&A	1.79	1.00	2.25	0.00	7.67	15
BIO	Invention quantity pre M&A	31.45	11.00	77.89	0.00	646.00	75
	Invention quantity post M&A	54.52	18.00	99.92	0.00	637.00	75
	Invention quality pre M&A	45.46	12.09	79.70	0.00	454.67	75
	Invention quality post M&A	73.54	23.14	122.82	0.00	599.71	75
	Citations per patent ratio pre M&A	8.73	5.45	12.00	0.45	88.01	75
	Citations per patent ratio post M&A	7.01	5.56	5.82	0.00	29.78	75
	Licensing pre M&A	0.01	0.00	0.05	0.00	0.38	75
	Licensing post M&A	0.02	0.00	0.08	0.00	0.40	75

PHARMA							
Invention quantity pre M&A	29.38	14.00	35.53	0.00	158.00	39
Invention quantity post M&A	88.92	32.00	289.42	0.00	1833.00	39
Invention quality pre M&A	38.57	15.13	54.29	0.00	242.20	39
Invention quality post M&A	103.88	27.00	320.07	0.00	2003.67	39
Citations per patent ratio pre M&A	6.35	4.87	4.86	0.75	18.92	39
Citations per patent ratio post M&A	7.24	4.50	9.67	0.48	56.25	39
Licensing pre M&A	0.02	0.00	0.04	0.00	0.20	39
Licensing post M&A	0.22	0.00	1.25	0.00	7.83	39

Five futher companies are involved in acquisitions in the biopharmaceutical industry in addition to those noted above, but not within these four main categories.

Source: Authors' elaboration.

where we observe an absolute decline in patenting and also a stronger reduction of average citations per patent in the post-M&A phase, respectively from 9.47 to 7.43. Considering the various industry segments, the best performers appear to be the big pharmas, followed by the big bios, the pharmas and finally the small bio firms.

In detail, we see that the annual citations per patent measure, in the case of big biotech firms, increases from a pre-M&A period of 6.93 citations per patent to a post-M&A period of 7.84 citations per patent (the highest level of quality in the post-acquisition period). Also the big pharmaceutical companies show an increasing trend of this indicator even starting from an inferior level (from 5.03 to 5.98). The quality of biotech patents is always higher than that of pharma and large pharma firms, in accordance with the greater capacity of those firms to generate breakthrough patents/inventions, given that these firms, generally, work in the most innovative technological areas and on the frontier of the creation of new scientific knowledge.

Big pharma companies, in contrast, are the strongest users of the modality of patent licensing in comparison with all other categories of companies. They rule the 'market of technology' and benefit from the exploitation of their knowledge generated internally from acquisitions through M&As and thus from the extensive utilization of patent portfolios held by such companies.

If we look at the smaller companies (both bio and pharma), we note much lower absolute levels of performance, even if quantity and quality indicators are in constant growth in the post-acquisition period. As a result of the acquisition process, pharma firms were able to triple the number of patents (from 29.38 to 88.92 patents) and the number of citations (from 38.57 to 103.88 citations) and to increase also the annual citations per patent ratio (from 6.35 to 7.24), but also the smaller biotechs, which represent the majority of our sample, moved up increasing both on average the number of patents (from 31.45 to 54.52) and the number of citations (from 45.46 to 73.54). However, small biotech firms denoted, on average, a decrease in patent citations from 8.73 to 7.01. Both small pharma and small biotech companies show a very low level in using the licensing modality.

Conclusions

Our study focused on the biopharmaceutical industry for two main reasons. First, competition in this industry is knowledge-based (Chang, 2008). Thus, firms' competitiveness relies largely on their dynamic capability (Teece, 2007), social capital and networking (Ghoshal and Moran, 1996) and absorptive capacity (Cohen and Levinthal, 1990). Second, the rise of biotechnology has stimulated firms in the biotechnological and pharmaceutical sectors to enter into M&As in order to balance their respective strengths and weaknesses (e.g. Rothaermel, 2001; Rothaermel and Boeker, 2008; Adegbesan and Higgins, 2011). A detailed dataset was constructed by integrating data from several sources. For each acquirer and target we collected all the patents granted between 1995 and 2011. Ultimately, the final sample resulted in 151 acquirers of biotech target firms (from biopharma and other sectors, but mainly biopharma) that completed 217 technological M&As between 2001 and 2005.

M&As can be interpreted as attempts portrayed by companies not only to increase control over the external environment but also to improve their knowledge bases by accessing and absorbing knowledge, resources and capabilities from external sources.

From these findings it is possible to affirm that our empirical analysis suggests that M&As, generally, increase the innovative performance of the acquiring firm. The effect of acquisitions seems to be higher on invention quantity than invention quality. Also, the use of open innovation strategies seems to increase in the post-acquisition period, although the level of this variable remains relatively low. North American companies seem to gain more benefits from acquisitions than European companies in terms of innovative performance and larger companies, such as the big pharmas and biotechs, seem to be able to absorb and better exploit the external knowledge generated through the acquired companies. These results, once again, confirm the dominant role played by the large pharmas in the sector and the increasing importance of the small number of larger biotech companies, as we have thoroughly discussed in Chapter 1.

Note

1 In the next chapter, a discussion about the drivers affecting absorptive capacity is developed.

References

Adegbesan J. A., Higgins M. J., 2011. The intra-alliance division of value created through collaboration. *Strategic Management Journal*, 32(2): 187–211.

Ahuja G., Katila R., 2001. Technological acquisitions and the innovation performance of acquiring firms: A longitudinal study. *Strategic Management Journal*, 22(3): 197–220.

Albert M. B., Avery D., Narin F., McAllister P., 1991. Direct validation of citation counts as indicators of industrially important patents. *Research Policy*, 20(3): 251–259.

Arora A., Gambardella A., 1990. Complementarity and external linkages: The strategies of the large firms in biotechnology. *Journal of Industrial Economics*, 38(4): 361–379.

Balakrishnan S., Koza M. P., 1993. Information asymmetry, adverse selection and joint-ventures: Theory and evidence. *Journal of Economic Behavior & Organization*, 20(1): 99–117.

Barney J., 1991. Firm resources and sustained competitive advantage. *Journal of Management*, 17(1): 99–120.

Bower J. L., 2001. Not all M&As are alike – and that matters. *Harvard Business Review*, 79(2): 93–101.

Buono A. F., Bowditch J. L., 1989. *The Human Side of Mergers and Acquisitions*, Jossey-Bass, San Francisco, CA.

Chang K., 2008. The strategic alliance performance of the biotechnology firm. *Applied Economics*, 40(23): 3089–3100.

Chatterjee S., Lubatkin M. H., Schweiger D. M., Weber Y., 1992. Cultural differences and shareholder value in related mergers: Linking equity and human capital. *Strategic Management Journal*, 13(5): 319–334.

Chesbrough H. W., 2003. *Open Innovation: The New Imperative for Creating and Profiting From Technology*, Harvard Business School Press, Cambridge, MA.

Cloodt M., Hagedoorn J., Van Kranenburg H., 2006. Mergers and acquisitions: Their effect on the innovative performance of companies in high-tech industries. *Research Policy*, 35(5): 642–654.

Cohen W. M., Levinthal D., 1990. Absorptive capacity: A new perspective on learning and innovation. *Administrative Science Quarterly*, 35(1): 128–152.

Cohen W. M., Nelson R. R., Walsh J. P., 2000. *Protecting Their Intellectual Assets: Appropriability Conditions and Why US Manufacturing Firms Patent (Or Not)*. Working Paper No. 7552, National Bureau of Economic Research, Cambridge, MA. Available at: http://www.nber.org/papers/w7552 (accessed 15 September 2014).

Conner K. R., Prahalad C. K., 1996. A resource-based theory of the firm: Knowledge versus opportunism. *Organization Science*, 7(5): 477–501.

Datta D. K., 1991. Organizational fit and acquisition performance: Effects of post-acquisition integration. *Strategic Management Journal*, 12(4): 281–297.

DeCarolis D. M., Deeds D. L., 1999. The impact of stocks and flows of organizational knowledge on firm performance: An empirical investigation of the biotechnology industry. *Strategic Management Journal*, 20(10): 953–968.

De Man A.-P., Duysters G., 2005. Collaboration and innovation: A review of the effects of mergers, acquisitions and alliances on innovation. *Technovation*, 25(12): 1377–1387.

Diestre L., Rajagopalan N., 2012. Are all 'sharks' dangerous? New biotechnology ventures and partner selection in R&D alliances. *Strategic Management Journal*, 33(10): 1115–1134.

Ghoshal S., Moran P., 1996. Bad for practice: A critique of the transaction cost theory. *Academy of Management Review*, 21(1): 13–47.

Goldman Sachs, 2001. *Strategic Alliances in Biotechnology*, Goldman Sachs, New York, NY.

Graebner M. E., Eisenhardt K. M., 2004. The seller's side of the story: Acquisition as courtship and governance as syndicate in entrepreneurial firms. *Administrative Science Quarterly*, 49(3): 366–403.

Grant R. M., 1996. Prospering in dynamically-competitive environments: Organizational capability as knowledge integration. *Organization Science*, 7(4): 375–387.

Greenwood R., Hinings C. R., Brown J., 1994. Merging professional service firms. *Organization Science*, 5(2): 239–257.

Griliches Z., 1998. Introduction to R&D and productivity: The econometric evidence, in *R&D and Productivity: The Econometric Evidence*, University of Chicago Press, IL, pp. 1–14.

Griliches Z., Schmookler J., 1963. Inventing and maximizing. *The American Economic Review*, 53(4): 725–729.

Hagedoorn J., 1993. Understanding the rationale of strategic technology partnering: Interorganizational modes of cooperation and sectoral differences. *Strategic Management Journal*, 14(5): 371–385.

Hagedoorn J., Schakenraad J., 1994. The effect of strategic technology alliances on company performance. *Strategic Management Journal*, 15(4): 291–309.

Hagedoorn J., Duysters G., 2002a. External sources of innovative capabilities: The preference for strategic alliances or mergers and acquisitions. *Journal of Management Studies*, 39(2): 167–188.

Hagedoorn J., Duysters G., 2002b. The effect of mergers and acquisitions on the technological performance of companies in a high-tech environment. *Technology Analysis & Strategic Management*, 14(1): 67–85.

Hagedoorn J., Wang N., 2012. Is there complementarity or substitutability between internal and external R&D strategies? *Research Policy*, 41(6): 1072–1083.

Hakanson L., 1995. Learning through acquisitions: Management and integration of foreign R&D laboratories. *International Studies of Management and Organization*, 25(1–2): 121–157.

Hall B. H., Jaffe A., Trajtenberg M., 2001. *NBER Patent Citations Data File: Lessons, Insights and Methodological Tools*. Working Paper No. 8498, National Bureau of Economic Research, Cambridge, MA. Available at: http://www.nber.org/papers/w8498 (accessed 7 September 2014).

Harhoff D., Scherer F. M., Vopel K., 2003. Citations, family size, opposition and the value of patent rights. *Research Policy*, 32(8): 1343–1363.

Haspeslagh P. C., Jemison D. B., 1991. *Managing Acquisitions: Creating Value through Corporate Renewal* (Vol. 416), Free Press, New York, NY.

Hitt M. A., Hoskisson R. E., Johnson R. A., Moesel D. D., 1996. The market for corporate control and firm innovation. *Academy of Management Journal*, 39(5): 1084–1119.

Lanjouw J., 1999. *The Quality of Ideas: Measuring Innovation with Multiple Indicators*. Working Paper No. 7345, National Bureau of Economic Research, Cambridge, MA. Available at: http://www.nber.org/papers/w7345 (accessed 10 September 2014).

Levitt B., March J. G., 1988. Organizational learning. *Annual Review of Sociology*, 14: 319–340.

Lindgren U., 1982. *Foreign Acquisitions: Management of the Integration Process*, Institute of International Business, Stockholm, Sweden.

Makri M., Hitt M. A., Lane P. J., 2010. Complementary technologies, knowledge relatedness, and invention outcomes in high technology mergers and acquisitions. *Strategic Management Journal*, 31(6): 602–628.

Malerba F., Orsenigo L., 1999. Technological entry, exit and survival: An empirical analysis of patent data. *Research Policy*, 28(6): 643–660.

Mowery D. C., Oxley J. E., Silverman B. S., 1996. Strategic alliances and interfirm knowledge transfer. *Strategic Management Journal*, 17(S2): 77–91.

Nahapiet J., Ghoshal S., 1998. Social capital, intellectual capital, and the organizational advantage. *Academy of Management Review*, 23(2): 242–266.

Narin F., 1993. Technology indicators and corporate strategy. *Review of Business*, 14(3): 19–23.

Narin F., Olivastro D., 1988. Science indicators: Their use in science policy and their role in science studies, in *Patent Citation Analysis: New Validation Studies and Linkage Statistics*, DSWO Press, The Netherlands, pp. 37–47.

Narin F., Noma E., Perry R., 1987. Patents as indicators of corporate technological strength. *Research Policy*, 16(2): 143–155.

Nonaka I., 1991. The knowledge-creating company. *Harvard Business Review*, 69(6): 96–104.

Pakes A., Griliches Z., 1984. Patents and R&D at the firm level: A first look, in *R&D, Patents, and Productivity*, University of Chicago Press, Chicago, IL, pp. 55–72.

Powell W. W., Koput K. W., Smith-Doerr L., 1996. Interorganizational collaboration and the locus of innovation: Networks of learning in biotechnology. *Administrative Science Quarterly*, 41(1): 116–145.

Rosenkopf L., Nerkar A., 2001. Beyond local search: Boundary-spanning, exploration, and impact in the optical disk industry. *Strategic Management Journal*, 22(4): 287–306.

Rosenkopf L., Almeida P., 2003. Overcoming local search through alliances and mobility. *Management Science*, 49(6): 751–766.

Rothaermel F. T., 2001. Complementary assets, strategic alliances, and the incumbent's advantage: An empirical study of industry and firm effects in the biopharmaceutical industry. *Research Policy*, 30(8): 1235–1251.

Rothaermel F. T., Deeds D. L., 2004. Exploration and exploitation alliances in biotechnology: A system of new product development. *Strategic Management Journal*, 25(3): 201–221.

Rothaermel F. T., Deeds D. L., 2006. Alliance type, alliance experience and alliance management capability in high-technology ventures. *Journal of Business Venturing*, 21(4): 429–460.

Rothaermel F. T., Boeker W., 2008. Old technology meets new technology: Complementarities, similarities, and alliance formation. *Strategic Management Journal*, 29(1): 47–77.

Shrivastava P., 1986. Postmerger integration. *Journal of Business Strategy*, 7(1): 65–76.

Singh A., 1971. *Take-overs: Their Relevance to the Stock Market and the Theory of the Firm*, Cambridge University Press, Cambridge, UK.

Sørensen J. B., Stuart T. E., 2000. Aging, obsolescence, and organizational innovation. *Administrative Science Quarterly*, 45(1): 81–112.

Teece D. J., 2007. Explicating dynamic capabilities: The nature and microfoundations of (sustainable) enterprise performance. *Strategic Management Journal*, 28(13): 1319–1350.

Trajtenberg M., 1990. A penny for your quotes: Patent citations and the value of innovations. *The Rand Journal of Economics*, 21(1): 172–187.

Trajtenberg M., Henderson R., Jaffe A., 1997. University versus corporate patents: A window on the basicness of invention. *Economics of Innovation and New Technology*, 5(1): 19–50.

Tuomo N., Raine H., Martti K., 2006. *Patent Citations Indicating Present Value of the Biotechnology Business*, ETLA Discussion Paper No. 1048, The Research Institute of the Finnish Economy (ETLA), Finland. Available at: https://ideas.repec.org/p/rif/dpaper/1048.html (accessed 10 September 2014).

Uhlenbruck K., Hitt M. A., Semadeni M., 2006. Market value effects of acquisitions involving internet firms: A resource-based analysis. *Strategic Management Journal*, 27(10): 899–913.

Vermeulen F., Barkema H., 2001. Learning through acquisitions. *Academy of Management Journal*, 44(3): 457–476.

Wernerfelt B., 1995. The resource-based view of the firm: Ten years after. *Strategic Management Journal*, 16(3): 171–174.

Yin X., Shanley M., 2008. Industry determinants of the 'merger versus alliance' decision. *Academy of Management Review*, 33(2): 473–491.

Zollo M., Reuer J. J., 2010. Experience spillovers across corporate development activities. *Organization Science*, 21(6): 1195–1212.

8 Post-M&A absorption-related invention capacity in the biopharmaceutical industry

Luigi Orsi, Andrea Ganzaroli and Ivan De Noni

Introduction

Recognizing the importance of external knowledge flows is fundamental in sectors characterized by dynamic information and strong intellectual property rights (Chesbrough, 2003). Consequently, firms have progressively forsaken the idea that new knowledge has to be generated through internal processes (Arora *et al.*, 2001; Gans and Stern, 2003) and have begun considering external knowledge appropriation. From this perspective, strategic alliances and mergers and acquisitions (M&As) are alternative organizational forms that, besides being renowned for their ability to promote entry into new markets and their effectiveness to achieve economies of scale and scope, have progressively become efficient means to access and assimilate knowledge from other organizations (De Man and Duysters, 2005).

Academic research concerning knowledge transfer through alliances and M&As has developed over recent years (Bresman *et al.*, 1999). The first to suggest that organizational learning could be a reason for the establishment of joint ventures was Kogut (1988). Specifically, he argued that a joint venture: 'is used for the transfer of organizationally embedded knowledge, which cannot be easily blueprinted or packaged thorough licensing or market transactions' (Kogut, 1988: 319). Related perspectives soon emerged (Westney, 1988; Hamel, 1991; Inkpen, 1992) and studies on the theme started to accumulate (e.g. Inkpen and Crossan, 1995; Doz, 1996; Mowery *et al.*, 1996), highlighting the importance not only of the transfer of knowledge but also of the ability to re-evaluate and learn from accessed knowledge in order to succeed – in other words, the crucial role of absorptive capacity. Some scholars have also considered the process of value creation through post-acquisition integration (Lindgren, 1982; Shrivastava, 1986; Haspeslagh and Jemison, 1991; Greenwood *et al.*, 1994; Hakanson, 1995), while Capron *et al.* (1998) concentrated on the role of resource redeployment and its impact on value creation in acquisitions.

Despite this work, however, little attention has been devoted to related modes of governance and poor results concerning their effects on knowledge transfer, absorptive capacity and innovation performance (Ahuja and Katila, 2001; Hagedoorn and Duysters, 2002b; Makri *et al.*, 2010). In fact, besides agreeing that the mere fact of exposure to flows of knowledge through interorganizational deals does not allow firms to benefit from them (Cohen and Levinthal, 1990), scholars have rarely focused on the assessment of benefits and returns of strategic alliances and technological acquisitions, of interorganizational deals established with the aim of acquiring external knowledge in order to exploit it and generate innovation. It is evident that firms engaged in strategic interorganizational agreements need to develop the ability first to recognize the value of new external knowledge and then to assimilate and employ such knowledge for commercial purpose (Cockburn and Henderson, 1998). The objective of this chapter, therefore, is to evaluate how a particular type of interorganizational agreement, M&As, allow the acquirer to exploit the target's knowledge base. In order to answer this question, we introduce the variable of 'absorption-related invention capacity' such as a measure of tangible firms' capacity to absorb, recombine and transform targets' knowledge bases, acquired in a specific M&A, in new knowledge and invention. We stress the fact that such capacity does not represent the company's whole absorptive capacity, which obviously depends on several organizational and dynamic aspects, but as the extent to which the target's knowledge base, acquired in M&A, has been assimilated and transformed into new knowledge.

We believe our study makes several contributions to the existing literature. First, it confirms the emphasis of prior work on the importance of the relatedness between the acquiring and the acquired knowledge bases in enhancing the ability of the acquiring firm to capture and reuse the knowledge produced by the target. However, this study goes beyond such results and introduces an element of novelty since it applies Makri *et al.*'s (2010) discrimination between the two main components of technological relatedness, similarities and complementarities, to the case of M&As in a specific environment: the biopharmaceutical industry. Second, the set of measures here employed goes beyond the literature, which has traditionally relied on patent counts, since our variables have been operationalized in terms of pre- and post-M&A cross-citations between patents of the acquirer and target involved in the M&A. We adopt this very specific measure as a proxy for absorption-related invention capacity of the acquiring firm, because it allows us to reach our goal of evaluating the ability of the acquirer to absorb a target's technological knowledge through the acquisition process, whereas other measures such as patent count, total citations, number of technological classes and their growth rates post M&A, are less adequate in depicting this aspect and reflect the influence of other factors. Third, this study indirectly corroborates the relevance of target selection, because it is through an appropriate selection of potential firms for acquisition or merger that it is possible to identify an adequate degree of technological relatedness to foster the innovative performance of the acquiring firm.

In the following section, we will first provide a literature review and a comprehensive explanation of our hypotheses. Next, we will illustrate our empirical analysis and our main results. The study then continues with a discussion of the main implications, after which some concluding remarks, limitations of the analysis and future research recommendations are presented.

The role of technological relatedness in absorption-related invention process

One of the primary elements to be considered when dealing with the acquirer's ability to internalize in the innovative process the knowledge created by the M&A partner using the target firm patents' portfolio, is the so-called technological relatedness of companies. Technological relatedness is generally conceived of in terms of similarities as: 'the degree to which companies are active in particular fields of technology that they share with (potential) partners in M&As' (Hagedoorn and Duysters, 2002a). In other words, technological relatedness is associated with the 'content' of the knowledge bases of the acquirer and target (Ahuja and Katila, 2001). Thus, two companies have a high technological relatedness when their knowledge bases belong to the same fields of technology, i.e. are similar to each other. The presence of a common ground is not only recommended but also necessary for companies involved in interorganizational collaborations (Lane and Lubatkin, 1998). Technological overlaps facilitate and strengthen absorptive capacity, exploitative learning and innovation, as well as enhance understanding of available information and resources and knowledge, enabling communication and learning (Cohen and Levinthal, 1990; Lane and Lubatkin, 1998; Ahuja and Katila, 2001). Thus, commonalities between the acquirer and target are likely to improve the former's ability to absorb and integrate the innovative knowledge stocks accessed through the M&A (Kogut and Zander, 1992; Grant, 1996), thereby fostering exploitation.

Phene *et al.* (2012) suggest, moreover, that overlaps might also increase exploration in the presence of technological uniqueness of the knowledge base of the target, since this is more likely to be recognized as valuable and easy to assimilate. The absorptive capacity perspective further suggests that when two firms with similar knowledge bases enter an M&A, they share analogous sets of 'know-whats' and 'know-hows' (Lubatkin *et al.*, 2001), facing fewer difficulties in absorbing, understanding and applying the new knowledge (Cohen and Levinthal, 1990; Lane and Lubatkin, 1998). Thus, knowledge similarity facilitates the exchange and combination of existing knowledge (Nonaka *et al.*, 1996) and encourages its exploitation, resulting in an increased number of post-M&A citations of the target pre-M&A granted patents, as well as in a growth of invention quantity in the technology areas in which the acquirer operated before the M&A. Therefore, we suppose:

Hypothesis 1:   *There exists a positive relationship between technological relatedness measured in terms of technological similarity of the acquirer and target and the absorption-related invention capacity of the acquirer.*

A second crucial factor closely connected to technological relatedness is its depth, better known as 'technological complementarity' (Hagedoorn and Duysters, 2002a). Technological complementarity refers to the degree to which research efforts of companies entering into M&As complement each other. Although it is obvious that distant and divergent knowledge bases are not always mutually complementary, it is equally clear that, when considering strategic collaboration deals involving companies within the same industry, dissimilar knowledge and competencies still have some elements of commonality and are likely to be complementary. Therefore, researchers on the theme rely on the assumption that resource heterogeneity between M&A participants fosters learning and innovation (Hagedoorn, 1993; Powell *et al.*, 1996; Ahuja, 2000; Rowley *et al.*, 2000; Rosenkopf and Almeida, 2003), notwithstanding the fact that previous literature has shown a tendency to overvalue the benefits of resource homogeneity.

An excessive focus on the undeniably positive effects of knowledge similarity might lead one to ignore the benefits of related variety (Frenken *et al.*, 2007; Boschma and Iammarino, 2009), such as enabling a broadening of the firms' cognitive base, further development of absorptive capacity due to the access to a greater variety of knowledge, exploration of new opportunities and stimulation of creativity and thus radical innovation (Burt, 2005). Conversely to similarity, complementarity in knowledge and technology bases enhances exploration and the subsequent creation of disruptive inventions (March, 1991). This holds in spite of the fact that complementary technology is more complex and challenging than similar knowledge and its efficient integration might require significant effort (Grant, 1996), with relied high integration costs (Katila and Ahuja, 2002). Consequently, we posit:

Hypothesis 2:   *There exists a positive relationship between technological relatedness measured in terms of the technological complementarity of the acquirer and target and the absorption-related invention capacity of the acquirer.*

Theoretical analysis and empirical evidences have stressed the complexity to balance similarity and complementarity by further suggesting a U-shaped relationship between technological relatedness and absorptive capacity (Hagedoorn and Duysters, 2002a; Makri *et al.*, 2010). In fact, the presence of common skills, shared languages and similar cognitive structures enables and simplifies technical communication and learning (Cohen and Levinthal, 1989; Lane and Lubatkin, 1998), while similar knowledge bases demolish integration barriers (Kogut and Zander, 1992; Grant, 1996). Nonetheless, when the target and acquirer knowledge bases are too similar, this might result in little contribution to subsequent innovation performance (Ahuja and Katila, 2001). Therefore, a moderate degree of relatedness generates the best benefits for innovation by improving absorption-related invention capacity, since it facilitates interaction between the acquirer and the targets because of the presence of some elements of commonality.

Similarly, although a certain degree of complementarity fosters exploration and innovation output variety (Ahuja and Katila, 2001), an excessive level, in which acquirer and target activities concern markedly different technological fields, will have negative effects on absorption-related invention capacity since few elements of commonality will be available to facilitate the process of acquisition, understanding and assimilation of external knowledge. Therefore, we suppose:

Hypothesis 3:   *Technological relatedness measured in terms of technological similarities of the acquirer and target is curvilinearly (inverted U-shape) related to absorption-related invention capacity.*

Hypothesis 4:   *Technological relatedness measured in terms of the technological complementarities of the acquirer and target is curvilinearly (inverted U-shape) related to absorption-related invention capacity.*

The effect of alliance and M&A experience in capturing the knowledge produced by the partner firm

Previous literature has proved relational capabilities – alliance and M&A management experience –play an essential role in interorganizational knowledge transfer by means of strategic alliances and M&As (Kogut and Zander, 1992, 1996). Besides the various possible reasons for failures of alliance and acquisition agreements, some contributions have provided evidence that firms with alliance and M&A management capabilities learn to create more value from such deals. Among other causes, failures might be due to a lack of relational capabilities and experience in managing alliances and acquisitions, which develop through repeated engagements in interorganizational collaborations (e.g. Simonin, 1999; Anand and Khanna, 2000; Rothaermel and Deeds, 2006). In fact, repeatedly engaging in alliances and/or M&As over time allows firms to create codified routines, procedures and tacit knowledge with respect to alliance management, from partner selection and alliance formation to deal management and termination (Rothaermel and Deeds, 2006).

Parallel to this, we suppose that the more developed an acquirer's relational capabilities – the more the acquiring firm has participated in R&D alliances and/ or completed M&As in the past – the better it is able to manage current deals in the form of both alliances and M&As. Hence, its post-M&A absorption-related invention capacity should increase, since it has already developed the ability to absorb external knowledge through several past engagements, having developed new routines and practices which should help in identifying, recognizing, understanding, absorbing, integrating and exploiting external knowledge. Therefore, we posit:

Hypothesis 5:   *There exists a positive relationship between the acquirer's alliance management capabilities and its absorption-related invention capacity.*

Hypothesis 6:   *There exists a positive relationship between the acquirer's M&A management capabilities and its absorption-related invention capacity.*

Concerning the acquirer's alliance and M&A management capabilities, some scholars have suggested that they might exhibit diminishing marginal returns (e.g. Hoang and Rothaermel, 2005). In other words, acquirers accumulating experience in managing alliances and M&As through repeated engagements in such collaborative deals initially outperform those with few or no such management capabilities, but this comparative gain for their economic returns and the capacity to absorb external knowledge gradually declines. In other words, interorganizational learning and knowledge accumulation depreciate over time (Darr *et al.*, 1995). In addition, companies usually enter the most promising collaborations first, with the consequence that the contribution of subsequent M&As in terms of opportunities and outcomes is relatively limited or even negative (Deeds and Hill, 1996; Silverman and Baum, 2002). Further, since these capabilities are path dependent, firms might tend to focus continuously on similar deals providing little or no additional learning (Sampson, 2002). Consequently, although alliance and M&A management capabilities allow firms to simultaneously engage in multiple agreements and obtain positive outcomes, beyond some optimum any additional deal will have declining benefits. Hence, we assume:

Hypothesis 7:   *The acquirer's alliance management capability is curvilinearly (inverted U-shape) related to its absorption-related invention capacity.*

Hypothesis 8:   *The acquirer's M&A management capability is curvilinearly (inverted U-shape) related to its absorption-related invention capacity.*

Methodology

Research setting

The hypotheses listed in Table 8.1 were developed and tested with reference to the biopharmaceutical industry. There were several reasons for this choice of industry. First, biotechnology is one of the most prominent technologies to have emerged over the last 40 years. Second, previous literature portrays biopharmaceuticals as a high-technology and knowledge-intensive industry, mostly because of its relatively recent birth and its complex and rapidly expanding knowledge base (Chang, 2008). Furthermore, biotechnology has proved to be competence-destroying in upstream R&D, although competence-preserving in downstream commercialization activities (Powell *et al.*, 1996) and its advent has determined a radical reshaping of the competitive basis (Schweizer, 2005). Third, the industry comprises heterogeneous networks of technology-devoted companies (Gottinger and Umali, 2008), with an extensive number of firms originally established as dedicated-biotech organizations having evolved into pharmaceutical companies in such a way, indeed, that a well-known joke states that: 'biotech companies are pharma companies without sales' (*The Economist*, 2003). Additionally, although not the only industry characterized by an important alliance activity,

Table 8.1 Hypotheses

Hypotheses		
Independent variable	*Dependent variable*	*Expected effect*
1 Technological similarity	Absortion-related invention	Positive
2 Technological complementarity	Absortion-related invention	Positive
3 Technological similarity	Absortion-related invention	Non-linear (inverted U)
4 Technological complementarity	Absortion-related invention	Non-linear (inverted U)
5 Alliance management capabilities	Absortion-related invention	Positive
6 M&A management capabilities	Absortion-related invention	Positive
7 Alliance management capabilities	Absortion-related invention	Non-linear (inverted U)
8 M&A management capabilities	Absortion-related invention	Non-linear (inverted U)

Source: Authors' elaboration.

the biopharmaceutical firm does have the highest alliance frequency (Hagedoorn, 1993; Senker and Sharp, 1997; Rothaermel, 2000). Support and empirical evidence have been provided by several studies confirming that alliances are frequently established within the industry with the aim of accessing capabilities and knowledge which are essential to achieve competitive advantage and thus a positive economic performance (e.g. Rothaermel, 2001, 2000; Rothaermel and Boeker, 2008; Adegbesan and Higgins, 2011).

Similarly, the industry has witnessed a considerable M&A activity (Goldman Sachs, 2001). M&As and strategic alliances occur for identical reasons: pharmaceutical companies need access to the knowledge and research capabilities embedded in biotech companies. Nonetheless, such capabilities have been shown to be context-specific and difficult to transfer, so many pharmaceuticals' acquisitions have not yet generated benefits (Bower, 2001). This has two main causes. On the one hand, there is the trade-off facing acquirers. They have to choose between the need to integrate acquired biotech companies in order to absorb and exploit their research and innovative capabilities and the need to preserve their autonomy, so as not to compromise the maintenance and development of these capabilities. On the other hand, there are the difficulties and negative outcomes that may arise from organizational and cultural differences between biotech and pharma companies. In general, biotech firms are dynamic, lean and effective in fostering innovation, since they are characterized by low levels of hierarchy, open communication and informal organizational structures, flexibility, risk taking inclination and significant ownership participation among employees; pharmaceutical companies, by contrast, usually have a formal structure, high levels of hierarchy and slow decision-making processes (Powell *et al.*, 1996).

Sample and data sources

We tested our hypotheses on a cross-sectional data set encompassing the acquisitions, patenting activities and R&D alliances of 152 firms from the biopharmaceutical industry engaged in 218 M&As completed during the period 2001–2005. We looked at companies in the biopharmaceutical and biotechnology industries that focused on human therapeutic and diagnostic applications – biomaterials and tissue regeneration, blood products, gene therapy, stem cell therapy, vaccines and bio-diagnostic products (Rothaermel and Boeker, 2008). We employed a three-step process that started from a list of all deals in the industry and extracted 229 firms, which were then reduced to the sample of 152 independent acquirers.

To begin with, a complete list of all deals in the biopharmaceutical industry without any filter regarding deal type, date, value or country was obtained from Medtrack. Medtrack was used because: (1) it provides a comprehensive view of the biopharmaceutical business panorama by offering insights into pharmaceutical pipelines, sales, epidemiology, patents and deals along with detailed profiles of 23,000 companies; (2) it automatically identifies all name variants of the acquirer and target firms (names of divisions, subsidiaries, previous names, etc.), which permitted us to directly match the list of contacts with that of deals, preventing time dissipation due to the standardization of alternative versions; and (3) other authors in previous works employed Medtrack to identify their samples (e.g. Diestre and Rajagopalan, 2012).

Next, we selected all M&As completed between 2001 and 2005 that involved either a North American or European company as an acquirer classified as active in 2005. As in the literature (e.g. Ahuja and Katila, 2001; Hagedoorn and Duysters, 2002a; Diestre and Rajagopalan, 2012), we selected a six-year window of observation, since the level of our analysis refers to the companies engaged in M&As and not to individual M&As. Furthermore, as Hagedoorn and Duysters (2002) pointed out, the combined effect of a number of acquisitions of a company is discernible, whereas that of a single agreement is rather difficult to ascertain. Lastly, we adopted the approach of Ahuja and Katila (2001) and Makri *et al.* (2010) and excluded all M&As unlikely to generate science and technology inputs, and thus innovative output, ignoring, therefore, deals that were concluded in order to gain access to distribution or entry into new markets, obtain financial synergies or increase market power. Hence, the sample resulting from the first step had 229 companies playing the role of acquirers and 401 companies playing the role of targets in 404 M&As.

In the second step, we considered information for the construction of our control variables. Medtrack provided these data for nearly the whole sample. Nonetheless, we proceeded with a double check of their verity and gathering of missing information. Three distinct data banks were employed for their different levels of detail: Amadeus, Compustat and Orbis. Financial and corporate data about European firms were obtained from Amadeus; Compustat was used to gather information about non-European listed companies; and Orbis was employed in order to obtain data on unlisted sampled firms. Additionally, missing data were directly obtained from the official websites of companies.

In the last stage we obtained data regarding patents of both the acquirer and target firms through the Orbit-QPat database. Although previous works (Ahuja and Katila, 2001; Hagedoorn and Duysters, 2002b; Makri *et al.*, 2010; Diestre and Rajagopalan, 2012) had utilized data on patents taken from US databases, we decided to employ Orbit-QPat, for two main reasons. First, our primary aim was to analyse a firm's ability to patent and protect its knowledge internationally and Orbit-QPat provides an extensive coverage with 95 patent authorities; second, this database is characterized by a great flexibility, which allowed us to identify and export fundamental data for the construction of our key measures.

By considering each firm in the sample, regardless of its role in the M&A, we specifically exported patents in the period 1995–2011 within the PlusPat collection. As expected, many companies had to be excluded from our sample because they were granted no patents in the time window determined. Hence, our ultimate sample was reduced to 152 acquirers engaged in 218 M&As.

Variables

Following the literature, the time lag required to effectively measure the influence of M&As on acquirers' innovation performance is approximately an average period of six years. Singh (1971) and Buono and Bowditch (1989) advocate it takes on average nearly five years before acquired organizations are assimilated and the benefits of an M&A emerge. These studies also indicate considerable variation in the assimilation process, since some companies are able to merge their organizations within one year, while others take considerably longer than the average. Furthermore, Pakes and Griliches (1984) and Ravenscraft and Scherer (1987) maintain that it typically takes about one year before R&D-derived inventions can become patent applications. Therefore, combining these two periods, we reach an average time lag of about six years (Hagedoorn and Duysters, 2002a). Both dependent and exploratory variables are defined with respect to the reference period. Moreover, to operationalize our measures relating to patents, we used the application date as reference.

Dependent variable

Absorption-related invention is a very specific measure of an acquirer's capacity to absorb, recombine and transform a target's knowledge base, acquired in an M&A, in new knowledge and invention. It is an indicator of the acquirer's ability to productively manage the M&A process and use a certain set of patents (more precisely, the targets' patents) to stimulate and support their invention and patenting activities (Makri *et al.*, 2010). During the process of M&A, if an acquirer firm is able to include in its patents, the patents of the target firm, this means that the realized acquisition has the benefit of the new knowledge discovered by the target. Thus, we are interested in seeing if a specific process of knowledge absorption is realized by the acquirer after its process of M&A and which factors affected this capability.

To operationalize this variable, we considered data on the patents of both of the M&A partners and specifically we looked at the application numbers and date of the target's patents. At this point, we observe if the target patents are cited in the acquirer's patent reference (looking also at the application date of the acquirer), always considering a time lag of one to six years in the pre-M&A and post-M&A periods. Orbit-QPat allowed us to match the patent numbers of the target and the acquirer in a simple manner, using the 'cross search patent number' (XPN) of the target with the 'cross search cited number' (XCT) contained in the patents' citations field of the acquirer patent portfolio. We then calculated the number of citations[1] that patents, granted to the target before the M&A, received by the acquirer in the post-M&A period.

It was difficult to calculate a growth rate between pre- and post-M&A citations, because of the number of zeros in pre-M&A acquirers' target citations that would have led to undetermined results of the change measure and a subsequent significant reduction in the sample size. To capture the change in acquirer-target citation outcomes in pre and post M&A, we calculated the total number of citations the target firm's patents receive from the acquiring firm's patents during the post-M&A period, dividing that by the total number of acquirer patents produced in the same period (i.e. we created an average citations-per-patent ratio post M&A). We did the same for the six-year window pre M&A creating an average citations-per-patent ratio pre M&A. Thus we constructed a continuous variable given by the difference between the citations per-patent-ratio pre and post M&A.

Absorption-related invention capacity =

$$\frac{\sum_{i=1}^{n} n.citing.post_j}{n.acq.pat.post} - \frac{\sum_{i=1}^{n} n.citing.pre_j}{n.acq.pat.pre}$$

where i is the ith acquirer patent; n is the total number of patents granted to the acquirer in the six-year window; $n.citing.post_j$ is the number of citations received by target patents in the six-year post-M&A period; $n.citing.pre_j$ is the number of citations received by target patents in the six-year pre-M&A period; and $n.acq. pat.post$ and *pre* are the total number of acquirers' patents in the two periods.

We assumed that the higher the value of this variable, the greater the ability of the acquiring firm to absorb the innovative knowledge created by the target firm. Absorption-related invention involved in multiple acquisition processes was estimated by considering an average value.

Exploratory variables

Technology similarity is introduced as a measure of technological relatedness between M&A partners, since it captures the extent to which the two firms patented in the same classes, i.e. they were employing similar technological knowledge (Ahuja and Katila, 2001; Rosenkopf and Almeida, 2003; Makri *et al.*, 2010; Diestre and Rajagopalan, 2012). Based on prior research, we operationalized this using the number of patents filed in the same four-digit subclasses one to six years before the M&A, in order to attenuate fluctuations and capture relevant knowledge stocks (Rothaermel and Boeker, 2008; Diestre and Rajagopalan, 2012). We calculated technological similarity numerically as the product between two ratios: (1) the first given by the total number of patents the partners applied for in the same technological subclasses divided by the total number of patents of the acquirer and target; and (2) the second by the total number of patents of the acquirer in all common subclasses divided by the total number of acquirer patents. The formula is the following:

$$Similarity = \frac{Overlap \, all \, patent \, subclasses}{Total \, patents \, acquirer + target}$$
$$* \frac{Total \, acquirer \, patents \, in \, common \, subclasses}{Total \, acquirer \, patents}$$

We computed technology similarity for companies engaged in multiple agreements as an average value. Additionally, we considered *technology similarity squared* to test assumptions of inverted U-shaped relationships.

Technology complementarity is a measure employed to capture the integrative potential of the M&A partners. As Makri *et al.* (2010) maintained, although technology similarity is an adequate proxy of the similarity of technological assets, it is only a part of the broad concept of technological relatedness and is not, in fact, able to capture possible technological complementarity existing between partners. Therefore, we introduced this second independent variable – here operationalized as the number of patents applied for in the same section (one-digit), but in different subclasses (four-digit), by the acquirer and target in the one- to six-year period preceding the M&A – using the following formula:

$$Complementarity = \frac{Overlap \, all \, patent \, sections}{Total \, patents \, acquirer + target}$$
$$- \frac{Overlap \, all \, patent \, subclasses}{Total \, patents \, acquirer + target}$$
$$* \frac{Total \, acquirer \, patents \, in \, common \, section}{Total \, acquirer \, patents}$$

We computed an average value for multiple agreements and also considered a squared measure, *technology complementarity squared*.

Alliance management capabilities is a measure that captures the acquirer's ability to manage deals with other firms. The literature classifies it as a dynamic capability that contributes to the achievement of a competitive advantage (Teece *et al.*, 1997) by increasing firms' capacity to manage several alliances (Rothaermel and Deeds, 2006). Although believing that a proxy based on the cumulative sum of the alliance duration for each of the firm's alliances, such as that developed by Rothaermel and Deeds (2006), is coherent with the theoretical assumption that at a firm level this kind of experience is accumulated through learning-by-doing over time, we adopted the traditional perspective (Shan *et al.*, 1994; Deeds and Hill, 1996; Anand and Khanna, 2000; Kale *et al.*, 2002; Sampson, 2002; Rothaermel and Deeds, 2004; Hoang and Rothaermel, 2005). Therefore, we measured alliance management capabilities using a simple count of each firm's alliances. Particularly, we considered the total number of R&D alliances (excluding alliances with the target) for the one to six years before the acquirer entered its first M&A in the focal period. We then squared the variable in order to test for diminishing marginal returns on technological performance.

Finally, a measure of *M&A management capabilities* was introduced, calculated as the number of acquisitions the acquirer completed in the period before completion of the first M&A process (Diestre and Rajagopalan, 2012).

Control variables

Several variables might be correlated with the firm's ability to capture the knowledge created by the target firm using the acquirer-target citation outcomes and, thus, with its innovative performance. Therefore, we controlled for some possible confounding effects, including *technological diversification of the acquirer* and *technological diversification of the target* (operationalized through a diversification measure based on the Shannon Entropy index:

$$\sum_{j=1}^{n} P_j * ln\left(\frac{1}{P_j}\right)$$

where P_j was defined as the percentage of a firm's patents in the four-digit patent classes j; $ln(1/P_j)$ was the weight for each patent classes j, with n as the total number of classes the firm patented in).

Other control variables were: *firm's size* (as the number of employees in the year of the first M&A); *firm's age*; *country of origin* (dummy 1 = North America, 0 = Europe); *public* (dummy 1 = firm's stock publicly traded in 2005, 0 = otherwise); *products* (number of drugs developed in the past); *post M&A* (number of M&As completed in the one to six years after the sampled M&A); *total M&As* (number of M&As completed in the focal period); and *international M&As* (share of international M&As in the total number of M&As in the focal period). Further, we considered pre-M&A citations, calculated as the number of citations that patents granted to the target before the M&A were received by the acquirer in the pre-M&A period. This allowed us to understand the influence of the stock of *citations* on the change in absorption-related invention capacity of the acquirer, according to the following formula:

Pre-M&A citations $\sum_{i=1}^{n} n.citing.pre_j$

where i is the ith acquirer patent, n is the total number of patents granted to the acquirer in the one- to six-year window pre M&A and *n.citing.pre$_j$* is the number of citations received by target patents in the one- to six-year window pre M&A.

Statistical analysis

As previously explained, the unit of our analysis is the acquirer firm. Since dependent variables, measuring the change in *absorption-related invention pre and post M&A*, are continuous variables, an ordinary least squares (OLS) model can be implemented.

Independent variables are not highly correlated among themselves or with control variables, with the exception of *technological similarity* and *complementarity*, whose correlation is large and negative (-0.765). However, this is not surprising, since we have argued that similarity and complementarity are the two fundamental components of technological relatedness and hence expected them to be somewhat correlated. In addition, it is reasonable to assume that if the acquirer and target knowledge bases are similar, their level of complementarity decreases, whereas in the case of dissimilarity, the likelihood of complementarity rises.

Some of the control variables show important correlations, notably *firm size* and *products* (0.777). This is plausible, since larger companies are likely to have more products on the market and this latter measure can be conceived as an alternative proxy of firm size. Hence, we decided to exclude the control variable *products* from our regression models.

Multicollinearity diagnostics were examined by applying additional tests to detect possible multicollinearity. We found that regressing each independent variable on all the other independent variables did not indicate multicollinearity (with the exception of the quadratic variables). In addition, we explicitly assessed potential multicollinearity in our model, finding that the variance inflation factors were well below the suggested cut-off point of ten (Kleinbaum *et al.*, 1988). Table 8.4 provides the results of this (reported with standard errors). The variables reflecting the hypothesized effects were entered individually into the regressions and adjusted R^2 as well as F tests are reported.

Although dealing with multiple years of data, a cross-sectional rather than panel data analysis was preferred, because many of the independent and control variables varied little or not at all over time. Hence, panel data analysis with almost identical explanatory variables would add very little information and increase dependence across residuals (Diestre and Rajagopalan, 2012). Moreover, the adoption of cross-sectional analysis is consistent with prior studies (Hagedoorn and Duysters, 2002b; Rothaermel and Boeker, 2008; Makri *et al.*, 2010).

Results

Our sample includes 59 European (Germany = 14, United Kingdom = 9, Switzerland = 9, Denmark = 5, Ireland = 4, Italy = 4, Netherlands = 4, Sweden = 4, Spain = 3, etc.) and 93 North American (US = 83 and Canada = 10) firms.

In our sample 36 companies were engaged in multiple M&As during the focal period (e.g. Johnson & Johnson = 7, Pfizer = 7, Abbott Laboratories = 5, Integra Lifesciences = 5, Genzyme Corp. = 4, Agilent Technologies = 4, Angiotech Inc. = 4, Cephanlon = 3), while the remaining were involved in only 1 acquisition. The average number of M&As in the focal period was 1.46 and varied from a minimum of 0 to a maximum of 7. The average acquirer firm was about 31 years old at the time of the first M&A in the focal period and had 7,821 employees. More specifically, the oldest company was founded in 1849 (Pfizer Inc.) and the youngest in April 2003 (Bioceros), which suggested its participation in an M&A immediately after its foundation. The minimum number of employees was recorded by Jazz Pharmaceuticals Plc, Nutra Pharma Corporation, and Whatman Plc, and was equal to 3, while the maximum was 127,600 people employed by Johnson & Johnson. Finally, with reference to the status of the acquirers in the sample, i.e. whether they were public or private companies, it resulted that 101 of them were listed on the stock exchange while the remaining 51 were unlisted. Table 8.2 displays descriptive statistics, with Table 8.3 providing correlations for each of the variables.

All econometric models are presented in Table 8.4. Model 1 includes only the control variables for this regression and shows that the acquisition, where both partners have diversified knowledge bases (especially the target knowledge base,

Table 8.2 Descriptive statistics

Variables	Mean	S.D.	Min	Max	Count
Absorption-related invention	0.044	0.271	−0.585	1.833	152
Technological similarity	0.452	0.329	0	1	152
Technological complementarity	0.309	0.238	−0.018	0.997	152
Alliance management capabilities	8.020	15.435	0	106	152
M&A management capabilities	0.454	1.190	0	8	152
Acquirer diversification	1.661	0.667	0	4.057	152
Target diversification	1.413	0.702	0	3.451	152
No. of citations pre M&A	9.961	30.710	0	185	152
Public	0.664	0.474	0	1	152
Region	0.579	0.495	0	1	152
Firm size	7821.908	20688.367	3	127,600	152
Products	121.599	259.954	0	1,653	152
Firm age	31.296	36.092	1	154	152
Year of foundation	1971	36.150	1849	2003	152
Year of the first M&A in focal period	2003	1.520	2001	2005	152
Total M&As in focal period	1.461	1.079	1	7	152
International M&A ratio	0.509	0.631	0	3	152

Source: Authors' elaboration.

Table 8.3 Pearson's correlation matrix

Variables	1	2	3	4	5	6	7	8	9	10	11	12	13	14	15
1 Absorption-related invention	1.000														
2 Technological similarity	0.131	1.000													
3 Technological complementarity	-0.009	-0.765	1.000												
4 Alliance management capabilities	0.160	0.066	0.016	1.000											
5 M&A management capabilities	0.074	-0.104	0.101	0.328	1.000										
6 Acquirer diversification	0.164	-0.165	0.090	0.183	0.219	1.000									
7 Target diversification	0.163	0.141	-0.105	0.075	0.143	0.231	1.000								
8 No. of citations pre M&A	0.071	0.303	-0.231	0.163	-0.017	0.087	0.082	1.000							
9 Public	0.085	0.112	-0.011	0.235	0.084	0.025	0.039	0.166	1.000						
10 Region	0.192	0.108	0.010	0.063	0.001	0.146	0.044	0.147	0.128	1.000					
11 Firm size	0.020	-0.091	0.105	0.537	0.367	0.307	0.042	0.058	0.210	0.047	1.000				
12 Products	0.012	0.042	0.051	0.579	0.268	0.085	-0.069	0.086	0.170	-0.041	0.777	1.000			
13 Firm age	-0.104	-0.166	0.012	0.335	0.271	0.091	-0.027	0.124	0.047	-0.061	0.434	0.372	1.000		
14 Total M&As in focal period	0.050	-0.165	0.165	0.322	0.306	0.271	-0.010	0.020	0.110	0.167	0.584	0.470	0.264	1.000	
15 International M&A ratio	-0.094	-0.008	-0.046	-0.123	0.170	-0.028	0.037	-0.107	0.032	-0.400	-0.003	0.003	0.114	-0.079	1.000

Source: Authors' elaboration.

Table 8.4 The effect of technological similarity and complementarity, alliance and M&A management capabilities on absorption-related invention

Variables	Model 1: control variable	Hypothesis 1	Hypothesis 3	Hypothesis 2
	Coeff. (Std. err.)	Model 2: similarity	Model 3: similarity^2	Model 4: complementarity
		Coeff. (Std. err.)	Coeff. (Std. err.)	Coeff. (Std. err.)
Intercept	−2.425** (0.831)	−3.037** (0.968)	−3.405** (1.06)	−2.387** (0.873)
Similarity		0.956** (0.366)	3.247*** (0.871)	
Similarity^2			−2.309** (0.773)	
Complementarity				−0.051 (0.873)
Complementarity^2				
Alliance management capabilities				
Alliance management capabilities^2				
M&A management capabilities				
M&A management capabilities^2				
Diversification acquirer	0.469* (0.215)	0.584† (0.311)	0.649† (0.371)	0.468* (0.226)
Diversification target	0.460** (0.156)	0.411** (0.197)	0.399* (0.203)	0.452** (0.139)
Public	0.377 (0.430)	0.342 (0.438)	0.325 (0.439)	0.362 (0.434)
Region	0.781** (0.277)	0.716** (0.215)	0.694* (0.269)	0.769** (0.289)
Size	0.022 (0.101)	0.026 (0.101)	0.019 (0.101)	0.02 (0.101)
Age	−0.293† (0.167)	−0.274† (0.149)	−0.264† (0.148)	−0.295* (0.147)
Total M&A	−0.004 (0.186)	0.026 (0.186)	0.003 (0.188)	0.001 (0.188)
International M&A ratio	−0.084 (0.365)	−0.118 (0.377)	−0.117 (0.381)	−0.075 (0.368)
No. of citations pre-M&A	0.003 (0.008)	0.002 (0.006)	0.001 (0.007)	0.001 (0.006)
Adjusted R squared	0.326	0.345	0.347	0.331
F (df)	2.289 (9)	2.283 (10)	2.230 (11)	2.282 (10)
p value	0.020	0.016	0.015	0.016

Significant codes: † $p<0.10$; * $p<0.05$; ** $p<0.01$; *** $p<0.001$

Source: Authors' elaboration.

Hypothesis 4	Hypotheses 5 and 6	Hypothesis 7	Hypothesis 8
Model 5: complementarity^2	*Model 6: alliance and M&A experience*	*Model 7: alliance experience^2*	*Model 8: M&A experience^2*
Coeff. (Std. err.)	Coeff. (Std. err.)	Coeff. (Std. err.)	Coeff. (Std. err.)
−2.412 (0.881)**	−2.072* (0.875)	−2.238** (0.861)	−2.421 (0.891)**
0.487 (2.638)			
−0.679 (3.145)			
	0.024*** (0.004)	0.061*** (0.016)	
		−0.001* (0.000)	
	0.084* (0.035)		1.245** (0.464)
			−0.219* (0.101)
0.457† (0.257)	0.473 (0.352)	0.389† (0.228)	0.463 (0.354)
0.446** (0.168)	0.423* (0.196)	0.476* (0.233)	0.499* (0.218)
0.358 (0.435)	0.23 (0.445)	0.109 (0.455)	0.587 (0.457)
0.771*** (0.219)	0.892** (0.273)	0.987** (0.324)	0.712** (0.256)
0.019 (0.101)	−0.019 (0.105)	−0.015 (0.105)	−0.038 (0.107)
−0.295† (0.177)	−0.383† (0.209)	−0.378 (0.210)†	−0.311* (0.155)
−0.004 (0.189)	−0.083 (0.193)	−0.041 (0.188)	−0.035 (0.201)
−0.074 (0.368)	0.041 (0.378)	0.107 (0.377)	−0.062 (0.383)
0.002 (0.006)	0.001 (0.006)	0.000 (0.006)	0.001 (0.006)
0.329	0.333	0.352	0.349
2.163 (11)	2.202 (11)	2.341 (11)	2.250 (11)
0.019	0.017	0.011	0.014

p < 0.01), is more likely to strengthen post-M&A absorption-related invention capacity. This result is consistent with the argument that a target's diversification increases acquirer R&D efforts and thus the development of its capacity to absorb new knowledge from the target in several fields, allowing a better evaluation and exploitation of available findings and opportunities (Cohen and Levinthal, 1990). Further, previous literature (Villalonga and McGahan, 2005) maintains that the likelihood of successful post-M&A integration is enhanced by the growth in the level of diversification because of the subsequent increase of commonalities between the participants. The model also signals that acquirers based in the US (p < 0.01), together with younger firms (p < 0.1), are more likely to further develop and enhance their post-M&A absorption-related invention. Generally, one would expect organizational age to be positively related to absorptive capacity, but older firms show a greater tendency to build on older technology when compared to younger firms. Moreover, innovations of older firms are generally less influential than those of younger firms (Sorenson and Stuart, 2000; Nooteboom *et al.*, 2007). The *size* of the firm, the *type of ownership*, the *international M&A ratio* and the number of citations before M&A, were not found to be significant. The results for the number of citations before M&A are especially interesting, because they suggest that a certain awareness of the target's knowledge base, resulting in pre-M&A citations from the acquirer, is not related to the change in post-M&A absorption-related invention capacity. Nonetheless, and rather surprisingly perhaps, we found that prior alliance experience with the target is not significant for the likelihood of an M&A (only two firms in our sample had made an R&D alliance before the M&A), meaning that having previously worked with a target firm in the biotech sector is not an essential element of the acquisition process.

Model 2 adds the first measure of technological relatedness: technological similarity. The results here depict a positive and statistically significant interaction between technology similarity and absorption-related invention capacity (p < 0.01), in support of Hypothesis 1. An inverted U-shaped relationship between technological similarity and absorption-related invention (Model 3) is highlighted and statistically significant in support of Hypothesis 3. Models 4 and 5 test Hypotheses 2 and 4. Contrary to our predictions, complementarity seems to have a negative impact on absorption-related invention capacity and an inverted U-shaped relationship is found; but none of these results has statistical significance.

Our findings, in model 6, corroborate Hypotheses 5, 6, 7 and 8, suggesting that higher levels of prior experience in dealing with R&D alliances (p < 0.001) and M&As (p < 0.05) strengthen post-M&A absorption-related invention capacity, but in both cases at the price of decreasing marginal returns beyond some optimum (models 7 and 8).

Discussion

The purpose of this study was to examine acquirer post-M&A absorption-related invention capacity, building on a measure based on patent citations. We focused on technological acquisitions in the biopharmaceutical industry. First, we observed the main effects of technological relatedness on our measure of absorption-related invention, discriminating between technological similarity and complementarity. Then, we focused on the impact of alliance and M&A management capabilities. As in previous studies (e.g. Makri *et al.*, 2010), our empirical results show that technological relatedness is complex and that, as well as conceiving of this in terms of technological similarity, other aspects of relatedness, particularly that of technological complementarity, should be considered.

Our findings on technological similarity are interesting and potentially relevant. Technological similarity has a positive linear effect on absorption-related invention capacity (Hypothesis 1) and an inverted U-shaped relationship (Hypothesis 3). These results are consistent with previous research (e.g. Lane and Lubatkin, 1998; Makri *et al.*, 2010), since it suggests that in the presence of a certain degree of similarity between acquirer and target knowledge bases, post-M&A absorptive capacity is enhanced and integration facilitated, although when the acquirer and target knowledge bases are too similar, this might result in little contribution to subsequent knowledge integration performance No statistical significance is found in support of either Hypotheses 2 or 4, indicating that complementary technology has no influence on acquirer post-M&A absorption-related invention capacity.

Finally, with reference to our third independent variable, alliance and M&A management capabilities, findings overall suggest that such capabilities are far more significant than technological similarity and complementarity in determining post-M&A absorption-related invention capacity. In fact, alliance management capabilities seems to strengthen post-M&A absorption-related invention capacity. M&A management capabilities have a less significant impact than the strategic alliances experience, but still positive and stimulating for the ability to absorb knowledge from the target. Both management capabilities and alliances' experience show an inverted U-shaped relationship with absorption-related invention. These results are consistent with previous literature and our assumptions. Firms create codified routines, policies, procedures and tacit knowledge with respect to partner selection and deal formation, management and termination through repeated engagements in strategic alliances (Rothaermel and Deeds, 2006). Hence, alliance and M&A management capabilities positively affect post-M&A absorption-related invention (e.g. Shan *et al.*, 1994; Deeds and Hill, 1996; Powell *et al.*, 1996; Anand and Khanna, 2000; Gray *et al.*, 2001; Takeishi, 2001; Sampson, 2002). Nonetheless, alliance and M&A management capabilities exhibit diminishing marginal returns, meaning that up to a certain point, companies having accumulated experience in the past outperform in the post-M&A period those with little or no capabilities, but beyond some optimum experience, dealing with alliances and M&A negatively influences their capacity to absorb knowledge directly from the target firm. As suggested, this might be due to the fact that interorganizational learning and knowledge accumulation depreciate over time (Darr *et al.*, 1995), as well as the fact that companies usually enter the most promising collaboration first, with the consequence that the contribution of subsequent M&As in terms of opportunities and outcomes is limited or even negative (Deeds and Hill, 1996; Silverman and Baum, 2002). Furthermore, since these capabilities are path dependent, firms might tend to focus continuously on similar deals providing little or no additional learning (Sampson, 2002). Consequently, although alliance and M&A management capabilities allow firms to simultaneously engage in multiple agreements and obtain positive outcomes, beyond some optimum level any additional deal will fail to significantly improve the firms' performances.

Theoretical and research implications

Looking at the theoretical and research implications of our findings, we believe that this research makes several important contributions. Essentially, it provides a deeper, context-specific understanding of a particular type of interorganizational knowledge transfer and resource redeployment (M&As). This study particularly improves our understanding of the role of knowledge complementarity in interorganizational learning, i.e. knowledge transfer. Past works conceived technological relatedness between partners' knowledge bases only in terms of similarity. Our results provide support for this perspective, since they show that complementarity is not relevant in determining post-M&A absorption-related invention. Another relevant and positive outcome of this analysis is the role attributable to alliance experience and M&A management capabilities. This means that, besides considering the features of potential targets (primarily the technological similarity and complementarity between knowledge bases), if an acquirer has already been engaged in R&D agreements, developing a certain degree of experience in dealing with these, then it is more likely that its post-M&A performances will increase.

Quadratic forms appear to play a particularly important role in post-acquisition technological performances, except in the case of technological complementarity. Similarity, alliance and M&A management capabilities exhibit diminishing marginal returns and beyond some optimum threshold, experience in dealing with alliances and M&A negatively influences absorption-related invention capacity.

Finally, our results are also relevant in an economic perspective. Although – or because – building and maintaining a competitive advantage based on technological knowledge is regarded as fundamental to succeed in high knowledge-intensive industries (Grant, 1996; Powell *et al.*, 1996), its realization has become more difficult in recent decades (Arora and Gambardella, 1994). Our findings show that obtaining technological assets from external sources and integrating them internally might effectively enhance firms' performances, at least from the specific aspect of absorptive capacity.

Managerial implications

The empirical results of this study have interesting managerial implications, drawing executives' attention to several aspects of the acquisition selection and integration process. In particular, this research indicates that M&A – and especially alliance management – capabilities play an important role. A moderate level of alliance and M&A management capability is preferable in order to avoid diminishing marginal returns and thus insignificant or even negative outcomes in terms of absorption-related invention capacity. Hence, we suggest that firms with a balanced number of previous agreements are favoured over those with few or excessively developed capabilities. Specifically, our findings imply that executives of highly skilled and broadly experienced companies might be unable to identify and select potential targets. Ironically, although strong skills provide a significant advantage over competitors in some dimensions of the innovation process, it might turn out to be a liability when looking for and trying to gain benefits from R&D-based firms' M&As.

From the perspective of partner selection, this study suggests that managers of companies willing to enter an M&A with the aim of accessing and integrating new knowledge to enrich their knowledge base and amplify their technological domains, might be able to better evaluate potential targets by focusing, in particular, on technological similarity and on target firms characterized by a diversified knowledge base. Therefore, besides traditional techniques to assess the financial indicators of a potential target, managers should implement analytical systems to identify its knowledge base.

Conclusion

M&As can be interpreted as attempts by companies not only to increase control over the external environment but also to improve their knowledge bases by accessing and absorbing knowledge, resources and capabilities from external sources.

From these findings it is possible to affirm that our empirical analysis suggests that technological similarity plays an important role in fostering absorption-related invention capacity and that diversified knowledge bases and alliance and M&A management capabilities are a critical determinant of the ability of the acquirer to exploit and enjoy benefits from the M&A. With the exception of the prior experience in R&D alliances' management, which has a high statistical significance, no strong and incontrovertible overall evidence is provided in terms of any general ability of M&As to enhance such capability. Thus, although firms still embark on a great number of M&As, especially within this industry, it is not obvious that long-term innovation benefits eventually come to outweigh the initial integration difficulties and costs. Further research needs to be carried out in order to better understand this phenomenon.

This study presents several limitations. First, we focus on a single industrial context from which we selected a population of companies headquartered in North America and Europe, observed over a period of six years. Although such a focus increases internal validity, our results might, therefore, reflect some industry- and period-specific factors that limit the generalizability of findings to other industries. For instance, the reliance on patents varies between industries and, thus, our measure, although appropriate for biopharmaceuticals, might not provide an accurate representation in other contexts. Although the number of industries where patents can be considered meaningful indicators of innovation has been growing in recent years (Makri *et al.*, 2010), a need for elaboration of the study in different settings is thus identified in order to confirm and generate further insights.

Second, we used patent citations and data to construct our dependent and independent variables. This led us to exclude from our sample any firms for which no data on patents was available in the consulted datasets. This is reasonable because: (1) acquisitions involving partners that do not own any patents generally take place for other purposes, such as manufacturing and marketing (Phene *et al.*, 2012) or simply to eliminate possible competitors from the market; and (2) similarly to other industries, like the semiconductor or high-tech industries, patenting in the biopharmaceutical context is actively and routinely pursued with the aim of acquiring an innovative visibility. However, although patents and patent citations are generally regarded as good indicators of innovative output and are related to the ability to acquire and exploit a target's knowledge base, they are also usually considered to be intermediate outcomes along the value chain. Hence, a better and comprehensive evaluation of knowledge relatedness effects on innovation and technological performances should rely not only on patents but also on products or processes generated by patent applications in the post-M&A period and effectively commercialized. In addition, the adequacy of patents as proxies of knowledge bases has been questioned, since these provide only a static representation and do not consider organizational routines as complementary factors in the absorption of external knowledge (Lane *et al.*, 2006).

Third, we reiterate Makri *et al.*'s (2010) argument that International Patent Classification, although fairly adequate and clear, has been created and developed for purposes other than providing researchers with a picture of firms' knowledge bases.

Fourth, as already mentioned, our sample of independent acquirers from North America and Europe necessarily provides no evidence from countries in other continents, such as those which are now emerging (e.g. as 'developing' and 'newly developed'). Fifth, the study might be biased due to undeniable general difficulties in obtaining broad data on firms' knowledge and R&D inputs and outcomes, as well as because of its reliance on data from the Medtrack dataset. The availability of more comprehensive datasets providing such information, not only with regard to the biopharmaceutical industry but also to other industrial contexts, would allow our research to be replicated, extended and improved.

Finally, with reference to patent citations, for US patents researchers have questioned the use of patent citations as a proxy for knowledge transfer, or organizational learning, on the basis that a non-trivial portion of citations are added by government officials or by legal experts along the patent filing process (Alcacer and Gittelman, 2006). This does not appear to be relevant here, because M&A partners get to know each other during the acquisition process. Thus, it is reasonable to assume that their citations follow a process of collecting information about the target knowledge bases.

Note

1 Patent citation is here defined as: 'the extent to which a firm's patents are cited in subsequent patents' (Makri *et al.*, 2010) applied for by other companies.

References

Adegbesan J. A., Higgins M. J., 2011. The intra-alliance division of value created through collaboration. *Strategic Management Journal*, 32(2): 187–211.

Ahuja G., 2000. Collaboration networks, structural holes, and innovation: A longitudinal study. *Administrative Science Quarterly*, 45(3): 425–455.

Ahuja G., Katila R., 2001. Technological acquisitions and the innovation performance of acquiring firms: A longitudinal study. *Strategic Management Journal*, 22(3): 197–220.

Alcacer J., Gittelman M., 2006. Patent citations as a measure of knowledge flows: The influence of examiner citations. *The Review of Economics and Statistics*, 88(4): 774–779.

Anand B. N., Khanna T., 2000. Do firms learn to create value? The case of alliances. *Strategic Management Journal*, 21(3): 295–315.

Arora A., Gambardella A., 1994. The changing technology of technological change: General and abstract knowledge and the division of innovative labour. *Research Policy*, 23(5): 523–532.

Arora A., Fosfuri A., Gambardella A., 2001. *Markets for Technology: Economics of Innovation and Corporate Strategy*. The MIT Press, Cambridge, MA.

Boschma R., Iammarino S., 2009. Related variety, trade linkages and regional growth in Italy. *Economic Geography*, 85(3): 289–311.

Bower J. L., 2001. Not all M&As are alike – and that matters. *Harvard Business Review*, 79(2): 93–101.

Bresman H., Birkinshaw J., Nobel R., 1999. Knowledge transfer in international acquisitions. *Journal of International Business Studies*, 30(4): 439–462.

Buono A. F., Bowditch J. L., 1989. *The Human Side of Mergers and Acquisitions*, Jossey-Bass, San Francisco, CA.

Burt R. S., 2005. *Brokerage and Closure: An Introduction to Social Capital*, Oxford University Press, Oxford, UK

Capron L., Dussauge P., Mitchell W., 1998. Resource redeployment following horizontal acquisitions in Europe and North America, 1988–1992. *Strategic Management Journal*, 19(7): 631–661.

Chang K., 2008. The strategic alliance performance of the biotechnology firm. *Applied Economics*, 40(23): 3089–3100.

Chesbrough H. W., 2003. *Open Innovation: The New Imperative for Creating and Profiting from Technology*. Harvard Business School Press, Cambridge, MA.

Cockburn I., Henderson R., 1998. Absorptive capacity, coauthoring behavior, and the organization of research in drug discovery. *The Journal of Industrial Economics* 46(2): 157–183.

Cohen W., Levinthal D., 1989. Innovation and learning: The two faces of R&D. *Economic Journal*, 99(397): 569–596.

Cohen W., Levinthal D., 1990. Absorptive capacity: A new perspective on learning and innovation. *Administrative Science Quarterly*, 35(1): 128–152.

Darr E. D., Argote L., Epple D., 1995. The acquisition, transfer, and depreciation of knowledge in service organizations: Productivity in franchises. *Management Science*, 41(11): 1750–1762.

De Man A.-P., Duysters G., 2005. Collaboration and innovation: A review of the effects of mergers, acquisitions and alliances on innovation. *Technovation*, 25(12): 1377–1387.

Deeds D. L., Hill C. W., 1996. Strategic alliances and the rate of new product development: An empirical study of entrepreneurial firms. *Journal of Business Venturing*, 11(1): 41–55.

Diestre L., Rajagopalan N., 2012. Are all 'sharks' dangerous? New biotechnology ventures and partner selection in R&D alliances. *Strategic Management Journal*, 33(3): 1115–1134.

Doz Y. L., 1996. The evolution of cooperation in strategic alliances: Initial conditions or learning processes? *Strategic Management Journal*, 17(S1): 55–83.

Frenken K., van Oort F., Verburg T., 2007. Related variety, unrelated variety and regional economic growth. *Regional Studies*, 41(5): 605–697.

Gans J., Stern S., 2003. The product market and the market for ideas: Commercialization strategies for technology entrepreneurs. *Research Policy*, 32(2): 333–350.

Goldman Sachs, 2001. *Strategic Alliances in Biotechnology*. Goldman Sachs, New York, NY.

Gottinger H.-W., Umali C. L., 2008. Strategic alliances in global biotech pharma industries. *The Open Business Journal*, 1(1): 10–24.

Grant R. M., 1996. Prospering in dynamically-competitive environments: Organizational capability as knowledge integration. *Organization Science*, 7(4): 375–387.

Gray D. O., Lindblad M., Rudolph J., 2001. University-based industrial research consortia: A multivariate analysis of member retention. *Journal of Technology Transfer*, 26(3): 247–254.

Greenwood R., Hinings C. R., Brown J., 1994. Merging professional service firms. *Organization Science*, 5(2): 239–257.

Hagedoorn J., 1993. Understanding the rationale of strategic technology partnering: Interorganizational modes of cooperation and sectoral differences. *Strategic Management Journal*, 14(5): 371–385.

Hagedoorn J., Duysters G., 2002a. External sources of innovative capabilities: The preference for strategic alliances or mergers and acquisitions. *Journal of Management Studies*, 39(2): 167–188.

Hagedoorn J., Duysters G., 2002b. The effect of mergers and acquisitions on the technological performance of companies in a high-tech environment. *Technology Analysis & Strategic Management*, 14(1): 67–85.

Hakanson L., 1995. Learning through acquisitions: Management and integration of foreign R&D laboratories. *International Studies of Management and Organization*, 25(1–2): 121–157.

Hamel G., 1991. Competition for competence and interpartner learning within international strategic alliances. *Strategic Management Journal*, 12 (S1): 83–103.

Haspeslagh P. C., Jemison D. B., 1991. *Managing Acquisitions: Creating Value through Corporate Renewal* (Vol. 416), Free Press, New York, NY.

Hoang H., Rothaermel F. T., 2005. The effect of general and partner-specific alliance experience on joint R&D project performance. *Academy of Management Journal*, 48(2): 332–345.

Inkpen A. C., 1992. *Learning and Collaboration: An Examination of North American-Japanese Joint Ventures*. National Library of Canada. Available at: http://ir.lib.uwo.ca/cgi/viewcontent.cgi?article=3110&context=digitizedtheses (accessed 14 April 2013).

Inkpen A. C., Crossan M. M., 1995. Believing is seeing: Joint ventures and organization learning. *Journal of Management Studies*, 32(5): 595–618.

Kale P., Dyer J. H., Singh H., 2002. Alliance capability, stock market response, and long-term alliance success: The role of the alliance function. *Strategic Management Journal*, 23(8): 747–767.

Katila R., Ahuja G., 2002. Something old, something new: A longitudinal study of search behavior and new product introduction. *Academy of Management Journal*, 45(6): 1183–1194.

Kleinbaum D. G., Kupper L. L., Muller K. E., 1988, *Applied Regression Analysis and Other Multivariate Methods*, 2nd edition, PWS-Kent, Boston, MA.

Kogut B., 1988. Joint ventures: Theoretical and empirical perspectives. *Strategic Management Journal*, 9(4): 319–332.

Kogut B., Zander U., 1992. Knowledge of the firm, combinative capabilities, and the replication of technology. *Organization Science*, 3(3): 383–397.

Kogut B., Zander U., 1996. What firms do? Coordination, identity, and learning. *Organization Science*, 7(5): 502–518.

Lane P. J., Lubatkin M., 1998. Relative absorption capacity and interorganizational learning. *Strategic Management Journal*, 19(5): 461–477.

Lane P. J., Koka B. R., Pathak S., 2006. The reification of absorptive capacity: A critical review and rejuvenation of the construct. *Academy of Management Review*, 31(4): 833–863.

Lindgren U., 1982. *Foreign Acquisitions: Management of the Integration Process*, Institute of International Business, Stockholm, Sweden.

Lubatkin M., Florin J., Lane P., 2001. Learning together and apart: A model of reciprocal interfirm learning. *Human Relations*, 54(10): 1353–1382.

Makri M., Hitt M. A., Lane P. J., 2010. Complementary technologies, knowledge relatedness, and invention outcomes in high-technology mergers and acquisitions. *Strategic Management Journal*, 31(6): 602–628.

March J., 1991. Exploration and exploitation in organizational learning. *Organization Science*, 2(1): 71–87.

Mowery D. C, Oxley J. E., Silverman B. S., 1996. Strategic alliances and interfirm knowledge transfer. *Strategic Management Journal*, 17(S2): 77–91.

Nonaka I., Takeuchi H., Umemoto K., 1996. A theory of organizational knowledge creation. *International Journal of Technology Management*, 11(7): 833–845.

Nooteboom B., Vanhaverbeke W., Duysters G., Gilsing V., Van den Oord A., 2007. Cognitive distance and absorptive capacity. *Research Policy*, 36(7): 1016–1034.

Pakes A., Griliches Z., 1984. Patents and R&D at the firm level: A first look, in *R&D, Patents, and Productivity*, University of Chicago Press, Chicago, IL, pp. 55–72.

Phene A., Tallman S., Almeida P., 2012. When do acquisitions facilitate technological exploration and exploitation? *Journal of Management*, 38(3): 753–783.

Powell W. W., Koput K. W., Smith-Doerr L., 1996. Interorganizational collaboration and the locus of innovation: Networks of learning in biotechnology. *Administrative Science Quarterly*, 41(1): 116–145.

Ravenscraft D. J., Scherer F. M., 1987. *Mergers, Sell-Offs, and Economic Efficiency*. Brookings Institution Press, Washington, DC.

Rosenkopf L., Almeida P., 2003. Overcoming local search through alliances and mobility. *Management Science*, 49(6): 751–766.

Rothaermel F. T., 2000. Technological discontinuities and the nature of competition. *Technology Analysis and Strategic Management*, 12(2): 149–160.

Rothaermel F. T., 2001. Complementary assets, strategic alliances, and the incumbent's advantage: An empirical study of industry and firm effects in the biopharmaceutical industry. *Research Policy*, 30(8): 1235–1251.

Rothaermel F. T., Deeds D. L., 2004. Exploration and exploitation alliances in biotechnology: A system of new product development. *Strategic Management Journal*, 25(3): 201–221.

Rothaermel F. T., Deeds D. L., 2006. Alliance type, alliance experience and alliance management capability in high-technology ventures. *Journal of Business Venturing*, 21(4): 429–460.

Rothaermel F. T., Boeker W., 2008. Old technology meets new technology: Complementarities, similarities, and alliance formation. *Strategic Management Journal*, 29(1): 47–77.

Rowley, T., Behrens, D., Krackhardt, D., 2000. Redundant governance structures: An analysis of structural and relational embeddedness in the steel and semiconductor industries. *Strategic Management Journal*, 21(3): 369–386.

Sampson R., 2002. *Experience, Learning and Collaborative Returns in R&D Alliances*. Working Paper. Stern School of Business, New York University, NY. Available at: http://papers.ssrn.com/sol3/papers.cfm?abstract_id=309944 (accessed 10 July 2013).

Schweizer L., 2005. Knowledge transfer and R&D in pharmaceutical companies: A case study. *Journal of Engineering and Technology Management*, 22(4): 315–331.

Senker J., Sharp M., 1997. Organizational learning in cooperative alliances: Some case studies in biotechnology. *Technology Analysis and Strategic Management*, 9(1): 35–52.

Shan W., Walker G., Kogut B., 1994. Interfirm cooperation and startup innovation in the biotechnology industry. *Strategic Management Journal*, 15(5): 387–394.

Shrivastava P., 1986. Postmerger integration. *Journal of Business Strategy*, 7(1): 65–76.

Silverman B. S., Baum J. A., 2002. Alliance-based competitive dynamics. *Academy of Management Journal*, 45(4): 791–806.

Simonin B. L., 1999. Ambiguity and the process of knowledge transfer in strategic alliances. *Strategic Management Journal*, 20(7): 595–623.

Singh A., 1971. *Take-overs: Their Relevance to the Stock Market and the Theory of the Firm*, Cambridge University Press, Cambridge, UK.

Sørensen J. B., Stuart T. E., 2000. Aging, obsolescence, and organizational innovation. *Administrative Science Quarterly*, 45(1): 81–112.

Takeishi A., 2001. Bridging inter- and intra-firm boundaries: Management of supplier involvement in automobile product development. *Strategic Management Journal*, 22(5): 403–433.

Teece D. J., Pisano G., Shuen A., 1997. Dynamic capabilities and strategic management. *Strategic Management Journal*, 18(7): 509–533.

The Economist, 2003. Climbing the helical staircase. 29 March, 3–7. Available at: http://www.economist.com/node/1647556 (accessed 14 April 2013).

Villalonga B., McGahan A. M., 2005. The choice among acquisitions, alliances, and divestitures. *Strategic Management Journal*, 26(13): 1183–1208.

Westney D. E., 1988. Domestic and foreign learning curves in managing international cooperative strategies. *Cooperative Strategies in International Business*, 21(2): 332–337.

9 Are M&As driving exploitation or exploration?

Fiorenza Belussi, Ivan De Noni,
Andrea Ganzaroli and Luigi Orsi

Introduction

Since the middle of the 1980s, there has been a rapid and steady increase in the number of technological mergers and acquisitions (M&As) and strategic alliances whose aim was technological learning and new knowledge creation (De Man and Duysters, 2005). The opportunity to gain access to complementary sources of innovation is often cited as a major reason for the increase in the number of M&As. This explanation is in line with both the resource-based view (Wernerfelt, 1984; Barney, 1986, 1991) and the knowledge-based view of the firms (Levitt and March, 1988; Nonaka, 1995; Conner and Prahalad, 1996; Grant, 1996; Cloodt *et al.*, 2006). The former defines firms as a bundle of idiosyncratic and difficult-to-trade assets and competencies (e.g. Grant, 1996). The latter, similarly, defines firms as social communities specialising in the effective and efficient creation and transfer of knowledge (Kogut and Zander, 1996). Both of these perspectives, however, point out path-dependency as a major driver in the development of firms' competitive advantage and in the transformation of firms' core competencies into firms' core rigidities (Teece, 2007). Thus, the capacity to acquire or gain access to external sources of knowledge, in order to complement and integrate internal processes of development and innovation, is seen as a dynamic capability useful in sustaining firms' competitiveness in fast-moving business environments.

Within this framework, absorptive capacity, defined as the ability of a firm to recognise the value of new external knowledge, assimilate it and apply it to commercial ends, plays an important role in explaining the capacity of a firm to transform knowledge from an external source into new exploitable knowledge (Cohen and Levinthal, 1990). Furthermore, it has been highlighted that the absorption of external knowledge may mitigate the trade-off between exploration and exploitation (Katila and Ahuja, 2002). Thus, in this chapter we investigate the extent to which technology-based M&As represent a viable strategy to support both explorative and exploitative innovation. Through M&As, firms gain access to external sources of innovation (Arora and Gambardella, 1990; Hitt *et al.*, 1996; Graebner, 2004), develop and extend their resources and capabilities (Vermeulen and Barkema, 2001; Uhlenbruck *et al.*, 2006), overcome local searching boundaries (Rosenkopf and Nerkar, 2001; Rosenkopf and Almeida, 2003) and gain the ability to respond to the increasing demand for rapid technological change in terms of both product-related technologies and process-related technologies in knowledge-intensive industries (Hagedoorn and Duysters, 2002a; Makri *et al.*, 2010).

In our study, this perspective is tested on a cross-sectional dataset consisting of data on 152 acquirer firms in the biopharmaceutical industry that completed 218 M&As in the period between 2001 and 2005. A negative binomial regression is operationalised to assess the factors affecting explorative and exploitative innovative performance.

The chapter is structured in three sections. The first is devoted to theory and hypothesis development. We review the main applied concepts and develop our hypotheses regarding their relationships. In the second section we present our sample, define our metrics and address the methodology applied to analyse data. Finally, in the third section, we present and discuss our major findings. The last section is indeed devoted to conclusions and further research directions.

Theoretical background and hypotheses building

Explorative and exploitative invention

Exploration and exploitation are two forms of organisational learning, which compete for organisational attention and resources (March, 1991; Levinthal and March, 1993). Exploitation refers to learning gained via local searches, experiential refinement and selection and reuse of existing routines. Exploration refers to learning gained through processes of concerted variation, planned experimentation and play (Baum *et al.*, 2000). On the basis of these two terms, it is also possible to characterise two different types of innovation (Benner and Tushman, 2003; Chakrabarti *et al.*, 2003; He and Wong, 2004; Jansen *et al.*, 2006). Exploitative innovations are incremental technological innovations or design improvements made to meet the needs of existing customers (Benner and Tushman, 2003). They build upon and broaden existing knowledge and skills and improve the efficiency of existing processes and structures (Abernathy and Clark, 1985; Levinthal and March, 1993; Lewin and Volberda, 1999; Benner and Tushman, 2003). In contrast, exploratory innovations are radical innovations or innovations designed to meet the needs of emerging customers and markets (Jansen *et al.*, 2006). They imply a shift to a different technological trajectory. Hence, they require new knowledge and a departure from existing skills (Benner and Tushman, 2003).

March (1991), in his original conceptualisation, defined exploration and exploitation as the two extremes of a single continuum. Exploration and exploitation compete for scarce organisational resources, as they are self-reinforcing and path-dependent and require radically different mindsets and sets of organisational routines. Therefore, there is a trade-off between exploration and exploitation. Furthermore, managing this trade-off within a single organisation is a very complex task. There are two possible organisational solutions to this trade-off (Chakrabarti *et al.*, 2003). The first solution is designing ambidextrous organisations. That is, designing an organisation composed of highly differentiated and weakly coupled subunits specialising in exploration and exploitation, respectively. Exploration units are small and decentralised, with loose cultures and processes. Exploitation units are larger and more centralised, with tight cultures and processes. The second solution is punctuated equilibrium; that is, a temporal and sequential cycling between long periods of exploitation and short bursts of exploration (Chakrabarti *et al.*, 2003).

However, recent literature points out that exploration and exploitation are not always at the extreme ends of a single continuum, but, in some circumstances, they can be orthogonal (Katila and Ahuja, 2002). There are different reasons why this might be the case. First, information and knowledge are not scarce resources (Varian *et al.*, 2008). Second, organisations do not have access only to resources they own, but also to resources in their external environments (Powell *et al.*, 1996) that are either public or shared/exchanged by contractual means such as licensing, contractual agreements, strategic alliances or M&As. Third, knowledge absorption requires that firms invest in solving complementary problems (Katila and Ahuja, 2002). Thus, the exploitation and development of existing knowledge may facilitate both the absorption and development of new knowledge.

Several studies have looked at strategic alliances as a mechanism for expanding the search boundaries of a firm. Rosenkopf and Nerkar (2001) emphasised that exploration spanning organisational boundaries has more impact on the subsequent technological evolution than exploration between the different domains. Rosenkopf and Almeida (2003) showed that strategic alliances are useful for stimulating learning across technologically distant contexts. Strategic alliances offer a wide range of organisational tools for interfirm interaction over a considerable period of time, which reduces the downside effects of knowledge transfer across divergent contexts. Similarly, Katila and Ahuja (2002) focused on the effect of knowledge reuse in the development of innovative products. They found that the frequency with which knowledge is cited and reused is significant in explaining the development of innovative products. Thus, our study contributes in a number of ways. First, it deepens our understanding of the role of cognitive distance in both explorative and exploitative innovative performance. Second, it focuses on the contribution of external knowledge to both exploration and exploitation. In particular, it focuses on a specific form of knowledge absorption based on a firm's capacity to absorb, recombine and transform target knowledge bases acquired in a specific M&A into both explorative and exploitative innovations. It looks at how back citing the acquired knowledge influences exploration and exploitation. Third, it investigates the effects of managerial capabilities and prior experience on innovative performance.

Cognitive distance

There is lively debate on how the distance between knowledge from an acquired source and knowledge from an owned source influence the innovative performance of the acquirer. The basic idea is that there is an inverted U-shaped relationship between knowledge distance and innovative performance. Similarity between acquired and owned sources of knowledge reduces the cognitive costs required to assimilate the acquired source of knowledge and transforms it into innovative combinations between acquired and owned knowledge (Nooteboom *et al.*, 2007). However, the more similar the two sources of knowledge are, the lower the number of innovative combinations available. On the contrary, the higher the degree of dissimilarity between acquired and owned sources of knowledge, the higher the number of innovative combinations potentially available. However, the accessibility of these opportunities for innovation decreases as the cognitive distance between the two sources of knowledge increases. There are two reasons for this. First, there are high costs involved in discovering, exploring and exploiting meaningful combinations between distant sources of knowledge. Second, even if, from a mathematical point of view, the number of combinations available increases exponentially with the distance between two sources of knowledge, only a limited number of these combinations are technically meaningful (Nooteboom *et al.*, 2007).

However, much of the current debate on the effect of knowledge distance on firms' innovative performance is related to how knowledge relatedness/distance is measured and how the type of metric used impacts on the sign, the strength and the shape of the relationship between knowledge distance and innovative performance. In this respect, Makri *et al.* (2010) argued that one of the main reasons there are conflicting results regarding the outcomes of relatedness is that relatedness has commonly been defined in broad terms, often using similarity and complementarity interchangeably (i.e. Davis *et al.*, 1992; Farjoun, 1998), or by means of incomplete or tautological definitions of complementarity (Mowery *et al.*, 1998) or the issue of complementarity has been completely ignored (Lane and Lubatkin, 1998; Ahuja and Katila, 2001). Larsson and Finkelstein (1999) clarified the distinction between these two concepts in the case of both scientific knowledge and technological knowledge. Abstracting from the two cases, two firms are said to be similar in terms of knowledge if their respective knowledge bases focus on the same narrowly defined areas of knowledge. On the other hand, two firms are said to be complementary in terms of knowledge if their respective knowledge bases focus on different narrowly defined areas of knowledge within a broadly defined area of shared knowledge. For example, two firms are similar in terms of technological knowledge if both firms have patents in the same narrowly defined technological area. They are complementary if they have patents in two different narrowly defined technological areas, but within the same broadly defined technological area. It is evident that the results derived from applying this metric also depend on what are considered narrowly defined and broadly defined areas of knowledge.

Similarity and complementarity are expected to impact differently on the innovative performance of the acquiring firm. Knowledge similarity is expected to have a positive influence on the number of exploitative inventions of the acquirer. The more similar the acquired base of knowledge is to the acquirer's established knowledge base, the easier it is for the acquirer to assimilate that knowledge base and transform it into innovative combinations and recombinations within the same narrowly defined area of knowledge. In other words, it is easier for the acquirer to transform the acquired base of knowledge into exploitative innovations. Furthermore, the cognitive proximity reduces the opportunities for radical innovations and explorative performance (Nooteboom *et al.*, 2007; Makri *et al.*, 2010). However, it should be taken into account that an excess of similarity between acquired and owned bases of knowledge may impact negatively on the number of innovative combinations potentially available (e.g. Zahra and George, 2002; Nooteboom *et al.*, 2007; Makri *et al.*, 2010). Thus, the relationship between knowledge similarity and exploitative invention is likely to be an inverted U-shape.

Hypothesis 1:   *Knowledge similarity is more positively associated with the level of post-M&A exploitative innovation (a) than explorative innovation (b) and the relationship is expected to be an inverted U-shape.*

Knowledge complementarity, different from knowledge similarity, implies, on the one hand, that the acquiring firms share some basic understanding of the bases of knowledge acquired with the acquired firm. Thus, the potential absorptive capacity of the acquiring firm with respect to the acquired knowledge should be stronger than in the case of completely unrelated knowledge. Consequently, exploitative invention should also benefit from an increase in the level of complementarity between acquired and owned bases of knowledge. On the other hand, the acquisition of a complementary base of knowledge should broaden the search scope of the acquirer and, indeed, its capacity to explore innovative paths of development and innovation. Discovering new routines, new modes of reasoning and challenges to existing understandings of cause–effect relationships helps a firm discover novel solutions to problems it has already identified. Furthermore, integration between complementary sources of knowledge provides the potential for a much greater portfolio of new and unique knowledge combinations. As with the argument for similarity, scarce or excessive complementarity may reduce the positive effects on innovation performance. Hence an inverted U-shaped relationship is to be expected.

Hypothesis 2:   *Knowledge complementarity is expected to affect post-M&A explorative innovation (b) more than exploitative innovation (a) more than exploitative and the relationship is expected to be an inverted U-shape.*

Invention capacity related to absorption of target's knowledge

Knowledge distance defines only the potential for innovation generated by the acquisition of an external source of knowledge. Its transformation into innovation, either explorative or exploitative, requires that firms invest in assimilation and transformation of that knowledge.

From this perspective, strategic alliances and, in particular, M&As are alternative organisational strategies that, besides being renowned for their ability to promote entry into new markets and their effectiveness for achieving economies of scale and scope, have progressively become an efficient means of accessing and assimilating knowledge from other organisations (De Man and Duysters, 2005). Cohen and Levinthal (1990) and Zahra and George (2002) have highlighted the key role played by absorptive capacity in the knowledge-acquiring process for innovation. Therefore, in M&As, absorptive capacity is crucial to choosing the right kind of partner for M&A. The efficiency with which the acquirer is able to transform the acquired knowledge into new exploitable knowledge and its efficiency in exploiting the newly created base of knowledge are of great importance.

To capture this particular side of the acquirer's capacity to absorb the target's knowledge base, we introduce the term *absorption-related invention capacity* as a tangible measure of firms' capacity to absorb, recombine and transform the acquired targets' knowledge bases into new knowledge and invention. Since absorptive capacity is theoretically supposed to positively influence post-M&A firms' innovation performance (Makri *et al.*, 2010), absorption-related invention capacity is expected to positively contribute to firms' global innovation capacity. Thus, we pose the following hypothesis:

Hypothesis 3:   *Absorption-related invention capacity positively influences both exploitative innovation (a) and explorative innovation (b).*

Managerial capabilities

The experience accumulated by a firm in managing the acquisition, assimilation, transformation and exploitation of an external source of knowledge is likely to play a major role in enhancing its innovative performance through M&As. Through the accumulation of experience, in fact, firms develop specific organisational routines that can be sources of competitive advantage and can make the firm proficient in the management of a particular task. Organisational routines play a crucial role in the formulation of a firm's strategic choices by supplementing, or even substituting for, calculative, formal strategic decision-making rules (March, 1991). Research on organisational learning suggests that experience and performance feedback drive the development of organisational routines and increase the likelihood that the same routines are reapplied in the future. Thus, the frequency with which external knowledge is acquired not only reflects the experience a firm has accumulated on that specific task but also the extent to which that firm has been successful in the management of that task in the past (Haleblian and Finkelstein, 1999).

There are three major strategies firms use to gain access to and exploit external sources of knowledge: (1) the acquisition of a patent or a pool of patents; (2) the development of strategic alliances; or (3) M&As. These strategies imply different levels of involvement of the firm in the acquisition of external knowledge and its integration into the existing base of knowledge. For instance, top management is involved only in the strategic evaluation of an opportunity to buy an external patent, but not in its integration into the company's existing knowledge base. In other words, strategic alliances and M&As are processes deeply involving the whole firm and they play a significant role in the history of a company. Thus, research on organisational learning has mainly focused on the effect of prior experience in the management of strategic alliances or M&As with respect to the innovative performance of the focal firms (Hoang and Rothaermel, 2005).

There is large agreement on the fact that prior experience of managing the absorption of external sources of knowledge through either strategic alliances or M&As is likely to enhance ex post firms' innovative performance (e.g. Simonin, 1997; Anand and Khanna, 2000; Rothaermel and Deeds, 2006). Prior experience enhances the capacity of a firm to select the appropriate partner to cooperate with or the appropriate firm to acquire. It provides specific insights on the right level of collaboration and integration. It also enhances a firm's capacity to stimulate access, assimilation and integration during the strategic alliances or in the post-M&A phase. However, it is also suggested that prior experience may exhibit diminishing returns on subsequent performance. Firms tend to enter the most promising partnerships and/or acquisitions first, leading to poorer outcomes in subsequent activities. Second, the continued reliance on established routines and procedures allows for little or no additional learning. Furthermore, it may crowd out necessary exploration and turn into core rigidity. Third, given that alliances and M&A relationships last for several years, firms may incur limitations in the managerial resources available to effectively manage an additional alliance or M&A.

Extant research has focused only on how the experience accumulated in the management of a specific form of integration/collaboration influences innovative performance generated by that specific form of integration/collaboration. This means that studies focusing on M&As have only analysed the influence of M&A management competence on innovative performance post M&A. However, the availability of specific competence in strategic alliances' management may also be useful in leveraging innovative performance post M&A. This is because stimulating the assimilation and transformation of knowledge in M&As may require either similar or complementary competencies with respect to strategic alliances. For instance, managing knowledge assimilation and transformation in strategic alliances may support the development of specific competencies on trust management that may also find application in the management of the same task in M&As. Thus, experience in the management of strategic alliances may contribute to enhancing innovative performance post M&A. Furthermore, for the reasons we have just seen, this relationship should be shaped like an inverted U.

Hypothesis 4: *Prior experience in management of alliances positively influences both exploitative innovation (a) and explorative innovation (b) and the relationship is expected to be an inverted U-shape.*

Hypothesis 5:   *Prior experience in M&A management positively influences both exploitative innovation (a) and explorative innovation (b) and the relationship expected will be an inverted U-shape.*

Methods

Data and sample

The hypotheses were tested on a cross-sectional dataset consisting of data for 152 acquirer firms in the biopharmaceutical industry that have completed 218 M&As in the period between 2001 and 2005.

There are several reasons for choosing this industry to test our set of hypotheses. First, competition in this industry is knowledge-based (Chang, 2008). Thus, firms' competitiveness largely relies on their dynamic capability (Teece, 2007), social capital and networking (Ghoshal and Moran, 1996) and absorptive capacity (Cohen and Levinthal, 1990). Second, this industry is the outcome of a combination and merging of two complementary sets of competencies. The development of biotechnology techniques has disrupted upstream R&D competencies in the pharmaceutical industry, but it has been competence-preserving in downstream commercialisation activities (Powell *et al.*, 1996). Thus, the rise of biotechnology has stimulated firms in the biotechnological and pharmaceutical sectors to enter strategic alliances and M&As in order to balance their respective strengths and weaknesses (e.g. Rothaermel, 2001; Rothaermel and Boeker, 2008; Adegbesan and Higgins, 2011). This is confirmed by the fact that the biopharmaceutical industry has the highest frequency of alliances (Hagedoorn, 1993), has witnessed considerable M&A activity (Goldman Sachs, 2001) and makes a great deal of investments in R&D and innovation activity (Rothaermel and Deeds, 2006).

We constructed our dataset integrating data from several sources according to the following procedure. First, we extracted firms from Medtrack. The following criteria were applied: (1) firms should have completed at least one M&A in the focal period (e.g. Ahuja and Katila, 2001; Hagedoorn and Duysters, 2002a; Diestre and Rajagopalan, 2012) between 2001 and 2005; (2) all firms not involved in technological M&As were excluded (Ahuja and Katila, 2001; Makri *et al.*, 2010); and (3) we excluded all firms that do not focus on human therapeutic and diagnostic applications – biomaterials and tissue regeneration, blood products, gene therapy, stem cell therapy, vaccines and bio-diagnostic products (Rothaermel and Boeker, 2008). We applied these last criteria in order to identify firms in the human in-vivo segment of biotechnology, which is unique in terms of its economic importance and potential, its regulatory environment and its consumer market (Powell *et al.*, 1996).

On the basis of these criteria, we identified 229 North American and European acquirers, which have completed 404 technological M&As between 2001 and 2005. Second, we collected the data required to calculate our set of control variables. These data were already available in Medtrack for almost the entire sample of firms. Nonetheless, the accuracy of these data was double checked. If data were missing, these have been collected from other sources. Due to their different levels of detail, three distinct databases were employed: Amadeus, Orbis and Compustat. First, financial and corporate data about European firms were obtained from Amadeus. Second, Compustat was used to gather information about non-European listed companies. Finally, we employed Orbis in order to obtain data on unlisted sample firms. Additionally, missing data were directly obtained from companies' official websites. Finally, we collected data about the acquirers' and the targets' patenting activities in Orbit-QPat. Although previous works (i.e. Ahuja and Katila, 2001; Hagedoorn and Duysters, 2002b; Makri *et al.*, 2010; Diestre and Rajagopalan, 2012) utilised data on patents taken from US databases, we decided to employ Orbit-QPat for two reasons. First, our major purpose was to analyse a firm's ability to patent and protect its knowledge at a worldwide level. Orbit-QPat provides extensive coverage with 95 patent authorities. Second, it is characterised by great flexibility, which allowed us to identify and export fundamental data for the construction of our key measures. Thus, for each target and acquirer we collected all the patents granted between 1995 and 2011. We excluded all the firms that had not been granted patents in the period between 1995 and 2011. In the end, our sample resulted in 152 acquirers that completed 218 technological M&As between 2001 and 2005.

Variables

In order to test our hypotheses, we considered several variables. Here we discuss and illustrate each of them.

Dependent variables

Coherent with previous literature on innovation performance (e.g. Nooteboom *et al.*, 2007; Gilsing *et al.*, 2008; Makri *et al.*, 2010) we developed two dependent variables to test our hypotheses, examining: (a) acquirers' technological distance; (b) technological spillover; and (c) alliances/M&As experience. We studied the influence of these explanatory factors on post-M&A technological performance.

Cumulative patent count was used to derive information about the existence of exploitative and explorative innovations. Thus, we recalculated the number of patents for the two dependent variables, 'explorative' and 'exploitative' (Gilsing *et al.*, 2008).

To analyse this process, we used a lagged variable of patents, assuming that, on average, the time lag between M&As and subsequent innovation performance covers a period of about six years. This choice was based on the extant literature. According to Singh (1971) and Buono and Bowditch (1989), it takes an average of nearly five years before acquired organisations are assimilated and acquirers benefit from the M&A. Obviously, these studies also indicate a considerable variation in the assimilation process, since some companies are able to merge their organisations within one year, whereas others take longer than the average of five years. Furthermore, Pakes and Griliches (1984) and Scherer (1984) maintained that it takes about one year on average before inventions through R&D lead to patent applications. Following the literature, in our study we considered a period from one to six years post M&A (Hagedoorn and Duysters, 2002a). In doing so, we counterbalanced the possible fluctuations of firms' innovation activity (Makri *et al.*, 2010).

To derive the dependent variables, the technological profiles of the acquirer firms were computed to find out if new patents in the five-year window post M&A could be categorised as 'exploitative' or 'explorative' (Gilsing *et al.*, 2008). The patent classes were determined at a three-digit level.

Exploitative patents is our first dependent variable. This variable is measured in terms of the number of patents a firm successfully applied for in the five-year window post M&A within patent classes in which the firm had been active in the five-year window prior to the M&A. In this way, we captured the innovation activity that followed the past trajectory of knowledge development in which only the exploitative processes appear. In the case of acquirers involved in multiple acquisitions, exploitative patents were estimated considering an average value.

Explorative patents is our second dependent variable. This variable is measured in terms of the number of patents a firm successfully applied for in the five-year window post M&A within patent classes in which the firm had not been active in the five-year window prior to the M&A. Thus, we measured the extension of innovation activity beyond the past technological domains. In the case of acquirers involved in multiple acquisition processes, explorative patents were estimated by considering an average value.

Independent variables

Technological similarity is a measure of technological relatedness between M&A partners, since it captures the extent to which the two firms patented in the same classes, i.e. employing similar technological knowledge (Ahuja and Katila, 2001; Rosenkopf and Almeida, 2003; Makri *et al.*, 2010; Diestre and Rajagopalan, 2012). Based on prior research, we operationalised technological similarity using the number of patents in the same three-digit subclasses, considering a lag time of one to six years before the M&A took place, in order to attenuate fluctuations and capture relevant knowledge stocks (Rothaermel and Boeker, 2008; Diestre and Rajagopalan, 2012). We calculated the value for technological similarity as the total number of patents the partners applied for in the same technological three-digit classes, divided by the total number of patents of both the acquirer and the target, weighted by the importance of each patent class for the acquirer. Coherent with prior studies (Hagedoorn and Duysters, 2002b; Dushnitsky and Lenox, 2005), we assumed that the higher this measure was, the more technologically related the partners were.

The formula is as follows:

$$Technological\ similarity = \frac{Overlap\ all\ patents\ in\ 3\text{-}digit\ classes}{Total\ patents\ acquirer + target}$$
$$* \frac{Total\ acquirer\ patents\ in\ common\ 3\text{-}digit\ classes}{Total\ acquirer\ patents}$$

When dealing with multiple agreements, we computed technological similarity for each of the agreements and then calculated an average value.

Technological complementarity is a measure that captures the integrative potential of the M&A partners. As Makri *et al.* (2010) maintained, although being an adequate proxy of the similarity of technological assets, technological similarity is only part of the broad concept of technological relatedness. In fact, it is not possible to grasp the technological complementarity existing between partners. Therefore, we introduced this second independent variable, here operationalised as the number of patents applied for in the same section (one-digit), but in different subclasses (one-digit), by the acquirer and the target, considering a time lag of one to six years preceding the M&A. Specifically, it was calculated as the previously discussed similarity index multiplied by the ratio between the number of patents of the acquirer in common sections (one-digit) and the total number of sections in which the acquirer applied for patents. Similar to the previous variable, the higher the value obtained, the higher the number of common sections, but when characterised by patents attributed to the different subclasses in which the acquirer applied for patents, the partners appeared to be more complementary.

The formula is as follows:

Technological complementarity =

$$\frac{Overlap\ all\ patent\ one\text{-}digit\ sections}{Total\ patents\ acquirer + target}$$
$$- \frac{Overlap\ all\ patent\ three\text{-}digit\ classes}{Total\ patents\ acquirer + target}$$
$$* \frac{Total\ acquirer\ patents\ in\ common\ one\text{-}digit\ section}{Total\ acquirer\ patents}$$

We computed an average value for multiple M&As.

Absorption-related invention capacity is another adequate indicator of the acquirers' ability to productively manage the M&A process and to use a certain set of patents (more precisely, the targets' patents) to stimulate and support their invention and patenting activities (Makri *et al.*, 2010). During the process of M&A, if an acquirer firm is able to quote in its patents the patents of the target firm, this means that the realised acquisition has the benefit of the past new knowledge discovered by the target. Thus, we are interested in seeing if a process of knowledge absorption is realised by the acquirer after the M&A process.

To operationalise this variable, we considered data on the patents of both the M&A partners and we looked specifically at the application numbers and dates of the target's patents. At this point, we observed whether the target patents were cited in the acquirer's patent reference (looking also at the application date of the acquirer), always considering a time lag of one to six years in the pre- and post-M&A periods. Orbit-QPat allowed us to match the patent numbers of the target and the acquirer in a very simple manner, using the cross-search patent number (XPN) of the target with the cross-search cited number (XCT) contained in the citations field of the acquirer. We then calculated the number of citations[1] for patents granted to the target before the M&A that were received by the acquirer in the post-M&A period. We chose to use a simple count variable, since it was difficult to calculate a growth rate between pre- and post-M&A citations, mainly because of the large number of zeros in the pre-M&A citations, which would have led to undetermined results for the change measure. We relied heavily on citations, since they provide good evidence of the link between an innovation and its technological antecedents and descendants. We proposed the following measure as a proxy for the technological spillover capacity of a firm:

$$Absorption\text{-}related\ invention\ capacity = \sum\nolimits_{i=1}^{n} n.citing.post_j$$

where i is the ith acquirer patent, n is the total number of patents granted to the acquirer in the one- to six-year window and $n.citing.post_j$ is the number of citations received by target patents in the one- to six-year window post M&A. We assumed that the higher the number of post-M&A citations, the greater the ability of the acquiring firm to absorb knowledge. Realised technological spillover involved in multiple acquisition processes was estimated by considering an average value.

Alliance management capabilities are a measure that captures the acquirer's ability to manage deals with other firms. Prior literature classifies it as a dynamic capability, which contributes to achieving a competitive advantage (Teece *et al.*, 1997) by increasing firms' capacity to manage several alliances (Rothaermel and Deeds, 2006). Although believing that a proxy based on the cumulative sum of the alliance duration (number of years) for each of the firm's alliances, such as that developed by Rothaermel and Deeds (2006), is coherent with the theoretical assumption that, at a firm level, this kind of experience is accumulated through learning-by-doing over time, we adopted the traditional perspective of a simple count variable for the cumulative number of alliances (Shan *et al.*, 1994; Deeds and Hill, 1996; Kale *et al.*, 2002; Sampson, 2002; Zollo *et al.*, 2002; Anand and Khanna, 2000; Rothaermel and Deeds, 2004; Hoang and Rothaermel, 2005). Therefore, we measured alliance management capabilities using a simple count of each firm's alliances. Particularly, we considered the total number of R&D alliances realised in the period of one to six years before the acquirer entered its first M&A.

M&A management capabilities is a measure of the number of M&As the acquirer completed in the period before the first M&A process was completed

(Diestre and Rajagopalan, 2012). It is a crucial independent variable, since the extant literature maintains that one of the main issues companies engaged in M&As have to deal with is the difficulty of acquiring adequate information on target firms. Furthermore, previous studies in the field have demonstrated that acquirers with some M&A management capabilities generally find it easier to assess the value of target firms. Thus, in terms of exploration and exploitation (Hagedoorn and Duysters, 2002a), there is a correlation between higher management capabilities and higher post-merger technological performance.

Control variables

Several variables might affect the exploitative/explorative innovation performance of firms.

Number of patents pre M&A was calculated as the total number of patents granted by the acquirer (one to six years before the M&A). This control variable allowed us to measure the influence of pre-M&A patents on the invention performance of the acquirer. Patents granted are used to measure, in an indirect way, the technological competence of a company (Narin *et al.*, 1987).

Relative patents portfolio size was calculated as a ratio between the acquirers' number of patents pre M&A (in the one- to six-year window) and the target number of patents applied for in the same period. This variable controls for the relationship between the degree of similarity in terms of the size of the patents' portfolio of companies involved in M&As and the technological performance of the acquiring firms (Hagedoorn and Duysters, 2002a). Higher scores of this ratio are associated with greater patents' portfolio dissimilarity, while scores near the value 1 represent patents' portfolio similarity between the acquirer and target.

Acquirer/target diversification ratio was operationalised through a ratio between two entropy measures. The numerator of this ratio measures the degree of diversification of the acquirer, while the denominator is the degree of diversification of the target. The entropy measures were calculated by considering the number of classes at a three-digit level in which each company applied for patents in the selected time window (one to six years pre M&A). The following formula was used to calculate the diversification measure:

$$\textit{Shannon entropy index} = \sum_{j=1}^{n} P_j * \textit{In}\left(\frac{1}{P_j}\right)$$

where P_j was defined as the percentage of firm patents in the three-digit patent classes *j*; and $\textit{ln}(1/P_j)$ was the weight for each patent class *j*; and *n* was the total number of classes in which the firm applied for patents (Ahuja and Katila, 2001; Miller, 2004).

In other words, a greater value for the technological diversification measure means that the acquirer firm had developed many more competencies across diverse technological areas relative to the acquired firm. This variable allowed us to understand how the diversification/specialisation of the acquirer and target influenced the technological performance of the acquirer post M&A. Average values were computed for companies engaged in multiple M&As.

Firm size is a critical control variable. Researchers have demonstrated that this factor has a direct effect on the production of innovative output (Acs and Audretsch, 1988; Freeman and Soete, 1997). Furthermore, it has been observed that the larger the firm is, the more likely it is to use and combine various R&D activities, hence knowledge and resources (Cassiman and Veugelers, 1999; Beneito, 2006). Coherent with this perspective, Kale *et al.* (2002) maintained that the possibility of success of large companies in managing an agreement is enhanced by the greater availability of resources with respect to smaller ones and that they generally have more alliance experience, because they have better opportunities to become involved in agreements. This variable is generally measured using financial data, such as revenues, assets or market share.

Nonetheless, we controlled for it by considering the number of employees. This is consistent with prior research in the biotechnology sector. In fact, Powell *et al.* (1996), Ahuja and Katila (2001), Rothaermel (2001), Kale *et al.* (2002), Deeds and Rothaermel (2003), Rosenkopf and Almeida (2003), Rothaermel and Deeds (2004, 2006), Rothaermel and Boeker (2008) and Hagedoorn and Wang (2012) adopted the number of employees as a proxy for firm size, since the use of more traditional size measures might be problematic. Dedicated biotechnology firms are mainly characterised by intangible assets (i.e. knowledge), or might not have products on the market. Thus, total assets and market share appear to be inadequate measures. We include the natural logarithm of 'employees', as a proxy for firm size.

It is worth noting that the number of employees was considered with reference to the year of the M&A and, in the case of multiple M&As, with respect to the year of the first deal.

Firm age was measured by the natural logarithm of years between a firm's foundation date and the year of the M&A, or the year of the first M&As that took place during the period considered for companies engaged in multiple M&As. Consistent with the extant literature, we supposed that the older the firm, the more likely it is to have intellectual property rights, products in development and experience in managing deals (Deeds and Hill, 1996; Sørensen and Stuart, 2000; Rothaermel and Deeds, 2004, 2006). Generally, one would expect organisational age to be positively related to innovation, but that older firms would show a greater tendency to build on older technology when compared to younger firms. Moreover, innovations of older firms are generally less influential than those of younger firms (Sørensen and Stuart, 2000; Nooteboom *et al.*, 2007).

Public is a dummy variable (0, 1) equal to 1 if the firm's stock was publicly traded in 2005 and equal to 0 otherwise.

Region is a dummy variable (0, 1) that scored 1 if the firm's country of origin was North America (i.e. it was either the US or Canada) and 0 if it was a European nation.

Model estimation

As previously explained, the unit of our analysis is the acquirer firm. Our dependent variables, exploitative patents and explorative patents, are count variables taking on discrete non-negative integer values, including zero, so a Poisson or a negative binomial specification is recommended (Hausman *et al.*, 1984; Henderson and Cockburn, 1996).

A negative binomial regression is the preferred estimation technique, because this technique relaxes the restrictive assumption of mean and variance equality inherent in the Poisson regression and accounts for omitted variable bias while estimating heterogeneity (Rothaermel and Boeker, 2008). We applied the following specification:

$$E[Y_i] = \lambda_i = exp\left(y_i = \mu + \beta x_i + \alpha_i + \varepsilon_i\right)$$

where $exp(\varepsilon_i) \sim \Gamma[1,\alpha]$ is assumed to have a gamma distribution. The subscript i indicates that the parameter λ is allowed to vary across individuals ($i = 1, \ldots ,n$). In this formulation of the negative binomial model, the parameter α is estimated directly from the data and captures overdispersion.

Results

Table 9.1 provides the descriptive statistics and the correlations between the variables for the 152 observations in our sample. All of the bivariate correlations between the independent variables fall below the 0.70 threshold, indicating acceptable discriminant validity. Nonetheless, multicollinearity diagnostics were examined by undertaking some additional tests to detect possible multicollinearity. We regressed each independent variable on all the other independent variables and this test did not indicate multicollinearity (Hagedoorn and Duysters, 2002a). In addition, we explicitly assessed potential multicollinearity in all models and found that the variance inflation factors were well below the suggested cut-off point of ten (Kleinbaum *et al.*, 1988).

Tables 9.2 and 9.3 show the results of the regression analysis using generalised linear model (GLM) negative binomial estimations to explain the exploitative and explorative innovation performance of the firms in our sample. Model 1 in Tables 9.2 and 9.3 represents the impact of the control variables on both exploitative and explorative patents. Models 2 to 6 include only one explanatory variable and its quadratic form, while model 7 provides the full representation. The coefficients are robust over the different models, so multicollinearity does not appear to be a particular problem in these regressions.

Technological similarity

Model 2 added the measure of technological similarity. The coefficients for the linear and quadratic terms of the technological similarity variable have the

Table 9.1 Descriptive statistics and correlation matrix (152 bservations)

Variables	Mean	S.D.	Min	Max	1	2	3	4	5	6	7	8	9	10	11	12	13	14
1 No. of exploitative patents	1189.49	3283.62	0	21397	1.000													
2 No. of explorative patents	18.24	62.84	0	703	0.162	1.000												
3 Technological similarity	0.76	0.28	0	1	0.264	0.008	1.000											
4 Technological complementarity	0.12	0.16	0	1	0.072	0.157	-0.499	1.000										
5 Absorption-related invention	16.48	54.77	0	404	0.364	0.246	0.125	-0.102	1.000									
6 Alliance management capabilities	8.02	15.43	0	106	0.472	0.258	0.098	-0.024	0.165	1.000								
7 M&A management capabilities	0.45	1.19	0	8	0.392	0.120	-0.085	0.100	0.035	0.328	1.000							
8 No. of patents pre M&A	906.74	2774.60	1	20648	0.862	0.138	0.006	0.013	0.111	0.479	0.359	1.000						
9 Relative patent portfolio size	92.32	577.57	0	6889.50	0.572	0.042	-0.191	0.150	-0.013	0.084	0.414	0.472	1.000					
10 Acquirer/target diversification ratio	1.87	2.77	0.04	18.58	-0.072	-0.028	-0.214	0.098	-0.057	-0.065	-0.065	-0.063	-0.010	1.000				
11 Size (No. of employees)	7821.91	20688.37	3	127600	0.567	0.313	-0.043	0.064	0.062	0.437	0.367	0.557	0.157	-0.016	1.000			
12 Age	31.30	36.09	1	154	0.275	0.318	-0.189	0.097	0.019	0.335	0.271	0.367	0.167	0.144	0.434	1.000		
13 Public (Yes=1)	0.66	0.47	0	1	0.147	0.057	0.034	0.019	0.147	0.235	0.084	0.157	0.082	0.026	0.210	0.047	1.000	
14 Region (US=1)	0.58	0.50	0	1	-0.017	0.059	0.054	-0.071	0.208	0.063	0.001	0.032	-0.066	0.186	0.047	-0.061	0.128	1.000

Source: Authors' elaboration.

expected sign and are significant (Table 9.2) with respect to the exploitative patents, while with respect to the explorative patents (Table 9.3), we found that the linear term is positive but not significant and the quadratic term is negative and significant (p < 0.1). The results confirm the basic hypothesis (Hypothesis 1a) that innovation performance is a parabolic inverted U-shaped function of technological similarity between M&A partners in the case of exploitative patents. In contrast, technological similarity has no significant effect in the case of explorative patents (Hypothesis 1b).

Technological complementarity

Model 3 measures the effects of technological complementarity on exploitative patents (Table 9.2) and on explorative patents (Table 9.3). There is no relationship between technological complementarity and innovative performance in terms of exploitative patents; the coefficients of the linear and quadratic term are not significantly different from zero. By contrast, the results show a U-shaped function of technological complementarity between M&A partners in the case of explorative patents: the linear term of the complementary index has a significant (p < 0.1) negative effect and the quadratic term has a significant (p < 0.05) positive effect.

Absorption-related invention capacity

We did not find an inverted U-shaped function for exploitative patents with respect to realised technological spillover. The linear term of the absorption-related invention capacity is positive and significant (p < 0.05), so firms with a high absorption-related invention capacity from the target patents portfolio have fewer problems dealing with exploitative innovation processes. The quadratic term is negative, but not significantly different from zero. By contrast, the results confirm the inverted U-shaped relationship between explorative patents and absorption-related invention capacity. The linear term has a positive and significant (p < 0.05) effect on the explorative innovation performance, while the quadratic term has a negative and significant (p < 0.10) effect on the explorative patents.

Alliance management capabilities

Hypothesis 4a states that the relationship between M&A partners' total number of R&D alliances and its exploitative patents is an inverted U-shape. The results obtained in model 5 (Table 9.2) support Hypothesis 4a. The linear term of the alliance management capabilities is positive and strongly significant (p < 0.001), while the squared term of the alliance capabilities is negative and strongly significant (p < 0.001).

Hypothesis 4b states that the relationship between M&A partners' total number of R&D alliances and its explorative patents is an inverted U-shape. Also in this case, the results obtained in model 5 (Table 9.3) support Hypothesis 4b.

Table 9.2 Results of GLM negative binomial regression predicting determinants of the number of firm patents in exploitative patent classes (152 observations)

Variables	Model 1: control variables	Hypothesis 1a	Hypothesis 2a
		Model 2: tech similarity	Model 3: tech complementarity
Intercept	4.121*** (0.405)	3.805*** (0.668)	4.112*** (0.404)
Technological similarity		2.948* (1.219)	
Technological similarity^2		−2.787*** (0.809)	
Technological complementarity			0.796 (1.568)
Technological complementarity^2			−0.539 (2.152)
Absorption-related invention capacity			
Absorption-related invention capacity^2			
Alliance management capabilities			
Alliance management capabilities^2			
M&A management capabilities			
M&A management capabilities^2			
No. of patents pre M&A	0.448*** (0.054)	0.383*** (0.054)	0.429*** (0.054)
Relative patent portfolio size	−0.415† (0.231)	−0.266 (0.236)	−0.395† (0.233)
Acquirer/target diversification ratio	−0.087† (0.044)	−0.094* (0.045)	−0.092* (0.045)
Size (ln size)	0.384*** (0.058)	0.380*** (0.057)	0.383*** (0.058)
Age (ln age)	−0.273* (0.113)	−0.294* (0.113)	−0.290* (0.112)
Public (Yes=1)	0.002 (0.257)	−0.020 (0.255)	0.020 (0.255)
Region (US=1)	−0.079 (0.245)	−0.047 (0.246)	−0.080 (0.244)
Log likelihood	−2277.8	−2251.4	−2275.2
Adjusted R squared	0.558	0.588	0.559
Mean VIF	0.649	0.649	1.057
Max VIF	0.809	0.809	2.431

Significant codes: † p<0.10; * p<0.05; ** p<0.01; *** p<0.001
Standard errors are reported in parentheses.
Absorption-related invention, alliance management capabilities, M&A management capabilities and number of patents pre-M&A have been divided by 100 in the respective explanatory variables and in quadratic form in order to have readable coefficients.

Source: Authors' elaboration.

| Hypothesis 3a | Hypothesis 4a | Hypothesis 5a | Model 7: All variables |
Model 4: Absorption-related invention	Model 5: Alliance capabilities	Model 6: M&A capabilities	
4.072*** (0.418)	3.762*** (0.354)	3.943*** (0.421)	3.609*** (0.721)
			2.874* (1.309)
			−3.043*** (0.875)
			−2.278 (1.636)
			2.175 (2.167)
1.000* (0.478)			0.532* (0.217)
−0.207 (0.210)			−0.122 (0.186)
	7.556*** (1.655)		7.192*** (1.901)
	−7.595*** (1.928)		−6.951** (2.122)
		0.573† (0.297)	0.401 (0.275)
		−0.097† (0.053)	−0.088† (0.048)
0.377*** (0.055)	0.206** (0.065)	0.343*** (0.056)	0.139* (0.068)
−0.276 (0.237)	−0.009 (0.221)	0.028 (0.332)	0.487 (0.308)
−0.077† (0.046)	−0.079* (0.039)	−0.084† (0.046)	−0.093* (0.042)
0.388*** (0.060)	0.417*** (0.051)	0.369*** (0.061)	0.407*** (0.056)
−0.263* (0.115)	−0.284** (0.099)	−0.229† (0.116)	−0.253* (0.105)
0.000 (0.264)	−0.136 (0.23)	0.176 (0.265)	−0.069 (0.245)
−0.218 (0.259)	−0.132 (0.214)	−0.151 (0.254)	−0.194 (0.232)
−2270.7	2219.6	2269.4	2194.4
0.567	0.606	0.568	0.638
1.605	1.294	1.677	3.223
4.991	3.147	5.436	6.963

Table 9.3 Results of GLM negative binomial regression predicting determinants of the number of firm patents in explorative patent classes (152 observations)

Variables	Model 1: control variables	Hypothesis 1b	Hypothesis 2b
		Model 2: tech similarity	Model 3: tech complementarity
Intercept	0.684 (0.606)	−0.456 (1.031)	0.743 (0.604)
Technological similarity		3.146 (1.916)	
Technological similarity^2		−2.176† (1.298)	
Technological complementarity			−1.348† (1.193)
Technological complementarity^2			2.038* (0.916)
Absorption-related invention capacity			
Absorption-related invention capacity^2			
Alliance management capabilities			
Alliance management capabilities^2			
M&A management capabilities			
M&A management capabilities^2			
No. of patents pre M&A	0.022* (0.012)	0.005* (0.002)	0.016* (0.094)
Relative patent portfolio size	−0.083 (0.317)	0.028 (0.329)	−0.055 (0.321)
Acquirer/target diversification ratio	−0.042 (0.069)	−0.013 (0.068)	−0.059 (0.07)
Size (ln size)	0.323*** (0.085)	0.325*** (0.085)	0.333*** (0.086)
Age (ln age)	0.061 (0.162)	0.092 (0.165)	0.067 (0.162)
Public (Yes=1)	−0.344 (0.376)	−0.289 (0.378)	−0.401 (0.375)
Region (US=1)	−0.134 (0.358)	−0.21 (0.363)	−0.134 (0.357)
Log likelihood	−1248.5	−1238.1	−1246
Adjusted R squared	0.287	0.304	0.291
Mean VIF	0.757	2.054	1.251
Max VIF	0.973	6.878	2.897

Significant codes: † $p<0.10$; * $p<0.05$; ** $p<0.01$; *** $p<0.001$
Standard errors are reported in parentheses.
Absorption-related invention, alliance management capabilities, M&A management capabilities and number of patents pre-M&A have been divided by 100 in the respective explanatory variables and in quadratic form in order to have readable coefficients.

Source: Authors' elaboration.

Hypothesis 3b	Hypothesis 4b	Hypothesis 5b	Model 7: All variables
Model 4: Absorption-related invention	Model 5: Alliance capabilities	Model 6: M&A capabilities	
0.969† (0.545)	0.920 (0.559)	0.655 (0.603)	−0.221 (1.149)
			3.999 (2.461)
			−3.073 (1.889)
			−1.842† (2.696)
			3.718* (3.518)
1.912* (0.853)			1.427* (0.924)
−0.502† (0.26)			−0.396† (0.275)
	5.504* (2.481)		2.281** (2.854)
	−4.765† (2.859)		−2.269* (3.159)
		0.491 (0.398)	0.155 (0.407)
		−0.08 (0.072)	−0.031 (0.07)
0.034 (0.068)	0.063† (0.051)	0.010* (0.044)	0.061† (0.039)
0.083 (0.286)	0.087 (0.319)	0.174 (0.443)	0.307 (0.447)
−0.015 (0.062)	−0.036 (0.064)	−0.033 (0.067)	−0.036 (0.068)
0.315*** (0.077)	0.310*** (0.079)	0.303*** (0.086)	0.324*** (0.086)
−0.029 (0.146)	−0.053 (0.152)	0.072 (0.161)	0.007 (0.159)
−0.473 (0.34)	−0.575 (0.359)	−0.302 (0.373)	−0.512 (0.378)
−0.393 (0.335)	−0.133 (0.331)	−0.191 (0.355)	−0.395 (0.357)
1210.3	−1219.9	−1244	−1249.3
0.339	0.321	0.297	0.299
1.824	1.47	1.894	1.983
5.539	3.545	6.064	6.974

The linear term of the alliance management capabilities is positive and significant (p < 0.05), while the squared term of the alliance capabilities is negative and significant (p < 0.1).

M&A management capabilities

In Hypothesis 5a, we postulated that the relationship between M&A management capabilities and exploitative innovation performance is an inverted U-shape. We find support for this hypothesis across model 6 in Table 9.2. The linear term of the M&A management capabilities is positive and significant (p < 0.1), while the squared term of the alliance capabilities is negative and significant (p < 0.1). We did not find an inverted U-shaped function for explorative patents with respect to M&A management capabilities. Neither of the two coefficients is significantly different from zero.

Control variables

Most of the controls have the expected effect on exploitative and explorative innovative performance. Concerning the effects of cumulative patents pre M&A on exploitative (Table 9.2) and explorative performance (Table 9.3), we found a positive and significant effect for pre-M&A cumulative patents in line with other research (Rothaermel and Deeds 2006; Nooteboom *et al.*, 2007). Firms with a larger patents' portfolio pre M&A should have fewer problems dealing with exploitative or explorative innovative processes.

The effect of the 'relative patent portfolio size' (which measures the degree of similarity between the acquirer and target patent portfolio size) on exploitative patents is negative and significant (Model 1, Table 9.2). In almost all the cases the acquiring firm was the larger of the two and, therefore, a lower ratio implies more similarity in patent portfolio size between firms. Previous studies show that large differences in the patent portfolio size of companies indicate dissimilarities in the organisational setting of the partners, which might disturb the post-merger knowledge integration process, affecting the innovative performance of firms involved in M&As (Hagedoorn and Duysters, 2002a). Our research shows that a large difference in patent portfolio size between the acquiring and the target firm, indicating a poor organisational fit, might produce weaker exploitative performance than in the case of greater organisational similarity among partners. Relative patent portfolio size seems not to have a significant effect as regards exploration in new technological areas (Table 9.3).

Similar to the relative patent portfolio size, the effect of the acquirer/target diversification ratio on exploitative patents is negative and significant (Model 1, Table 9.2). In almost all the cases the acquiring firm was the larger of the two and, therefore, a lower ratio implies more similarity in the breadth of technological knowledge among firms. Also in this case, a large difference in the breadth of technological patent classes between the acquiring and the acquired firm before M&A might lead to lower exploitative performance; instead, this variable seems not to have a significant influence on exploring new technological domains (Table 9.3).

Size, measured in terms of a natural logarithm of number of employees, has a positive and significant effect on innovative performance for exploiting the core technologies, as well as for exploring new technological domains. The log form of this variable enables us to interpret the coefficient in the negative binomial specification as the elasticity between firm size and the dependent variables. The coefficients in both tables (Tables 9.2 and 9.3) are smaller than 1, suggesting – all else being equal – that the frequency of patenting increases with firm size, but less than proportionately. Thus, small firms perform better than the larger ones.

Interestingly, the coefficient for firm size in the exploitation of current technologies is larger than in the case of the exploration of new technological domains. This difference shows that the smaller firms have a larger share of explorative patents (Nooteboom *et al.*, 2007). This is in line with previous studies that highlighted that new inventions are more likely to be originated by entrants rather than by incumbents (Cooper and Schendel, 1976; Foster, 1986; Nooteboom *et al.*, 2007).

Similar to the firm size, firm age is measured in terms of a natural logarithm of number of years since the foundation date of the firm. The log form of this variable allows us to interpret the coefficient as the elasticity between firm age and patenting activity. The coefficients in Table 9.2 are negative and smaller than 1 (exploitative performance), suggesting – all else being equal – that the frequency of patenting decreases with firm age, but less than proportionately; in fact, older firms perform better than the new ones.

Older companies that have had more time to develop capabilities in certain technological domains have a greater competitive advantage than new entrants, which still have to develop this technological skill (Nooteboom *et al.*, 2007). However, the positive but not significant coefficient for explorative patents (Model 1, Table 9.3) indicates that younger firms might have a small advantage in exploring new technological areas (although we have no conclusive evidence at all, because the value is not significant). This is in line with previous studies that have concentrated on the role of new firms in the creation of new technologies (Methe *et al.*, 1997; Sørenson and Stuart, 2000; Nooteboom *et al.*, 2007).

To check for differences between the type of ownership and the propensity to patent (both explorative and exploitative), we introduced a dummy variable (public=1 and private=0), but we found no significant coefficients.

Finally, the dummy variable 'Region', indicating in which economic area the firms are based (North America=1 or Europe=0), presents no significant coefficients in either Table.

Discussion

Cognitive distance

Our results highlight that knowledge distance affects knowledge performance measures differently in terms of explorative and exploitative innovation. On the one hand, knowledge similarity, as expected, positively influences exploitative innovation and this relationship is shaped like an inverted U. This confirms that there is an optimal distance in terms of similarity between acquired and available knowledge, which enables firms to maximise their productivity in terms of exploitative innovation. On the one hand, the acquisition of a base of know-how that is too similar to the available one reduces the potential for exploitative innovation available in the M&A. Thus, beyond a certain degree of distance between acquired and available knowledge, the cognitive costs of assimilation and integration become too high and there is less possibility for exploitative innovation.

Knowledge complementarity, different from what was expected, is negatively related to explorative innovation. However, there is a positive and stronger relationship between the square of knowledge complementarity and explorative innovation. This confirms that a minimum level of complementarity is required in order to support the development of exploitative innovation. Furthermore, beyond that minimum level, the relationship between complementarity and exploitative innovation is quadratic. There are two types of data supporting such a claim. First, knowledge similarity and complementarity are negatively correlated. This excludes the case that low level complementarity is strongly associated with a high degree of knowledge dissimilarity. Second, the quadratic relationship is more significant than the linear one.

Absorption-related invention capacity

Absorption-related invention capacity is positively associated both with explorative and exploitative innovation. This result is interesting from two points of view. First, it shows the relevance of assimilation and transformation in enhancing firms' productivity in terms of both explorative and exploitative innovation. Through these processes, the acquiring firms gain specific insights on how the acquired knowledge can be innovatively recombined with the available knowledge. Second, it also shows, as suggested by Katila and Ahuja (2002), that knowledge assimilation and transformation are also important for enhancing the explorative performance of firms. Thus, knowledge assimilation and transformation, different from what has been suggested in many other studies, do not contribute only to enhancing existing technologies but also to providing the ground for exploring new paths of innovation through the recombination of existing solutions and expertise.

Managerial capabilities

Our results concerning the effect of managerial experience are rather surprising. The experience accumulated in the management of strategic alliances displays a more significant effect on innovative performance than the experience accumulated in the management of M&As. Even more, previous experience in the management of M&As displays a weak significant effect only in relation to the level of exploitative innovation post M&A. This result, from our point of view, may have two possible and interconnected explanations. First, firms enter strategic alliances more frequently than they enter M&As. Thus, the number of strategic alliances entered into by a firm reflects its attitude towards the exploration and exploitation of external knowledge more than the number of M&As entered into by the same firms, which may depend more on casual factors. Second, being successful in a strategic alliance requires that firms mutually trust each other and collaborate under agreed terms of reference. Trust is also a critical factor in leveraging knowledge creation and recombination. Thus, accumulating experience in the management of strategic alliances may foster the development of a positive attitude towards the use of trust, which may strengthen the level of explorative and exploitative performance post M&As.

Managerial implications

Our study has several managerial implications. First, it shows that the absorption of external knowledge through M&As may mitigate the trade-off between exploration and exploitation. Therefore, technology-based M&As represent an alternative to the design of either an ambidextrous organisation or alternating between short-period exploration and long-period exploitation. However, it is not sufficient to enter into M&As to exploit the external sources of knowledge in order to leverage both exploration and exploitation. This depends on the specific conformation of the acquired knowledge base. On the one hand, knowledge similarity is relevant to feed exploitation. Thus, managers should merge with companies that have a similar knowledge base, but not too similar. In fact, there is an optimal level of dissimilarity between acquired and available knowledge, enabling firms to maximise their productivity in terms of exploitation. On the other hand, knowledge complementarity is important to feed the capacity of firms to develop explorative innovation. However, also in the case of complementarity, managers should consider that a minimum level of distance in terms of complementarity is required in order to support the development of explorative performance. Third, the exploitation of the acquired source of knowledge is not only relevant to support exploitative innovation but also explorative innovation. Moreover, managers should stimulate the internal experimentation and adoption of the acquired knowledge base in order to strengthen the development of innovative recombination between acquired and innovative knowledge.

Finally, we found that the experience accumulated in the management of strategic alliances is relevant to selecting the appropriate partner and to facilitating the flow of knowledge from the target to the acquirer. Therefore, in order to promote the accumulation and reuse of such experience, it is useful to either set up a team of managers who specialise in the management of M&As and strategic alliances or, especially in the case of small and medium enterprises, to rely on specialised temporary managers.

Conclusions

In this chapter we investigated whether technology-based M&As contribute to enhancing the capacity of firms to pursue both exploitation and exploration. Our analysis suggests that, under certain circumstances, this hypothesis is supported. More specifically, it highlights the importance of selecting the appropriate partner in terms of knowledge complementarity and knowledge similarity. Even more, it stresses knowledge assimilation and transformation as critical for enhancing exploitation and exploration post M&As. These two phases, differently from what has been suggested in the past, are found to contribute not only to exploitation but also to exploration. Finally, our study highlights the role of the experience accumulated in the management of technology-based M&As and, especially, strategic alliances in fostering innovative performance post M&As. In this respect, we suggest that the experience accumulated in the management of strategic alliances is more significant, because it reflects a positive attitude of the firms towards collaboration and open innovation.

This study presents several limitations. First, we focused on a single industrial context from which we selected a population of companies headquartered in North America and Europe, observed over a period of six years. Although such a focus increases internal validity, our results might reflect some industry- and period-specific factors that limit the generalisability of the findings for other industries. For instance, the reliance on patents varies between industries and, thus, our measure, although appropriate for biopharmaceuticals, might not provide an accurate representation in other contexts. Although the number of industries where patents can be considered meaningful indicators of innovation has been growing in recent years (Makri *et al.*, 2010), a need for elaboration of the study in different settings is thus identified in order to confirm or re-evaluate the findings and to generate further insights.

Second, we used patent citations and data to construct our independent variables. This led us to exclude from our sample any firms for which no data on patents was available in the consulted datasets. This is reasonable because: (1) acquisitions involving partners that do not own any patents generally take place for other purposes, such as manufacturing and marketing (Phene *et al.*, 2012) or simply to eliminate possible competitors from the market; and (2) similar to other industries, like the semiconductor or high-tech industries, patenting in the biopharmaceutical context is actively and routinely pursued with the aim of acquiring an innovative presence. However, although patents and patent citations are generally regarded as good indicators of innovative output and the ability to acquire and exploit a target's knowledge base, they are also usually considered to be intermediate outcomes along the value chain. Hence, a better and more comprehensive evaluation of the knowledge relatedness effects on innovation and technological performances should rely not only on patents but also on products or processes generated by patents obtained in the post-M&A period that are based on the pre-M&A target knowledge and also, perhaps, have been effectively commercialised. In addition, the adequacy of patents as proxies of knowledge bases has been questioned, since these provide only a static representation and do not consider organisational routines as complementary factors in the absorption of external knowledge (Lane *et al.*, 2006).

Third, we reiterate Makri *et al.*'s (2010) argument that International Patent Classification, although fairly adequate and clear, has been created and developed for purposes other than providing researchers with a picture of firms' knowledge bases.

Fourth, as already mentioned, our sample of independent acquirers from North America and Europe necessarily provides no evidence from countries in other continents, such as those that are now emerging (e.g. as 'developing' and 'newly developed').

Fifth, the study might be biased due to undeniable general difficulties in obtaining broad data on firms' knowledge and R&D inputs and outcomes, as well as because of its reliance on data from the Medtrack dataset. The availability of more comprehensive datasets providing such information, not only with regard to the biopharmaceutical industry but also to other industrial contexts, would allow our research to be replicated, extended and improved.

Finally, with reference to patent citations, for US patents, researchers have questioned the use of patent citations as a proxy for knowledge transfer or organisational learning on the basis that a non-trivial portion of citations is added by government officials or legal experts along the patent filing process (Alcacer and Gittelman, 2006). This does not appear to be relevant here, however, since M&A partners get to know each other during the acquisition process, so it is reasonable to assume that they directly cite their previous knowledge bases.

Note

1 Patent citation is here defined as: 'the extent to which a firm's patents are cited in subsequent patents' (Makri et al., 2010) applied for by other companies.

References

Abernathy W., Clark K. B., 1985. Innovation: Mapping the winds of creative destruction. *Research Policy*, 14(1): 3–22.

Acs Z. J., Audretsch D. B., 1988. Innovation in large and small firms: An empirical analysis. *The American Economic Review*, 78(4): 678–690.

Adegbesan J. A., Higgins M. J., 2011. The intra-alliance division of value created through collaboration. *Strategic Management Journal*, 32(2): 187–211.

Ahuja G., Katila R., 2001. Technological acquisitions and the innovation performance of acquiring firms: A longitudinal study. *Strategic Management Journal*, 22(3): 197–220.

Alcacer J., Gittelman M., 2006. Patent citations as a measure of knowledge flows: The influence of examiner citations. *The Review of Economics and Statistics*, 88(4): 774–779.

Anand B. N., Khanna T., 2000. Do firms learn to create value? The case of alliances. *Strategic Management Journal*, 21(3): 295–315.

Arora A., Gambardella A., 1990. Complementarity and external linkages: The strategies of the large firms in biotechnology. *The Journal of Industrial Economics*, 38(4): 361–379.

Barney J., 1986. Strategic factor markets: Expectations, luck, and business strategy. *Management Science*, 32(10): 1231–1241.

Barney J., 1991. Firm resources and sustained competitive advantage. *Journal of Management*, 17(1): 99–120.

Baum J. A., Li S. X., Usher J. M., 2000. Making the next move: How experiential and vicarious learning shape the locations of chains' acquisitions. *Administrative Science Quarterly*, 45(4): 766–801.

Beneito P., 2006. The innovative performance of in-house and contracted R&D in terms of patents and utility models. *Research Policy*, 35(4): 502–517.

Benner M. J., Tushman M. L., 2003. Exploitation, exploration, and process management: The productivity dilemma revisited. *Academy of Management Review*, 28(2): 238–256.

Buono A. F., Bowditch J. L., 1989. *The Human Side of Mergers and Acquisitions*, Jossey-Bass, San Francisco, CA.

Cassiman B., Veugelers R., 1999. *Importance of International Linkages for Local Know-How Flows: Some Econometric Evidence from Belgium*. Discussion Paper No. 2337, Centre for Economic Policy Research Discussion Papers, London, UK. Available at: https://ideas.repec.org/p/upf/upfgen/434.html (accessed 10 July 2013).

Chang K., 2008. The strategic alliance of the biotechnology firm. *Applied Economics*, 40(23): 3089–3100.

Cloodt M., Hagedoorn J., Van Kranenburg H., 2006. Mergers and acquisitions: Their effect on the innovative performance of companies in high-tech industries. *Research Policy*, 35(5): 642–654.

Cohen W. M., Levinthal D. A., 1990. Absorptive capacity: A new perspective on learning and innovation. *Administrative Science Quarterly*, 35(1): 128–152.

Conner K. R., Prahalad C. K., 1996. A resource-based theory of the firm: Knowledge versus opportunism. *Organization Science*, 7(5): 477–501.

Cooper A. C., Schendel D., 1976. Strategic responses to technological threats. *Business Horizons*, 19(1): 61–69.

Davis P. S., Robinson R. B. Jr., Pearce J. A. II., Park S. H., 1992. Business unit relatedness and performance: A look at the pulp and paper industry. *Strategic Management Journal*, 13(5): 349–361.

De Man A.-P., Duysters G., 2005. Collaboration and innovation: A review of the effects of mergers, acquisitions and alliances on innovation. *Technovation*, 25(12): 1377–1387.

Deeds D. L., Hill C. W., 1996. Strategic alliances and the rate of new product development: An empirical study of entrepreneurial biotechnology firms. *Journal of Business Venturing*, 11(1): 41–55.

Deeds D. L., Rothaermel F. T., 2003. Honeymoons and liabilities: The relationship between age and performance in research and development alliances. *Journal of Product Innovation Management*, 20(6): 468–484.

Diestre L., Rajagopalan N., 2012. Are all 'sharks' dangerous? New biotechnology ventures and partner selection in R&D alliances. *Strategic Management Journal*, 33(10): 1115–1134.

Dushnitsky G., Lenox M. J., 2005. When do firms undertake R&D by investing in new ventures? *Strategic Management Journal*, 26(10): 947–965.

Farjoun M., 1998. The independent and joint effects of the skill and physical bases of relatedness in diversification. *Strategic Management Journal*, 19(7): 611–630.

Foster R., 1986. *Innovation: The Attackers Advantage*, Summit Books, New York, NY.

Freeman C., Soete L., 1997. *The Economics of Industrial Innovation*, Psychology Press, London, UK.

Ghoshal S., Moran P., 1996. Bad for practice: A critique of the transaction cost theory. *Academy of Management Review*, 21(1): 13–47.

Gilsing V., Nooteboom B., Vanhaverbeke W., Duysters G., Van den Oord A., 2008. Network embeddedness and the exploration of novel technologies: Technological distance, betweenness centrality and density. *Research Policy*, 37(10): 1717–1731.

Goldman Sachs, 2001. *Strategic Alliances in Biotechnology*, Goldman Sachs, New York, NY.

Graebner M. E., 2004. Momentum and serendipity: How acquired leaders create value in the integration of technology firms. *Strategic Management Journal*, 25(8–9): 751–777.

Grant R. M., 1996. Toward a knowledge-based theory of the firm. *Strategic Management Journal*, 17(52): 109–122.

Hagedoorn J., 1993. Understanding the rationale of strategic technology partnering: Interorganizational modes of cooperation and sectoral differences. *Strategic Management Journal*, 14(5): 371–385.

Hagedoorn J., Duysters G., 2002a. External sources of innovative capabilities: The preference for strategic alliances or mergers and acquisitions. *Journal of Management Studies*, 39(2): 167–188.

Hagedoorn J., Duysters G., 2002b. The effect of mergers and acquisitions on the technological performance of companies in a high-tech environment. *Technology Analysis & Strategic Management*, 14(1): 67–85.

Hagedoorn J., Wang N., 2012. Is there complementarity or substitutability between internal and external R&D strategies? *Research Policy*, 41(6): 1072–1083.

Haleblian J., Finkelstein S., 1999. The influence of organizational acquisition experience on acquisition performance: A behavioral learning perspective. *Administrative Science Quarterly*, 44(1): 29–56.

Hausman J., Hall B., Griliches Z., 1984. Econometric models for count data with an application to the patents—R&D relationship. *Econometrica*, 52(4): 909–938.

He Z. L., Wong P. K., 2004. Exploration vs. exploitation: An empirical test of the ambidexterity hypothesis. *Organization Science*, 15(4): 481–494.

Henderson R. M., Cockburn I. M., 1996. Scale, scope, and spillovers: The determinants of research productivity in drug discovery. *The Rand Journal of Economics*, 27(1): 32–59.

Hitt M. A., Hoskisson R. E., Johnson R. A., Moesel D. D., 1996. The market for corporate control and firm innovation. *Academy of Management Journal*, 39(5): 1084–1119.

Hoang H., Rothaermel F. T., 2005. The effect of general and partner-specific alliance experience on joint R&D project performance. *Academy of Management Journal*, 48(2): 332–345.

Jansen J. J., Van Den Bosch F. A., Volberda H. W., 2006. Exploratory innovation, exploitative innovation, and performance: Effects of organizational antecedents and environmental moderators. *Management Science*, 52(11): 1661–1674.

Kale P., Dyer J. H., Singh H., 2002. Alliance capability, stock market response, and long-term alliance success: The role of the alliance function. *Strategic Management Journal*, 23(8): 747–767.

Katila R., Ahuja G., 2002. Something old, something new: A longitudinal study of search behavior and new product introduction. *Academy of Management Journal*, 45(6): 1183–1194.

Kleinbaum D. G., Kupper L. L., Muller K. E., 1988. *Applied Regression Analysis and Other Multivariate Methods*, 2nd edition, PWS-Kent, Boston, MA.

Kogut B., Zander U., 1996. What firms do? Coordination, identity, and learning. *Organization Science*, 7(5): 502–518.

Lane P. J., Lubatkin M., 1998. Relative absorptive capacity and interorganizational learning. *Strategic Management Journal*, 19(5): 461–477.

Lane P. J., Koka B. R., Pathak S., 2006. The reification of absorptive capacity: A critical review and rejuvenation of the construct. *Academy of Management Review*, 31(4): 833–863.

Larsson R., Finkelstein S., 1999. Integrating strategic, organizational, and human resource perspectives on mergers and acquisitions: A case survey of synergy realization. *Organization Science*, 10(1): 1–26.

Levinthal D. A., March J. G., 1993. The myopia of learning. *Strategic Management Journal*, 14(S2): 95–112.

Levitt B., March J. G., 1988. Organizational learning. *Annual Review of Sociology*, 14: 319–340.

Lewin A. Y., Volberda H. W., 1999. Prolegomena on coevolution: A framework for research on strategy and new organizational forms. *Organization Science*, 10(5): 519–534.

Makri M., Hitt M. A., Lane P. J., 2010. Complementary technologies, knowledge relatedness, and invention outcomes in high technology mergers and acquisitions. *Strategic Management Journal*, 31(6): 602–628.

March J. G., 1991. Exploration and exploitation in organizational learning. *Organization Science*, 2(1): 71–87.

Methe D., Swaminathan A., Mitchell W., Toyama R., 1997. The underemphasized role of diversifying entrants and industry incumbents as the sources of major innovations, in Thomas H., O'Neal D., (eds), *Strategic Discovery: Competing in New Arenas*. Wiley, New York, NY, pp. 99–116.

Miller D. J., 2004. Firms' technological resources and the performance effects of diversification: A longitudinal study. *Strategic Management Journal*, 25(11): 1097–1119.

Mowery D. C., Oxley J. E., Silverman B. S., 1998. Technological overlap and interfirm cooperation: Implications for the resource-based view of the firm. *Research Policy*, 27(5): 507–523.

Narin F., Noma E., Perry R., 1987. Patents as indicators of corporate technological strength. *Research Policy*, 16(2): 143–155.

Nonaka I., 1995. *The Knowledge-Creating Company: How Japanese Companies Create the Dynamics of Innovation*, Oxford University Press, Oxford, UK.

Nooteboom B., Vanhaverbeke W., Duysters G., Gilsing V., Van den Oord, A. (2007). Optimal cognitive distance and absorptive capacity. *Research Policy*, 36(7): 1016–1034.

Pakes A., Griliches Z., 1984. Estimating distributed lags in short panels with an application to the specification of depreciation patterns and capital stock constructs. *The Review of Economic Studies*, 51(2): 243–262.

Phene A., Tallman S., Almeida P., 2012. When do acquisitions facilitate technological exploration and exploitation? *Journal of Management*, 38(3): 753–783.

Powell W. W., Koput K. W., Smith-Doerr L., 1996. Interorganizational collaboration and the locus of innovation: Networks of learning in biotechnology. *Administrative Science Quarterly*, 41(1): 116–145.

Rosenkopf L., Nerkar A., 2001. Beyond local search: Boundary-spanning, exploration, and impact in the optical disk industry. *Strategic Management Journal*, 22(4): 287–306.

Rosenkopf L., Almeida P., 2003. Overcoming local search through alliances and mobility. *Management Science*, 49(6): 751–766.

Rothaermel F. T., 2001. Incumbent's advantage through exploiting complementary assets via interfirm cooperation. *Strategic Management Journal*, 22(6–7): 687–699.

Rothaermel F. T., Deeds D. L., 2004. Exploration and exploitation alliances in biotechnology: A system of new product development. *Strategic Management Journal*, 25(3): 201–221.

Rothaermel F. T., Deeds D. L., 2006. Alliance type, alliance experience and alliance management capability in high-technology ventures. *Journal of Business Venturing*, 21(4): 429–460.

Rothaermel F. T., Boeker W., 2008. Old technology meets new technology: Complementarities, similarities, and alliance formation. *Strategic Management Journal*, 29(1): 47–77.

Sampson R., 2002. *Experience, Learning and Collaborative Returns in R&D Alliances.* Working Paper. Stern School of Business, New York University, NY. Available at: http://papers.ssrn.com/sol3/papers.cfm?abstract_id=309944 (accessed 10 July 2013).

Scherer F. M., 1984. Corporate size, diversification, and innovative activity, in *Innovation and Growth: Schumpeterian Perspectives*, The MIT Press, Cambridge, MA, pp. 222–238.

Shan W., Walker G., Kogut B., 1994. Interfirm cooperation and startup innovation in the biotechnology industry. *Strategic Management Journal*, 15(5): 387–394.

Simonin B. L., 1997. The importance of collaborative know-how: An empirical test of the learning organization. *Academy of Management Journal*, 40(5): 1150–1174.

Singh A., 1971. *Take-overs: Their Relevance to the Stock Market and the Theory of the Firm*, Cambridge University Press, Cambridge, UK.

Sørensen J. B., Stuart T. E., 2000. Aging, obsolescence, and organizational innovation. *Administrative Science Quarterly*, 45(1): 81–112.

Teece D. J., Pisano G., Shuen A., 1997. Dynamic capabilities and strategic management. *Strategic Management Journal*, 18(7): 509–533.

Teece D. J., 2007. Explicating dynamic capabilities: The nature and microfoundations of (sustainable) enterprise performance. *Strategic Management Journal*, 28(13): 1319–1350.

Uhlenbruck K., Hitt M. A., Semadeni M., 2006. Market value effects of acquisitions involving internet firms: A resource-based analysis. *Strategic Management Journal*, 27(10): 899–913.

Varian H. R., Farrell J., Farrell J. V., Shapiro C., 2004. *The Economics of Information Technology: An Introduction*, Cambridge University Press, Cambridge, UK.

Vermeulen F., Barkema H., 2001. Learning through acquisitions. *Academy of Management Journal*, 44(3): 457–476.

Wernerfelt B., 1984. A resource-based view of the firm. *Strategic Management Journal*, 5(2): 171–180.

Zahra S. A., George G., 2002. Absorptive capacity: A review, reconceptualization, and extension. *Academy of Management Review*, 27(2): 185–203.

Zollo M., Reuer J. J., Singh H., 2002. Interorganizational routines and performance in strategic alliances. *Organization Science*, 13(6): 701–713.

Part III

Alliances in high-tech environments

10 Pasteur scientists meet the market

An empirical illustration of the innovative performance of university–industry relationships

Silvia Rita Sedita, Yasunori Baba and Naohiro Shichijo

Introduction

Many theoretical contributions have pointed out the need to take in serious consideration the relational nature of the innovation process, which implies the analysis of the interactions between firms, universities and public research organizations (PROs), stemming from the seminal contributions given by Edquist (1997) on the system of innovation approach and by Etzkowitz and Leydesdorff (1997) on the 'Triple Helix' model.

Some studies in the field of economic geography have mainly focused on the exploration of the spatial dimension of these interactions (the national system of innovation approach: Lundvall, 1992; and the regional innovation system approach: Cooke, 1992). The sociological approach to the innovation process provided researchers with the right tools to map the interorganizational networks for innovation (Owen-Smith *et al.*, 2002; Owen-Smith and Powell, 2004; Powell *et al.*, 2005) and to analyse the spatial knowledge spillovers, a concept that has been well developed by economists such as Breschi and Lissoni (2001). Management studies have been mainly concerned with the types of and vehicles for knowledge transfer (such as formal/informal agreements and alliances, inventors' mobility and so forth) and the impact of cognitive/spatial distance between the partners on their innovative performance (e.g. Almeida and Kogut, 1999; Rosenkopf and Almeida, 2003; Gittelman, 2007).

The investigation of the role of university–industry (U–I) research collaborations in shaping the innovative output of universities and firms has been a key issue in the debate on the relational nature of innovations (Agrawal and Henderson, 2002; Cohen *et al.*, 2002a; Feldman *et al.*, 2002; Murmann, 2003). The majority of the empirical works that have been published in this field attempted to explain the innovation patterns of firms operating in the life sciences sector (e.g. Owen-Smith *et al.*, 2002; Murray, 2002; Zucker *et al.*, 2002; Owen-Smith and Powell, 2004; Gittelman, 2007). Very few contributions shed any light on other innovation-intensive industries (such as nanotechnology: Meyer, 2006; Meyer, 2007; microelectronics and electronics: Balconi and Laboranti, 2006; Furukawa and Goto, 2006a), neglecting the possibility that results obtained by analysing the biotech and pharmaceuticals sectors could not be applied as such to the study of larger pools of innovation processes. Nevertheless, the heterogeneity of the innovation process leads us to investigate more broadly the technology transfer mechanism occurring in other knowledge intensive, but not purely science-based, industries such as the advanced materials sector.

As elaborated by Subramanian *et al.* (2013):

> [e]xisting studies on R&D alliances do not pay sufficient attention to the heterogeneity of scientific human capital in knowledge flows. The extant view is that firms employ scientists primarily to transform academic science into useful inventions, and they use R&D alliances as conduits to gain access to new scientific knowledge. (Subramanian *et al.*, 2013: 595)

The interaction effects between scientific human capital and R&D alliances is crucial and deserve attention. Accordingly, this work classifies researchers into three types to show their idiosyncratic attitudes towards entrepreneurial activities, including: (1) Edison scientists – researchers who, like Thomas Edison, conduct mainly applied research with the aim of discovering knowledge which can be applied to the real world, rather than extending basic science; (2) Bohr scientists – classified because of their similarity to Danish scientist, Niels Bohr, who contributed significantly to discoveries in quantum mechanics and atomic structure; these scientists are keener on pure research for its own sake and have little interest in the potential uses of their research; and (3) Pasteur scientists – such researchers are 'hybrid academics' like French scientist, Louis Pasteur, who had close links with the French distillation industry and from which his interests in fermentation originated. They are the most entrepreneurial, in that they aim to advance scientific understanding while contributing to solving real world problems.

Through some empirical evidence coming from the field of advanced materials in Japan, we are able to identify the performance of U–I relationships in terms of innovative capacity of firms engaged in research with universities. A case study of TOTO, the leading manufacturer of sanitary ceramics in Japan and the world market leader for toilet washing systems, is presented as empirical illustration. The indepth case study shows how company-specific orientation towards innovation and product differentiation strategies complement and lead the innovation strategies of the firm and the performance of U–I interactions.

Theoretical background

U–I collaborations have been long considered as crucial in finding industrial applications for scientific discoveries (Bonaccorsi and Piccaluga, 1994; Agrawal and Henderson, 2002; Cohen *et al.*, 2002a; Feldman *et al.*, 2002; Murmann, 2003; Baba *et al.*, 2009). Accordingly, firm networks and knowledge ecosystems have been proved to sustain the innovative output of firms, within an open innovation framework (Chesbrough, 2003, 2006).

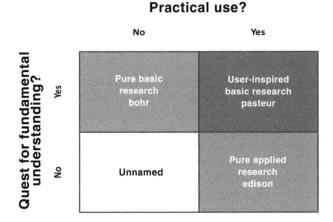

Figure 10.1 The Stokes' classification of scientists

Source: Stokes (1997).

For the purposes of clarifying the function of 'two-way' interaction between university and industry, research tradition makes use of the patenting and publishing performance of individual scientists and researchers (Narin and Breitzman 1995; Schmoch 1997; Murray 2002; Furukawa and Goto, 2006a, 2006b). The pioneering work of Zucker and Darby (1995, 1996, 2001) demonstrated the significance of an individual researcher as a unit of analysis and elected the 'star scientists', defined as those who had published 40 or more genetic sequence discoveries in GenBank, as the best corporate partners in biotechnology (Zucker and Darby 1995, 1996, 2001; Zucker *et al.*, 1998, 2002). Furukawa and Goto (2006a, 2006b) identified these 'core scientists' as corporate scientists who had collected an exceptionally large number of research papers and paper citations and who were, therefore, the most relevant firm innovation drivers in pharmaceuticals and electronics. Baba *et al.* (2009) investigated the role of 'Pasteur scientists' on the innovative performance of firms belonging to the advanced materials fields. Stemming from the seminal contribution of Stokes (1997), the authors of the paper proposed a classification of scientists based on their inclination towards science and technology (Baba *et al.*, 2009). Stokes identified mainly three types of scientists: (1) Edison scientists; (2) Bohr scientists; and (3) Pasteur scientists (see Figure 10.1).

Edison scientists, who are not well integrated within the scientific community, are at a disadvantage when they try to access advanced areas of science. Even if they are highly experienced in technological aspects due to their numerous patent applications, they are not able to offer significant advances in science.

Bohr scientists, who pursue basic research for understanding science for its own sake, have little interest in the potential uses of the research findings for industry. Although the two-way interaction between academic scientists and industry is expected to produce a series of mutual advantages in advanced materials, star scientists are reluctant to utilize U–I collaboration for raising their scientific productivity.

Pasteur scientists are those university scientists who have been involved in many patent applications, in addition to authoring many high-quality scientific papers. Pasteur scientists, in addition to traditional academic publishing, show a good patenting performance and they are inclined to work as bridges between scientific community and industry when it comes to finding the potential applications for a new scientific discovery. They facilitate the process of transforming the reservoir of applied knowledge into scientific knowledge and then increasing their scientific productivity (in terms of quantity and quality of publications, see Shichijo *et al.*, 2013). When firms engage in collaboration with Pasteur scientists, it is expected that knowledge interaction between academia and industry will become more advanced and scientific productivity of academic scientists will improve.

In the field of advanced materials, Pasteur scientists consider issues such as how to provide the new functions that have been made possible through the use of a material to end users with new services. For this purpose, Pasteur scientists consult with firms, aiming to resolve complex problems that involve numerous components, materials, performance constraints and interactions. Consulting is a two-way interaction between Pasteur scientists and corporate researchers, whose nature is found in the reciprocal expectation of gaining some advantages: industry partners receive the idea of how to use a material effectively in product development based on sophisticated scientific understanding; academic partners gain access to complimentary assets needed to advance their scientific activities such as process technology for testing a scientific hypothesis or financial support.

When illustrating the relevance of Pasteur scientists in shaping the innovative performance of companies, it is also crucial to investigate the characteristics of firms that engage in U–I collaborations. Not all companies have, in fact, the ability to conduct high-quality research, be able to embody forefront technologies in their products and successfully sell them in the market (it is a matter of, for example, absorptive capacity). This is why we provide an interesting case study where high-quality university research blends with high-quality industrial standards.

Methodology

Empirical evidence comes from a case study research approach focused on TOTO Ltd., the largest plumbing manufacturer in the world, based in Japan. Data come from primary and secondary data sources. Primary data come from indepth interviews with leading actors involved in TOTO's innovation process who see as crucial components, together with corporate researchers, two 'Pasteur scientists' from the University of Tokyo: Akira Fujishima and Kazuhito Hashimoto. Secondary data come from the company's website and the Orbit database.

Brief history of TOTO: blending Japanese culture, innovation and international opening

TOTO is Japan's leading producer of sanitary ware. Its technological innovations and high-quality standards have made it an iconic and much-loved brand in Japan and, with the increase in demand from European consumers, an ever more luxurious and fulfilling bathroom experience. TOTO Ltd. was established by Kazuchika Okura in 1917 in Kitakyushu, Japan, under the name Toyo Toki K.K. Okura had a vision more than a hundred years ago, in 1912, before the concept of public sewage systems was widespread in Japan. After seeing more advanced systems overseas, he was moved to establish a ceramic sanitary ware laboratory to develop healthier and cleaner living spaces. In 1914 the laboratory successfully produced Japan's first ceramic sanitary ware. In 1917 Toyo Toki K.K. (currently TOTO LTD.) was founded to permeate the market with these products. TOTO was founded on a commitment to provide a comfortable living space for people, while always protecting the planet and its water. Japan's rich artistic heritage in pottery and porcelain is alive in every TOTO product. Throughout its expansion worldwide, TOTO has remained true to the Japanese traditions that have shaped the company motto and philosophy. The TOTO motto, created in 1962, is: 'Take pride in your work, and strive to do your best'. After World War II, in 1946, TOTO began to manufacture metal fittings and taps as well as ceramics. In 1963 the company developed a construction method for the world's first prefabricated bathroom module. In 1980 it launched the WASHLET, which provides consumers with a new level of cleanliness and comfort. In 1985 TOTO created the 'Shampoo Dresser' bathroom vanity, which is used for washing hair. In 1989 TOTO U.S.A. was founded, the company having already expanded into Indonesia, Thailand, Taiwan and Hong Kong. In 1993 the NEOREST toilet was launched revolutionizing the principle of clean technology. In 2001 TOTO China opened. In 2005 the first system bathroom equipped with Karari flooring was introduced in Japan. In 2006 the TOTO Water Environment Fund was established and WASHLET shipments top 20 million. In 2008 TOTO opened the Universal Design Center to develop TOTO Total Design products accommodating users of all ages and physical abilities. TOTO U.S.A. was awarded the first EPA Water Efficiency Leadership Award. In 2009 TOTO Mexico opened. European headquarters are established in Germany and the Asian headquarters in Singapore.

In 2010 the NEOREST Hybrid Series used only 4.8 litres of water per flush. At the International Sanitary and Heating Trade Show in Frankfurt, Germany, this result was announced as a new global standard. Shipments of NEOREST reached 1 million units.

In 2011 TOTO Americas Holding is established, releasing new technologies: the 'Basic Plus' shower head with Air in Shower technologies, the 'GG' tank toilet with Twin Tornado Cleansing and the 'CRASSO' modular kitchen.

In 2012 TOTO Brazil and TOTO India opened; TOTO established TOTO (Fujian) Co., Ltd. In the same year TOTO participated in the UN Global Compact. In 2014 the company announced 'TOTO Global Environmental Vision'. TOTO has

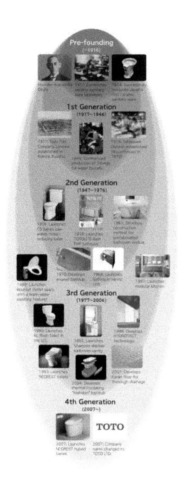

Figure 10.2 The evolution of TOTO products

Source: TOTO corporate report.

always embraced technology, pursued the highest levels of cleanliness, incorporated high aesthetic standards, protected the environment and worked to improve people's lifestyles. As a result of them continually innovating in all of these areas, TOTO has become the world standard of excellence for a quality bathroom experience. Figure 10.2 summarizes the evolution of TOTO products from its origins to the latest developments.

TOTO nowadays is the largest plumbing manufacturer in the world with ¥517 billion in annual sales (see Figure 10.3). The performance indicators are very positive and constantly increasing. During 2012 net sales increased by 5.2 per cent and during 2013 by 8.6 per cent.

To date, TOTO has produced more than 60 million plumbing fixtures. Today, this international company maintains 25,000 employees in 69 offices around the

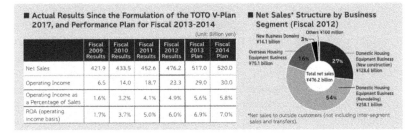

Figure 10.3 TOTO performance results

Source: TOTO corporate report 2013.

world and owns manufacturing facilities in Japan, Mexico, the US, China and Europe with an affiliated network of more than 80 production facilities worldwide. With over 1,500 engineers on the staff and three centres devoted solely to R&D, TOTO is the undisputed global leader in product innovation, precision engineering, high-design and sustainability in products that are designed to meet people's real world needs. Exemplified in the company's philosophy – People-First Innovation – TOTO offers consumers elegant luxury products that save money and water without sacrificing an ounce of performance and the peace of mind that comes from knowing that they purchased a brand that sets the standard for world-class performance, enduring quality and reliability. Winner of numerous domestic and international awards and recognitions, TOTO is the only plumbing manufacturer honoured as Water Efficiency Leader by the Environmental Protection Agency. TOTO continues to raise industry standards and consumer expectations as to what is possible in the bath space, as it connects people with water in ways that enrich the flow of their daily lives. Company mission, vision and values are described in Table 10.1.

TOTO values, besides being embodied in high-quality, high-design, eco-friendly products, are also made visible to clients and consumers through two

Table 10.1 TOTO mission, vision and values

Mission	Vision	Values
• 'Improve the lifestyle and culture of the people. Provide a healthy and civilized way of life'.	• New environmentally friendly products to be sold in new target markets • Willing to change the idea people have about bathrooms, exporting the Japanese culture	• Innovation (high quality product standards, differentiated products and top bathroom design) • Excellence (market leadership) • Saving natural resources (clean technology) • Well-being

Source: Authors' elaboration.

important initiatives: a company museum and a company gallery. TOTO established a company museum in 2007, the TOTO History Museum. The TOTO History Museum is located in the grounds of their headquarters in Kitakyushu displays sanitary wares dating from the Taisho to Showa eras, products that were used in the Diet Building and the original WASHLET, as well as eating utensils and other items. Since its opening, the museum has welcomed a total of some 60,000 visitors from around the world. Items on display include legacy examples of industrial modernization, architectural equipment technology and machinery of important historical value. Moreover, in order to underline its passion for design, in 1985 TOTO opened the TOTO Gallery 'MA'. This gallery, operated by TOTO in the Minami-Aoyama district of Tokyo, specializes mainly in architecture and design. Since its opening, the gallery has held to the objective of presenting high-quality information and it has conveyed the thinking and philosophy of architects and designers from Japan and other countries. In fiscal 2012 the gallery hosted a return exhibition of the 'Architecture. Possible here? Home-for-All' exhibit, which won the Japan Pavilion Golden Lion award for best national participation at the 13th Venice Biennale International Architecture Exhibition.

TOTO and the University of Tokyo: a fruitful collaboration

The collaboration between TOTO and the University of Tokyo is rooted in the discovery and development of properties and applications of the titanium dioxide (TiO_2) photocatalysts. When a photocatalyst, TiO_2, captures ultraviolet (UV) light, it forms activated oxygen from water or oxygen in the air. This process is similar to photosynthesis, in which chlorophyll captures sunlight to turn water and carbon dioxide into oxygen and glucose. The formed activated oxygen is strong enough to oxidize and decompose organic materials or smelly gas and kill bacteria. Recently, photocatalyst-coating technology has made it possible for a variety of building materials to incorporate advanced functions, i.e. sterilizing, deodorizing and anti-fouling properties.

In 1967 Japanese scientists from the University of Tokyo, Akira Fujishima (now Chairman of KAST – Kanagawa Academy of Science and Technology) and Kenichi Honda discovered the active cleansing effect of TiO_2 in photocatalysis. They researched this phenomenon, now known as the 'Honda-Fujishima Effect' and published a report entitled *The Effect of Photokatalysator TiO$_2$* in *Nature* magazine in 1972. Since then, TiO_2 photocatalysis has been studied on the subject of water cleavage, water treatment and air treatment. In 1990 Professors Akira Fujishima and Kazuhito Hashimoto of the University of Tokyo established the Fujishima-Hashimoto laboratory (now FH-Lab), in order to develop the idea of coating TiO_2 photocatalysts on two-dimensional solid surfaces, rather than mixing them with liquids as had been attempted previously. In 1991 they started to conduct joint research with the leading sanitary maker, TOTO, on the coating of TiO_2 photocatalysts on tiles and other building materials. When Hashimoto was collaborating with the company, he initially proposed using photocatalysis to clean yellowing of sanitary products. His partners at TOTO, however, insisted that just eliminating yellowing would not make their products more competitive; without the effect of removing odour, they argued, the products would not be marketable. Having gone through a process of intensive information exchange, they soon discovered that TiO_2 photocatalysts coated on solid surfaces have anti-dirt and antibacterial functions, which resulted in joint applications for patents. Unlike the so-called lotus effect (hydrophobia), water applied to the TiO_2-treated surface was able to eliminate even oily or greasy substances without leaving any dirty film behind. Thanks to this extraordinary discovery, TOTO successfully introduced the world's first photocatalytic antibacterial tiles to the Japanese market in 1994.

In 1995 TOTO researchers, collaborating with the FH-Lab, discovered another novel function of photocatalysts: superhydrophilicity. That opened up the possibility of utilizing the material for a much wider range of applications, including, among others, antifogging mirrors. Fogging occurs when steam cools down on a surface to form many water droplets. On a highly hydrophilic surface, no water drops are formed. Instead, a uniform thin film of water that prevents frogging is created. The FH-Lab and TOTO jointly applied for patents and TOTO developed self-cleaning tiles in the following year. Additionally, they published a paper in *Nature* in 1997 (Wang *et al.*, 1997).

Toilet hygiene plays a major role in sanitary facilities and TOTO has focused its efforts on this topic for decades. The company ushered in the era of the high-tech toilet 34 years ago when it produced its first WASHLET in 1980 and has manufactured 33 million units since. The Japanese manufacturer recently started using innovative photocatalytic technologies in its WASHLETs. The latest generation of WASHLETs, the 'NEOREST AC', offers familiar technologies and comfort functions such as the warm water spray, dryer and heated seat. It also has self-cleaning features that employ photocatalytics, which TOTO calls 'Actilight'. According to the company, the NEOREST AC is the first completely self-cleaning WASHLET. It makes additional cleansers practically unnecessary for the toilet bowl and far exceeds the previous standards achieved in the areas of hygiene and convenience. By using Actilight technology, TOTO has laid the foundation for a very special type of toilet hygiene. The oxygen activated in photocatalysis naturally breaks down all organic substances on the surface. This effect is never depleted, but continues to work effectively over the long term. The superhydrophilic properties of the zirconium coating on the toilet bowl further ensure the effortless elimination of waste and bacteria. The new zirconium coating also makes it easy to keep the WASHLETs clean, dramatically reducing the amount of chemical cleansers and time needed for cleaning. This reduces costs and, last but not least, protects the environment. Two components are responsible for producing the self-cleaning photocatalytic effect in the new WASHLET – UV light and a coating that contains TiO_2. The new NEOREST AC is equipped with an integrated UV light in the toilet lid. This automatically turns on for an hour once the sensor-based lid shuts following each use. An especially durable and long-lasting zirconium coating was chosen for the toilet bowl. Actilight also works in combination with another hygiene technology: 'ewater+'. The cleaning process in the toilet works as follows: When the sensor-based toilet lid rises prior to use, the

Table 10.2 The origin of the history of collaborations between the University of Tokyo and TOTO

Time	Step 1 Discovery – Science	Step 2 U-I collaboration	Step 3 Innovation – Technology	Step 4 Commercialization of products by TOTO Ltd.
1989	Discovery that TiO_2-coated materials exposed to weak UV light have the power to decompose various organic contaminants			
1990–1994		Hashimoto and Fujishima started to conduct joint research with TOTO Ltd. on tiles and other building materials coated with TiO_2 film photocatalyst	The U-I knowledge exchange led to the discovery that TiO_2 photocatalyst-coated two-dimensional surfaces have cleaning and antibacterial functions. Joint patent applications follow	
1994				Antibacterial tiles
1995	Discovery that UV irradiation makes the surface of TiO_2-coated materials become highly hydrophilic			
1995–1996		Hashimoto and Fujishima work with TOTO Ltd. corporate researchers on potential applications, including antifogging mirrors	Several other joint applications based on the new discovery	
1996				Self-cleaning tiles
1998				Coating for automobiles; films for door mirrors
Overall–10 years			27 joint patent applications and 4 joint publications	4 products

Source: Baba *et al.* (2009).

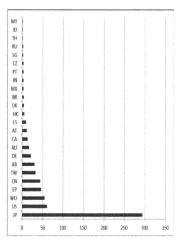

Figure 10.4 Distribution of search results by publication country

Source: Authors' elaboration on Orbit database.

entire toilet bowl is sprayed with water. After all, less waste sticks to wet ceramic surfaces. Once the toilet is flushed, the toilet bowl is sprayed once again with electrolysed water. This 'ewater' has a slightly acidic pH value and has cleansing as well as antibacterial properties. The food industry uses electrolysed water to clean fruit and vegetables. It is completely harmless, safe and can be returned to the water cycle without issue. Once the toilet bowl is sprayed with ewater, the lid closes automatically, the UV light turns on and the process of breaking down all organic substances begins. The superhydrophilic surface also ensures the thorough removal of waste and bacteria. According to TOTO, NEOREST AC is the most technologically sophisticated and hygienic toilet on the market today.

Table 10.2 shows how the history of collaboration between the University of Tokyo and TOTO originated and evolved from 1989, the date of the discovery of TiO_2-coated materials' properties.

We interrogated the Orbit database looking for all patent publications where TOTO Ltd. appeared as the applicant and 'TiO_2 photocatalysis' as keywords and obtained 496 records covering the period 1993–2013. Further analysis presented hereafter concerns this set of patent publications.

A first look at the geographical distribution of the records (in terms of country where the patent is registered, see Figure 10.4) shows the widespread diffusion of TOTO technologies, while underlining the strong research activities conducted and registered in Japan.

In order to evaluate the contribution of the two scientists from the University of Tokyo compared to other contributors to the innovative output of Tokyo, Figure 10.5 represents the list of inventors that patented TiO_2-related technologies for TOTO in the period 1993–2013. The role of Professors Hashimoto and

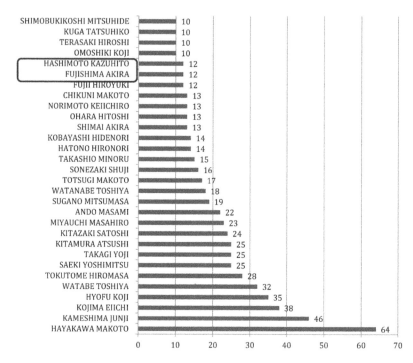

Figure 10.5 TiO$_2$ TOTO patent publications 1993–2013: top inventors

Source: Source: Authors' elaboration on Orbit database.

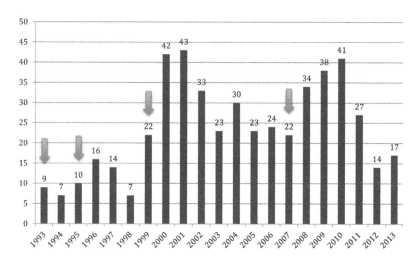

Figure 10.6 TiO$_2$ TOTO patent publications in the period 1993–2013

Source: Authors' elaboration on Orbit database.

Fujishima is more than evident. They signed 12 patents each as inventors and they are recognized as the top inventors for TOTO.

If we observe Figure 10.6, which shows the yearly number of patent publications from TOTO in the period 1993–2013, a sinusoidal distribution of the results appears.

Four triggering events, which originated four seminal patents, seem to have boosted further patent publications. These four patents were signed up by the two Professors at the University of Tokyo and a description of each follows.

1993: (US6277346)

A photocatalyst composite is provided which comprises a substrate having particles of a photocatalyst such as titanium oxide, adhered thereon via a less degradative adhesive such as a fluorinated polymer comprising a copolymer of a vinyl ester and/or vinyl ether and a fluoroolefin, or a silicon based polymer or cement. Furthermore, a process for producing the photocatalyst composite and a coating composition containing the photocatalyst composite are provided.

1995: (EP-816466)

A method of making the surface of a base material ultrahydrophilic, which comprises the step of coating the surface with a layer containing photocatalytic semiconductor material such as titania and the step of photoexciting the photocatalytic material to adjust the angle of contact of the surface of the above layer with water to about 10° C or less. When this method is applied to the surface of a base material such as mirror, lens or windowpane, the growth of water drops is prevented and the base material becomes highly antifogging. The articles treated by this method do not undergo any deposition of contaminants on the surfaces thereof and are readily cleaned by rainfall or washing with water.

1999: (JP2000100221)

PROBLEM TO BE SOLVED: To provide a compact lighting system even having an ultraviolet-ray absorbing function by integrating a device for the purpose of illumination and a device for the purpose of deodorization or disinfection. SOLUTION: This lighting system comprises a light emitting part 2 as a light source including ultraviolet rays, a cover member 3 that is so formed as to cover a part or all of the light emitting part 2 and reflects or transmits the light emitted from the light emitting part 2, and a semiconductor substance 4 that is arranged on the inside surface of the cover member 3, shows a photocatalytic reaction by the light from the light emitting part 2 and is formed of titanium oxide or the like decorated with palladium, platinum or the like. The emitted light from the light emitting part 2 is absorbed

(continued)

(continued)

by the semiconductor substance 4 and shows the photocatalytic reaction so that a gas releasing a bad smell and a poisonous gas in the vicinity of the semiconductor substance 4 are changed to odourless and harmless ones. Since the semiconductor substance 4 absorbs the ultraviolet rays in conjunction with the photocatalytic reaction, a less expensive fluorescent lamp including a lot of ultraviolet rays can safely be used.

2007: (JP4629700)

PROBLEM TO BE SOLVED: To provide a photocatalytic body which photocatalytic particles strongly adhere to over a long period of time without losing ability with extremely little degradation and deterioration of the binder caused by the photocatalytic particles. SOLUTION: A photocatalytic body keeps a first layer containing a persistent binder overlying a substrate, but no photocatalytic particles, and the first layer is coated or sprayed with a mixture of the persistent binder and the photocatalytic particles and dried at an ambient temperature of 200° C to provide a second layer. The volume of photocatalytic particles as a volume standard against a total amount of the photocatalytic particles and the persistent binder of the second layer is: (1) 5–40 per cent, if the persistent binder is cement and/or gypsum, (2) 20–98 per cent, if the persistent binder is not cement and/or gypsum.

Figure 10.7 shows the distribution by percentage of the TOTO patents according to the IPC adopted by the World Intellectual Property Office.

TiO_2 photocatalysis-related patents cover five main technological classes, which basically collect all the possible applications:

- A61: medical or veterinary science; hygiene;
- B01: physical or chemical processes or apparatus in general;
- B05: spraying or atomising in general; applying liquids or other fluent materials to surfaces, in general;
- B32: layered products;
- C03: glass; mineral or slag wool;
- C04: cements; concrete; artificial stone; ceramics; refractories;
- E04: building;
- H01: basic electric elements.

The top ten IPC subclasses are shown in Table 10.3:

Conclusions

This chapter sought to identify the effect of U–I collaborations on the innovative performance of firms operating in the advanced materials field and, by so doing,

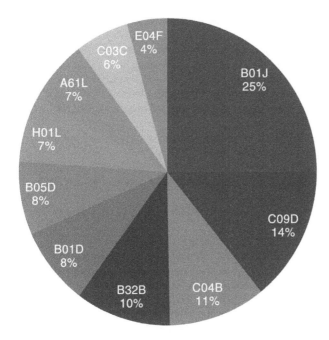

Figure 10.7 Distribution by percentage of the TOTO patents according to the IPC adopted by the World Intellectual Property Office

Source: Authors' elaboration.

it proposed to apply a framework inspired by the Stokes' (1997) classification of the research organization partners. The main contribution of the work resides in the illustration of the role played by Pasteur scientists in influencing the success of the U–I relationship. In contrast with previous studies, whose empirical setting was the life sciences industry or one of its components, in the advanced materials industry the most effective collaborations are not with Bohr scientists, but with Pasteur scientists (see Baba *et al.*, 2009). Engaging in research collaborations, measured as co-inventions, with Pasteur scientists increases firms' R&D productivity.

Moreover, the case study presented suggests evaluating carefully some important firm-specific assets, such as absorptive capacity (Cohen and Levinthal, 1990), which affect positively and significantly the firm's innovation performance.

Recent research shows that official channels play a limited role in the flow of knowledge between universities and industries by providing patent licences, while the open channel of academic paper publication, consulting and scientific advising, which occur informally between academic and corporate researchers, play a critical role in knowledge transfer (Cohen *et al.*, 2002b).

Our findings strongly support the importance of consulting as means for knowledge recombination and tacit knowledge flows between firms and universities

Table 10.3 Top 10 IPC subclasses

B01J	Chemical or physical processes, e.g. catalysis, colloid chemistry; their relevant apparatus
C09D	Coating compositions, e.g. paints, varnishes or lacquers; filling pastes; chemical paint or ink removers; inks; correcting fluids; wood stains; pastes or solids for colouring or printing; use of materials therefor
C04B	Lime; magnesia; slag; cements; compositions thereof, e.g. mortars, concrete or like building materials; artificial stone; ceramics; refractories; treatment of natural stone
B32B	Layered products, i.e. products built-up of strata of flat or non-flat, e.g. cellular or honeycomb, form
B01D	Separation
B05D	Processes for applying liquids or other fluent materials to surfaces, in general
H01L	Semiconductor devices; electric solid state devices not otherwise provided for
A61L	Methods or apparatus for sterilizing materials or objects in general; disinfection, sterilization, or deodorization of air; chemical aspects of bandages, dressings, absorbent pads, or surgical articles; materials for bandages, dressings, absorbent pads, or surgical articles
C03C	Chemical composition of glasses, glazes, or vitreous enamels; surface treatment of glass; surface treatment of fibres or filaments from glass, minerals or slags; joining glass to glass or other materials
E04F	Finishing work on buildings, e.g. stairs, floors

Source: Authors' elaboration.

through the contribution of Pasteur scientists who work as boundary spanners in charge of combining their science-based background with the knowledge, mainly ingrained in practice and trial-and-error procedures, of corporate researchers.

The ability to communicate with firms and to be orientated towards the commercialization of scientific discoveries is a peculiar characteristic of Pasteur scientists. Therefore, a direct managerial implication of the results of our investigation concerns the knowledge procurement strategy of the firm, which must be dependent on the industry knowledge base (Asheim and Coenen, 2005) and on the characteristics of the partnering scientists. In industries where an analytical knowledge base prevails, such as in the life sciences, the knowledge procurement strategy, at least initially, could be based upon contacts with star scientists through Technology Licensing Offices (TLOs). In contrast, in industries characterized by a combination of synthetic and analytical knowledge bases, such as in the field of advanced materials, the knowledge procurement strategy must be based upon the building of appropriate channels for two-way knowledge interaction between Pasteur scientists and corporate researchers, the latter playing an active role in the transfer of prior firm-specific and market knowledge. The ability of Pasteur scientists leads to a kind of customization process of science-based knowledge, which takes place only through a strong, bilateral U–I communication, facilitated by a proactive attitude of both the research partners. A common language and mutual understanding is, in fact, a prerequisite to the success of the joint research activity, which is sustained not only by formal agreements but by informal commitment rooted in friendship and reciprocal trust, as the case of Professors Fujishima and Hashimoto revealed.

In advanced materials, firms should look for experts orientated towards technology (reporting lots of patents) as well as science (reporting well-cited papers) – the Pasteur scientists. This is due to the fact that Bohr scientists may be the key actors in innovation carried out in biotech or sectors alike, but they lack the important quality of being able to play as boundary spanners between university and industry, which is very important in the field of advanced materials.

The success of U–I collaboration proved to be strictly connected to the absorptive capacity of the industrial partner (see also Schmoch, 1997). Moreover, the overall company orientation towards not only innovation per se, but also newness, is important. The case of TOTO is particularly informative showing a company whose competitive advantage is to leverage the Japanese culture relative to the bathroom experience (tradition) and create new spaces of experimentation and development through investing in basic research, design and consumer experience (newness). In terms of technological innovation strictly speaking, our recommendation to managers in the advanced materials field is to cultivate their corporate researchers in order to be an active part in the U–I knowledge transfer process. Adequate search strategies are also needed in order to find the appropriate Pasteur scientist whose knowledge and experience match the firm's requirements. Participation in industrial gatherings and scientific conferences might be good channels to establish direct contacts with candidates of Pasteur scientists, but industrial proposals to universities for specific material designs might work as well.

We acknowledge some limitations in our work, which are mainly related to the national boundary of our research design and to the very narrow sector of analysis: photocatalysts. Nevertheless, we believe that our findings contribute to the present understanding of firms' innovation strategies, pinpointing the role played by the company's culture and the type of U–I collaborations. Further research is needed to evaluate the extent to which the results of our analysis can be extended to other industrial segments, geographical contests and national systems of innovation.

References

Agrawal A., Henderson R., 2002. Putting patents in context: Exploring knowledge transfer from MIT. *Management Science*, 48(1): 44–60.

Almeida P., Kogut B., 1999. Localization of knowledge and the mobility of engineers in regional networks. *Management Science*, 45(7): 905–917.

Asheim B. T., Coenen L., 2005. Knowledge bases and regional innovation systems: Comparing Nordic clusters. *Research Policy*, 34(8): 1173–1190.

Baba Y., Shichijo N., Sedita S. R., 2009. How do collaborations with universities affect firms' innovative performance? The role of "Pasteur scientists" in the advanced materials field. *Research Policy*, 38(5): 756–764.

Balconi M., Laboranti A., 2006. University–industry interactions in applied research: The case of microelectronics. *Research Policy*, 35(10): 1616–1630.

Bonaccorsi A., Piccaluga A., 1994. A theoretical framework for the evaluation of university–industry relationships. *R&D Management*, 24(3): 229–247

Breschi S., Lissoni F., 2001. Knowledge spillovers and local innovation systems: A critical survey. *Industrial and Corporate Change*, 10(4): 975–1005.

Chesbrough H. W., 2003. *Open Innovation: The New Imperative for Creating and Profiting from Technology*, Harvard Business School Press, Cambridge, MA.

Chesbrough H. W., 2006. *Open Business Models: How to Thrive in the New Innovation Landscape*, Harvard Business School Press, Cambridge, MA.

Cohen W. M., Levinthal D. A., 1990. Absorptive capacity: A new perspective on learning and innovation. *Administrative Science Quarterly*, 35: 128–152.

Cohen W. M., Nelson R. R., Walsh J. P., 2002a. Links and impacts: The influence of public research on industrial R&D. *Management Science*, 48(1): 1–23.

Cohen W. M., Goto A., Nagata A., Nelson R. R., Walsh J. P., 2002b. R&D spillovers, patents and the incentives to innovate in Japan and the United States. *Research Policy*, 31(8): 1349–1367.

Cooke P., 1992. Regional innovation systems: Competitive regulation in the new Europe. *Geoforum*, 23(3): 365–382.

Edquist C., (ed.), 1997. *Systems of Innovation: Technologies, Institutions and Organizations*, Pinter/Cassell, London, UK.

Etzkowitz H., Leydesdorff L., (ed.), 1997. *Universities in the Global Economy: A Triple Helix of University–Industry–Government Relations*, Pinter/Cassell, London, UK.

Feldman M., Feller I., Bercovitz J., Burton R., 2002. Equity and the technology transfer strategies of American research universities. *Management Science*, 48(1): 105–121.

Furukawa R., Goto A., 2006a. Core scientists and innovation in Japanese electronics companies. *Scientometrics*, 68(2): 227–240.

Furukawa R., Goto A., 2006b. The role of corporate scientists in innovation. *Research Policy*, 35(1): 24–36.

Gittelman M., 2007. Does geography matter for science-based firms? Epistemic communities and the geography of research and patenting in biotechnology. *Organization Science*, 18(4): 724–741.

Lundvall B.-A., (ed.), 1992. *National Systems of Innovation: Towards a Theory of Innovation and Interactive Learning*, Pinter, London, UK.

Meyer M., 2006. Are patenting scientists the better scholars? An exploratory comparison of inventor–authors with their non-inventing peers in nano-science and technology. *Research Policy*, 35(10): 1646–1662.

Meyer M., 2007. What do we know about innovation in nanotechnology? Some propositions about an emerging field between hype and path-dependency. *Scientometrics*, 70(3): 779–810.

Murmann J. P., 2003. *Knowledge and Competitive Advantage*, Cambridge University Press, Cambridge, UK.

Murray F., 2002. Innovation as co-evolution of science and technological networks: Exploring tissue engineering. *Research Policy*, 31(8): 1389–1403.

Narin F., Breitzman A., 1995. Inventive productivity. *Research Policy*, 24(4): 507–519.

Owen-Smith J., Powell W. W., 2004. Knowledge networks as channels and conduits: The effects of spill-overs in the Boston biotechnology community. *Organization Science*, 15(1): 5–21.

Owen-Smith J., Riccaboni M., Pammolli F., Powell W. W., 2002. A comparison of U.S. and European university–industry relations in the life sciences. *Management Science*, 48(1): 24–43.

Powell W. W., White D. R., Koput K. W., Owen-Smith J., 2005. Network dynamics and field evolution: The growth of interorganizational collaboration in the life sciences. *American Journal of Sociology*, 110(4): 1132–1205.

Rosenkopf L., Almeida P., 2003. Overcoming local search through alliances and mobility. *Management Science*, 49(6): 751–766.

Schmoch U., 1997. Indicators and the relations between science and technology. *Scientometrics*, 38(1): 103–116.

Shichijo N., Sedita S. R., Baba Y., 2013. How does the entrepreneurial orientation of scientists affect their scientific performance? Evidence from the Quadrant Model. *Marco Fanno Working Papers* 0156, Dipartimento di Scienze Economiche "Marco Fanno". Available at: http://economia.unipd.it/sites/decon.unipd.it/files/20130156.pdf (accessed 10 November 2014).

Stokes D. E., 1997. *Pasteur's Quadrant—Basic Science and Technological Innovation*, Brookings Institution Press, Washington, DC.

Subramanian A. M., Lim K., Soh P.-H., 2013. When birds of a feather don't flock together: Different scientists and the roles they play in biotech R&D alliances. *Research Policy*, 42(3): 595–612.

Wang R., Hashimoto K., Fujishima A., Chikuni M., Kojima E., Kitamura A., Shimohigoshi M., Watanabe T., 1997. Light-induced amphiphilic surfaces. *Nature*, 388(6641): 431–432.

Zucker L. G., Darby M. R., 1995. *Virtuous Circles of Productivity: Star Bioscientists and the Institutional Transformation of Industry*. Working Paper, No. 5342, National Bureau of Economic Research, Cambridge, MA. Available at: http://www.nber.org/papers/w5342 (accessed 10 November 2014).

Zucker L. G., Darby M. R., 1996. Star scientists and institutional transformation: Patterns of invention and innovation in the formation of the biotechnology industry. *Proceedings of the National Academy of Sciences of the United States of America*, 93(23): 12709–12716.

Zucker L. G., Darby M. R., 2001. Capturing technological opportunity via Japan's star scientists: Evidence from Japanese firms' biotech patents and products. *Journal of Technology Transfer*, 26(1–2): 37–58.

Zucker L. G., Darby M. R., Brewer M. B., 1998. Intellectual human capital and the birth of U.S. biotechnology enterprises. *The American Economic Review*, 88(1): 290–306.

Zucker L. G., Darby M. R., Armstrong J. S., 2002. Commercializing knowledge: University science, knowledge capture, and firm performance in biotechnology. *Management Science*, 48(1): 138–153.

11 The relational models of the software industry in Italy and Spain relative to Germany

Francesca Gambarotto, Stefano Solari and Luigi Orsi[1]

Introduction

In this chapter we compare the software industry of three European countries – Italy, Spain and Germany – applying and further developing the three fundamental dimensions of a business model, i.e. strategy, finance and organization. Our aim is to detect a structural profile of this industry in countries with a different model of capitalism – 'Central European' versus 'Southern European' – and to study the characteristics of the business model of the Southern countries, Italy and Spain, known for their strong institutional inertia.

ICT is a key sector that is increasing the competitive potential, both globally and locally, through a radical change in the business model of innovative firms. Started in the US, the ICT industry has flourished and crowded out the old capitalism structure thanks to a completely new market organization. In contrast to the old economy based on segmented firms' organization, the new economy has inspired new product strategies, new finance and new organizing production and distribution systems (Lazonick, 2009). During the 1990s, the American ICT industry grew very rapidly and laid the foundations for new knowledge and competences, new organized venture capital and new labour market dynamics (Jaakkola, 2009; Lazonick, 2009). The diffusion of ICT products in other industries by embedding technological components or new technological production processes has changed the institutional structure of the American economy and its international competitiveness.

The evolution of the American ICT industry is quite representative in order to understand the reliance of a country's growth on the institutional system's capability to forecast and implement a technological trajectory, giving birth to a social innovation system (Amable *et al.*, 1997; Rodríguez-Pose, 1999; Hall and Soskice, 2001; Amable, 2003; Lundvall, 2007). In countries with a capitalism model based on decentralized market coordination, such as the USA, the UK and the Netherlands, growth is addressed by stimulating the domestic demand of ICT and by maintaining a very competitive ICT market. This means that low barriers to entry and the financial support for new ideas have stimulated industry enlargement and activated a multiplier effect on the whole economy. However, institutional strategies for a more efficient market are not equally adoptable in diverse configurations of capitalism. Countries with a capitalism model shaped by the satisfaction of social needs, as in Germany and social-democratic countries, pursue the goal of growth through policies based on a coordinated institutional upgrading. In this way they build a context enabling the introduction of ICT into citizens' lifestyles and firms' strategies. This is in contrast to countries with a market-orientated capitalism for which the role of the state is subordinated to the market and policies are mainly devoted to reducing market failures.

In between these two different models of capitalism we find the Mediterranean (or Southern European) capitalism, where the development trajectory of the ICT industry apparently is not well-shaped (Lippoldt and Stryszowski, 2009). This result depends on the co-existence of items of the old business model, such as the financing model, and items of the new one, such as human capital (Grimaldi and Torrisi, 2001). In these countries the development of the ICT industry is constrained by the lack of that enabling context necessary to build firms' confidence in investment and to promote specific capital accumulation. In order to exit this deadlock, the Mediterranean countries appear to benchmark the growth model of the continental capitalism based on a mixed private–public capital accumulation system and they look for a balance between social needs and freedom of individual economic plans. It is pretty clear that the evolution of the ICT industry in the Mediterranean countries is not a straightforward process. It depends on the production organization of the socio-economic system and on the set of conditions concerning the domestic economic environment.

In this chapter we investigate differences and similarities of the ICT industry business model between Italy, Spain and Germany. In this paper we assume that Germany represents a desirable configuration of the economic system, given that in the Mediterranean countries the state plays a positive and proactive role.

To attain our goal, i.e. to analyse the different relational patterns of the business model in each one of these countries, we have interviewed a group of firms belonging to the ICT industry. As a consequence, this paper endorses one of the main conclusions of the variety of capitalism models: growth is not easily coerced into a one-way social development, so that there does not exist a main evolutionary pattern as well as a general recipe to incentivize the development of an industry. Simply put, in this paper it is assumed that institutions matter and affect the capability of the economy to fit the changing environment. Starting from this viewpoint, the chapter points out the features and different trajectories of the business models in Spain and Italy compared to what has been achieved in Germany. Finally, some conclusions will follow in terms of the sustainability and contribution of ICT to the growth of Mediterranean capitalism.

The different paths of ICT development in Europe

The ICT industry is an umbrella sector, which includes all those activities concerning communication applications and devices. Software is one of these activities and represents a large market share of the sector itself. The US and European market quotas are quite similar – each is around one-third of the OECD sectoral value added. However, European countries contribute quite differently to the creation of the software economy in terms of value added, employment, R&D and export; this is the result attained by the ICaTSEM (Institutional Changes and Trajectories of Socio-Economic development Models)[2] European research project composed of a team of European researchers and devoted to analysing, using a comparative-institutional framework, the trajectories of socio-economic development models. In the research report, differences and similarities of the software industrial dynamics have been summarized in different industry configurations. Using value added, employment and investment variables in 2007, the research distinguishes countries with an exporter profile (Germany, the Netherlands and Austria), those with an exporter profile but also with a sectoral specialization (the UK and Sweden), countries that are R&D orientated (Denmark, Finland and Norway), those with a low specialization, low competitiveness and low exports (Portugal, Spain, Italy and Greece) and, finally, those orientated to the domestic market (Belgium and France). A factor analysis disclosed that the software industry structure within the EU has remarkable differences and there is no unique software industry profile in Europe (Bécue and Coris, 2011).

Regarding employment in the ICT industry, Germany, France and the UK employ about 1.5 million workers, while Italy and Spain employ about 0.4 million each. In contrast to the US, the dimension of European companies is extremely small (mainly companies with 1–9 and 10–19 employees). The average size of German ICT firms listed in the Amadeus database[3] (year 2010, Table 11.1) is 55.2 employees; in Italy it is considerably lower at 34.4 and in Spain it reaches 48.6. As regards turnover, in Germany the average size is €0.55 million, while it reaches €0.32 million in Italy and €0.29 million in Spain. The average growth of turnover reflects greatly the evolution of the national internal market, with higher rates of growth in Spain. This suggests that the size of the software industry depends particularly on domestic demand.

Combining industry features with the different models of capitalism in Europe (Amable, 2003) we observe that each model owns a specific sectoral trajectory. This difference is particularly relevant because the software industry is both very pervasive in the whole economy and a pillar of the knowledge economy. The Southern European model is presently suffering from a peripheral position in the EU and is over-exposed to lower-income countries' competition (Gambarotto and Solari, 2015). The European software industry is also suffering from the emerging pressure of developing countries. The latter can threaten the domestic industry either in terms of labour cost of specialized competences or of the ease of R&D investments.

The production models of European ICT

The main aim of the notion of a *production model* adopted here concerns the study of the micro–macro dependencies connecting firms' organization and strategy to the general institutional configuration of the economic system (Boyer, 1998; Boyer and Freyssenet, 2000). In fact, the growth model of an economy is shaped

Table 11.1 Descriptive statistics

Variable	Country	Mean (Sample data)	Mean (Amadeus data)	S.D.	Min	Max	Sample	Valid
Number of employees	Germany	151.61	55.21	319.78	15.00	1422.00	30	18
	Italy	164.27	34.37	480.80	5.00	1900.00	32	15
	Spain	74.92	48.56	40.86	23.00	151.00	30	12
	Total	135.38		338.93	5.00	1900.00	92	45
Turnover (€m)	Germany	27.81	0.55	57.73	4.50	158.70	30	7
	Italy	34.24	0.32	81.96	0.80	237.00	32	8
	Spain	6.38	0.29	1.38	4.50	8.50	30	6
	Total	24.14		59.09	0.80	237.00	92	21
Turnover growth rate % (2005–2010)	Germany	0.25	n.a.	0.08	0.15	0.36	30	5
	Italy	0.14	n.a.	0.15	−0.20	0.33	32	11
	Spain	0.38	n.a.	0.24	0.18	1.00	30	8
	Total	0.24		0.21	−0.20	1.00	92	24

Source: Authors' elaboration.

by two institutional levels: that defining the national set-up and that specifically developed at the firm level in order to find a viable agreement between factors of production. Institutions do not directly determine the production model. They rather represent the structural elements shaping the evolution of organizations in their specific environment. Therefore the shape of an industry, such as ICT, is given both by structural economic conditions and the institutions that play a coordination role. The consequence is that different institutional set-ups shape differently the development opportunities of an industry.

Institutions are normally grouped by regulation school scholars in five sets corresponding to the main sectors of the economy: finance, industrial relations, market regulation, state intervention and international relations. With regard to the actual difference in the structuring of institutions in Germany (continental model) and Italy and Spain (Mediterranean model) we refer to Amable (2003). Both models are characterized by an intermediated financial system, i.e. 'bank-based', but the banks in Germany are more directly involved in companies' control and management. Industrial relations are traditionally more conflict-ridden in the South and the labour market more regulated and rigid. The latter aspect has recently undergone deep reform that has led to a massive rise in precarious labour in both models, but with a deeper precariousness in the South. Market regulation is traditionally more pervasive in the South, but our sector is new and not as subject to specific national rules. State intervention has been important in both models, even if differently shaped. In Germany the ownership of firms by local states is important, whereas in the South state expenditures are relatively more relevant. International relations do not differ much due to the adhesion to the EU and to monetary union.

A specific dimension of the *production model* is the way enterprises organize to exploit their resources in relation to the interacting actors. As this model is focused on the consistency of connections between internal organization and the institutional configuration of the economy, the relational dimension of firms' interaction with partners, suppliers and competitors is the fundamental variable to be studied. Therefore we study five sets of relationships of the specific firms:

- financial relationships;
- industrial relations and human capital management;
- relationships with suppliers;
- relationships with clients;
- relationships with competitors.

The structural differences of the industries will be highlighted and such relationships will be studied relative to the different institutional set-ups.

Research setting and design

We verified the consistency of the five relational areas in a pilot study and pre-test. More generally, the purpose of the exploration was to assess the validity of the relational sets and to further adjust scales if necessary, and to verify the language translation of the questionnaire to test its quality before conducting the survey. The final version of the survey was firstly developed in Italian and then translated into Spanish and German in order to facilitate understanding and answering. This research adopted a web-based email survey design to collect the data.

Participating firms were selected in the following way. First, they were extracted using the Amadeus database. We identified the software industry through NACE code 72 (Software production, Software consulting and related activities) and obtained a sample of 19,644 Italian firms, 15,076 Spanish firms and 26,958 German firms. Second, we randomly contacted firms by telephone to establish whether the firm actually belongs to the software industry. In the case that the firm actually belonged to this industry and was willing to participate in the survey, we noted the name and email address of the top managers. Finally, a total of 90 completed (30 for each country), valid questionnaires were collected (yielding, however, a low response rate).[4]

The questionnaire was divided into five sections devoted to analysing how the five types of relationships previously discussed are linked to different institutional set-ups. The first section is devoted to understanding financial relationships, the second section to understanding industrial relationships, the third is the relationships with clients, the fourth is the relationships with suppliers and the last one is the relationships with competitors. In the final part of the questionnaire, data on the structure of the company and personal data of the respondents were collected.

Two types of analysis were implemented – a preliminary exploration based on a descriptive analysis of the phenomenon and an analysis of variance (Anova) in order to investigate the existence of significant differences between the detected form of relationships and the specific institutional set-up. The first column of each table (highlighted in grey) reports the average scores for German firms. German firms therefore represent the reference group and we focus on how the firms belonging to the two other economic systems differ from them. The next columns show the differences between the means of the reference group and those of the further groups. The sign '−' before the scores shows that the average value of a given group is lower than the corresponding average of the reference group. The asterisks highlight whether differences in averages are statistically significant due to random sampling.

In this section, we report the description of the firms in our sample. The average number of partners that control the company is about 35 for the German firms, 7 for the Italian and 4 for the Spanish ones. This means that company ownership is more widespread in Germany and consequently also the presence of larger companies, compared to the Mediterranean countries taken into account. In Table 11.2 we analyse the governance structure and product typology. The control structure of the German companies is wider than that of the Italian and Spanish ones, the latter two presenting only ownership of relatives or institutional partners. Being a member or leader of a group of enterprises is almost the same in all the three countries analysed, but German companies, when they claim to belong to a group, in 77 per cent of the cases this is a multinational group. This contrasts with the firms in the Mediterranean countries that generally belong to national groups.

The main software activities of the firms in our sample are almost the same in all countries analysed and are focused on the activities of development (including contract programming), maintenance and consulting. When we look at the product category, German companies are more focused on development software (compiler, editor, framework, libraries, etc.), while the Italian and Spanish companies are more orientated on application/utility software (individual productivity, communication, database analysis, scientific package, etc.), enterprise software (including ERP, inventory, customer, etc.) and mobile/online applications. Another difference between German firms and those belonging to the Mediterranean countries is the kind of code they use to develop software. German firms operate principally with their own proprietary source code and an autonomously developed or contributed open source code, while the Italian and Spanish firms claim to use also third-party open source and third-party proprietary source codes. Software companies in Mediterranean countries seem to then use all types of available code, while German firms prefer the internal development of software codes.

The comparative analysis of the software production model: empirical findings

The empirical analysis shows that a different production model exists between Mediterranean countries and Germany. However, between Italy and Spain some relevant differences also emerge due to the different trajectory and intensity of growth. The organization of production is quite specific to each country and also

Table 11.2 Governance structure and product typology

	Variable	Country	Germany		Italy		Spain	
Governance structure	q3. The control is performed by:	Natural persons	25	86%	32	100%	27	90%
		Other companies	4	14%	0	0%	3	10%
		Total	29	100%	32	100%	30	100%
	q4. Who controls the company?	Relatives	3	33%	11	48%	9	50%
		Other companies	4	44%	1	4%	1	6%
		Bank	0	0%	0	0%	0	0%
		Institutional partners	2	22%	11	48%	8	44%
		Total	9	100%	23	100%	18	100%
	q5. Are you a member/leader of a group of companies?	Yes	9	30%	8	27%	9	30%
		No	21	70%	22	73%	21	70%
		Total	30	100%	30	100%	30	100%
Product typology and features	q7. What are the main software activities of the company? (multiple choice question)	Development	24	29%	27	26%	28	29%
		Maintenance	15	18%	24	23%	26	27%
		Training	10	12%	11	10%	8	8%
		Documentation	6	7%	4	4%	3	3%
		Reselling	13	16%	11	10%	5	5%
		Consulting	14	17%	28	27%	28	29%
		Total	82	100%	105	100%	98	100%
	q8. Which category of products is your target? (multiple-choice question)	Development software	15	30%	12	13%	5	5%
		Infrastructure software	4	8%	5	6%	4	4%
		Applications	7	14%	24	27%	28	26%
		Enterprise software	10	20%	16	18%	29	27%
		Application-specific custom software	12	24%	17	19%	24	22%
		Mobile/online applications	2	4%	16	18%	17	16%
		Total	50	100%	90	100%	107	100%

q9. Which kind of source code do you use? (multiple-choice question)	Third-party open source code	6	21%	21	24%	23	23%
	Third-party proprietary source code	1	3%	16	18%	26	26%
	Own proprietary source code	16	55%	25	29%	26	26%
	Autonomously developed or contributed open source code	6	21%	25	29%	25	25%
	Total	29	100%	87	100%	100	100%

Source: Authors' elaboration.

depends strongly on firms' dimensions. This notwithstanding, some specific characteristics of the business model clearly emerge from the interviews.

Financial relationships

A preliminary question concerns the amount of R&D expenditure on turnover. This is necessary to better understand any subsequent issues in financial relationships. Contrary to what is normally understood, Italian and Spanish firms invest a large share of their turnover. This fact can be explained by the relative delay in the development of this sector in the respective economies. On the other hand, this fact shows that even in the South this industry is not passively pulled by the structural change of the economy. Moreover, this result implies that in the South there is a greater need for external financing compared to Germany.

Looking at the structure of financing, a clear pattern emerges: German firms rely very much on self-financing or take advantage of other sources within their business group; Italian firms definitely do not rely on these sources; Spanish are in between, because reinvesting profits is relevant for innovation activity. Italy and Spain mainly rely on bank credit, but only in Italy on bonds. The entire sample of German firms answer that they have recently increased their capital stock. There is no such pressure for financial consolidation in the South (however, deflationary policies began earlier in Germany).

Regarding the relational dimension of the business model (Table 11.3 and Figure 11.1), when Southern companies need financial support, they ask banks or other financial institutions and they enjoy the support of medium- to long-term bank loans (q22). However, banks tend to finance specific firms' projects in Germany,

Table 11.3 Anova test on financial relationships

Variable	Germany	Italy	Spain
q20. Invest in R&D (% investment/sales)	0.145(0.033)***	0.165(0.045)***	0.108(0.046)*
q21.1. Projects to innovate technological equipment	0.429(0.179)***	−0.022(0.198)	0.338(0.199)
q21.2. Projects for new product development	0.5(0.172)**	0(0.193)	−0.241(0.196)
q21.3. Projects for technological partnerships with other companies	0.286(0.103)**	−0.251(0.115)*	−0.202(0.117)
q21.4. Projects for technological transfer with universities	0.286(0.129)*	−0.148(0.143)	−0.206(0.146)
q21.5. Projects to open new markets	0.429(0.174)*	−0.153(0.194)	−0.169(0.195)
q21.6. No. of projects at all	0.667(0.197)**	−0.394(0.222)*	−0.067(0.233)
q22. Medium- or long-term bank loan	0.429(0.177)*	0.363(0.201)*	0.18(0.202)

Significant codes 0 '***' 0.001 '**' 0.01 '*' 0.05 ' ' 1
Standard errors are reported in parentheses.

Source: Authors' elaboration.

while in the South there is no compact answer, i.e. financing tends to be general purpose and short term. Italian and Spanish companies appear to engage less in partnerships with other firms to have access to technological innovation financing (q21.3).

The conclusion is that a more structured set of financial relationships exists in Germany. In the two other countries, besides some small differences, firms rely on a looser, more flexible set of relationships. The German case is evidently characterized by codified and institutionalized relationships assuring a shared standard. This pattern is in part explained by the fact that Southern business tends to assume the status of 'family capitalism'.

Industrial relationships

Flexible labour contracts (Table 11.4 and Figure 11.2) are perceived as relevant in Italy, less so in the other countries (q14). That could be the result of a psychological reaction to past rigidities, but it nonetheless affects industrial relations. When German firms recruit employees, they require some basic technical competencies as well as some industry-specific competencies, some teamwork propensity, learning and problem solving capability and capabilities to achieve results and responsibility (q12.1–7). In the two other countries such competences appear less fundamental to employment, in particular technical capabilities.

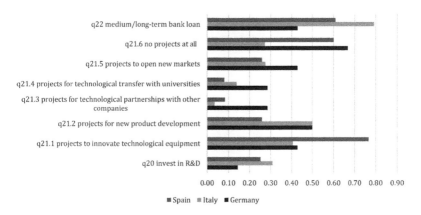

Figure 11.1 Financial relationships

Source: Authors' elaboration.

Table 11.4 Anova test on industrial relationships

Variable	Germany	Italy	Spain
q12.1. Basic technical	4.238(0.218)***	−0.613(0.281)*	−2.038(0.285)***
q12.2. Specific technical	4.727(0.201)***	−0.884(0.261)**	−1.294(0.265)***
q12.3. Teamwork propensity	3.913(0.195)***	−0.007(0.256)	0.32(0.26)
q12.4. Learning capability	4.048(0.172)***	0.327(0.221)	−0.414(0.224)*
q12.5. Problem solving capability	4.238(0.169)***	−0.832(0.218)***	−0.238(0.222)
q12.6. Capability to achieve the result	4(0.222)***	−0.031(0.289)	−0.367(0.292)
q12.7. Responsibility	4.261(0.189)***	−0.073(0.248)	−0.094(0.251)
q13.1. Inside on the job	2.963(0.083)***	−0.244(0.113)*	−0.296(0.115)*
q13.2. Inside internal specific courses	2.444(0.115)***	−0.507(0.156)**	0.256(0.159)
q13.3. Outside ad hoc courses	2.111(0.115)***	0.139(0.157)	0.189(0.159)
q14. Flexible labour contracts to produce software	2(0.149)***	0.406(0.188)*	−0.6(0.19)**

Significant codes 0 '***' 0.001 '**' 0.01 '*' 0.05 ' ' 1
Standard errors are reported in parentheses.

Source: Authors' elaboration.

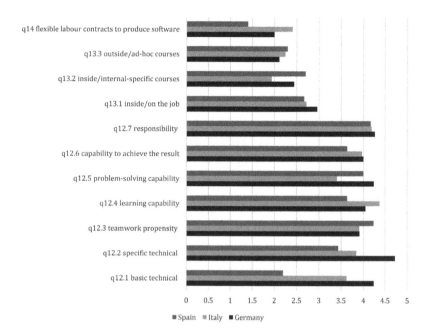

Figure 11.2 Industrial relationships

Source: Authors' elaboration.

But there are exceptions: in Italy learning capability is valued more than in Germany, and teamwork is valued more in the Southern industries. The behavioural aspects that qualify the problem-solver profile and that concern the employees' accountability are mainly a German concern. The learning practice is mainly on-the-job in Germany, but it is more importantly conducted on specific courses and outside the firm in Spain (q13.1–3).

Relationships with clients

Looking at relationships orientated to define the position of companies in the business environment (Table 11.5 and Figure 11.3), customization is relevant in Germany and Spain, but is less of a homogeneous characteristic of Italian companies. In Spain prices tend to be set by clients, or bargained, which highlights a more personal type of relationship. The idea of an impersonal 'market price' is more evident in the Italian and German markets (q30.3).

The quality of service is a fundamental variable in Germany (q31.1), while low price is the main factor of success in Spain. Italians tend to rely on personnel training, assistance and customization (q31.3 and q31.5–6). Assistance security and customization are also important for Spain (q31.3–5). We can say that in the Mediterranean countries trust is the institutional key factor to staying in the

Table 11.5 Anova test on relationships with clients

Variable	Germany	Italy	Spain
q28.2. Most sold is a customization of standard service product	3.348(0.21)***	0.027(0.275)	−0.2(0.286)
q28.3. Most sold is design and development of custom product service	3.043(0.251)***	0.238(0.329)	0.994(0.341)**
q30.1. Price set by the customer	1.05(0.168)***	0.138(0.214)	1.283(0.227)***
q30.2. Price bargained with the customer	3.312(0.211)***	−0.248(0.26)	1.021(0.273)***
q30.3. Price fixed by market	4.056(0.188)***	−0.774(0.235)**	−0.328(0.253)
q31.1. Success factor quality of product service	4.45(0.17)***	−0.356(0.217)	0.086(0.223)
q31.2. Success factor low prices	2.15(0.161)***	0.038(0.205)	2.004(0.214)***
q31.3. Success factor maintenance and assistance	3(0.219)***	0.687(0.274)*	0.897(0.279)**
q31.4. Success factor product reliability and security	3.389(0.243)***	0.486(0.304)	0.646(0.309)*
q31.5. Success factor customization	3.001(0.242)***	0.906(0.3)**	0.69(0.305)*
q31.6. Success factor personnel training	2.687(0.243)***	1.937(0.297)***	0.384(0.304)
q32.1. Difficulty in definition of service	2.6(0.231)***	−0.697(0.281)*	0.757(0.286)**
q32.2. Difficulty in exploitation of product	2.2(0.222)***	0.316(0.271)	1.443(0.275)***
q32.3. Difficulty in finding the needed competences	1.867(0.261)***	1.101(0.319)***	1.455(0.324)***
q32.4. Difficulty in being paid	1.877(0.212)***	1.573(0.269)***	0.455(0.263)*

Significant codes 0 '***' 0.001 '**' 0.01 '*' 0.05 ' ' 1 Standard errors are reported in parentheses.

Source: Authors' elaboration.

market. This is also due to the fact that ICT in these economies is more directly linked to the final producers of consumer goods.

A question on the difficulties encountered with new clients reveals that all issues are relevant for Germans. In Spain enterprises may find more difficulties

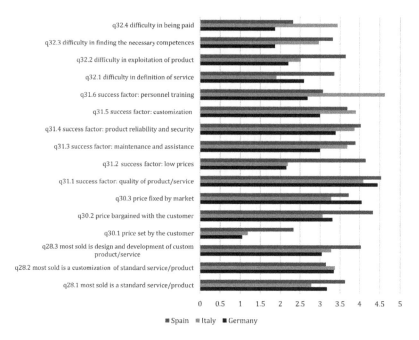

Figure 11.3 Relationships with clients

Source: Authors' elaboration.

in defining the service or exploiting the product (q32.1–2). In both the Italian and Spanish ICT industries, it can be a problem to find the needed competences and this is a sign that the market is not standardized (q32.3). Italian and Spanish producers have remarkable difficulties in being paid and this is an element reinforcing the relational dimension (which also explains the higher need for short-term bank financing). As a consequence, besides some marked diversity, more precarious markets and more uncertainty dominate the Southern industries. That can be connected to the lower propensity to have a more structured set of relationships with input suppliers.

Relationships with suppliers

There is no very clear result (Table 11.6 and Figure 11.4) regarding the existence of habitual suppliers, even if the tendency is more clearly positive in the South, particularly in Spain (q34). The continuity of the relationship is given by the quality of product and all other variables in Germany, but by respect for the terms of delivery in Spain (q35.2) and by collaboration with the design of software in Italy (q35.4). Germans set up partnerships for product certification and for sharing strategic suppliers (q36.1–2); no clear answers appear for the South.

Local networks are less relevant in Germany. The software industry is related to suppliers at the European or international level (e.g. Asia). On the other hand, in Italy regional or national partners are relevant (q37b.2), while the Spanish have mainly European partners (q37b.3). Partnerships include software and hardware producers in Germany (q38.1–2), while they are less important in Italy and Spain. A consulting partnership is typical of Southern countries (q38.4). These relationships sometimes bring difficulties in sharing the knowledge for Germans (q39.1); Italians have difficulties with suppliers as regards standards and payments (q39.2–3); the latter point is shared with Spanish firms, all of which testify to a less structured environment. German firms underline that several aspects are relevant in their conventions with clients (q40.1–4). They value non-disclosure agreements more than Southern firms (q40.4), while Italian companies tend to focus on technological standards and training activities as being more relevant (q40.2–3).

Germans subcontract more (q41) and in the same area (q42.1); subcontracting in Germany is used in general to reduce costs (q43.5), but also to have access to specific knowledge and, in part, to be punctual and to reach different, specific competences (q43.1–4). In Italy subcontracting is not used for cost reasons but, similarly to Spain, there are no homogeneous answers to the questions. Improvisation and precariousness, together with specificity, individuality and non-standardization, are the emerging characteristics of relationships with input suppliers in the South.

Relationships with competitors

The competition (Table 11.7 and Figure 11.5) perceived by firms tends to be national and global in the case of German firms, while it is more relevantly local and national in the case of Southern companies (q44.1–3). Collaboration with competitors is important in Germany, particularly at the national level. On the other hand, it is not declared to be important by Italian firms at any level. Some local and national level collaboration with competitors to develop standards exists in Germany (q48.1–2). Italian firms clearly affirm this relationship is absent, while in Spain there is some at the national and global level (q48.2–3). In Germany communities are created for all the reasons proposed in the questionnaire, mainly for receiving some feedback from users, or communities of users or developers. In Italy only some community develops around the service or product (q49.1, 49b.3).

The results are, therefore, interesting for revealing an ability to collaborate, in view of the developing of standards by German firms that is scarce and very specific in Southern countries.

Final remarks

The relational dimension of the software industry's production model stemming from our panel of interviews is significantly different in the three countries. There are some characteristics that are clearly common to Italy and Spain: the financial

Table 11.6 Anova test on relationships with suppliers

Variable	Germany	Italy	Spain
q34. Important habitual supplier	0.476(0.085)***	0.257(0.111)*	0.524(0.115)***
q35.1. Quality of product	2.75(0.119)***	−0.063(0.139)	0.147(0.141)
q35.2. Respect of terms of delivery	2.333(0.149)***	−0.177(0.175)	0.598(0.178)**
q35.3. Capability to contribute to the solution of problems	2.167(0.21)***	0.052(0.246)	0.109(0.249)
q35.4. Capability to collaborate in the design	2.083(0.204)***	0.417(0.24)*	0.089(0.243)
q35.5. Price	1.917(0.165)***	0.052(0.193)	0.049(0.196)
q36.1. Partnerships on product service user certification programs	0.692(0.138)***	−0.144(0.164)	−0.077(0.169)
q36.2. Partnership in commercial networks of strategic suppliers	0.769(0.137)***	−0.269(0.166)	−0.192(0.168)
q36.3. Privileged partnerships	0.154(0.132)	0.191(0.159)	0.402(0.16)*
q37. Suppliers located in your area	0.267(0.127)*	0.133(0.155)	0.126(0.157)
q37b.1. Suppliers in the same region	1.667(0.259)***	1.569(0.32)***	−0.222(0.366)
q37b.2. Suppliers in the same country	1.2(0.228)***	2.078(0.284)***	0.086(0.355)
q37b.3. Suppliers in Europe	2.6(0.273)***	0.047(0.344)	2.15(0.409)***
q37b.4. Suppliers in the US	2.111(0.326)***	N.A.	0.556(0.652)
q37b.5. Suppliers in Asia	2.778(0.224)***	N.A.	−1.278(0.525)*
q38.1. Software	3.786(0.2)***	−1.341(0.267)***	−0.593(0.248)*
q38.2. Hardware	3.857(0.211)***	−1.413(0.281)***	−0.697(0.263)*
q38.3. Body.rental	1.4(0.227)***	−0.2(0.293)	0.373(0.274)
q38.4. Consulting	1.667(0.234)***	1.333(0.314)***	0.949(0.283)**
q39.1. Difficulty in sharing knowledge	2.143(0.232)***	−0.393(0.257)	−0.18(0.261)
q39.2. Difficulty in adoption of technological standards	1.333(0.288)***	0.979(0.314)**	0.556(0.318)

q39.3. Difficulty with payments	1.167(0.248)***	0.927(0.271)**	0.685(0.275)*
q39.4. Difficulty in fixing prices	1(0.224)***	1.094(0.244)***	0.84(0.25)**
q40.1. Trade conventions	2.5(0.222)***	−0.031(0.249)	−0.672(0.251)**
q40.2. Technological standards	2.286(0.217)***	0.464(0.24)*	−0.286(0.242)
q40.3. Guarantee of training activities	2.111(0.21)***	0.405(0.238)*	0.027(0.24)
q40.4. Non-disclosure agreements	2.571(0.222)***	−0.821(0.245)**	−0.675(0.247)**
q41. Subcontract work	2.571(0.222)***	−0.821(0.245)***	−0.675(0.247)
q42. Subcontractors located in your area	0.667(0.18)***	−0.267(0.266)	0.152(0.203)
q42b.1. Subcontractors in the same region	2.5(0.829)*	−0.5(1.436)	−1(1.016)
q42b.2. Subcontractors in the same country	N.A.	N.A.	N.A.
q42b.3. Subcontractors in Western Europe	3.5(0.5)	−2.5(0.866)	−0.5(0.866)
q42b.4. Subcontractors in Eastern Europe	N.A.	N.A.	N.A.
q42b.5. Subcontractors in the US	1.5(0.5)	−0.5(0.866)	1.5(0.866)
q42b.6. Subcontractors in Asia	N.A.	N.A.	N.A.
q43.1. Respect the terms of delivery	1.714(0.297)***	0.619(0.543)	0.286(0.348)
q43.2. Specific technical competences	2.286(0.257)***	0.714(0.47)	0.135(0.301)
q43.3. Specific commercial competences	1.857(0.234)***	−0.524(0.427)	−0.226(0.273)
q43.4. Specific managerial competences	1.859(0.242)***	−0.19(0.442)	−0.068(0.283)
q43.5. Lower costs	2.5(0.286)***	−1.5(0.495)**	0.026(0.328)

Significant codes 0 '***' 0.001 '**' 0.01 '*' 0.05 ' ' 1
Standard errors are reported in parentheses.

Figure 11.4 Relationships with suppliers

Source: Authors' elaboration.

dependence on banks, the low propensity for formal networking and the more individual reliance on the market with less industrial organization. The different institutional configurations clearly affect the labour and financial structuring of the companies' models of interaction with their environment. In particular, we can perceive the signs of a deinstitutionalized labour market in the South and the different behaviour of the banking system, which is more orientated towards general purpose lending. The consequence is the reliance on standardized or codified

Table 11.7 Anova test on relationships with competitors

Variable	Germany	Italy	Spain
q44.1. Local competition with other firms	1 538(0.173)***	0.962(0.206)***	0.502(0.214)*
q44.2. National competition with other firms	1.923(0.158)***	0.639(0.188)***	0.357(0.195)*
q44.3. Global competition with other firms	2.3(0.209)***	0.231(0.239)	−0.411(0.244)*
q47.1. Local collaborations with competitors	2.5(0.38)***	−1.352(0.42)**	0.042(0.425)
q47.2. National collaborations with competitors	2.833(0.323)***	−1.611(0.373)***	−0.667(0.373)
q47.3. Global collaborations with competitors	2.375(0.254)***	−1.327(0.299)***	−0.375(0.297)
q48.1. Local community with other firms for standards	2(0.262)***	−0.913(0.314)**	−0.091(0.316)
q48.2. National community with other firms for standards	1.5(0.204)***	−0.463(0.239)*	0.591(0.246)*
q48.3. Global community with other firms for standards	1(0.136)***	0(0.164)	0.917(0.162)***
q49. Development of communities around the service product	1.429(0.126)***	0.321(0.158)*	0.271(0.164)
q49b.1. Communities of developers	3(0.358)***	−0.5(0.526)	−1.429(0.506)*
q49b.2. Community of users	3.75(0.269)***	−2.25(0.347)***	−2.25(0.347)***
q49b.3. Feedback from users	4.25(0.508)***	−2.25(0.656)**	−0.821(0.637)
q49b.4. Debugging community	1.667(0.45)**	−0.167(0.551)	−0.095(0.537)

Significant codes 0 '***' 0.001 '**' 0.01 '*' 0.05 ' ' 1
Standard errors are reported in parentheses.

Source: Authors' elaboration.

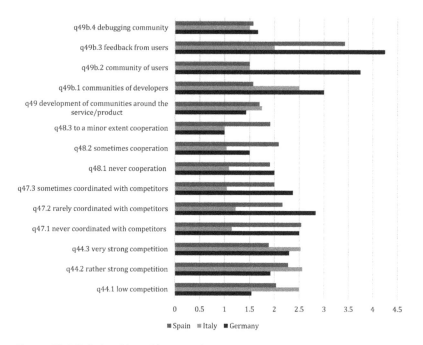

Figure 11.5 Relationships with competitors

Source: Authors' elaboration.

forms of interaction in Germany and the higher reliance on informality, flexibility and the ability to learn in Italy and Spain.

While German firms often find relevant the variables proposed in the questionnaire, Southern companies tend to attribute less importance to them and supply very diversified results. A likely reason is that German enterprises belong to a more solid institutional environment and to a more structured industrial organization, while Southern companies rely more on flexibility. The spatial dimension of the suppliers' network and the relationships with the clients' community also supply interesting results; they point to a different horizon of the business and a different way of coordination. The most relevant result is the higher level of uncertainty within which Southern firms live, even regarding payments. This uncertainty can be understood as either a mirror of the weak structuring of economic relations' space or as the cause of it – this is difficult to decide from the data. On the other hand, there are relevant differences between the two Mediterranean ICTs. These are due to the different contexts, which in Italy are dominated by specialized consumer quality productions and machinery that induce specific and differentiated strategies for the Italian software industry. That notwithstanding, the Spanish ICT is growing more rapidly, in part due to its delay, in part due to the growth of the internal market.

All these differences can also be related to firms' dimensions: in Germany firms are, on average, definitely larger than in the other two countries. This basic element affects all the connections inside the industry and also connections with the rest of the economy. Larger firms are more organized, look for dynamic efficiency, care for customer and supplier relationships, differentiate strategies with respect to different functions (development, customization, etc.) and invest in cognitive competences. In the Southern countries, firms are smaller, face national or regional markets and look for short ties and local networks. However, smaller size can hardly be regarded as a cause; it is rather/also a consequence of uncertainty. Therefore, uncertainty reinforces the destructuring of relationships and informal relations have a further feedback on companies, thereby reinforcing the small size.

These differences confirm that a single production model does not exist in Europe and that institutional solutions that are successful in one industrial system can fail in another. In other words, benchmarking and comparative analyses can be misleading if institutional conditions and organizational rules of firms are not observed. We can conclude that, even if the software industry is growing in Southern countries, its potential is constrained by the structure of the market, the difficult access to finance and the uncertain conclusion of transactions with clients and suppliers. All these elements enlighten the strong structural difference between Mediterranean and Continental capitalism models. The conclusion is that a convergence in the industry trajectories is a long way off.

Notes

1 This study is based on research, which received funding from the European Community's Seventh Framework Programme FP7/2007–2013 under grant agreement number 225349.
2 ICaTSEM is a project funded by the European Commission as part of the Seventh Framework Programme (FP7/2007–2013).
3 Amadeus is developed by Bureau van Dijk, a consulting company that collects balance sheet data and contacts' data for more than 11 million active firms in 41 European countries (2008 version).
4 The representativeness of our sample is not very high, but comparisons of average values did not identify significant differences between questionnaires that were returned early and those that were returned later. Therefore, in accordance with Armstrong and Overton (1977), we did not assume a significant non-response bias.

References

Amable B., 2003. *The Diversity of Modern Capitalism*, Oxford University Press, Oxford, UK.

Amable B., Barré R., Boyer R., 1997. *Les Systèmes d'Innovation à l'Ère de la Globalisation*, Paris, Economica.

Armstrong J. S., Overton T. S., 1977. Estimating nonresponse bias in mail surveys. *Journal of Marketing Research*, 14(3): 396–402.

Bécue M., Coris M., 2011. *The European Software Sector: Statistical Profiles*. ICaTSEM project funded by the European Commission as part of the Seventh Framework Programme (FP7/2007–2013), under Socio-Economic Sciences and Humanities. Grant agreement number 225349. Available at: http://icatsem.u-bordeaux4.fr/sites/icatsem/IMG/pdf/icatsem_deliverable_d4.2_v1.pdf (accessed 10 December 2014).

Boyer R., 1998. Evolution des modèles productifs et hybridation, CEPREMAP couverture orange, no. 9804. Available at: http://www.cepremap.fr/depot/couv_orange/co9804.ps (accessed 10 December 2014).

Boyer R., Freyssenet M., 2000. A new approach of productive models. The world that changed the machine. *Industrielle Beziehungen*, 7(4): 385–413.

Gambarotto F., Solari S., 2015. The peripheralization of Southern European capitalism within the EMU. *Review of International Political Economy*, forthcoming.

Grimaldi R., Torrisi S., 2001. Codified-tacit and general specific knowledge in the division of labour among firms. A study of the software industry. *Research Policy*, 30(5): 1425–1442.

Hall P. A., Soskice D., 2001. *Varieties of Capitalism. The Institutional Foundations of Comparative Advantage*. Oxford University Press, Oxford, UK.

Jaakkola H., 2009. Towards a globalized software industry. *Acta Polytechnica Hungarica*, 6(5): 69–84.

Lazonick W., 2009. The new economy business model in the crisis of U.S. capitalism. *Capitalism and Society*, 4(2): 1–67.

Lippoldt D., Stryszowski P., 2009. *Innovation in the Software Sector*, OECD, Paris, France.

Lundvall B., 2007. National Innovation Systems. Analytical concept and development tool. *Industry and Innovation*, 14(1): 95–119.

Rodríguez-Pose A., 1999. Innovation prone and innovation averse societies: Economic performance in Europe. *Growth and Change*, 30(1): 75–105.

12 How alliances in biotech are shaping the national systems of innovation in three European countries

Maria Francesca Savarese, Stefania Michelazzo, Fiorenza Belussi and Kristina Rakic

Introduction: the national systems of innovation literature and the development of the biotech niche

The biotech sector represents a broad area of scientific and technological knowledge applied to the processing of materials by biological agents through the usage of rRNA, cell fusion and novel bio-processing engineering. The science related to genomics and DNA recombination was first developed during the 1970s. It was the premise for the discovery of novel technologies in the fields of pharmacy, agriculture and industrial treatments. While, at the beginning, the relevant science was conducted within the leading public research organizations (PROs) as 'pure science', very soon, through a process of business creation and new university start-ups, a new market niche was created based on the commercialization of science (Feldman, 2000, 2004). The application of these discoveries to new drugs could, in principle, substitute the old pharmaceutical technological paradigm, furnishing the markets of health and agriculture with new products as alternatives to chemical compounds (Arora and Gambardella, 1994; Gambardella, 2002). Since the late 1970s, universities, venture capitalists, pharmaceutical firms and governments have supported the evolving biotechnology firms by providing critical resources and developing an institutional environment that has enabled the growth of life sciences activities within universities and dedicated science parks (Baglieri and Belussi, 2009). Since all the relevant skills are rarely found under a single roof, the participants are frequently linked through a network of interorganizational agreements. In the US and Europe the biotech sector was created around poles of scientific excellence, witnessing a movement of researchers from academic laboratories towards the private sector. Most of the biotech firms are young, science-based firms and are high R&D-intense organizations or dedicated biotechnology firms (DBFs). An interesting body of literature (Benner and Löfgren, 2007), has discussed the evolution of this 'emerging bio-economy' in different countries, examining the role of the state and the constitution of a specific national innovation system. Comparing the patterns of governance of the biotechnology sector in various countries, such as Finland, Sweden, the US, the UK and Australia, it has been argued that the bio-industry sector does not fit with the 'variety of capitalism' paradigm (Hall and Soskice, 2001), which postulates

Table 12.1 Models of innovation in the life sciences industry

• The French model of Genopole: Locally planned clusters throughout a national governance
• The Bioregion of Medicon Valley: Spontaneously emerging regional clustering with interactive research institutions framed within a national governance
• The weak science-cluster in Italy: A spontaneous model with local boundaries and local governance

Source: Authors' elaboration.

coherence within, and systemic divergences between, national models of economic governance (for instance in relation to: labour market regulation, industrial support and ethical restrictions). On the other hand, it displays a trend towards convergence, in particular considering the high level of expenditure of public investments in health care, in financing R&D and in sponsoring university start-ups.

Despite these similarities, our work presented here contrasts the idea of a prevailing uniformity of the life sciences sector in various countries and underlines the existence of three separate European models. In particular, we will study the case of Biopoles in France, where there is a mixed model of multilevel (national and local) governance; the case of the Medicon Valley located in Sweden and Denmark (where a regional innovation system is at work); and the case of Lombardy in Italy, based on a local dynamic of a science cluster. Our work is based on qualitative information collected in the specialized press and on an original analysis based on a selected sample of 75 firms (24 Danish and Swedish, 27 French and 24 Italian firms), extracted by using the Bioscan database (Bioscan, 2005). We analysed the typology of firms, the intensity and types of alliances developed between firms and between firms and institutions, the relationships of DBF firms with pre-existing pharma and the role of financing. In contrast to the previous literature, which has emphasized the predominant role of clustering as a spontaneous growth mechanism, we put at the centre of our reflections some institutional key factors, such as the level of public investment in the sector and the presence of extra local (regional or national) active institutions, in support of the development of the local biotech system, which are not necessarily classical venture capital (VC) firms. Our findings showed three models of innovation (see Table 12.1): (1) the French model of Genopole: this model is composed of locally planned clusters realized throughout a national governance; (2) the Bioregion of Medicon Valley: this is a spontaneously emerging regional clustering with interactive research institutions framed within a national governance; and (3) the weak science cluster in Italy: this is a spontaneous model on innovation with local boundaries and local governance.

A review of the literature on cluster and regional innovation systems

The French model of Genopoles

The development of the biotechnology industry in France has been the focus of attention within the mission innovation strategies launched by the various governmental

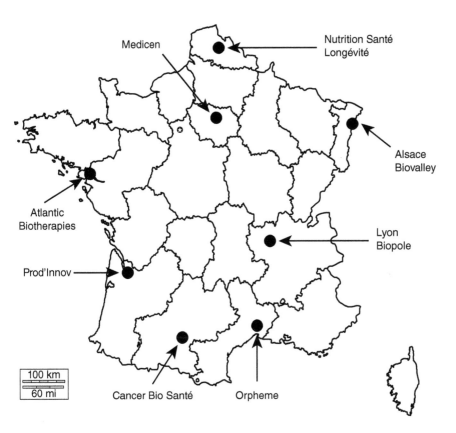

Figure 12.1 The French Genopoles

Source: Authors' elaboration.

programmes during the 2000s. France traditionally has assigned to the state a central role in the planning of industrial policy and, in the past, has always supported the development of large 'national champions' in sectors considered to be strategic.

In a line of continuity with the vision of Jean Baptiste Colbert (1619–1683), since the early 1990s the Agence Nationale de Valorisation de la Recherche (ANVAR) has promoted many interventions and funding (with an estimated allocation of €230 million) for the creation of various biotechnology clusters, the so-called 'Genopoles', in which to concentrate public research and private enterprises. ANVAR provides funds for biotech companies that are committed to maintaining a level of investment in R&D equal to or greater than 15 per cent of total spending, providing tax breaks for staff involved in research, tax credits and special funding for specific projects. It also allows tax exemptions for young entrepreneurs. In addition, at a local level, there are available other grants and additional tax breaks. Currently eight clusters (Monsan, 2000) have been created in health and biotech, as shown in Figure 12.1. The Biopole governance is centralized, so that only the government takes the final decision on the actors and firms allowed to obtain the status of being part of the 'poles of competitiveness'. Clearly, the entire coordination and development of research strategies are subject to the examination of public structures. The role of these 'poles of competitiveness' is not limited to tax incentives and funding, but also passes through the support and enhancement of corporate networks, investment in human resources and infrastructures (through founding universities and R&D centres), supporting links between industry and research and promoting technology transfer from university to industry. In addition, there are specific provisions allowing public researchers to participate in the creation of new businesses. This strong growth of R&D is undoubtedly linked to the government policy of support that has allowed the creation of the status of 'Jeunes Entreprises Innovantes' (JEI), which was adopted in 2004.

From the BioInItaly report (2011) we have extracted the information that in France in 2008 there were 461 DBF enterprises active in biotech (Table 12.2) in an exclusive modality, 43 per cent of which – 198 – were pure red biotech. The number of R&D personnel was 3,000 employees. The most important public companies in 2008 realized about €700 million in sales (Table 12.3). According to the report by France Biotech (www.france biotech.org) in 2008, the sector accounts for 66 products under R&D, of which most (34) are in the preclinical phase, 11 in clinical phase 1, 14 in phase 2 and 7 in phase 3.

The presence of many actors in the public sector specializing in research, such as the Institut Pasteur, INSERM, INRA, the IFREMER and CEA, together with an efficient network of public hospitals, has greatly facilitated the development of new projects, linking the public sphere to the private initiatives. Private funds are, however, quite restricted, although in recent years the trend of investment has been growing (between 2006 and 2008 it realized an increase of 14 per cent per year, with new investments of about €200 million per annum). Financial transactions in the early stages were supported by 19 VC funds ranging from €500 million to €2.8 billion per annum. Since 2005 investment in the later stages, i.e. the less risky, has risen to €140 million per annum. Actually the sector comprises relatively mature medium-large companies that, through the stock exchange, have obtained a good supply of capital. In April 2008 the launch of the European stock exchange index 'Next Biotech' was a means of further support. The index consists of 26 European

Table 12.2 The French biotech

Biotech firms	461
Firms active in biotech	824
Employees	6,000
R&D employees	3,000
Industry output (€m)	14.6
Investment in R&D (€m)	1.4
% of output on R&D expenditure	9.6%

Source: Authors' elaboration on Ernst & Young-Assobiotech 2011 data.

Table 12.3 The first French biotech firms (public companies)

First 15 firms in 2008	Sales in 2008 (€m)
LFB1	352.4
Ethypharm	147.4
Cerep	30.8
Transgene	26.0
Flamel Technologies	23.8
Nicox	3.3
Innate Pharma	14.2
Idenix	12.4
Genfit	8.7
Porsolt & Partners Pharmaco	8.1
Genoway	6.7
Exonhit	4.2
Vivalis	5.4
Iris Pharma	5.0
Total	648.4

Source: Authors' elaboration on Ernst & Young-Assobiotech 2011 data.

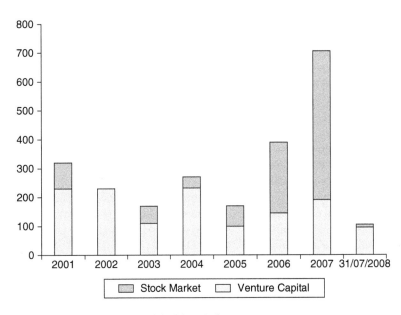

Figure 12.2 The financing of the biotech firms

Source: Authors' elaboration on French biotech.

companies listed on Euronext, Alternext and NYSE Euronext. Out of the 26 firms there are 12 French companies: BioAlliance Pharma, Cellectis, Cerep, Eurofins Scientifique, Exonhit Thérapeutiques, Genfit, Genoway, Hybrigenics, Innate Pharma Prom, Nicox, Transgenic and Vivalis. In Figure 12.2 we see that in the mid-2000s the financial market, through initial public offerings (IPOs), started to finance biotech firms in a consistent way.

The bioregion of Medicon Valley

The area of Malmö-Lund is the second in order of importance in Europe for the development of biotech after Cambridge in the UK, and is called Medicon Valley. It is a cross-border cluster, created from the region of Skåne (southern Sweden) and Copenhagen (Denmark) to stimulate the integration of firms and knowledge flows of biotech.

These two countries have formed a single 'regional innovation system' that has been able to plan long-term excellence in the field. The background of Medicon Valley is still that of an area that after the end of World War II based its economic development on the development of knowledge and high-tech sectors. In particular, it should be noted that Sweden invests 4 per cent of its GDP on average on research activities, being the second leading industrialized country after Israel. Sweden hosts a full complementary array of related actors that form a biotech cluster: DBFs, universities and leading institutions, large pharmas, leading research hospitals, such as the Karolinska Institute, and medical technology firms. In the cluster reside some of the most important pharmaceutical and biopharma companies known worldwide, among them Beaufort Ibsen, Biogen, Ferring Pharmaceuticals, Pfizer subsidiary, Yamanouchi Pharmaceuticals, Eli Lily subsidiary, GlaxoSmithKline subsidiary, Bristol Myers Squibb and AMGen Medicon Valley, who have chosen to locate in the area as the basis for their production and research, stimulating a high level of competitiveness. About 60 per cent of Scandinavian pharmaceutical and biotechnology companies are located in the Medicon Valley, where there are also 26 hospitals including 11 university hospitals, 14 universities including the University of Lund, a total of 41,000 professionals employed in the field of life sciences and 5,000 researchers, 135,000 students and 4 science and technology parks (Table 12.4).

The medical technology for hospital equipment, diagnostic equipment and medical equipment is developed by 130 companies, followed by red biotech with 125 companies and 3,300 employees. Among the major biotech companies are Active Biotech, BioInvent, Biora and Clinical Data Care Concentrate. Despite the many parties involved, this cluster is highly integrated: there is a consortium of 14 universities in the Øresund region – Zealand (Denmark) and Skåne (Sweden) – with a strong coordination among the sponsored research programmes.

Recently there has been a process of hyper-specialization around four medical areas (diabetes, inflammatory diseases, neurosciences and cancer) that revolve around centres such as the Copenhagen Biocenter, the Biotech Research & Innovation Center in Copenhagen, the Center for the Biology of Stem Cells

Table 12.4 The Medicon Valley regional system

Cluster composition	
Actors	Firms or employees
Biotech industry	125
Pharma industry	70
Medical technology	130
Research organizations	15
Investors and services	250
Hospitals/clinical	26
Universities	14
Pharma and biotech	41,000
Students	135,000
Science parks	4

Source: Authors' elaboration on Techpath data.

and Cellular Therapy in Lund (Sweden), the Center for Diabetes and Stem Cell Research at Lund (Sweden) and the Proteomics Centre SweGene-Lund (Sweden). Other important fields of research concern biotechnology instrumentation, bioinformatics, diagnostics and 'functional food'. One of the strengths appears to be intense collaboration with hospitals that provide excellence in the clinical trials phase. Regarding the relationship between universities and industry, it should be stressed that Swedish legislation provides academic researchers with the opportunity to retain the rights from the patents of their findings and provides strong collaboration between academia and industry. According to the latest data provided by the Swedish innovation agency (VINNOVA), 95 per cent of biotechnology companies collaborate in research projects conducted by academics. From a financial point of view, there are numerous institutional and private investors, including many venture capitalists attracted by the biomedical and major brands who have settled in the area. In recent years there has been created a new type of venture capitalist from the Novo Nordisk Foundation, Novo A/S, with the aim of supporting the most brilliant ideas in the field of biotechnology. This area also attracts foreign investors and companies by offering them a range of services that include:

- contacts with potential industrial partners and research;
- support during and after settlement in Medicon Valley;
- contacts with venture capitalists;
- information on business opportunities;
- guided tours within the area.

An important role is also played by the connection of networks that integrate the research system, industry (both large and small businesses) and public bodies. Among the various networks in the area the Medicon Valley Academy, which specializes in biotechnology and life sciences sectors, stands out. The 227 members include companies, research institutes, partners and public bodies. Members are evenly distributed between Sweden (40 per cent) and Denmark (60 per cent). As mentioned previously, in all biotech clusters, public funding and tax incentives are part of a 'long-term commitment' and play an important role.

In particular, despite the crisis that has affected all countries, the flow of funding for strategic research in the field of life sciences is allocated at around 3.6 per cent of GDP. In addition, the corporate tax rate is quite small – since 2009 it has been lowered to a threshold of 26.3 per cent on profits, lower than that of France (34.4 per cent) and Italy (32.5 per cent). Fiscal deduction in tax and a long-term industrial policy are the determinants of significant private investment in the area. Contrary to what happens in Italy, it appears that R&D is financed by VC, two-thirds of which (at about 9 per cent) comes from abroad. (This share has increased significantly since the early 1990s, when it represented only 1.5 per cent.) Of this 9 per cent, 77 per cent comes from firms and groups with subsidiaries in Sweden and only 24 per cent of the funding comes from the public sector.

The weak biotech cluster in Italy

The Italian biotech sector appears to be a slowly growing business, which includes both 'pure biotech', i.e. companies with 'core business' activities related exclusively to biotechnology, and biopharmaceutical companies, which are the Italian subsidiaries of foreign multinational companies, science parks and incubators. The report Assobiotech 2011 shows that the sector consists of 375 firms, of which 221 are dedicated companies that fall into the category of 'pure biotech' (Table 12.5), employing about 6,000 people.

None of the products has yet reached the market, given the weakness of the Italian biotech industry. Looking at the pipeline of the biotech industry as a whole, there are 337 drugs in development, of which 82 are in the preclinical phase, 30 in the clinical stage, 167 in phase 2 and 58 in phase 3. However, if we apply the success rates quoted by TD Securities to the entire Italian pipeline, probably in the next 10–15 years we should not expect to see more than 10 new biotech drugs deriving from Italian R&D on the market.

While pharmaceutical companies cover their self-financing through stock exchange or private banking and over 90 per cent of expenditure on R&D is

Table 12.5 The Italian biotech

	All biotech firms	Pure biotech
Firms	375	221
Employees	52,411	6,000
R&D employees	6,400	2,248
Biotech sales	7,400 (€m)	1,184 (€m)
Investment in R&D	1,800 (€m)	533 (€m)

Source: Authors' elaboration on Ernst & Young-Assobiotech 2011 data.

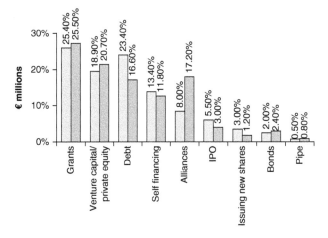

Figure 12.3 The sources of financing for red Italian biotech firms

Source: Authors' elaboration on Ernst & Young-Assobiotech 2011 data.

internally supported by past profits, the analysis of sources of funding for biotech companies in Italy shows that they mainly resort to various sources of funding, but primarily public grants. Access to finance is a critical priority for most of the biotech industry, especially in the early stages of their drug development, but the role played by VC or private equity investors, appears low (Figure 12.3).

In 2010, at the European level, €2.532 billion were collected, of which 52 per cent was through a capital increase by private equity, 40 per cent from VC operations and 7 per cent from IPOs. However, domestic business angels were virtually absent from the market.

Science and technology parks play an increasingly important role in the whole process of R&D in biotechnology, both in the initial phase and in the technology transfer when the results of scientific research take the road towards industrial applicability. The location in an incubator or science park is often the only chance of birth and growth for a business in the biotech sector for a number of reasons among which are the availability of financial instruments, the possibility of finding the right competencies and easier access to a network of national and international operators. The national support to the biotech industry has been absent or scarcely influential since the early 1990s. When industrial policies have been delegated to the regions, some uncoordinated initiatives have been taken. After 2005 a €5 million project organized by MIUR (Ministry of Research – Lombardy Region) was launched, but there was a systematic delay in the provision of the real monetary flows to firms.

In Italy about 50 per cent of the employees of Italian biotech firms are located in Lombardy and about 50 per cent of firms are located inside the structures of science parks. Thus Lombardy emerges in a dominant position with its three dedicated science parks: 'Insubrias Biopark Gerenzano', 'Science Park San Raffaele'

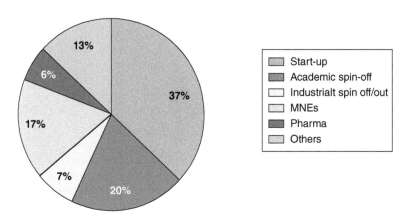

Figure 12.4 Genesis of Italian pure red biotech

Source: Authors' elaboration on Ernst & Young-Assobiotech 2011 data.

and 'Parco Tecnologico Padano'. In total there are five poles: (1) Polo Bresso (BioCity) with the firms: Cell Therapeutics, Newron Pharmaceuticals, Nicox, Zambon Z-Cube and Arsan; (2) Polo Baranzate: with the firms Nikem and a subsidiary of Glaxo R&D; (3) Polo of San Rafael (Science Park Raf): with the firms DIBIT, Molmed, BioXell, Axxam, Primm and Telbios; (4) Polo via Ripamonti Milan (Campus IFOM-IEO and IEO-IFOM; and (5) Biopolo with the firms Genextra, State University, Institute of Cancer, Mario Negri Institute and Semm (European School of Molecular Medicine). In Italy there are only three listed companies and they are all located in Lombardy: Vicuron, CTI and Nicox. In Lombardy there are 78 biotech firms of different sizes, mainly specializing in the development of anti-cancer drugs and rare diseases.

The genesis of Italian pure red biotech companies is classical: most of them began as start-ups (37 per cent) and university spin-offs (20 per cent), as shown in Figure 12.4. Companies of this type and size (small) also appear to be essential to the location within a cluster.

Network of innovation in 'life sciences': a comparison between three models

According to Cooke (2005) the life sciences industry is characterized by an 'open innovation system', where the source of knowledge does not come only from the firm itself, but from the interaction with other companies, research institutes, universities and organizations (Chesbrough, 2003).

This new knowledge, created through different types of collaboration, does not spread equally across geographical boundaries (Moodysson *et al.*, 2008), but leads to a variety of networks of innovation. This difference is reflected in the three national systems of innovation presented in this chapter.

The three networks generated by the three models of innovation combined together represent well the idea of an open system characterized by numerous collaborations between firms and other actors involved in the innovation process. This differentiation represents the basis for the evolution of three systems, equal in scope but different in nature, that reflects the peculiarity of the country in which they are located.

Going through the analysis of every single network, we can understand the rise of these differences by scrutinizing the type of firm, collaborations and partners. In particular, the French case represents a network with a high number of national firms involved, where large, leading firms, such as Sanofi-Aventis, are at the centre of this big network of collaborations with French public organizations, such as ANRS (National Research Agency on Aids/HIV) and partners located abroad. This highlights a well developed and established model with respect to the Italian model characterized by a few firms that collaborate with just one Italian public organization, the CNR (National Research Center), some Italian universities (University of Milan and University of Urbino) and other firms, mostly located abroad.

In the third case, the Denmark-Swedish model, the so-called Medicon Valley, is dominated by the presence of collaboration with big foreign firms. For example, Biovitrum AB has agreements with AMGen and GlaxoSmithKline, or Affibody, which collaborates with GE. The three national cases show great differences in innovation patterns, even if they are all considered as open innovation systems. The reason can be found in the distinction between the R&D systems, the role of the public sector, policy systems, financial systems and inter-firm collaborations.

In particular, what types of agreement do these firms prefer when shaping their network of innovation?

As Table 12.6 shows, the alliance bio-to-bio is the most relevant in terms of innovative output measured by the number of patents for the three models, even if they present different characteristics. The country of origin, size and age of the firm have no impact on innovative performance.

Table 12.6 The characteristics of innovative output

Variables	Coefficient	Standard error	T	P-value
Marketing agreements	−5.72474	4.76396	−1.20168	0.2338
Bio-to-bio agreements	7.69426	3.19981	2.4046	0.019
Denmark	4581.13	2928.32	1.56442	0.1226
France	4540.02	2928.32	1.55039	0.1259
Italy	4554.75	2933.55	1.55264	0.1254
Sweden	4627.15	2926.04	1.58137	0.1186
Firm's age	−2.27353	1.46696	−1.54983	0.126
M&A (passive)	39.9059	19.9612	1.99917	0.0498
Size	0.024364	0.0110302	2.20885	0.0307

Source: Authors' elaboration on data from Bioscan.

Conclusion

The innovative performance of a country depends upon the synergies between different factors such as firms, public institutions and universities that collaborate to create a common system of knowledge. Moreover, the way all the actors combine this knowledge shapes the national system of innovation.

As Freeman (1995) states, the importance of a national system of innovation derives from the networks of relationships that are necessary for any firm to innovate. Therefore, besides external international connections, the influence of the national education system, industrial relations, technical and scientific institutions, government policies and cultural traditions are all very important. It is the combination of actors and factors that has led to the creation of three different models in Europe in the biotech sector. Every model is well integrated at the national level, but there is no evidence of integration between them at the European level.

The reason for this lack of evidence can be found in some institutional mechanisms to support the biotech sector evolution and, more generally, in the innovation system of every specific country. For example, in a country such as France, the government plays a central role in defining industrial policies. The Genopole model is the result of a long-run strategy, planned at the beginning of the 1990s, with the idea of bridging public and private research. Its main characteristic is the high number of agreements with a few big pharmas.

The bioregion of Medicon Valley in Sweden and Denmark seems to be very similar to the case of Genopole, but the government there does not have a crucial role as in France. The firms of Medicon Valley are more dynamic, being more able to attract private and public investment, both national and international.

The Italian model presents completely different characteristics. It is not the result of a specific governmental plan, but emerged naturally. The lack of an overall plan to support biotech firms reflects the inability to attract investments and the continuous search for agreements, especially M&A, with big pharmas.

Another interesting result of this research is the positive relationship between the bio-to-bio agreements in terms of innovative performance (measured by the number of patents). It is not the relationship with big firms in the sector that spurs innovation, but the agreement with the same typology of firm. Even if the biotech firms are small and lack resources, they can lead a change in the biopharmaceutical industry and the starting point can be represented by their alliances with similar partners.

In very brief terms, there is no single, ideal type of national system of innovation that can be considered better than another, as every model is the reflection of the idiosyncratic characteristics of the country in which it is based.

References

Arora A., Gambardella A., 1994. The changing technology of technical change: General and abstract knowledge and the division of innovative labour. *Research Policy*, 23(5): 523–532.

Baglieri D., Belussi F., 2009. Strategie localizzative delle imprese biotech italiane: Il ruolo dei parchi scientifici e tecnologici, in Sorrentino M., (ed.), *Le Imprese Biotech Italiane. Strategie e Performance*, Il Mulino, Bologna, Italy.

Benner M., Löfgren H., 2007. The bio-economy and the competition state: Transcending the dichotomy between coordinated and liberal market economies. *New Political Science*, 29(1): 77–94.

BioInItaly report, 2011. *Rapporto sulle biotecnologie in Italia. Farmindustria*, Ernst & Young. Available at: http://www.biotechinitaly.com/Allegati/download_rapporto.pdf (accessed 5 December 2014).

Bioscan, 2005. *Biotech Database*, Padua University, Italy. CD-ROM resource.

Chesbrough H. W., 2003. *Open Innovation: The New Imperative for Creating and Profiting from Technology*. Harvard Business School Press, Cambridge, MA.

Cooke P., 2005. Rational drug design, the knowledge value chain and bioscience megacentres. *Cambridge Journal of Economics*, 29(3): 325–341.

Feldman M., 2000. Where science comes to life: University bioscience, commercial spin-offs, and regional economic development. *Journal of Comparative Policy Analysis: Research and Practice*, 2(3): 345–361. Available at: http://www.druid.dk/uploads/tx_picturedb/ds2002-678.pdf (accessed 3 December 2014).

Feldman M., 2004. *Knowledge Externalities and the Anchor Hypothesis: The Locational Dynamics of the US Biotech Industry*. Paper presented at the Annual Meeting of the Association of American Geographers, Philadelphia, PA, 14–17 March.

Freeman C., 1995. The 'National System of Innovation' in historical perspective. *Cambridge Journal of Economics*, 19(1): 5–24.

Gambardella A., 2002. 'Successes' and 'failures' in the markets for technology. *Oxford Review of Economic Policy*, 18(1): 52–62.

Hall F., Soskice D., 2001. In, Soskice D., (ed.), *Varieties of Capitalism: The Institutional Foundations of Comparative Advantage*, Oxford University Press, New York, NY.

Monsan P., 2000. Twenty years of biotech in France. *Biofutur*, Special issue: 27–31.

Moodysson J., Coenen L., Asheim B., 2008. Explaining spatial patterns of innovation: Analytical and synthetic modes of knowledge creation in the Medicon Valley life-science cluster. *Environment and Planning A*, 40(5): 1040–1056.

Part IV

Case studies

13 Evolving through innovation and knowledge reutilization

The case of L'Oréal

Fiorenza Belussi, Silvia Rita Sedita, Andrea Ganzaroli and Luigi Orsi

Introduction

Conventional theories on innovation have tried to explain the technological trajectory of firms, stressing the discontinuities existing in the firm innovation process (Tushmann and Anderson, 1986; D'Aveni, 1994). As highlighted over the years by the Schumpeterian tradition, radical innovations emerge erratically by chance when dynamic entrepreneurs, exploring new market opportunities, introduce 'new combinations' moving the entire economic system far from equilibrium (Schumpeter, 1934, 1947). This process, described in an imaginative mode by Schumpeter himself, has been termed 'creative destruction', where new technologies and new methods of production displace the old modus operandi in the economy. Schumpeter never discussed in his writings the interplay between discontinuities and continuities in firms' innovation activity, despite it being obvious that a great deal of technological change and product improvements consist of marginal and incremental innovations (Arrow, 1962; Malerba, 1992; Freeman, 1994). It was the innovation literature of the 1980s and 1990s, focused prevalently on basic radical inventions and innovations, which provided a standard definition of invention and innovation (Clark *et al.*, 1984, who elaborated on Jewkes *et al.*, 1958). The innovation literature was integrated with the Usher (1955) theory of inventions, which distinguishes 'acts of insights' and 'acts of skills', separating the inventive activity into four stages: the perception of a problem, the setting of the analysis, the primary act of insight and the critical revision. At the time, innovation literature disregarded the impact of all novelties arising from what Usher (1955) was defining as 'acts of skills', being the consequence of the skilled activities of engineers and technicians undertaken within the environment of established processes. But Usher himself would have agreed. He argued clearly that the results of those acts do not constitute any invention. As Johnson (1975) clarifies:

> [t]o some extent the distinction between the two finds its legal embodiment in patent laws, where obviousness is a ground of exclusion from patentability. Acts of skills will be normally obvious in the sense that they will usually be apparent to those who are skilled in the art' (Johnson, 1975: 30).

Academia, at that time, focused mainly on the analysis of breakthrough innovations. Even Schmookler (1966), who is acknowledged for his contributions to the role of demand growth in pulling inventions into the economic system, for instance, when referring to the Usher theory, called these 'acts of skills' minor changes introduced by technicians; in other words, mainly, as 'sub inventions'. After the end of the 1970s the economic importance of marginal technical improvements for sustaining innovation in firms became largely acknowledged (Rosenberg, 1976, 1982; Dosi, 1982; Freeman, 1982, 1984; Basalla, 1988).

But what drives innovation? Schumpeter clearly answered the question. It is the introduction of a new combination of production means (not necessarily new ideas deriving from new scientific knowledge). The subsequent Schumpeterian traditions focused, in contrast, on the new knowledge brought about by science and by the application of new technical knowledge to productive activities. But old and new pieces of knowledge can be recombined to trigger inventions and innovations. This aspect is of paramount importance, because it shows an underestimated aspect of the innovation activities within the most recent innovation literature and the role of multiple sources in feeding the innovation activity of firms, which has been discussed for instance in the dismantling of the linear model and in the popular alternative innovation models such as the chain-linked model (Kline and Rosenberg, 1986). We completely agree with the statement of Mokyr (2000): 'Much if not most creativity comes from the manipulation of what is already known, rather than an addition of totally new knowledge' (Mokyr, 2000: 18). Often innovations are only fed by a continuous recombination of flows of pre-existing knowledge, coming from different sectors or firms through cumulative learning processes as Pavitt (1984, 1999) authoritatively showed. Another critical aspect is how old and new knowledge is integrated by firms and applied to new domains.

While Dosi (1982) has described the continuous development of technology (with incremental and radical innovations strengthened together) as a path towards a specific technological trajectory that during the time incorporates important stylized fact, Levinthal (1998) and Adner and Levinthal (2000, 2002) argued that the crucial event is not the transformation of the technology, but the application of an existing technology to a new domain, through a 'speciation process'. Within the economic system there is an overwhelming amount of old knowledge that firms reuse and recombine for new needs, but there is also an overwhelming production of new knowledge and the presence of dissipative processes with knowledge obsolescence. Old knowledge might be 'exapted' to new uses in other domains, or the firms might acquire existing knowledge from outside to feed their internal innovation activities, along with an open innovation strategy (Chesbrough, 2003). This is clearly important for firms in traditional sectors, which innovate through knowledge acquisition from the producers of technologies (Pavitt, 1984; Von Tunzelmann and Acha, 2005; Hirsch-Kreisen et al., 2006; Hirsch-Kreisen and Jacobson, 2008).

We assist to an exaptation each time a previous artefact/technology is reused with a new function, more or less, distant from the one it was originated for.

We develop a theoretical framework, which adds to previous contributions on the economic implications of exaptation (Dew et al. 2004; Marquis and Huang,

2010) by introducing some important features of the exaptation process for innovation. Our analysis discusses the following two issues: first, how exaptation relates to the evolutionary theory of technological change; second, how innovation cascades are formed by a variety of exaptive processes, which can be classified according to the degree of newness embodied in the new products generated, distinguishing between narrow and extensive exaptation.

This chapter is focused on the analysis of the modalities by which firms reuse knowledge, derived from internal development and external acquisition, which are later co-opted into the creation of new products in new market niches. Old knowledge might be embodied in different products, processes and technologies not necessarily owned by the innovative firm and later moved into other domains by the firm's ability to intercept new, and often hidden, demand needs. This process occurs not exclusively by chance, but can be interpreted within a strategic and intersectoral technological trajectory of the firm, which may lead, as in the case of L'Oréal, to innovation cascades (Lane, 2011).[1] This is a new approach and adds to previous contributions over the issues, such as, for instance, the Corning case (Cattani, 2006), where the innovation strategy of the firm is shaped by pre-adaptive processes of internal knowledge reuse for accomplishing new market demand. Our work shows that triggering factors of exaptation processes can be unused patents or dormant business agreements with leading firms operating in other close or distant sectors, generating opportunities for narrow or extensive internally- or externally-driven exaptation.

The empirical setting is L'Oréal, the world leader in the beauty industry. We reconstruct the historical pattern of innovations developed by the firm, by means of a collection of information coming from secondary sources.[2] In particular, we identify the conditions that allowed L'Oréal to enter the nutricosmetics arena, by means of the creation of a new product out of an exaptation process.

The next section introduces our theoretical background, followed by a discussion of our methodological approach. Thereafter we show our empirical evidence coming from the long-term qualitative and quantitative analysis of L'Oréal. The final section puts forward some concluding remarks.

Theoretical background

Exaptation and the evolutionary theory of technical change

A combination of alertness and effectual behaviour (Mastrogiorgio, 2013) allows entrepreneurs to look at resources and technologies as 'interpretative flexible' entities (Bijker, 1987), in other words as entities whose services are a: 'function of the ways in which they are used' (Penrose, 1959: 25). Indeed, as Dew *et al.* (2004) have suggested, there is evidence that entrepreneurs behave effectually, namely they: 'act to fabricate their own environments and futures' (Dew *et al.*, 2004: 55). Our criticism of Levinthal (1998) is that his approach obscures the creative drift and the post-application dynamics of cascade innovations that an exaptive process can generate (Lane, 2011).

We think that it is important to distinguish between: (a) adaptive evolutionary patterns related to new variants triggered by the process of variation, retention and environmental selection (technical change involving adaptation); and (b) exaptive reuses of knowledge in new domains that give rise to the phenomena of innovation, percolation and cascades (Watts, 2002).

The aim of this chapter is to discuss the latter point within the analysis of evolutionary technological trajectories of firms involving exaptation. Our contribution is rooted in the evolutionary theory of the firm. The evolutionary theory of the firm is part of a research program, known as universal Darwinism, aimed at showing that the schema variation selection and retention can be extended, at some level of abstraction, to other fields of research (Breslin, 2011) and that these apply a dialectical thinking, where organizational adaptation is recombined with strategic choices, as discussed by Abatecola (2015).

There are two theoretical perspectives on the evolution of firms. Our approach allows us to integrate two important research traditions in organizational analysis. The first is the theory of population ecology (Hannan and Freeman, 1977; Volberda and Lewin, 2003), which explains evolution of organizational forms as a consequence of market competition and selection. Incumbents are expected to lose their capacity to adapt to their environmental changes over time. Thus, evolution is driven by the entry of new firms, which are more efficient and effective in sighting, seizing and exploiting emerging technological and market opportunities. In this perspective, therefore, almost no attention is devoted to technological change, which is taken as exogenous, and internal adaptability, which is the capacity of incumbents to sight, seize opportunities and threats and change accordingly.

The second is the evolutionary theory of economic change, which, in its original form was proposed by Nelson and Winter (1982). In this second perspective, change is made endogenously in the model. Environment structure is not taken as given, but as the emergent construct of market competition. Firms not only adapt to external changes, but proactively co-construct their competitive environment. The evolutionary theory of economic change is mostly used to explain discontinuities in the firm innovation process. In contrast, a great deal of attention has been devoted to the adaptation of the organization and to the continuous evolution of technical change.

The concept of dynamic capabilities (Teece *et al.*, 1997; Eisenhardt and Martin, 2000; Winter, 2003; Helfat *et al.*, 2007; Teece, 2007) stays in some ways in the middle, but it has been mostly used to explain continuities in the firm innovation process. Recent literature has pointed out that we need a better investigation of the existing 'interregnum' between discontinuous and continuous innovation patterns, and radical and incremental changes, in terms of gradualism (Levinthal, 1998; Antonelli, 2007), pre-adaptation (Cattani, 2006), the reconfiguration process in technological transition (Geels, 2002; Meyer and Stensaker, 2006), the reconfiguration of operational and dynamic capabilities (Di Stefano *et al.*, 2010; Helfat and Winter, 2011) and adaptation and selection of capabilities (Fortune and Mitchell, 2012).

In the evolutionary theory of technical change and in its biological metaphors, a great deal of effort has been targeted at the narrow evolution of innovation within the firm. Scant attention has been devoted to the ways in which firms absorb external innovations and use externally created new knowledge. We have decided, therefore, to enlarge here the analysis of the forms of niche creation and use of exaptation processes, which involve the external acquisition of knowledge and innovation. This is an important and often disregarded point, in our view, once we agree on the importance of the open innovation model.

The term 'exaptation', even if not mentioned and acknowledged by Levinthal (1998), can be considered as an element of the theory of technological speciation. This theory has been proposed on the grounds of the theory of speciation of Gould and Eldridge (1977). It is suggested that, differently from what Darwin originally proposed, new species are not always born from the long-term, gradual accumulation of diverging adaptive changes that are positively selected by the environment (Gould, 1982), but as consequence of a speciation event that consists of a punctuated equilibrium, i.e. an event such as the migration in a new niche that triggers a divergent evolutionary path. Thus, the same form of life – the same phenotype – exposed to a different competitive pressure may evolve into a new species. The same evolutive process applies to technology where it may be activated not by a blind variation, but by an active strategy selected by firms of knowledge redeployment in new niches and in new variants. Exaptation mirrors the application of existing technology into a new domain of application, precipitating a process of evolution of prior technologies into new innovative artefacts.

A similar theoretical approach has been proposed by Cattani (2006). According to him, part of a firm's prior experience and knowledge, which is accumulated without the anticipation of subsequent uses, can be co-opted into new domains. To this end, he introduces the notion of pre-adaptation. This notion was originally introduced by Darwin to explain the evolution of complex organs, which are combinations of parts working together as a complex whole. None of these parts has a function independently from the others. Thus, how does it happen that these parts were originally developed? According to Darwin, these functions were co-opted to their present role from a precedent function, which originally selected and shaped these parts. While for Gould and Vrba (1982), in the field of evolutionary biology, pre-adaptation refers solely to features that promote fitness and they are built to perform the same function, features that evolved for other usage (or for no function) and that were later co-opted should be called exaptation.

Moving the argument from biology to business, this means that exaptation must be referred to in the co-evolution of a firm and its business ecosystem. We adopt an approach to exaptation that takes into account both of these two key aspects. This approach can be helpful in explaining the emergence of discontinuous and continuous change as an historical sequence of knowledge recombination, new inventions and exaptation.

Innovation cascades and exaptation forms

In the analyses of the history of technology we find that technological innovations frequently involve the use of an artefact or a process in a new domain. But clearly very often it is difficult to prove a net switch from one use to another, which cannot be ascribed to multiple selective market pressures, rather to a non-blind process of functional shift.

Technological evolution is always directed by an element of foresight or guided variation, despite the preference of some authors, including Cattani (2006), for depicting it as a combination of luck and serendipity. Larson *et al.* (2013) emphasize that often the terms adaptation and exaptation overlap and that it can be claimed that all adaptations can also be said to be exaptations. Some other authors (Dew *et al.*, 2004; Bonifati, 2010; Lane, 2011; Bonifati and Villani, 2013), in contrast, clearly define exaptation as a new pattern of interaction among agents around the use of new kinds of artefacts leading to the emergence of a new functionality. In order to distinguish adaptation from exaptation, Bonifati and Villani (2013) suggest that while adaptation processes can be derived by their actual functionality, the origin of the artefacts created by exaptation processes cannot be derived from their current utility. Dew *et al.* (2004) specify that exaptation refers to connecting a technology with a new domain of use, not to technology-technology combinations. Exaptation processes include an initial exaptation followed by subsequent processes of 'aptation', characterized by continuous positive feedbacks, innovation cascades and interactions.

In addition to the internal firm's efforts directed to innovation, novelties may arise by absorbing capability, by interactive learning and by the leading role played by users, as argued in the past by Rosenberg (1982) and by von Hippel (1986). However, next to these forms, we can also conceptualize various forms of exaptation, such as user-producing exaptation or exaptation by fusion (Sedita, 2012). Exaptation serves, here, as an excellent introduction to another aspect of the innovation theory, because as all the new functionalities attributed to possible uses of a technology (or to an old piece of knowledge) are still unknown at the time of its introduction, we are experimenting with the existence of what Lane and Maxfield (2005) called ontological uncertainty. In our view, three important issues must be tackled in order to deepen the study of innovation processes through exaptation, which is an event but also a process that may occur within a firm in multiple stages:

1   Exaptation is the result not only of the reuse of internal knowledge for new uses (internal exaptation) but also of the acquisition of external knowledge for new uses (external exaptation).
2   Exaptation occurs throughout the reuse of knowledge either in the same technological classes, or in the same sector (narrow exaptation), or in distant classes or in different sectors (extensive exaptation).
3   Exaptation may sustain the creation of a complex and multilevel dynamic innovation ecosystem leading to innovation cascades.

Therefore, three phases characterize the process of exaptation: (1) accumulation of knowledge from internal and external sources (this process can be either emergent or deliberate); (2) existing knowledge is co-opted for new uses in new market domains (different degrees of exaptation might exist according to the distance between the old and the new market domain); and (3) the co-opted knowledge expands the innovation ecosystem of the firm, creating new venues for innovation cascades. We distinguish between narrow and extended domains of exaptation, which correspond to a small or large technological distance existing between the old and the new use of knowledge.

Dynamic capabilities and relational dynamic capabilities are fundamental to identify, combine and deploy internal and external knowledge (Keil, 2004). Dynamic capabilities have been originally defined as the ability of a firm to integrate, build and reconfigure internal and external competencies. They reflect the ability of an organization to achieve new and innovative forms of competitive advantage given path dependencies and market positions (Leonard-Barton, 1992). There is an ongoing debate in the literature that attempts, after more than a decade of strategic management research, to clarify both the meaning and scope of this theoretical construct. In particular, recent contributions on the topic have pinpointed the importance of external relational capabilities (Inkpen, 2000; Hagedoorn and Duysters, 2002; Helfat *et al.*, 2007), which can be developed through strategic alliances and acquisitions. External relational dynamic capabilities are not only the capabilities required to adapt to changing customer and technological opportunities but also embrace the enterprise's capacity to shape the ecosystem it occupies, develop new products and processes and design a viable business model (Teece, 2007). A firm can be seen as a nexus of network relationships with partners, clients and suppliers, which build the business ecosystem (Powell, 1990; Powell *et al.*, 1996; Hargadon and Sutton, 1997; Sorenson *et al.*, 2006). The network position of the firm (Cattani and Ferriani, 2008) affects its propensity to be involved in knowledge flows that can be potential drivers of exaptation.

Figure 13.1 represents the spaces for exaptations. Organization A develops over time some core competencies and abilities, which lead it to some innovative output. This can be the result of internal research and development (R&D) effort (closed innovation model), or collaboration and interaction with external organizations (open innovation model – ABCDEFG). In both cases, innovations can have the characteristics of exaptations; in the first case it will be internal exaptation, in the second external exaptation. Moreover, the reuse of knowledge at the basis of the exaptive event might be from adjacent or distant technological classes, giving rise to two spaces for potential exaptations (respectively narrow or extended, see Table 13.1). The creation of an innovation ecosystem, where generative relationships (Lane and Maxfield, 1997) can take place, is the consequence of a series of exaptive events. The relationships with external organizations might, in fact, generate new attributions of functionality that help in shaping a new artefact.[3]

Figure 13.2 represents the evolutive dynamics of an innovation cascade. Key variables in explaining this evolution are time – in the x-axes, and the technological artefact – in the y-axes. The exploitation of an innovation may follow a specific technological trajectory (i.e. 1), which is linearly explained by a continuous innovation path that develops over time (Dosi, 1982). Accidentally, an exaptive event can lead to an exaptation 1, which extends and multiplies the technological trajectory

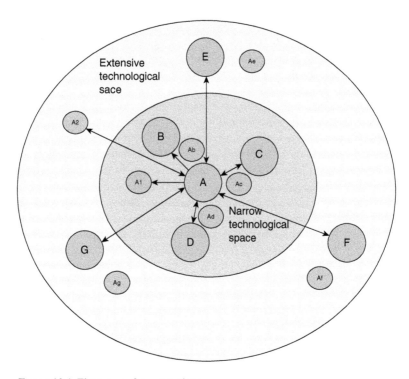

Figure 13.1 The spaces for exaptations

Source: Orbit database: https://www.orbit.com

Table 13.1 Description of spaces for exaptations

	Technologically adjacent*	*Technologically distant***
Internal	A1 Narrow internal driven exaptation	A2 Extensive internal driven exaptation
External	AB; AC; AD Narrow extensive driven exaptation	AE; AF; AG Extensive external exaptation

*Citation of patents within the same 3-digit patent class.
** Citation of patents within outside the 3-digit patent class.

Source: Authors' elaboration.

of innovation A, creating eventually the venue for a new exaptive pattern, giving rise to exaptation 2. As a result, we observe an innovation cascade along a variety of technological trajectories. Generative collaborations (within an innovation ecosystem) that enlarge the space of possibilities and identify new systems of use alongside the discovery of new functionalities are crucial (Bonaccorsi, 2011).

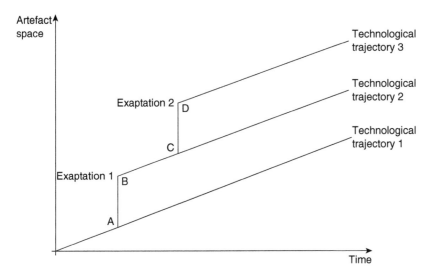

Figure 13.2 The evolutive dynamics of an innovation cascade

Source: Authors' elaboration.

The exaptation process is evolutionary in nature and exists alongside the firm and is able to build a dynamic innovative ecosystem, where external and internal knowledge may interplay. An innovative ecosystem, which is a specific form of business ecosystem (Moore, 1993), is a broad community of organizations, institutions and individuals that impact on the innovation capacity of the enterprise and the enterprise's customers and suppliers (Carayannis and Campbell, 2009). Therefore, as spelled out by Teece (2007), a company can be viewed not as a member of a single industry, but as part of an innovation ecosystem that crosses a variety of industries; an environmental context where complementary firms, suppliers, regulatory authorities, standard-setting bodies, the judiciary and educational and research institutions all play a relevant role in the choice of the strategic orientation of the firm. Network position and absorptive capacity (Cohen and Levinthal, 1990) are two fundamental conditions that favour the innovation process. In order to absorb external knowledge, the firm must develop learning abilities. However, the purpose and result of the interaction might not be clear from the beginning. Innovation can therefore be the result of an exaptation process where existing knowledge, belonging to one or more actors, is leveraged on and co-opted in an unexpected way to eventually generate new products in new market domains. This aligns with the open innovation argument (Chesbrough, 2003). A random component, but also a guided strategy, shape the way in which two or more nodes interact within a network. The breadth, diversification and liquid property of the innovation ecosystem together determine the probability of exaptation. The more ample, diversified and liquid the network of the firm, the greater the possibilities of random encounters and exaptation.

Methodology

We adopted a case study research design, because of the need to explore a phenomenon that is still underrepresented in the business and economic literature (Yin, 1984) and asks for an exploratory more than a confirmatory research approach. A combination of qualitative and quantitative data from a variety of sources allows us to produce an illustrative case study that informs on the exaptation process in L'Oréal (Jick, 1979; Miles and Huberman, 1994). Triangulated data were jointly considered in order to frame the innovation strategies of L'Oréal, gathered from: (a) the L'Oréal website and press releases collected in the period 2009–2012; (b) journal articles and books on the global cosmetics industry; and (c) patent data from the Orbit-QPat database registered in the period 1904–2012. The main reference for the history of the global beauty industry is Jones (2008, 2010). Concerning the patent data, we elaborated data from the Orbit-QPat database, which is a Questel/Orbit internet database providing the searchable full text of world patents from 1974 to the present day in about 80 countries. Examining patent information for a given firm or industry will highlight important trends and directions within the firm and within the industry (Lambert, 2004). We identified the patents' population of L'Oréal in the Orbit-QPat database and obtained 12,380 family patents and 50,509 single patents from 1904 to 2012.

The case of L'Oréal

L'Oréal in a nutshell

L'Oréal is one of the largest cosmetic companies in the world. It produces and markets a range of make-up, perfume, hair and skin care products in over 130 countries. It is headquartered in Clichy (a suburb of Paris), France and employed 66,600 people in 2010 (they employed 50,500 worldwide in 2008). The company recorded revenues of €19,495.8 million (US$25,865.1 million) during the financial year ended December 2010. Presently, L'Oréal accounts for 500 brands (23 international), 5,000 new formulas developed annually, 18 research laboratories worldwide, 100 active research agreements with prestigious universities and public research organizations and have about 13,000 patents registered (our analysis from the Orbit-QPat database). The company is now a large multinational.

L'Oréal was founded in 1909 by Eugène Schueller,[4] a French chemist who graduated from the Institut de Chimie Appliqué de Paris in 1904 and who created his first hair dye formula under the name Oréal in 1907, using a blend of harmless chemical compounds. Schueller filed for a patent (no. 383920) on 24 March 1908. This product became very popular with Parisian hairdressers. Two years later, Schueller established L'Oréal, which was originally named Société Française des Teintures Inoffensives pour Cheveux. The company became L'Oréal in 1939. In 1963 the company entered the stock market. At the beginning L'Oréal pursued its growth through the haircare products, but in quick succession added shampoos and soaps to its product portfolio. The growth of the company is linked to the idea of developing a 'market of beauty'. To continue this growth, L'Oréal also activated a series of key acquisitions in the cosmetics, pharmaceuticals and publishing sectors (fashion journals). It recently entered (and created) the business of nutricosmetics where the necessary knowledge was 'exapted' by Nestlé with which it made a strategic alliances (Innēov).

Innēov is utilizing the expertise in nutrition and food security of the Nestlé R&D, to combine it with the dermatological knowledge of the skin (physiology of cutis and experience in monitoring the effects of the components) accumulated in the past, in a newly created niche market – nutricosmetics – where new pills for hair and skin treatment are conceptualized. In particular, L'Oréal is benefiting from Nestlé's R&D because it uses the firm's unique expertise to select raw materials and components, to optimize their absorption and to verify the quality of safety and of their conservation. More details on this case of exaptation follow later.

The innovative path of L'Oréal

Over time, the creation of the 'market of beauty' process has implied some crucial steps for L'Oréal. The first was the 1909 breakthrough innovation: a product for synthetic hair dye using safe compounds invented by Schueller. Before his invention the Romans, ancient Egyptians and Greeks were experimenting with different forms of hair dyeing. Most of the early forms of hair dyes were henna, indigo, sage and camomile, but these methods could only darken the hair. Blond hair continued to be desirable, with potassium lye or caustic soda being use to bleach the hair. Venetian women used large hats with an open top to expose their treated hair to the strong sun. In the 1800s chemists discovered para-phenylenediamine (PPD) and its use in the creation of synthetic dye. At the same time, it was found that hydrogen peroxide was a gentler and safer chemical for hair bleaching. These two discoveries paved the way for Schueller, who created the first commercial chemical hair dye. He was a French chemist who started to manufacture his own products, selling them initially to Parisian hairdressers. L'Oréal soon became a leading firm in Europe, while other firms such as Clairol in the US explored similar technologies, becoming the top selling brand in hair colouring up to the 1950s (Sherrow, 2006). After the 1950s, and thanks to its reputation, research activity and marketing efforts, L'Oréal also conquered the US market and become in the 1970s a global company. During the 1920s and 1930s Schueller patented few inventions related to hair dyeing, but later on innovation in L'Oréal become an institutionalized activity, managed by a large R&D laboratory. In hair dyeing L'Oréal now has (end 2011) 432 patents, which is about 20 per cent of all patents, registered in this technological area. L'Oréal is the number one for the extension of patenting activity in this area (Figure 13.3). Top assignees are Kao (240), Henkel (119), Wella (99), Clairol (88), Shiseido (56) and Procter & Gamble (52).

The second important step (1928) of the company was the acquisition of Monsavon, a firm specializing in the production of soap. At that time, soap was at the basis of many detergents and liquid shampoos. This explains how L'Oréal, after the acquisition of the knowledge possessed by Monsavon, was able to enter

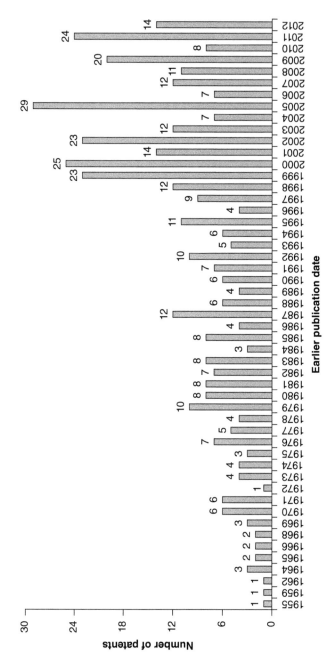

Figure 13.3 L'Oréal's registered patents related to shampoo reported in the Orbit-QPat database

Source: Authors' elaboration on Orbit Database.

Table 13.2 L'Oréal patents in shampoo

	Patents		Patent citations of L'Oréal	L'Oréal patents self-citations	External citations
	L'Oréal	All firms (including L'Oréal)			
Hair dye	432	2,553	2,386	222	2,164
Shampoo	660	9,224	4,768	1,067	3,701
Bath foam	5	143	–	–	–

Source: Authors' elaboration on Orbit Database.

quickly into the production and commercialization of new types of synthetic shampoo in the market of beauty.[5]

The invention of very commonly used products is often uncovered by the scientific literature. Since then L'Oréal has registered 660 patents related to shampoo out of a total number of 9,224 total inventions reported in the Orbit-QPat database (Figure 13.3 and Table 13.2). L'Oréal covers only about 6 per cent of the total technological area, but its leadership in the market is indisputable. L'Oréal patents related to shampoo have received 4,768 citations, 3,701 coming from external organizations. Other top assignees are Kao (373), Procter & Gamble (373), Unilever (279), Colgate (222), Henkel (138) and Shiseido (120).

Step three is related to the invention of a new product. Schueller is credited as the inventor of the modern sunscreen. L'Oréal released sunscreen Ambre Solaire in 1935. Others, wrongly, give that honour to Austria's Franz Greiter who, in 1938, was inspired to create a product named Gletscher Crème (Glacier Cream) as a result of sunburn he received while mountain climbing at Piz Buin (in 1962 Franz Greiter re-emerged, developing a way to measure a product's ability to block ultraviolet rays, known as the Sun Protection Factor, (SPF)). The L'Oréal sun tanning oil and cream became another milestone for the company.

Step four is related to the creation of an ecological niche in the market of beauty. Already during the 1930s its market of beauty extended from hair to skin. Thus, L'Oréal became a world leader specializing both in hair and skin treatments. Moreover, in 1933 Schueller published Votre Beauté, the first monthly women's health and beauty magazine. We cannot imagine a better communicative and marketing strategy for a cosmetic company than to 'organize' directly the consumption of its products, dictating the fashion, helping to create the female identity and, consequently, influencing the demand for its new goods. In order to become the leader in the market of beauty, L'Oréal activated many acquisitions of important firms that specialized in similar products. Thus the company built new competencies thanks to the external acquisitions of new knowledge and patents. This step was organized around the absorption of various skin cream producers, pharmaceutical and beauty firms. In this context, L'Oréal also set up numerous R&D agreements with several international labs. In 1954 L'Oréal signed the first technical agreement with a pharma company: the Société d'Hygiène Dermatologique de Vichy. We can now observe a shift towards a more scientific concept of beauty. All the products were at that time patented, in order to avoid imitation and the entry of substitutive products. L'Oréal became a giant company, spending a huge amount of money on marketing and advertising. Thus, it maintained its leadership through its presence in women's journals and through agreements with various commercialization networks. During the 1960s and 1970s, growth occurred mainly through acquisitions: the prestigious firm Lancôme in 1964 and Garnier in 1965. In 1970 followed the acquisition of Biotherm and, in 1973, L'Oréal acquired a majority interest in the pharmaceutical companies Synthélabo and Gemey. Then (in 1979), it started to be a knowledge-intensive firm, becoming a high-level R&D performer through the dermatology research centre established in Sophia Antipolis, in France. It is important to note that through Synthélabo L'Oréal also holds 10.41 per cent of the shares of the big French pharma Sanofi-Aventis. Between 1984 and 1996 another group of leading companies was integrated into the giant company L'Oréal: Marie Claire, Helena Rubinstein, La Roche-Posay, Maybelline and Biomedic. Another interesting feature of its strategy was the agreement signed in 2006 with Diesel to launch a line of fragrances (Diesel is a cult brand for the 18–35 age group worldwide, featuring bold, modern and unconventional casual chic).

Step five was dedicated to the intensification of its innovation trajectory. In 1945 the company introduced its first 'cold perm' – a 'chemical way' to transform the form of the hair, rendering it soft and curly.

Step six was the co-option of its internal knowledge on hair (cold perm and hair dyeing) and skin in the generation of radically new products. In 1955, from the R&D labs of the company, came Colorelle: the first colour-enhancing shampoo where, again, we see the exaptation of an existing competence into a new use. This process of expanding into new niches occurred, again, in 1963, with the launch of OBAO, the first foam bath. L'Oréal patented this product in 1969. During the 1970s several other improvements were registered and patented.

Step seven is again related to the introduction of permed and dyed hair shampoo. In the early 1970s Proctor & Gamble challenged the L'Oréal leadership, revolutionizing the hair care market with the introduction of the two-in-one shampoo plus conditioner. Many other manufacturers followed with two-in-one formulas, including L'Oréal. As a reaction, in 1972, L'Oréal launched the first Elsève shampoo for permed and dyed hair. Combining its knowledge on perming (and the possible damaging effects of its use) and on shampoo, L'Oréal invented a new product. The strategy this time was to introduce a product for the mass market made with an original innovative formula. Subsequently the company diversified its range of shampoos, emphasizing various distinctive characteristics. Figure 13.4 shows the intense innovative activity of L'Oréal in shampoo, which is at the basis of the company's market success. In the shampoo market Proctor & Gamble with their products never exceeded 20 per cent of sales, while L'Oréal, through its various brands, Elsève, Fructis, Ultra Doux (all acquired in 1970s) and Laboratoires Garnier (a company born in 1904 and acquired in 1965) became dominant with about 40 per cent of the whole shampoo market (www.lOréal.esade.edu).

Step eight, occurring during the 1980s, is strictly related to the previous phase of firm acquisitions (phase four). As a consequence, L'Oréal, mainly a cosmetic firm,

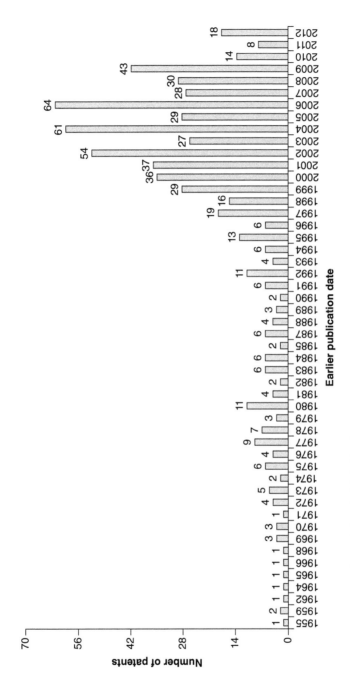

Figure 13.4 Innovative activity of L'Oréal in shampoo

Source: Orbit database: https://www.orbit.com

was able to launch several pharmaceutically-based revolutionary products: in 1982 the sunscreen, Mexoryl SX; in 1994 the ingenious molecule that repairs damaged hair, Céramide R; and in 1996 the molecule that combats hair loss, Aminexil.

Step nine is at the basis of the formation of a new, futuristic sector: nutri-cosmetics. Nutricosmetics refers to nutritional supplements, which can improve individuals' aesthetics. Products generally focus on three areas: skin, hair and beauty. Nutricosmetics are available in pill, tablet, liquid and food formats. To be able to create this new sector, and in order to modify its core competences, L'Oréal chose to enlarge the firm's knowledge base through signing an agreement with a food company, Nestlé. L'Oréal selected Nestlé, deepening its previous, purely financial relationship. Strategically, in 2002, L'Oréal moved, therefore, into a completely new field: the new area of nutricosmetics. In 2003 The Research Institute for Ethnic Skin and Hair opened up in Chicago (US). In 2005 L'Oréal acquired Skinceuticals and Pro-Xylane in the subsequent year (2006), the latter being a firm with a product which contains the anti-ageing gene, and SkinEthic, one of the major international specialists in tissue engineering. During the same year (2006), in order to grow in the organic sector as well, L'Oréal acquired a well-known British retail chain, The Body Shop, and subsequently Sanoflore, a leading name in organic skincare.

The evolution of L'Oréal is not inscribed into a linear process of growth. Each step realized has increased the synergies between the existing segments of the firm and also increased the possibility of realizing the processes of knowledge recombination, exaptation and learning. Thus, a scale effect of increasing returns intervened.

The huge investments in internal R&D (calculated to be about 3 per cent of sales annually), dispersed among 18 R&D labs in the US, Europe, China and Japan, with about 2,350 researchers in different disciplines (e.g. chemistry, biology, medicine, physics and toxicology), are complemented by an extended network of external R&D collaborations.

L'Oréal adopted a sophisticated model of open innovation, which combines the development of internal competencies and the speciation of new market niches, where both narrow and extensive exaptation occurs. The reutilization of knowledge in new market niches, through exaptation, was complemented by a flow of new knowledge internally generated in its R&D laboratory. Exploration and exploitation processes extended the firm's boundaries. L'Oréal can be considered a very creative firm that has been able during its long existence not only to produce very innovative products but to create a completely new market niche: the market of beauty.

Exploring the role of exaptation in the evolution of L'Oréal's technological trajectory and the reutilization of knowledge in new market niches

The objective of this section is to investigate the role of exaptation in the evolution of L'Oréal's technological trajectory. In this section we have studied technological exaptation at the level of technological artefacts. As discussed by Basalla

(1988), we agree that technological artefacts are central in any debate on technology and innovation. To perform our analysis we consider a technological artefact as a patent. In this approach we followed Mastrogiorgio (2013).

Our statistical approach is based on patent data. A critical starting point of any patent-based analysis is clearly related to the availability of reliable data, according to two important dimensions: the coverage of the database and the quality of the data available for patents. QPat database is one of the currently available patent databases that satisfy all these characteristics across the world. QPat is Questel/Orbit's internet database providing the searchable full text of world patents from 1974 to the present day in about 80 countries. For the industrial researcher, QPat offers invaluable competitive intelligence and market knowledge. Often, examining a competitor's patents will provide indepth and comprehensive information about strategies, production costs and product limitations. In a more general sense, examining patent information for a given firm or industry will highlight important trends and directions within the firm and within the industry (Lambert, 2004).

We identified the patents' population of L'Oréal in the QPat database and we obtained 12,380 family patents and 50,509 single patents from 1904 to 2012.

Mastrogiorgio (2013) proposes a modified version of Trajtenberg *et al.*'s (1997)[6] distance metric to capture serendipitous and non-connected discoveries. We hypothesize that non-connected discoveries occurring in remote technological areas can be considered as proxies of the 'exaptation potential' of a patent. If knowledge is used in the same technological area, it can be classified in the spillover category. In contrast, when knowledge is used in other technological areas it can be at the basis of a potential exaptive process. Thus, our idea is to measure the 'exaptation potential' of a patent by looking at the number of citations obtained across different technological classes. We conceive each technological 'jump' as a potential technological exaptation. We calculate the exaptation score using the detailed information contained in patents, relying on citations to other patents, since these citations provide good evidence of the links between an innovation and its technological antecedents and descendants (Trajtenberg *et al.*, 1997).

The World Intellectual Property Organization divides the entire set of patents into searchable collections based on the technology claimed (International Patent Classification (IPC) in the QPat database). The primary groupings are referred to as classes. Classes are divided into relatively small collections of patents called subclasses. We use 3-digit patent subclasses to capture the patent spread across different technological classes and calculate the potential exaptation of the entire L'Oréal patents' portfolio. We utilize the entire patent portfolio of L'Oréal as a reference to calculate the degree of exaptation for each patent. We construct, accordingly, two sets of measures: (1) 'backward-looking' measures, which are derived from the relationship between a given patent and the body of knowledge that preceded it; and (2) 'forward-looking' measures, which are derived from the relationship between a patent and subsequent technological developments that build upon it. We use the patent citations obtained by each patent to identify its antecedents and the subsequent patents that cite it to identify its descendants. For each of these patents we have information on their technological and temporal location, the number of citations that they received and the identity of the assignee (Trajtenberg *et al.*, 1997).

We have about 20,000 family patents cited by L'Oréal and about 25,000 family patents citing L'Oréal patents. The major difficulty of this type of analysis, besides the enormous amount of data to analyse, has been the matching of data from the classes of the L'Oréal patents with the classes of cited and citing patents, because many patents have multiple subclasses to match and because there may be more citations per patent so as to significantly increase the number of possible combinations.

$$\text{Backward exaptation potential of a L'Oréal patent } p = \sum_{x=1}^{n^\circ \text{ cited by } p} \frac{dummy_x}{no.cited \text{ by } p}$$

$$\text{Forward exaptation potential of a L'Oréal patent } p = \sum_{x=1}^{n \text{ cited by } p} \frac{dummy_x}{no.cited \ p}$$

where:

p = a patent belonging to L'Oréal's patent portfolio from 1904 to 2012
no. cited by p = number of citations made by patent p up to the end of 2012
no. citing p = number of citations received by patent p up to the end of 2012

$$dummy_x = \begin{cases} 0 \text{ if class of citing or cited patent } x \text{ is} = \text{class of patent } p \\ 1 \text{ if class of citing or cites patent } x \text{ is} \neq \text{class of patent } p \end{cases}$$

The values vary in the [0 1] interval; a score close to 1 indicates higher exaptation potential while 0 indicates the absence of exaptation potential. We expect an important number of citations between patents which do not share the same technological class, hence a high exaptation potential.

We analyse the patents at three analytical levels: country (country group), assignee institution and technology field (represented by subclass IPC categories) to calculate the degree of potential exaptation for each patent with respect to the patents cited by L'Oréal and those citing L'Oréal's.

Figure 13.5 shows the total number of patents published in the last 100 years. It is worth noting that L'Oréal patents reached their peak starting from 2010–2011. After an initial smooth, little and slow increase in patent applications, L'Oréal registered an exponential growth. In fact, from 2000 patent applications rapidly grew after stabilizing for four years and it is still increasing.

In Figure 13.6 and Table 13.3 we represent the distribution by kind of IPC codes in L'Oréal's patent portfolio.

The most important technological subclasses in R&D of new products represent also the L'Oréal core business. The two subclasses in which the company patented the most are A61K and A61Q representing preparations for medical,

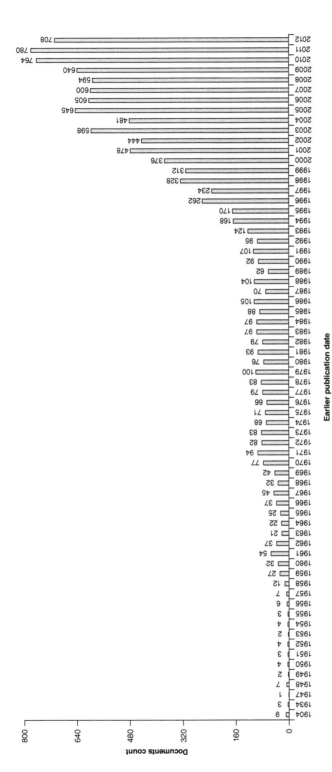

Figure 13.5 The total number of patents published in the last 100 years

Source: Authors' elaboration on Orbit Database.

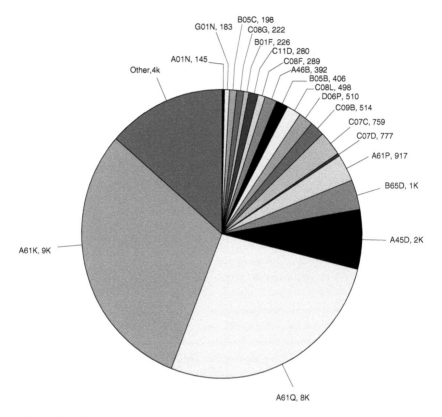

Figure 13.6 The distribution by kind of IPC codes in L'Oréal's patent portfolio

Source: Authors' elaboration on Orbit Database.

dental or toilet purposes and the use of cosmetics or similar toilet preparations, followed by A45D representing hairdressing or shaving equipment, manicuring or other cosmetics treatment. Table 13.4 shows the ten IPC 3-digit subclasses where we count more technological 'jumps' and so potential exaptation with respect to cited patents by L'Oréal. It should be noted that the two subclasses in which the number of exaptations is the most are not core in L'Oréal's technological trajectory. However, it should also be noted that these two subclasses are dealing with more fundamental knowledge compared to the core ones. Thus, the productivity of these subclasses in terms of exaptation may be a consequence of the wider applicability of the patented knowledge.

In Table 13.5 we represent the top 10 IPC 3-digit subclasses where we count more technological 'jumps' with respect to citing patents of L'Oréal patent portfolio. As we can see from a first descriptive analysis of the subclasses, the classes that contain the largest number of potential exaptations are C07 'acyclic or carbocyclic compounds, heterocyclic compounds', A61 'use of cosmetics or similar toilet preparations', A45 'hairdressing or shaving equipment; manicuring or other

Table 13.3 Top 20 IPC codes

Code	Description	Doc. no.
A61K	Preparations for medical, dental or toilet purposes	9165
A61Q	Use of cosmetics or similar toilet preparations	7914
A45D	Hairdressing or shaving equipment; manicuring or other cosmetic treatment	2026
B65D	Containers for storage or transport of articles or materials, e.g. bags, barrels, bottles, boxes, cans, cartons, crates, drums, jars, tanks, hoppers, forwarding containers; accessories, closures or fittings therefor; packaging elements; packages	1207
A61P	Therapeutic activity of chemical compounds or medicinal preparations	917
C07D	Heterocyclic compounds	777
C07C	Acyclic or carbocyclic compounds	759
C09B	Organic dyes or closely-related compounds for producing dyes; mordants; lakes	514
D06P	Dyeing or printing textiles; dyeing leather, furs or solid macromolecular substances in any form	510
C08L	Compositions of macromolecular compounds	498
B05B	Spraying apparatus; atomizing apparatus; nozzles	406
A46B	Brushes	392
C08F	Macromolecular compounds obtained by reactions only involving carbon-to-carbon unsaturated bonds	289
C11D	Detergent compositions; use of single substances as detergents; soap or soap-making; resin soaps; recovery of glycerol	280
B01F	Mixing, e.g. dissolving, emulsifying, dispersing	226
C08G	Macromolecular compounds obtained otherwise than by reactions only involving carbon-to-carbon unsaturated bonds	222
B05C	Apparatus for applying liquids or other fluent materials to surfaces, in general	198
G01N	Investigating or analysing materials by determining their chemical or physical properties	183
A01N	Preservation of bodies of humans or animals or plants or parts thereof; biocides, e.g. as disinfectants, as pesticides, as herbicides; pest repellants or attractants; plant growth regulators	145
B67D	Dispensing, delivering or transferring liquids, not otherwise provided for	143

Source: Authors' elaboration on Orbit database.

Table 13.4 Top 10 3-digit IPC subclasses with respect to cited patents by L'Oréal

IPC cited	Freq	Description
C07	70773	Acyclic or carbocyclic compounds, heterocyclic compounds
C11	22527	Detergent compositions; use of single substances as detergents; soap or soap-making; resin soaps; recovery of glycerol
A61	22209	Use of cosmetics or similar toilet preparations
B01	20996	Mixing, e.g. dissolving, emulsifying, dispersing
A45	20205	Hairdressing or shaving equipment; manicuring or other cosmetic treatment
D06	19372	Dyeing or printing textiles; dyeing leather, furs or solid macromolecular substances in any form
A01	9622	Disinfectants, as pesticides, as herbicides; pest repellants or attractants; plant growth regulators
B67	8380	Dispensing, delivering or transferring liquids, not otherwise provided for
G01	5505	Investigating or analysing materials by determining their chemical or physical properties
D21	2395	Paper making; production of cellulose

Source: Authors' elaboration on Orbit database.

cosmetic treatment', B01 'mixing, dissolving, emulsifying, dispersing', B67 'dispensing, delivering or transferring liquids' and C11 'detergent compositions; use of single substances as detergents; soap or soap-making; resin soaps; recovery of glycerol'. The three technological classes A61, A45 and C07 also constitute the core business of the company as we saw in Table 13.3. There are also IPCs that contain many technological jumps, but they do not represent the core business of the company. They are intermediate IPCs that are halfway between the core and peripheral classes such as G01 'investigating or analysing materials by determining their chemical or physical properties', B67 'dispensing, delivering, or transferring liquids' or D06 'dyeing or printing textiles; dyeing leather, furs, or solid macromolecular substances in any form'.

The IPC structure is also similar between the citing and cited patents' subgroups. There are, however, some differences, for example B44 'decorative arts' for the citing group and D21 'paper making; production of cellulose' for the cited one. As a second step of analysis, Table 13.6 reports mean, standard deviation, minimum, maximum and sample size of exaptation potential scores among different subsamples.

The first descriptive analysis represents the distinction between the average score of the cited group and the citing one. We can observe that the average score of the cited (0.385) is higher than the citing group (0.357).

The second analysis represents the division between the average score of internal exaptation potential, external exaptation potential and the score of the group

Table 13.5 Top 10 3-digit IPC subclasses with respect to citing patents of L'Oréal's patent portfolio

IPC citing	Freq	Description
C07	39598	Acyclic or carbocyclic compounds, heterocyclic compounds
A61	20668	Use of cosmetics or similar toilet preparations
A45	10996	Hairdressing or shaving equipment; manicuring or other cosmetic treatment
B01	7505	Mixing, e.g. Dissolving, emulsifying, dispersing
B67	6690	Dispensing, delivering or transferring liquids, not otherwise provided for
C11	5802	Detergent compositions; use of single substances as detergents; soap or soap-making; resin soaps; recovery of glycerol
D06	2902	Dyeing or printing textiles; dyeing leather, furs, or solid macromolecular substances in any form
A01	2546	Disinfectants, as pesticides, as herbicides; pest repellants or attractants; plant growth regulators
B44	2525	Decorative arts
G01	2427	Investigating or analysing materials by determining their chemical or physical properties

Source: Authors' elaboration on Orbit database.

Table 13.6 Descriptive statistics of exaptation potential score

Variable	Mean	S.D.	Min	Max	Sample
Cited (all patents)	0.385	0.327	0	1	70853
Citing (all patents)	0.357	0.263	0	1	70853
Internal (all patents)	0.362	0.102	0	1	70853
External (all patents)	0.376	0.119	0	1	70853
Co-assignee (all patents)	0.338	0.107	0	1	70853
Internal (only cited)	0.317	0.321	0	1	33065
External (only cited)	0.446	0.275	0	1	33065
Co-assignee (only cited)	0.379	0.199	0	1	33065
Internal (only citing)	0.377	0.267	0	1	37828
External (only citing)	0.333	0.214	0	1	37828
Co-assignee (only citing)	0.325	0.313	0	1	37828

Source: Authors' elaboration on Orbit database.

with the presence of a co-assignee as a patent owner. Internal exaptation potential is defined as the number of citations received or made by patent p, up to the end of 2012, by patents owned by the same firm owning patent p; external exaptation potential is defined as the number of citations received or made by patent p, up to the end of 2012, by patents owned by a different firm owning patent p; and co-assignee exaptation potential is defined as the number of citations received or made by patent p, up to the end of 2012, by patents owned with a co-assignee. The external exaptation potential score (0.376) is higher than the internal (0.362) and the co-assignee score (0.338) with respect to all patents considered. If we consider only the average score with respect to the cited patents' group (third analysis), also in this case, the external exaptation potential is the highest (0.446), followed by the co-assignee score (0.379) and the internal score (0.317). In the case of the citing patents' group (fourth analysis), the internal exaptation average score (0.377) is higher than the external score (0.333) and the co-assignee score (0.325).

As a third step of the analysis we conducted an analysis of variance test (Anova) on the statistical significance of the differences between different groups with respect to the exaptation potential score. The one-way Anova compares the means between the groups one is interested in and determines whether any of those means are statistically significantly different from each other. Specifically, it tests the null hypothesis:

$$H_0: \mu_1 = \mu_2 = \mu_3 \ldots = \mu_\kappa$$

where μ = group population mean and k = number of groups.

Estimates represent the difference between the mean of the first group (taken as a reference) and the mean of each other group. The results of the test are reported in Table 13.7.

The Anova test highlights some interesting characteristics of the role of exaptation in L'Oréal's technological trajectory. First, it shows that, on average, there is a slight but significant difference in the exaptation potential of backward cited patents and forward citing patents. This result could be affected by the asymmetry existing between cited and citing patents in terms of probability of being cited, following a certain year. However, in the case of L'Oréal, this distortion is minimal due to the long time series of patents available. This may reflect the scientific orientation and exploitive capacity of the firm, which invests in the production and acquisition of scientific knowledge and transforms it into market products. In fact, as we have already argued, the exploitation potential of scientific knowledge is higher than that of applicative knowledge. This is due to the abstract nature of scientific knowledge, which may find application in many different technological classes and subclasses.

Second, it shows that firms' boundaries and control are relevant for the exaptation potential of both cited and citing patents. In case of cited patents, exaptation potential is affected negatively by the level of control exercised by the company in the production of that knowledge. It is the highest when the cited patent is granted to an external assignee, who is not directly related to L'Oréal. This implies that

Table 13.7 Anova test results

Variable	Coeff. (Std. err.)
Cited (all patents)	0.385 (0.351)
Citing (all patents)	−0.055 (0.021)*
Internal (all patents)	0.365 (0.573)
External (all patents)	+0.011 (0.733)
Co-assignee (all patents)	−0.027 (0.611)
Internal (only cited)	0.317 (0.493)
External (only cited)	+0.129 (0.015)***
Co-assignee (only cited)	+0.062 (0.025)*
Internal (only citing)	0.367 (0.212)
External (only citing)	−0.331 (0.115)**
Co-assignee (only citing)	−0.462 (0.037)***

Significant codes 0 '***' 0.001 '**' 0.01 '*' 0.05 ' ' 1

Source: Authors' elaboration on Orbit database.

L'Oréal has the capacity to perceive the potential embedded in the application of knowledge developed outside of the company and translate (exapt) it into potential value in technological subclasses that are different from the original ones. It is the lowest when the cited patent is owned by L'Oréal itself. This implies that innovation is more adaptive. Thus, there is more strategic foresight in the exploitation of internal patents, which may bind the capacity of the company to perceive alternative technological applications for the same knowledge. It is intermediary when L'Oréal is co-assignee. The interaction with an external partner seems to affect positively the exaptive capacity of the firm, but to a lesser extent than the market.

The opposite is true in the case of citing patents. The exaptation potential is the lowest in the case of citing patents granted to an external assignee. This implies that external parties find it difficult to exploit the potential embedded in patents owned by L'Oréal in different technological subclasses. This may be consequence of an aggressive patent strategy applied by L'Oréal, which aims to protect the value of the patents' portfolio and is more orientated to exploit internally the knowledge either produced or acquired. It is the highest when the assignee is L'Oréal. It is again intermediary when L'Oréal is co-assignee of the citing patents.

L'Oréal and the acquisition of externally-based dynamic capabilities

The acquisition path relates to an important feature of the L'Oréal modality through which exaptation was pursued: when new desired competencies were not internally available, they were acquired in the market. In 1973 the company diversified into pharmaceuticals and publications through two acquisitions: a French pharmaceutical firm, Synthélabo, and a French publication house, Marie Claire. Synthélabo made products for arterial diseases and hospital equipment and its acquisition allowed L'Oréal to become the third largest pharmaceutical company in France. Nevertheless, L'Oréal's investment in the pharmaceutical industry never translated into a source of innovation in beauty products until the 1990s. At that time many companies in the pharmaceutical industry tried to enter into the 'cosmetic' market of beauty, competing directly with L'Oréal. However, after a while, they were out of the market and many of them (or the technicians from their laboratories) were absorbed by L'Oréal (Jones, 2008).

Thus, for a long time, the new scientific competence acquired in the area of the pharma industry remained 'silent'. In 1974 François Dalle, managing director of L'Oréal since 1954, was looking for a large company to invest in L'Oréal and, after trying to reach an agreement with Unilever, (which in the end rejected his offer), successfully persuaded Nestlé to acquire a 25 per cent stake in the L'Oréal business. Thus, nearly by serendipity (historical accident), Nestlé became a significant shareholder in L'Oréal. In addition, Nestlé also became the majority owner of Cosmair, a private US company, which had the exclusive licence to distribute L'Oréal's brands in the US. This was an important step towards the internationalization of L'Oréal, but also set out their future technological collaborations. In 1979 L'Oréal, together with Nestlé, founded a new research centre, the International Dermatology Research Centre (CIRD) in Sophia Antipolis, France, with the aim of conducting fundamental research into skin physiology. The acquisition of a pharma firm in 1973 was thus developed into something more demanding and innovative. After the complete debacle of many pharma firms that have tried to enter into the cosmetic market, which is well protected by the cosmetic leader, L'Oréal entered into the pharma market, bringing its accumulated experience. Thus, in 1981, Nestlé and L'Oréal formed a joint venture that became one of the world's leading dermatology players: Galderma. From the 1980s onwards, L'Oréal strengthened its presence in the global beauty industry by acquiring different companies in a variety of geographical locations and product segments. Yet, in the 1990s, L'Oréal still remained primarily a hair care company, with skin care and cosmetics confined to the smaller luxury component of the company and heavily dependent on the European market. When François Dalle retired in 1988, he chose as the new chief executive of the company Lindsay Owen-Jones, who was able to boost the globalization of L'Oréal and enlarge its product portfolio. The effects are clearly visible in Table 13.8, where, from 1993 onwards, we see a huge expansion of L'Oréal through acquisitions of American brands (Cosmair, Redken, Matrix, Maybelline, etc.). While in the mid-1990s, L'Oréal still generated 63 per cent of its sales in Western Europe and 20 per cent in North America, by 2008 these proportions had changed to 45 per cent and 23 per cent respectively. L'Oréal, therefore, became a truly global company, well established in the new emerging markets. L'Oréal's acquisitions and joint ventures are shown in Table 13.8.

Table 13.8 L'Oréal acquisitions and joint ventures

Year	Company	Country	Product segment
1928	Monsavon*	France	Soap business
1961	Cadoricin	France	Shampoos
1965	Lancôme	France	Skin care – luxury products
1970	Biotherm	France	Skin care – luxury products
1973	Marie Claire** (equity investment)	France	Publication (magazine)
	Synthélabo (53% stake)	France	Pharmaceuticals
1984	Canal Plus (10% stake)	France	Pay television
	Warner Communications' fragrance and cosmetics business (Gloria Vanderbilt and Ralph Lauren Fragrances)	US	Perfumes and cosmetics
	Helena Rubinstein (first operations in Latin America and Japan, acquisition completed in 1988)	US	Cosmetics
1988	Mennen	US	Cosmetics
	Laboratories Pharmaceutiques La Roche-Posay	France	Cosmetics
	Lanvin***	France	Fashion house
1990s	Liechtenstein Pharmazeutica	Germany	Generic Drug Co.
	Irex	France	Make up
1991	Laboratories Delagrange	France	Pharmaceuticals
	Delalande	France	Pharmaceuticals
	Vita Farmaceutici	Italy	Pharmaceuticals
1993	Redken	US	Professional hair care
1994	Cosmair	US	Professional hair care
1996	Maybelline	US	Make up
1998	Soft Sheen	US	Ethnic hair care
	Carson	US	Ethnic hair care
2000	Matrix Essentials	US	Hair care (salon only)
	Kiehl's	US	Hair care, skin care
	Shu Uemura (35% stake, majority control in 2003)	Japan	Make up
	Respons	US	Shampoos, hair care
	Dermablend	US	Cosmetics
2001	Colorama	Brazil	Make up, hair care
	Biomedic	US	Skin care
2002	ARtee	US	Hair care
2003	Innēov (joint venture with Nestlé)	US	Marketing for nutritional supplements for skin & hair skin care

(continued)

Table 13.8 (continued)

Year	Company	Country	Product segment
2004	Yue-sai	China	Make up and skin care
2005	SkinCeuticals	US	Professional skin care
	Delial	US	Suncare
2006	The Body Shop	GB	Natural beauty
	Sanoflore	France	Natural beauty
	SkinEthic	France	Tissue engineering
2007	PureOlogy	US	Professional hair care
2008	YSL Beauté	France	Perfumes, cosmetics, skin care

*L'Oréal sold Monsavon to P&G in 1961 and used the cash to invest in research and other acquisitions.
**L'Oréal divested 49% stake in Marie Claire in 2001.
***L'Oréal divested 100% stake in Lanvin in 2001.

Sources: Our adaptation on http://www.loreal.com/ and Jones (2010).

L'Oréal and Innēov: how to perform an activity of extensive exaptation, creating a complex dynamic innovation ecosystem

As consumers worldwide increasingly seek out new ways to stay healthy and maintain a youthful appearance, cosmeceuticals and nutricosmetics have been hailed as the next 'big thing' in the beauty industry. Euromonitor International estimates that sales of beauty supplements totalled more than US$2.7 billion in 2009, equating to 8 per cent of global retail expenditure on dietary supplements.

The cooperation of L'Oréal and Nestlé was initially only based on finance issues (in 1974 Nestlé became a significant shareholder in L'Oréal) but over time the two organizations have started to cooperate at the productive level as well. In the 1970s Nestlé expanded its product portfolio to include pet foods, pharmaceutical products and cosmetics too. Thus the two organizations started to become technologically more similar.

The alliance with L'Oréal was kept alive through a common investment in the creation of CIRD in Sophia Antipolis, France, in 1979. The collaboration gave rise to a joint venture based in Switzerland: Galderma, a global leading pharmaceutical company specializing in the research, development and marketing of innovative medical solutions in dermatology. The two industry giants joined forces to set up another joint venture based in France: Laboratoires Innēov, in 2003.

Innēov, the joint venture between L'Oréal and the Nestlé Group, was organized with the aim of exploring the new niche market, that of nutricosmetics, through a line of new products (functional foods, mainly available in pills, tablets, creams and beverages) that are supplements to a person's diet. It represents the research laboratory where the knowledge on properties and conservation of foodstuffs has been exapted into the cosmetic sector knowledge for the creation of nutritional health and beauty supplements. L'Oréal was interested in what has been generally known as 'beauty pills' for a number of years, but it waited until a clear

EU directive framework was formalized before making its move. Actually, one of the major recent launches of Innēov includes the lycopene-containing supplement Innēov Fermeté. Lycopene was initially marketed on the basis of its cancer-fighting properties; however, it is now promoted as a beauty/skin health enhancer. Innēov Fermeté, designed to be taken daily, reportedly slows the effects of skin ageing. It is currently being sold in parts of Europe, Latin America and the UK.

Nearly all of the 26 patents registered in the last decade by Innēov, L'Oréal and Nestlé share the common feature of being classified both as cosmetic (A61K) and toilet (A61Q) preparations, but in 13 cases they incorporated new knowledge related to therapeutic preparations (see Table 13.9) and, in 9 cases, the new knowledge is related to the conservation of foodstuffs.

Thus, nutraceutical supplementary diet tablets exapt knowledge from distant technological domains. These beauty and functional pills develop a new functionality in comparison with the typical L'Oréal products. In particular, elements of natural products such as green and roasted coffee beans are reused to extract phenols to support skin regeneration and regulation of pigmentation disorders. Old ingredients like vanillin in this context are used as important preservative compounds. We have also analysed the collaboration network for the cited patents by Innēov from one side and the collaboration network for the cited patents by L'Oréal and Nestlé on the other. We have seen that the previous patents registered by Innēov are only a small subcluster in comparison with the wide structure of the entire network, which is dominated by two large cliques related to nutritional food stuffs. In reference to the second network of collaborations, we have seen the marginal position of the self-citation of L'Oréal and Nestlé in generating the new knowledge in comparison with wide co-assignees' networks. This new niche

Table 13.9 Descriptions of patent codes of the 13 Innēov patents and the nutraceutical patents of L'Oréal (7) and L'Oréal and Nestlé (6)

Code	Description	Number of patents in the class
A61K	Preparations for medical, dental or toilet purposes	25
A61Q	Use of cosmetics or similar toilet preparations	23
A61P	Therapeutic activity of chemical compounds or medicinal preparations	16
A23L	Foodstuffs and preservation	9
C07C	Acyclic or carbocyclic compounds	7
C07D	Heterocyclic compounds	1
C08G	Macromolecular carbon-to-carbon	1
C11C	Fatty acids	1
C11D	Detergent compositions	1

Source: Authors' elaboration on Orbit database.

in nutraceuticals has arisen from the recombination of knowledge deriving from multiple external research groups. This supports the important role played by the exaptation of old knowledge derived from the complex recombination of competences of various research groups.

The possibility of cooperation between food and personal care manufacturers has been around for a long time; nevertheless, in the 1970s this alliance opened up new niche markets for health and beauty food supplements. The venture established draws on key strengths from each participant. The new products – dietary supplements – are intended to improve the appearance of hair, nails and skin, mainly by combining Nestlé's nutritional know-how with the dermatological expertise of L'Oréal. Aside from the benefits of sharing knowledge, one advantage of entering the cosmeceuticals industry is that there is no necessity for the rigorous health and safety testing routinely applied to new drugs in pharmaceuticals. Nestlé and L'Oréal have taken the risk of being the first to move into this industry. There are clear advantages to this: there will be less regulation in the market then in pure pharma markets, no competition during the market entry phase and the opportunity to establish a brand name and win consumer loyalty early on. Nestlé, by aligning its interests in nutricosmetics with other partners, has spread its risk. Colgate-Palmolive has teamed up with Nestlé to develop portable oral care products. The new partnership aims to build up the distribution of Colgate dental gum and the development of new oral care confectionery products. The venture has proved to be successful and the two companies have launched innovative, portable oral care solutions worldwide. Colgate has brought its expertise in oral care to the table. Nestlé, meanwhile, has knowledge of the confectionery market and, crucially, has a strong distribution network with both highly fragmented confectionery vendors and multiples.

The potential for functional confectionery solutions is strong. Most confectionery products are available in single serve portions, are typically small and easy to eat on the move and are not excessively intrusive into people's diets. The popularity of sugar-free chewing gums to combat tooth decay has been a worldwide success, monopolizing the share of sugared gum in almost all markets. Future developments of functional chewing gums may stretch beyond oral care to focus on delivery of medical care, personal care or performance boosts. Whatever new products are dreamt up in the future, Nestlé is keen to spearhead the development of functional foods in a big way. By aligning its interests in nutricosmetics with other partners it can spread risk, speed up development and share expertise. Up until now the functional foods' segment has been a tough market to crack, with much promise and only a handful of success stories, such as Yakult drinks. Nestlé is clearly keen to boost its own chances of success by bringing several parties to the table and there may be opportunities for other companies to team up with them in their next potential functional food joint venture. The network of Nestlé partners can, in turn, be very useful also for the development of new products by L'Oréal. One example is that of the partnership with Coca-Cola. In the early 1990s, Nestlé entered into an alliance with Coca-Cola in ready-to-drink teas and coffees in order to benefit from Coca-Cola's worldwide bottling system and expertise in prepared beverages. In 2007 Coca-Cola signed an agreement with L'Oréal to launch a new skin-enhancing beverage. The product will be called Lumaé and will be a beverage based on tea targeted towards women over 25 years old who want to take care of their skin wellbeing. This very active involvement within the niche market of nutricosmetics did not limit the overall innovation activity of the firm, that during recent years has intensified in terms of registered patents.

Conclusions

In this study, through the lenses of the evolutionary theory of the firm, we examined how the exaptation process can shape a firm's innovative capabilities. A combination of knowledge accumulation, external relationships, luck and foresight might be seen as part of an exaptation process, which allows the firm to create new products and enter or generate new market niches. Our arguments are validated through the analysis of the L'Oréal case, the giant of the beauty industry that more than others has played a crucial role in the evolution of the beauty ecosystem, being able to co-evolve with the business environment. We reconstructed the historical pattern of innovations developed by the firm, by means of a collection of information coming from secondary sources. An important mechanism of exaptation has been described through which the firm evolved, forming a complex system of research alliances and embarking on numerous acquisitions. In the case of L'Oréal, we highlighted two types of exaptive processes based on acquisitions: narrow and extensive exaptations. They were both based on strategic acquisitions, for acquiring external knowledge to sustain the innovation strategy of the firm. The latter was the case of nutricosmetics innovation, where the competencies of Nestlé were combined with those of L'Oréal to create a new market niche: nutricosmetics.

We contribute to existing literature on innovation by offering a new typology of the exaptive processes, giving an accurate description of the interface between exaptive innovations, depending upon the reuse of knowledge for other functionalities and non-exaptive, internal R&D-based innovations. We pinpoint the interplay between internal and external resources as drivers of exaptation. In our view, exaptation works not only with resources that are internally created by the firm but also within the complex net of external research collaborations and acquisitions that dynamic firms are able to create and settle. The capacity of the firm to co-evolve with its business ecosystem is another relevant element.

The quantitative analysis clearly pointed out that the L'Oréal exaptation potential related to its own patents and, also, to external patents, is significantly higher than other firms' exaptation potential regarding L'Oréal's patents. This means that the profound knowledge of its own technological base, joined with several acquisitions/R&D collaborations, can lead to a greater capability in the reuse of a technological artefact in different technological areas and for different functions, more or less, distant from the one it was originated for. From a managerial point of view, acquisitions and R&D collaborations seem to be the essential ingredients to maximize the exaptation potential inside a firm.

Shifting from biology to business, we were able to demonstrate that exaptation is not only a single event but can manifest itself within a process, which can be articulated by firms in their long period of development. Moreover, we showed that exaptation may originate from outside the acquired resources (through relational dynamic capabilities) and that innovation can be linked to a complex spiral of continuous and discontinuous innovation that characterizes the specific evolutionary trajectory of a firm, giving rise to a complex and multilevel dynamic business ecosystem. In this chapter we approached the analysis of the exaptation process by applying a case study methodology. We studied, through a qualitative historical reconstruction, the firm innovation activity and how competence, knowledge and capabilities were reused and recombined into new products, generating market niche speciation à la Adner and Levinthal (2000).

Notes

1 The shift of the concept of exaptation from biology to economics needs to acknowledge that firm behaviour cannot be seen as a completely random phenomenon, but can be interpreted as the consequence of the capacity to exploit visible and latent opportunities hidden in technologies, processes and market needs, in Gould and Vrba's (1982: 6) words, pushing characters (old knowledge) towards fitness.
2 Mainly the company website, Jones (2010) and the QPat database.
3 The generation of a new artefact from an enlarged agent/artefact space might be confused with a diversification process, but it is not if the artefact is not only new to the firm (in the case of Figure 13.1, organization A) but also new to the market.
4 He only had one daughter, Liliane, who married the French politician, André Bettencourt, in 1950. In 1957 Liliane Bettencourt inherited the L'Oréal fortune when her father died, becoming the principal shareholder of L'Oréal.
5 The products known as shampoos derive from the Hindi word for massage and date back to 1877 when English hairdressers boiled soap in soda water and added herbs for health, fragrance and manageability. During the Victorian age, their use was widespread in thermal baths in England. Originally, soap and shampoo were very similar products: both containing surfactants, a type of detergent.
6 For the details on the original measure, see Trajtenberg *et al.* (1997: 28).

References

Abatecola G., 2015. Research in organizational evolution. What comes next. *European Management Journal*, forthcoming.
Adner R., Levinthal D. A., 2000. Technology speciation and the path of emerging technologies, in Day G., Shoemaker P., Gunther R. E., (eds), *Wharton on Emerging Technologies*, John Wiley & Sons, New York, NY.
Adner R., Levinthal D. A., 2002. The emergence of emerging technologies. *California Management Review*, 45(1): 50–66.
Antonelli C., 2007. The system dynamics of collective knowledge: From gradualism and saltationism to punctuated change. *Journal of Economic Behavior & Organization*, 62(2): 215–236.
Arrow K., 1962. The economic implications of learning by doing. *Review of Economic Studies*, 29(3): 155–173.
Basalla G., 1988. *The Evolution of Technology*, Cambridge University Press, Cambridge, UK.

Bijker W. E., 1987. The social construction of Bakelite: Toward a theory of invention, in Bijker W. E., Hughes T. P., Pinch T., (eds), *The Social Construction of Technological Systems: New Directions in the Sociology and History of Technology*, The MIT Press, Boston, MA.

Bonaccorsi A., 2011. A functional theory of technology and technological change, in Antonelli C., (ed.), *Handbook on the Economic Complexity of Technological Change*, Edward Elgar, Cheltenham, UK.

Bonifati G., 2010. 'More is different', exaptation and uncertainty: Three fundamental concepts for a complexity theory of innovation. *Economics of Innovation and New Technology*, 19(8): 743–760.

Bonifati G., Villani M., 2013. Exaptation in innovation processes: Theory and models, in Antonelli C., (ed.), *Handbook of Economic Organization: Integrating Economic and Organization Theory*, Edward Elgar, Cheltenham, UK.

Breslin D., 2011. The evolving organizational routine, in Belussi F., Staber U., (eds), *Managing Networks of Creativity*, Routledge, London, UK.

Carayannis E. G., Campbell D. F. J., 2009. 'Mode 3' and 'Quadruple Helix': Toward a 21st century fractal innovation ecosystem. *International Journal of Technology Management References*, 46(3–4): 201–234.

Cattani G., 2006. Technological pre-adaptation, speciation and emergence of new technologies: How Corning invented and developed fiber optics. *Industrial and Corporate Change*, 15(2): 285–318.

Cattani G., Ferriani S., 2008. A core/periphery perspective on individual creative performance: Social networks and cinematic achievements in the Hollywood film industry. *Organization Science*, 19(6): 824–844.

Chesbrough H. W., 2003. *Open Innovation: The New Imperative for Creating and Profiting from Technology*, Harvard Business School Press, Cambridge, MA.

Clark J., Freeman C., Soete L., 1984. Long waves, inventions and innovations, in Freeman C., (ed.), *Long Waves and the World Economy*, Frances Pinter, London, UK.

Cohen W., Levinthal D., 1990. Absorptive capacity: A new perspective on learning and innovation. *Administrative Science Quarterly*, 35(1): 128–152.

D'Aveni R., 1994. *Hypercompetition*, The Free Press, New York, NY.

Dew N., Sarasvathy S. D., Venkataraman S., 2004. The economic implications of exaptation. *Journal of Evolutionary Economics*, 14(1): 69–84.

Di Stefano G., Peteraf M. A., Verona G., 2010. Dynamic capabilities deconstructed: A bibliographic investigation into the origins, development, and future directions of the research domain. *Industrial and Corporate Change*, 19(4): 1187–1204.

Dosi G., 1982. Technological paradigms and technological trajectories. *Research Policy*, 11(3): 147–162.

Eisenhardt K., Martin J., 2000. Dynamic capabilities: What are they? *Strategic Management Journal*, October–November Special Issue 21(10–11): 1105–1121.

Fortune A., Mitchell W., 2012. Unpacking firm exit at the firm and industry levels: The adaptation and selection of firm capabilities. *Strategic Management Journal*, 33(7): 794–819.

Freeman C., 1982. *The Economics of Technical Change*, Frances Pinter, London, UK.

Freeman C., 1984. *Long Waves in the World Economy*, Frances Pinter, London, UK.

Freeman C., 1994. *The Handbook of Industrial Innovation*, Edward Elgar, Cheltenham, UK.

Geels F. W., 2002. Technological transitions as evolutionary reconfiguration processes: A multi-level perspective and a case-study. *Research Policy*, 31(8–9): 1257–1274.

Gould S. J., 1982. Darwinism and the expansion of evolutionary theory. *Science*, 216(4544): 380–387.

Gould S. J., Eldridge N., 1977. Punctuated equilibria: The tempo and mode of evolution reconsidered. *Paleobiology*, 3(1): 115–151.

Gould S. J., Vrba E. S., 1982. Exaptation – a missing term in the science of form. *Paleobiology*, 8(1): 4–15.

Hagedoorn J., Duysters G., 2002. External sources of innovative capabilities: The preference for strategic alliances or mergers and acquisitions. *Journal of Management Studies*, 39(2): 167–188.

Hannan T., Freeman J., 1977. The population ecology of organization. *American Journal of Sociology*, 82(5): 929–964.

Hargadon A., Sutton R. I., 1997. Technology brokering and innovation in a product development firm. *Administrative Science Quarterly*, 42(4): 716–749.

Helfat C. E., Winter S., 2011. Untangling dynamic and operational capabilities: Strategy for the (n)ever-changing world. *Strategic Management Journal*, 32(11): 1243–1250.

Helfat C. E., Finkelstein S., Mitchell W., Peteraf M. A., Singh H., Teece D. J., Winter S. G., 2007. *Dynamic Capabilities: Understanding Strategic Change in Organizations*, Blackwell, Oxford, UK.

Hirsch-Kreisen H., Jacobson D., 2008. *Innovation in Low-Tech Firms and Industries*, Edward Elgar, Cheltenham, UK.

Hirsch-Kreisen H., Jacobson D., Robertson P., 2006. 'Low-tech' industries: Innovativeness and development perspectives—a summary of a European research project. *Prometheus: Critical Studies in Innovation*, 24(1): 3–21.

Inkpen A., 2000. Learning throughout joint ventures: A framework of knowledge acquisition. *Journal of Management Studies*, 37(1): 1019–1043.

Jewkes J., Sawers D., Stillerman R., 1958. *The Sources of Inventions*, Macmillan, London, UK.

Jick T. D., 1979. Mixing qualitative and quantitative methods: Triangulation in action. *Administrative Science Quarterly*, 24(4): 602–611.

Johnson P. S., 1975. *The Economics of Invention and Innovation*, Martin Robertson, London, UK.

Jones G., 2008. Blonde and blue-eyed? Globalizing beauty, c.1945–c.1980. *Economic History Review*, 61(1): 125–154.

Jones G., 2010. *Beauty Imagined. A History of the Global Beauty Industry*. Oxford University Press, Oxford, UK.

Keil T., 2004. Building external corporate venturing capabilities. *Journal of Management Studies*, 41(5): 799–825.

Kline S. J., Rosenberg N., 1986. An overview of innovation, in Landau R., Rosenburg N., (eds), *The Positive Sum Strategy*, National Academy Press, Washington, DC.

Lambert N., 2004. *Internet Patent Information in the 21st Century: A Comparison of Delphion, Micropatent, and Qpat*. 2004 International Chemical Information Conference Exhibition. CD-ROM resource.

Lane D., 2011. Complexity and innovation dynamics, in Antonelli C., (ed.), *Handbook on the Economic Complexity of Technological Change*, Edward Elgar, Cheltenham, UK.

Lane D., Maxfield R., 1997. Foresight, complexity, and strategy, in Arthur W. B., Durlauf S. N., Lane D. A., (eds), *The Economy as an Evolving Complex System II*, Addison-Wesley, Reading, MA, pp. 169–198.

Lane D., Maxfield R., 2005. Ontological uncertainty and innovation. *Journal of Evolutionary Economy*, 15(1): 3–50.

Larson G., Stephens P. A., Tehrani J. J., Layton R. H., 2013. Exapting exaptation. *Trends in Ecology & Evolution*, 28(9): 497–498.

Leonard-Barton D., 1992. Core capabilities and core rigidities: A paradox in managing new product development. *Strategic Management Journal*, 13(S1): 111–125.

Levinthal D., 1998. The slow pace of rapid technological change: Gradualism and punctuation in technological change, *Industrial and Corporate Change*, 7(2): 217–247.

Malerba F., 1992. Learning by firms and incremental technical change. *The Economic Journal*, 102(2): 845–859.

Marquis C., Huang Z., 2010. Acquisition as exaptation: The legacy of founding institutions in the U.S. commercial banking industry. *Academy of Management Journal*, 53(6): 1441–1473.

Mastrogiorgio M., 2013. *Technological Exaptation: Evidence From Patent Data*. Paper presented at the Academy of Business Conference, Orlando, FL, August. Available at: http://proceedings.aom.org/content/2013/1/11872 (accessed 24 November 2014).

Meyer C. B., Stensaker I. G., 2006. Developing capacity for change. *Journal of Change Management*, 6(2): 217–231.

Miles M. B., Huberman M. A., 1994. *Qualitative Data Analysis: An Expanded Source Book* (2nd ed.). Sage, London, UK.

Mokyr J., 2000. Natural history and economic history: Is technological change an evolutionary process? In Ziman J., (ed.), *Technological Innovation as an Evolutionary Process*, Oxford University Press, Oxford, UK.

Moore J. F., 1993. Predators and prey: A new ecology of competition. *Harvard Business Review*, 71(3): 75–86.

Nelson R. R., Winter S. G., 1982. *Evolutionary Theory of Economic Change*, Belknap, Cambridge, MA.

Pavitt K., 1984. Sectoral patterns of technical change: Towards a taxonomy and a theory. *Research Policy*, 13(6): 343–373.

Pavitt K., 1999. *Technology, Management and Systems of Innovation*, Edward Elgar, Cheltenham, UK.

Penrose E., 1959. *The Theory of the Growth of the Firm*, John Wiley & Sons, London, UK.

Powell W., 1990. Neither market nor hierarchy: Network forms of organization. *Research in Organizational Behavior*, 12: 295–336.

Powell W. W., Koput K. W., Smith-Doerr L., 1996. Interorganizational collaboration and the locus of innovation: Networks of learning in biotechnology. *Administrative Science Quarterly*, 41(1): 116–145.

Rosenberg N., 1976. *Perspectives on Technology*, Cambridge University Press, Cambridge, UK.

Rosenberg N., 1982. *Inside the Black Box. Technology and Economics*, Cambridge University Press, Cambridge, UK.

Schmookler J., 1966. *Invention and the Economic Growth*, Harvard University Press, Cambridge MA.

Schumpeter J. A., 1934. *The Theory of Economic Development*, Harvard University Press, Cambridge, MA. (Oxford University Press, New York, NY, 1961.) First published in German, 1912.

Schumpeter J. A., 1947. The creative response in history. *Journal of Economic History*, 7(2): 149–159.

Sedita S., 2012. Leveraging the intangible cultural heritage: Novelty and innovation through exaptation. *City, Culture and Society*, 3(4): 251–259.

Sherrow V., 2006. *The Encyclopaedia of Hair, a Cultural History*, Greenwood Publishing Group, Westport, CT.

Sorenson O., Rivkin J. V., Fleming L., 2006. Complexity, networks and knowledge flow. *Research Policy*, 35(7): 994–1017.

Teece D. J., 2007. Explicating dynamic capabilities: The nature and microfoundations of (sustainable) enterprise performance. *Strategic Management Journal*, 28(13): 1319–1350.

Teece D. J., Pisano G., Shuen A., 1997. Dynamic capabilities and strategic management. *Strategic Management Journal*, 18(7): 509–533.

Trajtenberg M., Henderson R., Jaffe A., 1997. University versus corporate patents: A window on the basicness of invention. *Economics of Innovation and New Technology*, 5(1): 19–50.

Tushmann M., Anderson P., 1986. Technological discontinuities and organizational environments. *Administrative Science Quarterly*, 31(3): 439–465.

Usher A. P., 1955. Technical change and capital formation, in *Capital Formation and Economic Growth*, NBER, reprinted in Rosenberg N., (ed.), 1971, *The Economics of Technological Change*, Penguin Books, Middlesex, UK.

Volberda H. W., Lewin A. Y., 2003. Co-evolutionary dynamics within and between firms: From evolution to co-evolution. *Journal of Management Studies*, 40(8): 2111–2136.

Von Hippel E., 1986. Lead users: A source of novel product concepts. *Management Science*, 32(7): 791–805.

Von Tunzelmann N., Acha V., 2005. Innovation in 'low tech' industries, in Fagerberg J., Mowery D., Nelson R., (eds), *The Oxford Handbook of Innovation*, Oxford University Press, Oxford, UK.

Watts D., 2002. A simple model of global cascades on random networks. *Applied Mathematics*, 99(9): 5766–5771.

Winter S., 2003. Understanding dynamic capabilities. *Strategic Management Journal*, 24(10): 991–995.

Yin R. K., 1984. *Case Study Research: Design and Methods*, Sage Publications, Newbury Park, CA.

14 The implementation of a new game strategy in biotech form

From start-up to acquisition: the case of Fidia Advanced Biopolymers (now Anika Therapeutics) of Abano Terme

Fiorenza Belussi

Introduction

In this chapter we will illustrate in detail the case of an Italian biotech firm, Fidia Advanced Biopolymers srl ('Fidia'), now Anika Therapeutics ('Anika'), located in the Veneto region of Italy, near Padua. The firm was spun out from a pharmaceutical firm specializing in neurological treatments to utilize some unused patent regarding hyaluronic acid, extracted initially from the cockscomb plant. But the technology behind it was quite advanced: in tissue engineering, firms were looking for materials to support and replace cell growth in skin, tendons and bones. This firm entered with impetus into the field of biological research and built an open model of innovation collaborating with several European universities, research centres and hospitals. During this time it became the largest producer of tissue engineering in Europe. But the long-term economic sustainability of the model of a contract-research biotech firm was at risk and also its capability to reach the market with standardized and cheap products. Thus, to profit from its innovation capability, the firm decided to enter into an acquisition deal with an American firm, Anika Therapeutic (ANK on the New York stock exchange), specializing in the same technological area, but with greater commercial experience and capability. The acquisition, realized at the end of 2009, was successful. Fidia received US$17.5 million in cash, but also ownership rights. Fidia became the largest shareholder of Anika, but after a few years the Italian investors (and Lanfranco Callegaro) liquidated their shareholdings, profiting from the 100% increase in the Anika stock value. Thus, Anika remained in the hands of the US company, but its products could finally enter into the complex and heavily regulated US market. This case portrays a singular business model in which, in order to survive and profit from innovation, firms must enter not only into alliances but also into acquisitions. In this case we do not analyse the acquisition motivations from the acquirer, but those of the target and the synergies that were created. In terms of R&D management prescriptions, the case of Anika shows the risks in following a pure research path, without considering the commercial application of science. True science-based firms cannot survive in the long term without a strong market penetration of their products. In the next section some theoretical reflections are presented on the paradigm shift from closed to open models of innovation. Thereafter, the literature on acquisition is briefly discussed followed by the presentation of the story of Fidia and its acquisition by Anika. In the final section we draw some conclusions.

From a closed to an open model of innovation

Since the first industrial revolution, science and technology have become the engine of capitalist development (Nelson, 1990) and firms have shown their autonomous capacity to absorb and recombine the new knowledge generated by public institutions, dealing with the development and diffusion of science and technology.

Firms, in particular, have been responsible for the improvement of production processes through the invention of new machinery and for the introduction of new goods into the market. In essence, technological progress in enterprises is linked to the creation of specific technological capabilities (Rosenberg, 1982) that innovative firms develop over time and that bring about new technological developments, as occurred for instance, in the case of the US's Edison, AT&T and IBM, or the German chemical firm BASF. More recently, in the US, the growth of the biotechnology industry has portrayed a new radical technological shift towards a novel class of therapeutics products deriving from biotech and genomic science (Mowery and Rosenberg, 1989; Gambardella, 1995; Tollman *et al.*, 2001). In these developments, public science (Arrow, 1994) and new technologies developed by public research institutions have obviously played an important role (Nelson, 1993). However, in biotech the contribution of firms to the advancement of the new knowledge frontiers has been crucial. Here, new developments in science and technology overlap (Rosenberg, 1990; Pisano, 2006; Sampat, 2006) and new entrepreneurs are often star scientists (Shan *et al.*, 1994; Zucker *et al.*, 1998). New science and novel technologies have been developed within open research networks, within a non-linear model of knowledge exploration and exploitation (Kline and Rosenberg, 1986; March, 1991).

While in the first phase of capitalist development, the technological development of the company was based on the insights of individual entrepreneurs, especially artisans and 'amateurs', in the next step, which ended with the emergence of Fordism, the firms' R&D laboratories, located in the most dynamic large enterprises (Mowery, 1983), placed for instance in the chemical and electro-mechanical areas, become the locus of the discovery of new innovative applications (Freeman, 1986). It was the introduction of a continuous flow of innovations (Winter, 1987; Audretsch *et al.*, 2002) to generate monopoly profits (Schumpeter, 1934, 1942) and asymmetries, giving rise, in the economic systems of the most developed economies, to the growth of large corporations (Chandler, 1990) and to a mechanism of protected and routinized 'innovations' (via the patenting system as discussed, among others, by Basberg, 1987; Narin *et al.*, 1987).

In the post-Fordist era, the laboratories of R&D companies have witnessed both increasing R&D costs and significant falls in R&D productivity, in particular in the biopharma industry (Grabowski and Vernon, 1994; DiMasi and Grabowski, 2007). The exponential growth of knowledge, which we have witnessed in modern times, constrains firms to scan the external environment to find the 'useful' knowledge and expertise necessary to design and develop new products or processes (Chesbrough, 2003; Laursen and Salter, 2006). Connected with that, firms must develop specific absorption capabilities (Cohen and Levinthal, 1989, 1990). Investments in R&D are characterized by a high level of uncertainty, therefore companies have decided that they have to dismantle giant laboratories, dilute their risk and multiply their research path options. The foundational elements of the new emerging business model in the biotech industry (McKelvey, 1996; De La Mothe and Noisi, 2000) have, thus, become those of technological alliances (Pisano *et al.*, 1988), cost-sharing research and the external search for complementary capabilities (Powell, 1998), R&D outsourcing (Howells *et al.*, 2008), 'focal' extended enterprises (Kinder, 2003), developing networks (Zaheer *et al.*, 2000) and large global chains (Coe and Bunnell, 2003). Often innovative activities have clustered around districts (Saxenian, 1996; Scott, 2006) or innovative regions (Coenen *et al.*, 2004). Clusters have also stimulated temporary cooperation between multiple agents with complementary capabilities (Grabher, 2001, 2002).

Thus, the characterization of the old innovation model in which companies were just heavily investing in internal R&D and their innovations were protected by an expensive (and aggressive) strategy of full control of their intellectual property, has lost its effectiveness over time. Companies cannot maintain total control of their ideas, experiences and technologies; the mobility of scientists and technicians spread innovation and new knowledge around. The economic environment (knowledge spill-over) and the new funding opportunities (such as venture capital) easily allow the creation of spin-offs from R&D labs (Chesbrough and Rosenbloom, 2002). However, the value of the new knowledge created is soon constrained by a rapid obsolescence. Procter & Gamble has established a strategy by which every idea originating from its laboratories will be offered outside, even to competitors, if it is not used within three years, preventing promising projects from being lost on the street without creating profits.

As argued by Chesbrough (2003), in order to generate more value, companies should market their knowledge, either physically embedded in products or in property rights, selling their patents to others, or developing licensing agreements, or cross-licensing or establishing a novel business, if their new patents are not in tune with their main specific activity.

In fact, nowadays, in the high-tech industry, the so-called 'market for technology' is expanding in an impressive way (Arora *et al.*, 2001a, 2001b). The open innovation model is based on the principle that the vast knowledge available in one enterprise must be fully used within a short time.

One of the major differences between the closed and open innovation 'research model', lies in the way in which companies need to move from one project to another, betting not only on the results of their compelled limited R&D laboratory but on the knowledge generated through alliances and mergers and acquisitions (M&As) and thus on a distributed model of knowledge creation. In the ongoing evaluation of R&D projects, researchers and managers are often incapable of separating good ideas from poor ones. They might eliminate the so-called 'false positives' (i.e. those projects that initially look promising) and save the 'false negatives' (i.e. those projects which initially do not seem important, but which are proved the second time round to be surprisingly good). This means that firms need to keep more projects in their pipeline. Furthermore, in a highly uncertain environment, such as that of the biotech and pharma industries, innovation activity is a long journey from the proof of a concept up to the public foreign direct investment approval of the innovation that has passed various clinical trials. Thus, success is not only determined by the achieving of an innovation (a new drug development, which must contain an innovative component – new or better treatments in the market) but it is also realized when a firm legally achieves market exclusivity because the US Food and Drug Administration (FDA) approves the new treatment. Hence, innovation is not enough. Firms must develop a marketable innovation targeting therapeutically more effective drugs. Innovators are not by definition 'winners' in the market and the logic of science and research might conflict with the managerial development and selection of R&D projects, requiring difficult to find managerial R&D capabilities and new business models (Kim, 2014).

A new game strategy in biotech: creating value from M&As

In management theory, the creation of competitive advantage has been traditionally developed around three concepts: (1) the Porter 'value chain' approach, where firms position themselves as focal actors against suppliers, competitors, distributors, potential entrants and regulators, gaining value by reaching monopolistic power over them; (2) the theory of the 'dynamic capabilities' (Teece, 1986) in which firms create value by investing in innovation and in building distinctive resources and, hence, overcoming competitors as a result of their innovative effort; and (3) the recent theoretical reflections on the business models, where the creation of value is connected to the realized specific strategy of the firm in meeting customers' needs (Amit and Zott, 2001; Casadesus-Masanell and Ricart, 2010). Osterwalder (2004) made the most practical description of the business model's structure, further transformed by Osterwalder and Pigneur (2013) into the 'business model canvas', a managerial tool for business model construction, describing the architecture of the various elements (in product design, marketing and delivering) responsible for generating a revenue stream.

Thus, these three concepts alternatively stress different aspects. In the first case, we look at the power of the focal firm over the constellation of competitors, suppliers and clients. Here, the 'value chain' approach refers typically to verticalized organizations, but nowadays production cycles are highly fragmented, geographically dispersed among different agents and firms typically focus only on a few tasks. Thus, the design (and its economic sustainability) of each phase of the 'value chain' must be analysed alone, along the various connections organized by markets, as is clearly suggested in the case of the biopharma business, where many agents, in a long-lasting period of about ten years, participate in the conceptualization, financing, developing, legally approving and marketing of a new drug.

The second approach is only interested in analysing the innovative capabilities of firms, disregarding all other strategic managerial aspects. Innovation is often a catch-all phenomenon and, as discussed by many authors, firms with similar patterns of technological innovations (or with no technological innovation at all) may reach very different competitive capabilities. Here we can contrast the Benetton case with the Zara one, or the success of Ryanair in a sector where the main companies do not make a profit at all.

The third approach is still in its infancy in describing a clear set of alternative business models and it suffers from an over proliferation of models (Afuah and Tucci, 2000). In the biopharma industry, strategic alliances and acquisitions can be considered the prevailing business model utilized by firms to seize the opportunity to market a new drug, as we studied particularly in Chapters 4 and 6.

Current research, such as the valuable work of Dyer *et al.* (2004), focuses on the acquisition versus alliance decision, but it relies primarily on analysis from a focal firm perspective. Others have tentatively measured alliances' occurrence or performance (Sampson, 2007), not value created for the target (or alliance partner). Sampson (2007) found that alliances (and acquisitions) contribute far more to firm innovation when technological diversity is moderate, rather than low or high. In contrast, De Man and Duysters (2005) suggest that studies using output measures have shown that companies engaging in M&As face a decline in innovation.

Wang and Zajac (2007) have applied a dyadic perspective to the same issue, but they look at the similarities or complementarities of capability. They advocate that with high levels of resource similarity, firms will choose acquisition rather than alliance and vice versa. On the issue of value creation, the article by Kang and Afuah (2010) is illuminating in providing an explanation for why innovators often do not profit from their innovations. Their article argues that, instead of looking to the existence of complementary capabilities, as in Teece (1986), we must examine the innovator's positioning vis-à-vis customers, suppliers, competitors and coopetitors and, thus, to their business model associated with the firm strategy (Dagnino and Rocco, 2009). In the case of Lipitor, one of the world's best-selling drugs, Kang and Afuah (2010) linked the ability of profiting from innovation to the strategies of cooperation and commercialization developed in the alliance of the biotech firm with the large pharma, Pfizer. It was the synergy created within the alliance that allowed their new drug to become the most sold treatment against cholesterol in the world, surpassing all other competitors. In 2000 Pfizer acquired (through a hostile acquisition), the Warner Lambert shares, paying the astronomical sum of US$90 billion. This 'forced' exit strategy was clearly associated with a very rewarding model of value creation.

But how common is this case in representing the reality of the biotech industry? Rasmussen (2009) has maintained that pharmaceutical companies have successfully adjusted their business models to meet the challenge of biotechnology and have, therefore, retained their powerful position in the industry. Central to this has been the breadth and depth of knowledge transfer through alliance formation. This been critical both to the adjustment process for the large pharmaceutical companies and for the development of the many biopharmaceutical start-ups. Nonetheless, Rasmussen (2009) emphasizes:

> [t]he business models of these smaller companies have many weaknesses, which have led to the erosion of the value of their initial strategic assets. Despite the poor financial performance of the vast majority of these companies, the biopharmaceutical sector, as a whole, has created significant value. This has been captured disproportionately by a handful of large, fully integrated biopharmaceutical firms and, to a lesser extent, by the largest dozen pharmaceutical firms' (Rasmussen, 2009: 4).

But the hostile acquisition by Pfizer represents more the exception than the norm. Within the biotech industry, non-hostile acquisitions have constituted the main tool of a diffused growth model in which firms were pursuing obtaining larger scale economies in research, increasing the number of products in the pipeline, acquiring new synergies, reducing redundant resources and having a higher control of R&D risky investment. The case of Anika has been selected to better illustrate this path.

The Fidia Advanced Biopolymers case[1]

Anika is a small business, a dedicated biotechnology firm (DBF), founded in 1992 and located in Abano Terme, Province of Padua, in Italy. This is one of the few Italian companies specializing in tissue engineering, an important segment of the biotech industry, according to the OECD definition (Allansdottir *et al.*, 2002). It was created as a spin-off of Fidia SpA, founded in 1946, a pharmaceutical company specializing in the production and extraction of active neurological ingredients from animal organs, including bovine organs. In 1975, after a period of high investment in R&D, Fidia launched Cronassial (a ganglioside mixture) and in 1987 Sygen (derived from a single ganglioside): these drugs were the root of the company's success both in the domestic and international markets. After 1993, at the height of the scandal of 'mad cow' disease, due to numerous pressures from the Ministry of Health, Fidia had to remove the two drugs which were accounting for almost 80% of their total sales. The company was unable to prove the safety of bovine source of the extracts used. Notwithstanding the numerous articles published in leading international journals of neuroscience, it was difficult for Fidia to demonstrate the clinical safety of its product. Thus, the company went into crisis and its balance sheet fell in one year from 350 billion lire (of which 20% was invested in research) to 40 billion lire. Since that period Fidia has recovered, consolidating its traditional market of pharmaceutical products. In 2005 it realized a turnover of €94 billion, thanks to the acquisition of a company that produced antibiotics and due to its expansion in the Chinese market.

During 1992, the director of the Fidia R&D, Lanfranco Callegaro (employed previously in Sorin Medical, part of the Fiat group), decided to open up a new department that was working on some research funded by the National Ministry of Research (Law 46) using some Fidia patents on hyaluronic acid that were retained by the firm. The twin company soon started to specialize in the production of hyaluronic acid (Hyalgan is the main Fidia product that can be used for intra-articular knee injections and Connettivina for the treatment of skin ulcers). In 1993 Fidia had a market of 14 billion lire. Subsequently, the firm developed other products, such as hyaluronic acid Hyaff, Hyalofill, Hyalograft and Merogel. These products have been licensed to corporations. On the basis of the rapid development of Fidia is the fact that these new technologies were considered medical devices and clinical trial standards were less stringent. While at the beginning the business was only supported by public funding, after 1996 Fidia obtained its first royalties from Medtronics and Baxter. During the 2000s the company developed new biomaterials, tissue engineering and bio-surgery products. Since its beginning Fidia has specialized in autologous tissues, cultivating cells that come directly from the patient (in the form of a biopsy) and that could be multiplied in bioreactors and subsequently re-implanted in the same patient (its 'cell factory' was capable of reproducing tissue with dermal fibroblasts, epidermal with condrociti and adipose tissue lymphocytes). Lastly, efforts were devoted to the regeneration of articular cartilage (Hyalograft C) and bone. The Fidia plant for tissue engineering was the largest in Europe during the 2000s. The turnover in 2006 was about €10.4 billion, resulting from the sale of approximately 40 products and Fidia employed about 50 researchers.

Over the years, research alliances have been established with more than 50 Italian and foreign universities. The company developed a significant number of proprietary technologies and more than 150 international patents (Figure 14.1). In Italy 160 hospitals and 25 in Europe were using Fidia's products, but the use of cell culture as reconstructive therapy requires mainly a service directed to the domestic market (human tissue development requires complex logistics facilities, including required authorizations that depend on different European and international laws). Technological innovation in this area depends on the combination of very different capabilities in the fields of chemistry, engineering, new materials, technologies, biotech and medical. In particular, new products must be able to overcome a long validation period, clinical testing and acceptance by the scientific medical community. During the 2000s Fidia was involved in seven major European projects dedicated to tissue engineering and in five acted as a coordinator. From 1993 to 2007 the research network of Fidia received European funding for approximately €32 billion, of which €13 billion were related to STEPS projects. The competitors of Fidia were some large US biotech firms (e.g. Genzyme, now acquired by the French Sanofi-Aventis) and small US and European companies (Smith & Nephew, co.don, Aastrom Biosciences). US biotech companies opted, during the 2000s, mainly for allogeneic tissue engineering technologies, or in vitro cell proliferation or in vivo tissue engineering based on biological tissues derived from donors (or cadaveric tissue), but this issue is still controversial.[2]

The development of these technologies was once promising, but it was later discovered that patients developed rejection or infection. Within the US market, both technologies, i.e. autologous and allogeneic, are now in use (Mason, 2007; Hellman, 2008). So far, few companies have been able to move from experimental research to the production of products available on the market, such as Fidia who uses autologous technologies (Dotto, 2007). However, despite its technological leadership, Fidia was unable to enter the US market, which for a biotech firm is by far the most important country in which to display its visibility and competitive position. During 2009, after a long reflection, Fidia's managers and Callegaro Lanfranco, the chief operating officer and one of the most productive inventors in Fidia (Figure 14.2), approached the US firm Anika Therapeutics of Boston, a biotech firm specializing in tissue engineering and ranked by the Nasdaq in New York, to discuss the possibility of a deal with P&R (the holding company which controlled Fidia). Mauro Brunelli, responsible for the M&A of Mittel (the deal advisor, located in Milan), helped Fidia to terminate the acquisition, promoting an exchange of shares (Fidia could then become the main shareholder in Anika with 1,981,000 shares, representing about 14.7% of the total capital and having a value of about US$20 million)[3] and a payment of US$17.1 million in cash. In this transaction who was the most innovative partner, in terms of patenting? Anika had a patent portfolio of 29 patents, while Fidia could count 161 (Figure 14.1). Anika's first patent in tissue engineering dates back to 1989 (biosynthesis of hyaluronic acid), but it was first registered in 1993 by Medchem and then assigned in 1993 to Anika. On the other hand, Fidia declared a constant flow of innovations starting from the 1985 patent on 'Process for preparing salt of hyaluronic acid with a pharmaceutically active substance', registered by Fidia and the several patents registered in its name during the 1990s regarding biopolymers, biomaterials, injectable hyaluronic, graft technologies, membranes, bone substitute, graft to be implanted in cartilage, meniscus, spinal cord and gellan. Thus, we can observe that a pure contract-research biotech was acquired by a dynamic but less innovative organization, with more commercial power in the international market. But tissue engineering as a whole, clearly, is having a difficult transition period from a development stage industry to one with a successful product portfolio and this is often the case for breakthrough medical technologies.

Taking into account the market of Fidia, we turn back to the analysis of Franco Mazzoleni, Director of Plastic Surgery at the Padua Hospital. Padova (Moro, 2000), a patient with 30% burns to the skin, could be cured with 30 pieces of artificial tissue, starting from a 2 cm square of derma. They could build in two weeks the necessary skin to cover him and the patient would recover in 45 days, instead of the 3 months necessary with traditional therapy: the only limitation is the cost of this process, i.e. about €9,000.

Drug discovery companies, when they are contract research firms, do not fully understand the real potentiality of their market and tend to undervalue the issue related to the marketability of their inventions, while upstream pharmaceutical or biotech companies are more in tune both with the regulatory frameworks and with the possible commercial use of their inventions. Thus, the best strategy for

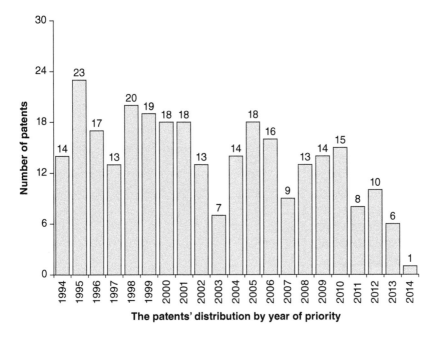

Figure 14.1 The patents' distribution by year of priority

Source: Author's elaboration from Orbit database: https://www.orbit.com

maximizing the value of the firm, considering the difficulties in building an efficient independent business, is the condition of being acquired by one of the existing larger pharmaceutical or biopharmaceutical firms (Rasmussen, 2009: 276). After the acquisition, the strategy of Anika was to further invest in the Italian subsidiary, spending about €10 million for a new plant investment in Padua (it will be completed during 2016). A great restructuring took place after 2010. Employment levels fall from 120 to 60. The productive tissue plant was closed, because the unit costs of tissue regeneration with autologous methods (implying a double chirurgical extraction) were too expensive for Europe and for the US market. Some activities were moved to the newly opened US tissue plant in Bedford (MA). In Italy the production was concentrated on R&D activities and on the production and commercialization of Hyalofast – a leading product that does not require two invasive operations but that operates with a method of tissue regeneration based on the regeneration of filaments of skin. Hyalofast® is a biodegradable, hyaluronan based (HYAFF®) scaffold for one-step surgical treatment of chondral and osteochondral defects. In Abano Terme, near Padua, total employment at Anika in 2015 has decreased to about 20, but the firm has become very profitable.

In 2014 Anika announced it had received marketing approval for Monovisc[4] from the US FDA. Monovisc is a single injection used to treat pain and improve joint mobility in patients suffering from osteoarthritis of the knee. While Anika has

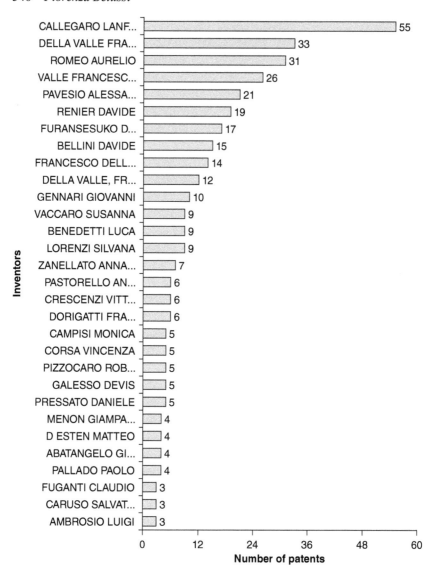

Figure 14.2 Inventors

Source: Author's elaboration from Orbit database: https://www.orbit.com

marketed Monovisc internationally since 2008 (the product is currently sold in a variety of territories, including Canada, the UK and several countries in the Middle East, Europe and Asia), until now it was not able to commercialize it in the US, because a competitor, Genzyme, launched a strong patent dispute in the past, that was concluded during February 2013 with Anika triumphing over Genzyme. As shown in Figure 14.3 the share price of Anika reached a peak of US$60 per share

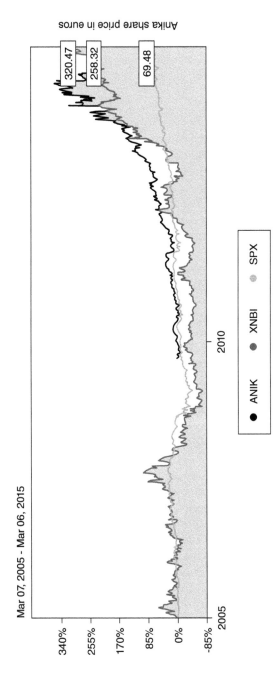

Figure 14.3 The share value of Anika

Source: Author's elaboration from Morningstar: http://quotes.morningstar.com

in 2013 and in 2014 the market capitalisation of Anika reached US$591 million, an increase in market value of 320% over 2005. In conclusion, it can be confirmed that the game strategy implemented by Fidia of profiting from innovation by being acquired was successful: the firm lacked significant capabilities for the commercialization of its innovation, but it found a knowledgeable partner who was able to do it.

Some conclusions

In this chapter we have presented the case of an important Italian biotech firm that has fully followed an open innovation model in its development. A further step in its growth was the decision to be sold to (and merged with) another international organization. Fidia, the largest European company in tissue engineering, is now part of Anika. Its technological evolution is still remarkable (while after the acquisition Anika has registered only 1 international patent, Fidia has applied for 24 new inventions) and it is now the R&D laboratory of the US biotech firm, whose patent portfolio is now composed of 63.3% of patents co-assigned with Fidia, (Orbis database, authors' estimation). Despite the acquisition, the original group of researchers and scientists remained attached to Fidia, thus the risk of losing the most crucial human capital of the firm was avoided (Ranft and Lord, 2000; Malik, 2009).

Anika's operating profit has been strongly positive in recent years (in 2013 US$14 million out of US$60 million of sales). The closing of the unprofitable tissue engineering factory product line in Padua in 2011 was considered by Anika to be necessary, as well as terminating the development of the Hyalograft C autograft product, while the transfer of gel-based production from Italy to the Bedford (MA) manufacturing facility was completed. Anika also sponsored the regenerative product Hyalofast™ for the repair of chondral and osteochondral, or cartilage lesions, invented in Padua, expanding the sales of Fidia's Hyalobarrier®, a post-surgical anti-adhesion product for use in abdominal and pelvic procedures, as well as Hyalomatrix®, a biodegradable dermal substitute for the treatment of highly complex wounds, such as traumatic, chronic wounds and severe burns. Interestingly, Anika withdrew the most complex technologies of Fidia from the market, considering that they were technologically too complex, while it is still delaying putting on the market some more mature products. Typically the literature that studies acquisitions, with few exceptions (Fernald *et al.*, 2015), devolves its attention to the performance of the acquirer. In contrast, analysing this case, we focused on the motivations of the target for 'being acquired', and the synergies that were created between the acquirer and the target. Was Fidia right in looking around the world for a new owner? The answer is, yes. This appears to be the right modality of profiting from innovation, particularly in a high-tech sector such as the biopharma industry.

Notes

1 The information elaborated in this section is derived from some interviews undertaken with a member of the research team of Fidia Advanced Polymers srl, now Anika Therapeutics, during 2008 (Alessandra Pavesio) and from recent articles (2011–2014)

reported in the local press and from internet sources. On this topic the author has also published a case study (Belussi, 2008). Our last – and in depth interview – was conducted with Nicola Tiozzo Caenazzo, the human resource director of Fidia Advanced Biopolymers of Abano Terme, in mid-February 2015. His comments and reflections were extremely useful for validating the general interpretative framework.

2　http://biomed.brown.edu/Courses/BI108/BI108_2007_Groups/group03/sources.html

3　The value of the shares has been calculated at an average of US$10 per share (see Figure 14.3).

4　Monovisc is the first FDA approved single injection product with HA from a non-animal source. It is composed of a sterile, clear, biocompatible, resorbable, viscoelastic fluid composed of partially cross-linked sodium hyaluronate (NaHA) in phosphate buffered saline.

References

Afuah A., Tucci C., 2000. *Internet Business Models and Strategies*, McGraw-Hill Higher Education, New York, NY.

Allansdottir A., Bonaccorsi A., Gambardella A., Mariani M., Orsenigo L., Pamolli F., Riccaboni M., 2002. Innovation & competitiveness in European Biotechnology. *European Commission, Enterprise Papers*, no. 7.

Amit R., Zott C., 2001. Value creation in e-business. *Strategic Management Journal*, 22(6–7): 493–520.

Arora A., Fosfuri A., Gambardella A., 2001a. *Markets for Technology: The Economics of Innovation and Corporate Strategy*, The MIT Press, Cambridge, MA.

Arora A., Fosfuri A., Gambardella A., 2001b. Markets for technology and their implications for corporate strategy. *Industrial and Corporate Change*, 10(2): 419–451.

Arrow K., 1994. The production and distribution of knowledge, in Silverberg G., Soete L., (eds), *The Economics of Growth and Technical Change*, Edward Elgar, Aldershot, UK.

Audretsch D. B., Bozeman B., Combs K. L., Feldman M., Link A. N., Siegel D. S., Wessner C., 2002. The economics of science and technology. *The Journal of Technology Transfer*, 27(2): 155–203.

Basberg B., 1987. Patents and the measurement of technological change: A survey of the literature. *Research Policy*, 16(2): 131–141.

Belussi F., 2008. Il modello dell' '*open innovation*' in un caso di successo: la FAB di Abano Terme (Padova), in Belussi F., (ed.), *Strategie Innovative, Modelli di Impresa e Comportamenti Organizzativi*, Cleup, Padua, Italy.

Casadesus-Masanell R., Ricart J. E., 2010. From strategy to business models and onto tactics. *Long Range Planning*, 43(2): 196–215.

Chandler A., 1990. *Scale and Scope. The Dynamics of Industrial Capitalism*, Belknap Press, Cambridge, MA.

Chesbrough H., 2003. The era of open innovation. *The MIT Sloan Management Review*, 44(3): 35–41.

Chesbrough H., Rosenbloom R. S., 2002. The role of the business model in capturing value from innovation: Evidence from Xerox Corporation's technology spin-off companies. *Industrial and Corporate Change*, 11(3): 529–555.

Coe N., Bunnell T., 2003. Spatializing knowledge communities: Towards a conceptualisation of transnational innovation networks. *Global Networks*, 3(4): 437–456.

Coenen L., Moodysson J., Asheim B., 2004. Nodes, networks and proximity: On the knowledge dynamics of the Medicon Valley biotech cluster. *European Planning Studies*, 12(7): 1003–1018.

Cohen W. M., Levinthal D. A., 1989. Innovation and learning: The two faces of R&D. *Economic Journal*, 99(397): 569–596.

Cohen W. M., Levinthal D. A., 1990. Absorptive capacity: A new perspective on learning and innovation. *Administrative Science Quarterly*, 35(1): 128–152.

Dagnino G., Rocco E., 2009. *Coopetition Strategy. Theory, Experiments, and Cases*, Routledge, Oxford, UK.

De La Mothe J., Noisi J., (eds), 2000. *The Economic and Social Dynamics of Biotechnology*, Springer, Heidelberg, Germany.

De Man A.-P., Duysters G., 2005. Collaboration and innovation: A review of the effects of mergers, acquisitions and alliances on innovation. *Technovation*, 25(12): 1377–1387.

DiMasi J. A., Grabowski H. G., 2007. The cost of biopharmaceutical R&D: Is biotech different? *Managerial and Decision Economics*, 28(4–5): 469–479.

Dotto M., 2007. *Business Strategies of the Tissue Engineering Sector.* Tesi presentata all'Università di Padova, AA 2006/07, Corso di Laurea di Biotecnologie, Padua, Italy. CD-ROM resource.

Dyer J. H., Kale P., Singh H., 2004. When to ally and when to acquire. *Harvard Business Review*, 82(7–8): 109–115.

Fernald K., Pennings E., Claas E., 2015. Biotechnology commercialization strategies: Risk and return in interfirm cooperation. *Journal of Product Innovation Management*, forthcoming.

Freeman C., 1986. *The Economics of Industrial Innovation*, The MIT Press, Boston, MA.

Gambardella A., 1995. *Science and Innovation in the US Pharmaceutical Industry*, Cambridge University Press, Cambridge, UK.

Grabher G., 2001. Locating economic action: Projects, networks, localities, and institutions. *Environment and Planning A*, 33(8), 1329–1331.

Grabher G., 2002. Cool projects, boring institutions: Temporary collaboration in social context. *Regional Studies*, 36(3): 205–214.

Grabowski H., Vernon J., 1994. Returns to R&D on new drug introductions in the 1980s. *Journal of Health Economics*, 13(4): 383–406.

Hellman K. B., 2008. Tissue engineering: Translating science to product. *Topics in Tissue Engineering*, 4: 1–28.

Howells J., Gagliardi D., Malik K., 2008. The growth and management of R&D outsourcing: Evidence from UK pharmaceuticals. *R&D Management*, 38(2): 205–219.

Kang J., Afuah A., 2010. Profiting from innovations: The role of new game strategies in the case of Lipitor of the US pharmaceutical industry. *R&D Management*, 40(2): 124–137.

Kim H. R., 2014. Formulation of a success model in pharmaceutical R&D: Efficient innovation model. *Sage Open*, January–March: 1–9.

Kinder T., 2003. Go with the flow – a conceptual framework for supply relations in the era of the extended enterprise. *Research Policy*, 32(3): 503–523.

Kline S. J., Rosenberg N., 1986. An overview of innovation, in Landau R., Rosenberg N., (eds), *The Positive Sum Strategy*, National Academic Press, Washington, DC.

Laursen K., Salter A., 2006. Open innovation: The role of openness in explaining innovation performance among UK manufacturing firms. *Strategic Management Journal*, 27(2): 131–150.

Malik N. N., 2009. Biotech acquisitions by big pharma: Why and what is next. *Drug Discovery Today*, 14(17): 818–821.

March J., 1991. Exploration and exploitation in organizational learning. *Organization Science*, 2(1): 71–87.

Mason C., 2007. Regenerative medicine 2.0. *Regenerative Medicine*, 2(1): 11–18.

McKelvey M., (ed.), 1996. *Evolutionary Innovation: The Business of Biotechnology*, Oxford University Press, Oxford, UK.

Moro A., 2000. Biotecnologie al Servizio della Medicina: Il Derma Artificiale. *Il Sole 24 Ore*, 2 March. Available at: http://www.mediamente.rai.it/mediamentetv/mmquotidiano/nuovamente/docs/020300.asp (accessed 2 March 2015).

Mowery D., 1983. The relationships between contractual and intrafirm forms of industrial research in American manufacturing, 1900–1940s. *Explorations in Economic History*, 20(4): 351–374.

Mowery D., Rosenberg N., 1989. *Technology and the Pursuit of Economic Growth*, Cambridge University Press, Cambridge, UK.

Narin F., Noma E., Perry R., 1987. Patents as indicators of corporate technological strength. *Research Policy*, 16(2): 143–155.

Nelson R., 1990. Capitalism as an engine of progress. *Research Policy*, 19(3): 193–214.

Nelson R., (ed.), 1993. *National Innovation Systems: A Comparative Analysis*, Oxford University Press, Oxford, UK.

Osterwalder A., 2004. *The Business Model Ontology – A Proposition in a Design Science Approach*, University of Lausanne. Available at: http://www.hec.unil.ch/aosterwa/PhD/ Osterwalder_PhD_BM_Ontology.pdf (accessed 2 March 2015).

Osterwalder A., Pigneur Y., 2013. Designing business models and similar strategic objects: The contribution of IS. *Journal of the Association for Information Systems*, 14(5): 237–244.

Pisano G. P., 2006. *Science Business: The Promise, the Reality and the Future of Biotech*, Harvard Business School Press, Cambridge, MA.

Pisano G. P., Shan W., Teece D. J., 1988. *Joint Ventures and Collaboration in the Biotechnology Industry*, Ballinger Publishing, Cambridge, MA.

Powell W. W., 1998. Learning from collaboration: Knowledge and networks in the biotechnology and pharmaceutical industries. *California Management Review*, 40(3): 228–240.

Ranft A. L., Lord M. D., 2000. Acquiring new knowledge: The role of retaining human capital in acquisitions of high-tech firms. *The Journal of High Technology Management Research*, 11(2): 295–319.

Rasmussen B., 2009, Creating and capturing value in the biopharmaceutical sector, PhD Thesis, unpublished. Available at: http://vuir.vu.edu.au/1946/ (accessed 5 March 2015).

Rosenberg N., 1982. *Inside the Black Box. Technology and Economics*, Cambridge University Press, Cambridge, UK.

Rosenberg N., 1990. *Why do Firms do Basic Research (With Their Own Money)?* Department of Economics, Stanford University, Stanford, CA.

Sampat B. N., 2006. Patenting and US academic research in the 20th century: The world before and after Bayh-Dole. *Research Policy*, 35(6): 772–789.

Sampson R., 2007. R&D alliances and firm performance: The impact of technological diversity and alliance organization on innovation. *Academy of Management Journal*, 50(2): 364–386.

Saxenian A., 1996. *Regional Advantage. Culture and competition in Silicon Valley and Route 128*, Harvard University Press, Boston, MA.

Schumpeter J. A., 1934. *The Theory of Economic Development*, Harvard University Press, Cambridge, MA. (Oxford University Press, New York, NY, 1961.) First published in German, 1912.

Schumpeter J. A., 1942. *Capitalism, Socialism, and Democracy*, Harper and Brothers (Harper Colophon edition, 1976), New York, NY.

Scott A., 2006. Origins and growth of the Hollywood motion-picture industry: The first three decades, in Braunerhjelm P., Feldman M., (eds), *Cluster Genesis: Technology-Based Industrial Development*, Oxford University Press, Oxford, UK, pp. 17–37.

Shan W., Walker G., Kogut B., 1994. Interfirm cooperation and startup innovation in the biotechnology industry. *Strategic Management Journal*, 15(5): 387–394.

Teece, D. J., 1986. Profiting from technological innovation: implications for integration, collaboration, licensing, and public policy. *Research Policy*, 15(6): 285–305.

Tollman P., Guy P., Altshuler J., Flanagan A., Steiner M., 2001. *A Revolution in R&D: How Genomics and Genetics are Transforming the Biopharmaceutical Industry*. Boston Consulting Group. Available at: http://www.bcg.com/documents/file13745.pdf (accessed 5 March 2015).

Wang L., Zajac E., 2007. Alliances or acquisitions? A Dyadic perspective on interfirm resource combinations. *Strategic Management Journal*, 28(13): 1291–1317.

Winter S., 1987. Knowledge and competence as strategic assets, in Teece D., David P., (eds), *The Competitive Challenge – Strategies for Industrial Innovation and Renewal*. Ballinger, Cambridge, MA, pp. 159–184.

Zaheer A., Gulati R., Nohira N., 2000. Strategic networks. *Strategic Management Journal*, 21(3): 203–215.

Zucker L. G., Darby M. R., Brewer M. B., 1998. Intellectual human capital and the birth of U.S. biotechnology enterprises. *The American Economic Review*, 88(1): 290–306.

Index

For Product Safety Concerns and Information please contact our EU
representative GPSR@taylorandfrancis.com
Taylor & Francis Verlag GmbH, Kaufingerstraße 24, 80331 München, Germany